MASS MURDER

GARLAND REFERENCE LIBRARY
OF SOCIAL SCIENCE
(Vol. 427)

MASS MURDER
An Annotated Bibliography

Michael Newton

GARLAND PUBLISHING, INC. • NEW YORK & LONDON
1988

Library of Congress Cataloging-in-Publication Data

Newton, Michael, 1951–
Mass Murder: An Annotated Bibliography/Michael Newton.
p. cm.—(Garland Reference Library of Social Science; vol. 427)
ISBN 0–8240–6619–7 (alk. paper)
1. Mass Murder—United States—Bibliography.   2. Murder—
Psychological aspects—United States—Bibliography.   3. Crime and
criminals—United States—Registers.   I. Title.   II. Series:
Garland Reference Library of Social Science; v. 427.

Z5703.4.M87N49   1987   [HV6529]   016.3641′523—dc19   87-24588   CIP

Printed on acid-free, 250-year-life paper
Manufactured in the United States of America

To
Eddie Cole, *for showing me the dark side,*
and to
Judy, *for tending the light.*

CONTENTS

PREFACE

America today is caught up in the grip of what one expert calls a "homicidal mania." The Federal Bureau of Investigation estimates that during 1983, 5,000 victims--or an average of thirteen each and every day, year-round--were slaughtered by so-called "recreational killers," a lethal breed who select their victims at random, for the sport of killing. Dozens, perhaps hundreds more Americans will die each year in homicidal outbursts by mass murderers who crack beneath life's pressures and relieve their private demons with the slaughter of a family, co-workers, even strangers in a shopping mall.

The changing face of murder in America has frightened law enforcement experts into looking long and hard for patterns in the way we kill each other--and the patterns which emerge are worrisome, indeed. Since World War II, the national solution rate for homicides has dropped from 90% to an average of only 76%--indicating that one out of every four killers escapes, unidentified. American police are cognizant of some 120 recreational killers over the past 20 years--the ones who were identified and apprehended--as compared to only forty for all the other nations. Of those in custody, some 92 percent are male, the vast majority Caucasian, and a terrifying one in ten are doctors, dentists, or some other health professional.

The problem is as old as history, but only in the past five years has it attracted widespread public notice--and, indeed, statistics do appear to indicate an escalation in the number of random, senseless murders. How much of this new "homicidal mania" is fact, and how much should be written off to the computer age, with its improved techniques of cataloguing and recording crimes?

Unfortunately, lagging scholarship makes this and other vital questions difficult, if not impossible, to answer with authority. The recent deluge of publicity, producing several excellent biographies along with much that is sensational and cheap, has failed to offer answers or solutions to the problem which endangers every man and woman in America today.

ix

Initially, we run afoul of definitions. Prior to 1980 multicides were lumped together as "mass murders," with no viable distinctions for the varied motivations or techniques of the criminals in question. Thus, a strangler in Boston and a sniper at the Texas university, in Austin, were "mass murderers," their crimes dismissed identically as symptoms of a passing aberration.

With official recognition of a growing problem in the 1980s, jargon raced ahead of understanding, and a host of instant experts quarreled among themselves about the proper terminology for this or that atrocity. "Mass murder," most conceded, should apply exclusively to individuals who slaughter groups of relatives or strangers simultaneously, in a single and continuing transaction. The repeaters, those who claim their solitary victims over months or years, became "serial killers"--and cound never graduate to "mass," no matter what their final body count.

Within these general semantic guidelines, chaos reigns supreme, as "experts" jockey for position, grappling for the "final word." Some stolidly maintain that serial killers choose strangers as victims exclusively, though many have annihilated parents, siblings, spouses, and acquaintances, as well. A number of the "experts" bicker over time spans, logging intervals between successive homicides. (One self-proclaimed authority denies serial status to Charles Starkweather, based on the fact that ten of his eleven homicides occurred within a five-day span, while applying the label to Christopher Wilder in almost identical circumstances.) Still others insist that serial killers are exclusively male, despite substantial evidence of lethal ladies who asphyxiated, poisoned, stabbed, and otherwise dispatched prodigious numbers through the years, without apparent motive.

For the purposes of clarity, I have adopted certain definitions from the FBI's Behavioral Science Unit. Henceforth, "mass murder" shall refer to any multicide in which the several victims are assaulted simultaneously, or in swift succession as a series of related incidents. "Serial murders," conversely, are committed separately (although there may be several victims in a single incident), are unrelated as to choice of victims, time, and place, and are primarily compulsive, lacking any "normal" motive such as private gain. (Again, we must be cautious, as a number of the "classic" serial killers also boast arrests for robbery, auto theft, and other crimes.)

With the foregoing definitions fresh in mind, I have eliminated certain killers from consideration here. First off were the professionals--assassins, Dillinger-type robbers, hit-men for the Mafia--who kill by contract, or else incidentally, in the performance of their other crimes. Collective zealots likewise are excluded--Klansmen, Nazis, terrorists and members of established cults--because their violence, while considerable, is a "logical" extension of religious or political beliefs. Some cases finally accepted for inclusion may be borderline: children or domestics slaughtering whole families in the hope of an inheritance; Fred Cowan, self-styled fascist, gunning down his former co-employees in a sudden fit of rage; Henry Lucas, brutally eliminating witnesses to petty robberies. But in the last analysis, a wanton disregard for human life distinguishes these cirmes from other, common mayhem. Homicide becomes the end, with greed or crack-pot ideology reduced to window dressing on the side. As a Texas Ranger working on the Lucas case astutely remarked, "The motive is murder itself."

The present work includes both serial and simultaneous mass murderers, and is divided into three subsections: first, a list of general or encyclopedic works on homicide: a second list of works directed toward the psychological or psychiatric roots of murder; and a final section listing individual killers alphabetically, with brief case histories preceding each specific list of sources. The notation (S) or (M) beside a killer's name distinguishes between the serial and mass (or simultaneous) murderers. Some famous unsolved multicides have been included, with their entries listed either under well-known nicknames for the murderer (the "Zodiac," etc.) or the location of the crime (e.g., Chicago child murders, 1956-57). Entries are cross-indexed where a pair or group of killers were involved in several homicides; case histories are offered for the leader of the group or team (if one had been identified), including notes on the participation of accomplices. If there is no apparent leader, entries are appended alphabetically to the first member of the group (e.g., "Beck" for entries on the team of Martha Beck and Ray Fernandez).

Sources listed have been chosen with an eye toward comprehensive coverage. Two notable exceptions, here omitted, are the local press and pulp "detective" magazines. No study of mass murder is complete without resort to both, but they have been omitted from the present volume in the interest of space, and because of the general absence of reliable indices. (Serious students should consult the excellent NEW YORK TIMES INDEX for a yearly survey of outstanding cases.) While "the pulps" contain a wealth of information (and misinformation), they are neither indexed nor preserved by any major public library. Die-hard students of the subject may take a subscription or find the latest issues readily available at any newsstand; older issues can be found, with effort, in some used-book stores. Exclusion of these bountiful but highly perishable sources has necessitated the omission of some fascinating cases--the Toledo Clubber for example, sought by the authorities, without success, since 1931--but any effort to compile a comprehensive listing of the many weeklies, dailies, and "police gazettes" was clearly an unmanageable task. Other sources here omitted are the countless volumes which contain some passing mention of specific multicides, but which contribute no substantial information. Any text on vampirism, for example, doubtless will include some reference to Countess Bathory or Peter Kurten, but material contained therein has generally been extracted from the classic sources cited here.

What follows is a personal attempt to bring some order out of chaos in the field of literature on multicides. The glaring lack of any such compendium was driven home when I began the research for a pair of criminal biographies in 1985, and found that no collective bibliography existed in the subject area. If the present volume fills that gap, at least in part, it has achieved its purpose.

Mass Murder

PART 1
GENERAL AND ENCYCLOPEDIC WORKS

Books

1. ABC News. "20/20: Can They Be Caught?" New York: American
   Broadcasting Companies, 1984.

   Transcripts of a "20/20" documentary on serial killers,
   broadcast on July 5, 1984. Correspondent Sylvia Chase
   interviews Henry Lucas, together with various detectives
   and psychiatrists.

2. Boar, Roger, and Nigel Blundell. THE WORLD'S MOST INFAM-
   OUS MURDERS. New York: Exeter Books, 1983.

   Presents capsule case histories of thirty-five notorious
   homicide cases, with footnote references to many more,
   including several multicides. Prepared by British authors
   in sensational tabloid style, this volume is one entry in
   a paperback series recounting the "world's greatest"
   mysteries, disasters, UFO sightings, "fantastic freaks,"
   etc. Primarily of interest as the only English-language
   source of information on the case of Pedro Lopez, "The
   Monster of the Andes."

3. Brian, Dennis. MURDERERS DIE. New York: St. Martin's
   Press, 1986.

   Examines modern and historical applications of the death
   penalty, with capsule case histories of thirty-one condemned killers, including several famous multicides.

4. CRIMES AND PUNISHMENT: A PICTORIAL ENCYCLOPEDIA OF ABER-
   RANT BEHAVIOR. (20 Volumes) Paulton, England: The
   Symphonette Press, 1974.

   Treats a wide variety of crimes by topic (swindlers,
   pirates, cannibals, etc.), including numerous individual
   case histories of multicide. An added feature, at the
   end of every volume, is an alphabetical presentation of

infamous cases and criminals. Fully indexed.

5. Demaris, Ovid. AMERICA THE VIOLENT. New York: Cowles
   Book Co., 1970.

   Dedicated "to Peace," this narrative history of American violence from Colonial times through the 1960s is
   clearly written more to entertain than to instruct. A
   chapter on "The Gun and the Sociopath" recounts case histories of several multicides, but serious researchers
   should recall the author's previous involvement with pro-
   duction of assorted highly sensational and heavily fictionalized gangster "biographies."

6. Douthwaite, L.C. MASS MURDER. New York: Holt, Rinehart
   and Winston, 1929.

   An early study of the subject, with attempts to dissect
   motives of some infamous contemporary killers. Interesting primarily from a historical perspective.

7. FACTS ON FILE. (Annual volumes from 1941). New York:
   Facts on File Publications, 1941-1986.

   Records significant news on a weekly basis, bound and
   published in annual volumes, fully indexed. Includes
   reports of major homicides as they occur, providing a
   convenient back-up system for students lacking instant
   access to the major daily papers.

8. Gaute, J.H.H., and Robin Odell. THE MURDERERS' WHO'S
   WHO. London: Harrap, 1979.

   Presents outstanding murder cases in an encyclopedic
   format, with inclusion of some European cases overlooked
   by similar volumes published domestically. A valuable
   work, with sources cross-referenced to facilitate further
   study of individual cases.

9. ———. MURDER, "WHATDUNIT." London: Harrap, 1982.

   A companion volume to THE MURDERERS' WHO'S WHO.
   Approaches famous homicides from the unique perspective
   of examining the weapons used. Indexed to assist the
   student who may know "whodunit," but who may not be
   precisely sure "whatdunit" prior to reading this informative and entertaining volume.

10. Godwin, John. MURDER USA. New York: Ballantine, 1978.

Attempts to pick out patterns and suggest solutions for the American "murder epidemic" of the 1970s. Godwin's readable account includes case histories of several fascinating multicides, with chapters devoted to homosexual murders and a "chamber of horrors" for especially bizarre cases. Inclusion of some major psychiatric theories makes this volume well worth reading.

11. Green, Jonathon. THE GREATEST CRIMINALS OF ALL TIME. New York: Stein and Day, 1982.

Presents abbreviated histories of famous criminals, including 90 separate multicides, in chapters broken down by topic (i.e., swindlers, sex crimes, cannibals, etc.). Incorporates a few case histories not covered in the other literature to date.

12. Hurwood, Bernhardt J. VAMPIRES, WEREWOLVES, AND GHOULS. New York: Ace Books, 1968.

Presents case histories of several famous multicides within a lurid paperback examination of the "human monsters" who inspired beliefs in vampirism and lycanthropy. Ostensibly designed to seek "the facts" behind primitive superstitions, this volume relies primarily on cases from the 19th and 20th centuries. Cover blurbs describe the author as an "internationally recognized expert on the Strange, the Uncanny, the Bizarre!"

13. Jones, Ann. WOMEN WHO KILL. New York: Holt, Rinehart and Winston, 1980.

Approaches homicides by women from a modern feminist perspective, cataloguing female murderers from Colonial times to the present. Jones concludes that "[s]ociety is afraid of both the feminist and the murderer, for each of them, in their own way, tests society's established boundaries."

14. Kuncl, Tom, and Paul Einstein. LADIES WHO KILL. New York: Pinnacle, 1985.

Presenting case histories of twelve female murderers, this paperback includes three separate multicides not covered in the other literature. Sensational at times, in the style of "pulp" detective magazines, the

acknowledgments make it clear that case histories were
lifted more or less intact from files of various local
dailies around the country.

15. Levin, Jack, and James Alan Fox. MASS MURDER: AMERICA'S
    GROWING MENACE. New York: Plenum Press, 1985.

    Recent and readable, this excellent primer for begin-
    ning students of the subject reviews major psychiatric
    theories and refers to more than sixty major multicides,
    with cases as current as 1984. The single weakness—if
    it is a weakness—is the authors' tendency to lump pro-
    fessional killers and religious cultists with compulsive
    multicides as related subjects of inquiry. Probably the
    best beginning point for any general study of the field.

16. Leyton, Elliott. COMPULSIVE KILLERS. Washington Square,
    N.Y.: New York University Press, 1986.

    Opens with the author's frank admission that "this
    book contains no new data of any kind." Rather, it is
    a "revision" of the work prepared by other writers "who
    have labored so mightily on my behalf." Copious foot-
    notes save Leyton from a charge of plagiarism as he
    examines half a dozen major multicides, deciding of his
    subjects that "[t]heir only value is as objects of study."
    For Leyton's part, her prefers to study from afar, with-
    out leaving home to endure "the nightmare of enforced
    sociability." As Leyton himself admits, other writers
    have done the job before him. They have also done it
    better.

17. Logan, Guy B.H. MASTERS OF CRIME: STUDIES OF MULTIPLE
    MURDERS. London: Stanley Paul & Co., 1928.

    Extracts case histories from the annals of British and
    French authorities, treating twenty separate multicides
    of the nineteenth century. Logan concludes that "[t]he
    one common characteristic all the world over of murder-
    ers of the type described ... is their utter and complete
    insensibility"—i.e., their lack of conscience and re-
    morse.

18. Masters, R.E.L., and Eduard Lea. PERVERSE CRIMES IN
    HISTORY. New York: The Julian Press, 1963.

    Focusing on sex crimes, including several bizarre

multicides, this volume may frustrate researchers through
its heavy reliance on anonymous, undated case histories.
Primary concentration on European cases, with some Third
World examples. A point of particular interest is the
introduction by Dr. John Cassity, one-time senior psychiatrist at Bellevue, who examined cannibal Albert Fish
in 1934-35.

19. Nash, Jay Robert. ALMANAC OF WORLD CRIME. Garden City,
     N.Y.: Anchor Press, 1981.

Examines worldwide crime by categories—murder, arson,
prison breaks, etc.—with numerous case histories included. Better than a number of the author's works, this
volume features essays on mass murder, lethal arsonists,
and medical practitioners of homicide.

20. ————. BLOODLETTERS AND BADMEN. New York: M. Evans
     & Co., 1973.

The first and best of many "crime encyclopedias" from
Nash, including numerous case histories from Colonial
times through the early 1970s. Frequently sensational,
reflecting the author's background as a newsman with
Chicago's dailies, BLOODLETTERS avoids most of the gross
inaccuracies which characterize Nash's later books.
Even so, perusal of the lengthy bibliography reveals a
strong reliance on "pulp" detective magazines, and serious researchers should proceed with caution.

21. ————. CRIME CHRONOLOGY, 1900-1983. New York: Facts
     on File, 1984.

The latest—and among the most confused—of Nash's
several works, this volume is essentially an expanded
version of the chronology contained as an appendix to
item 23 below. Nash presents a wealth of information
and misinformation in time line format, repeating most
of the errors from his previous books and throwing in
some new ones for good measure. Cases erroneously
described as unsolved in item 24 below are still "open"
here, although Nash was informed of his errors a year
before the present volume went to press. Clumsy typo-
graphical errors are accompanied by more substantial
errors of fact. (The David Berkowitz confessions are
placed by Nash in 1976, a year before Berkowitz's arrest,
and Ottis Toole is described as serving time for the
murder of his mother, who died of natural causes in 1981.)

Researchers with an eye for accuracy will avoid this volume energetically.

22. ———. LOOK FOR THE WOMAN. New York: M. Evans & Co., 1981.

A sequel to item 20 above, this encyclopedic volume concentrates on female criminals, including several multicides, selected from around the world. Less careful with his data than in his first encyclopedia, Nash fumbles simple facts, misdating cases by as much as a decade, and occasionally veers off into fantasy, once describing 1930s outlaw "Ma" Barker as a lesbian serial killer with scores of victims to her credit. Primarily of value in disputing claims that women are incapable of multicide, this volume offers more as entertainment than as history.

23. ———. MURDER, AMERICA. New York: Simon & Schuster, 1980.

An anecdotal history of homicide in the United States spanning two centuries, the volume includes chapter-length accounts of nine notorious multicides. An appended chronology of murder, later expanded to book length in a separate volume, briefly recounts some 100 cases of multicide with varying degrees of accuracy. Based on Nash's reputation, serious researchers should beware.

24. ———. OPEN FILES. New York: McGraw-Hill, 1984.

Perhaps the worst of Nash's various encyclopedic volumes, OPEN FILES distorts or totally misrepresents the facts concerning several famous multicides. At least five separate serial murders described by Nash as "unsolved" had resulted in suspect arrests and convictions before publication—in some cases years before Nash unilaterally chose to "reopen" defunct investigations. ("Texas Strangler" Johnny Meadows, for example, confessed and was imprisoned during 1972, twelve years before Nash reported the case as "unsolved.") Other cases are distorted to the point that basic facts become unrecognizable. (The "3X" gunman, sought for shooting two men in New York, in 1930, becomes a "mad bomber" here, accused of detonating charges all around Manhattan in a four-year period!) This volume will impede and frustrate serious researchers in the field.

25. Pearson, Edmund L. "Rules for Murderesses." MASTER-
     PIECES OF MURDER. Edited by Gerald Gross. New York:
     Bonanza Books, 1963.

     Presents a light, facetious view of several famous fe-
     male murderers, including half a dozen well-known multi-
     cides. Pearson's articles are generally considered
     classics of the true crime genre, with tongue-in-cheek
     approach more popular before the 1970s.

26. Purvis, James. GREAT UNSOLVED MYSTERIES. New York:
     Grosset & Dunlap, 1978.

     A popular compendium of "open" cases, this includes
     four famous unsolved serial murder cases from the United
     States and Britain. Brief chapters, quickly written,
     manage to incorporate the classic errors of fact from
     other published sources, but Purvis still manages to do
     a better job, with less, than Nash in OPEN FILES. Light
     reading, geared primarily for entertainment.

27. Scott, Sir Harold. THE CONCISE ENCYCLOPEDIA OF CRIME
     AND CRIMINALS. London: Andre Deutsch, Ltd., 1961.

     As promised by the title, an informative encyclopedia
     of notorious cases, especially intriguing for the British
     point of view.

28. SERIAL MURDERS—HEARINGS BEFORE THE SENATE SUBCOMMITTEE
     ON JUVENILE JUSTICE, JULY 12, 1983. Washington, D.C.:
     U.S. Government Printing Office, 1984.

     Incorporates the testimony of assorted witnesses sup-
     porting the establishment of VICAP, the FBI's Violent
     Criminal Apprehension Program. Includes several case
     histories, together with discussion of techniques for
     "profiling" killers still at large.

29. Sifakis, Carl. THE ENCYCLOPEDIA OF AMERICAN CRIME. New
     York: Facts on File, 1982.

     Surpasses the assorted works of Nash in thoroughness
     and accuracy. Numerous case histories of multicide are
     catalogued with sundry other crimes, dating from Colonial
     times.

30. Steiger, Brad. THE MASS MURDERER. New York: Award
     Books, 1967.

Quickie paperback examination of the subject from an author who has previously specialized in books on UFOs and "Star People," cashing in on free publicity provided by the likes of Richard Speck and Charles Whitman.

31. Tobias, Ronald. THEY SHOOT TO KILL: A PSYCHO-SURVEY OF CRIMINAL SNIPING. Boulder, Colo.: Paladin Press, 1981.

A fascinating and instructive study of criminal snipers, offered by a publisher best known for military manuals. Despite pretentious forays into amateur psychiatry, the work stands up as a valuable reference source, including many multicides, a few of which are covered in no other published work.

32. Tullet, Tom. STRICTLY MURDER. New York: St. Martin's Press, 1979.

An episodic history of Scotland Yard's most famous homicide investigations, through the 1970s, including several British multicides. Written in the style of a police procedural, the volume is designed to showcase Scotland Yard's techniques, but it is still instructive in an area too often overlooked by American sources. Worth reading.

33. Wilson, Colin. A CASEBOOK OF MURDER. New York: Cowles, 1969.

The second volume in Wilson's classic "murder trilogy," picking up where item 35 below left off, with a survey of social trends in homicide through history. Wilson examines the roles of pornography and "magical thinking" as causes of homicide, noting the shift from economic or "rational" murders to the "motiveless" crimes of recent years. Instructive.

34. ————. A CRIMINAL HISTORY OF MANKIND. New York: G.P. Putnam's Sons, 1984.

Relates the history of man "in terms of that counterpart between crime and creativity, and to use the insights it brings to try to discern the next stage of human evolution." The first 150 pages theorize on the psychology of violence; the remainder is a tour of man's deliberately forgotten history, relating trends in crime to various specific eras of development.

35. ————, and Patricia Putnam. THE ENCYCLOPEDIA OF MURDER.
     New York: G.P. Putnam's Sons, 1961.

     The best encyclopedia of homicides in print. Case
     histories, including many multicides, are drawn from the
     United States and foreign countries, with the cases laid
     out alphabetically. Special attention is paid to certain
     sexually-motivated killers. Superior to Nash's several
     efforts in both scope and accuracy, this volume provides
     a decent overview of the subject for beginning students.

36. ————, and Donald Seaman. THE ENCYCLOPEDIA OF MODERN
     MURDER, 1962-1982. New York: G.P. Putnam's Sons,
     1983.

     A completely new companion volume to the 1961 encyclo-
     pedia, with many new case histories of multicide. On a
     par with Wilson's other work, informative and entertain-
     ing.

Articles

37. "Are Serial Killers on the Rise?" U.S. NEWS & WORLD
     REPORT 99 (September 9, 1985): 14.

     Examines the serial murder phenomenon in light of the
     search for California's "Night Stalker" and discusses
     general trends.

38. "Case of the Sudden Murderers." SCIENCE DIGEST 53 (June
     1963): 41.

     A sketchy look at impulse killers.

39. Curtis, L.A. "What's New in Murder?" NEW REPUBLIC 182
     (January 26, 1980): 19-21.

     Takes a look at changing trends in homicide and reaches
     no reliable conclusions on prevention or causality.

40. Darrach, Brad, and Joel Norris. "An American Tragedy."
     LIFE 7 (August 1984): 58-74.

     A timely overview of the serial killer phenomenon, with
     major case histories and a survey of current psychiatric
     opinions on causality. Profusely illustrated, this
     article is a good starting point for beginning students
     of the subject area.

41. "Death Follows Art." TIME 107 (March 22, 1976): 47.

    Examines allegations of multiple murders committed by members of hospital staffs in Michigan and New Jersey.

42. Egger, Steven A. "A Working Definition of Serial Murder and the Reduction of Linkage Blindness." JOURNAL OF POLICE SCIENCE AND ADMINISTRATION (September 1984).

    Egger's definitions of serial murder have been adopted by the FBI's Behavioral Science Unit in coordinating the new Violent Criminal Apprehension Program. Concise and specific, the article includes a brief discussion of the "linkage blindness" which too often prevents police from connecting serial crimes in the early stages.

43. "Further Reflections on Mass Murder." AMERICA 115 (October 15, 1966): 443.

    An editorial overview of the problem, as perceived in 1966, with reference to headline cases of the period.

44. Futch, J.D. "Mass Murder Bourgeois Style." NATIONAL REVIEW 26 (August 30, 1974): 980.

    Compares Dean Corll with Gilles de Rais, concluding that the former lacks "the old charm of aristocratic snobbery." Futch laments "the drabness of an egalitarian era" which produces mundane homicides.

45. Garelik, G., and G. Maranto. "Multiple Murderers." DISCOVER 5 (July 1984): 26-29.

    A survey of the American "murder epidemic."

46. Gest, Ted. "On the Trail of America's Serial Killers." U.S. NEWS & WORLD REPORT 96 (April 30, 1984): 53.

    Examines recent trends, case histories, and efforts to initiate the VICAP program as a means of tracking serial murderers.

47. ————, and Douglas C. Lyons. "Behind a Nationwide Wave of Unsolved Murders." U.S. NEWS & WORLD REPORT 90 (March 16, 1981): 58.

    A survey of contemporary multicides, all of which were subsequently solved.

48. Kagan, D. "Serial Murderers." OMNI 6 (August 1984): 20+.

    An overview of the phenomenon from a periodical normal-
ly devoted to UFOs and science fiction. Adequate, but
no surprises.

49. "Little Murderers." TIME 88 (August 12, 1966): 102.

    Examines children who kill, in light of contemporary
headline cases.

50. Lubenow, G.C. "When Kids Kill Their Parents." NEWSWEEK
    101 (June 27, 1983): 35-36.

    Discussion on the theme of parricide, with attention
to motivations and root causes, inspired by recent notorious cases.

51. "Mass Murder in the US, Why?" U.S. NEWS & WORLD REPORT
    61 (August 15, 1966): 34-35.

    Why, indeed? An interview with psychologist H.A. David-
son, discussing causes of then-recent headline cases.
Inspired by the notoriety of Richard Speck and Charles
Whitman, the interview reaches no lasting conclusions.

52. Meredith, N. "The Murder Epidemic." SCIENCE '84
    5 (December 1984): 4, 42-48.

    Examines changing trends in domestic homicide, with
speculation on causality and remedies.

53. "Murders by Poison." HARPER'S WEEKLY 46 (November 8,
    1902): 1643.

    An early, lightweight overview of "classic" poisoners,
with primary focus on serial killer Jane Toppan, arrested
five months prior to publication.

54. Saltus, E., "Champion Poisoners." COSMOPOLITAN 32 (Feb-
    ruary 1902): 399-402.

    Another early anecdotal history of classic poisoners,
ironically produced before the Chapman and Toppan cases
were announced in flamboyant headlines.

55. Sonnenschein, Allan. "Serial Killers." PENTHOUSE (Feb-
    ruary 1985): 32+.

An adequate overview of the phenomenon, interesting
for its inclusion of an interview with author and self-
styled expert Ann Rule. Particularly fascinating is an
interview with killer Henry Lucas, recorded by author
Hugh Aynesworth two months before Aynesworth's infamous
turnabout, denouncing Lucas's confessions as contrived
and false. The interview, recorded fourteen months after
Lucas allegedly confessed his "hoax," reveals another
side of Aynesworth not apparent in his subsequent self-
righteous "expose."

56. Stanley, A. "Catching a New Breed of Killer." TIME 122
     (November 14, 1983): 47.

     Focuses primarily upon the case of Ottis Toole and
     Henry Lucas, as examples of the serial killer phenomenon
     in America. Brief coverage of the "Hillside Strangler"
     and others.

57. Starr, Mark. "The Random Killers." NEWSWEEK 104 (Novem-
     ber 26, 1984): 100-106.

     An overview of the serial killer phenomenon, with special
     emphasis on Lucas, Toole, and other recent headliners.
     Coverage of major psychiatric opinions is included.
     Instructive.

58. "Symptoms of Mass Murder." TIME 88 (August 12, 1966):
     18-19.

     A journalistic effort to predict mass murder and deter-
     mine causal factors in the wake of the Speck and Whitman
     cases. Contains few viable conclusions, in the light of
     later evidence.

59. "These Brutal Young." NEWSWEEK 49 (March 25, 1957): 36+.

     Examines some contemporary cases of adolescent homicide,
     inspired by Charles Starkweather and publicity concerning
     "juvenile delinquents."

60. Walker, G. "Why Children Kill." COSMOPOLITAN 143 (Oc-
     tober 1957): 48-51.

     Inspired by Charles Starkweather's Nebraska murder
     spree, the article attempts to fathom youthful violence
     from a 1950s viewpoint. Interesting primarily as history,
     since relatively few of the determined causal factors

are in vogue today.

61. "Wife Killers." NEWSWEEK 43 (May 24, 1954): 81.

Reveiws the methodology and motivations of contemporary spouse killers.

PART 2
SPECIALIZED/PSYCHOLOGICAL WORKS

Books

62. Abrahamson, David. THE MURDERING MIND. New York: Harper and Row, 1973.

Freudian in perspective, Abrahamson stresses the sexual nature of "all" violent acts. Four years after publication of this book, he was involved in the psychiatric evaluations of David Berkowitz—the "Son of Sam." Abrahamson found Berkowitz sane and competent for trial, despite a diagnosis of paranoid schizophrenia.

63. Brussel, James A. CASEBOOK OF A CRIME PSYCHIATRIST. New York: Bernard Geis Associates, 1968.

An interesting volume, written from the viewpoint of a working crime psychiatrist involved in tracking killers to detection and arrest. The author was involved in preparation of official "profiles" on the Boston Strangler, New York's Mad Bomber, and other multicides, some unsolved at the time of publication. The pitfalls of attempting to describe an unknown killer are explored, with the exuberance of victory and the traumatic cost of failure. Well worth reading.

64. Fredericks, Carlton. PSYCHO-NUTRITION. New York: Grosset and Dunlap, 1976.

The author, a vitamin specialist, asserts that chemicals in common tap water may produce "mental disturbances" in certain individuals. He reaches firmer ground in stating that selected vitamin deficiencies may contribute to depression, or even schizophrenia. An interesting, if unusual, perspective on the possible physiological causality of multicides and other violent crimes.

65. Fromm, Erich. THE ANATOMY OF HUMAN DESTRUCTIVENESS.
     New York: Holt, Rinehart and Winston, 1973.

     Argues that a need for dominance derives from feelings
     of inadequacy or the lack of self-fulfillment. Even at
     the time, it was a less than startling conclusion. Routine.

66. Krafft-Ebing, Richard. PSYCOPATHIA SEXUALIS. Chicago:
     W.T. Kenner & Co., 1900.

     The original study of sex crimes, still regarded as a
     classic. Krafft-Ebing coined the term "sadism," and
     pioneered in the study of "lust murder," along with other
     less lethal perversions. A fascinating slice of history.

67. ———. ABERRATIONS OF SEXUAL LIFE. (Edited by Alexan-
     der Hartwich.) London: Staples Press, 1959.

     Selected excerpts from the work of a recognized pioneer
     in the study of sex crime and lust murder.

68. Lunde, Donald T. MURDER AND MADNESS. San Francisco:
     San Francisco Book Co., 1976.

     A Stanford University psychiatrist, Lunde has been
     employed as a consultant on numerous homicides. His book
     relies extensively upon his own first-hand experience,
     including interviews with Edmund Kemper, Herbert Mullin,
     John Linley Frazier, and other mass killers. He describes
     two general types of repeat killers: the paranoid schizo-
     phrenic and the rarer sadistic sociopath. An interesting
     and instructive launching point for students in the field.

69. Palmer, Stuart. THE PSYCHOLOGY OF MURDER. New York:
     Thomas Y. Crowell, 1960.

     Based upon the author's study of fifty-one (non-multiple)
     murderers, this volume traces lethal violence to the
     childhood of the prepetrator, finding roots in early ill-
     ness, child abuse, poverty, and other environmental
     factors. Written by a sociologist, the text is limited
     by its restriction to one-time killers, but it is none-
     theless instructive as a primer of established thought
     before the "homicidal mania" of the 1970s and '80s
     became headline news.

70. Reinhardt, James Melvin. THE PSYCHOLOGY OF STRANGE
     KILLERS. Springfield, Ill.: Charles C. Thomas, 1962.

A Nebraska professor of criminology presents nine "strange" cases, including eight multicides. Reinhardt's introduction draws a vague distinction between "lust" killers and those who kill for pleasure, breaking new ground for its time by discussing "chain killers"—i.e., serial murderers—twenty years before most authorities recognized the distinction.

71.   ———.   SEX PERVERSIONS AND SEX CRIMES.   Springfield, Ill.: Charles C. Thomas, 1957.

Author Reinhardt examines sex crimes from the viewpoint of the 1950s.   Interesting, but dated.

72.   Shah, Saleem A.   "The 47, XYY Chromosomal Abnormality: A Critical Appraisal with Respect to Antisocial and Violent Behavior."   ISSUES IN BRAIN/BEHAVIOR CONTROL. Edited by W. Lynn Smith and Arthur Kling.   New York: Spectrum, 1976.

Provides a comprehensive overview of the "XYY syndrome" debate.   A useful primer in the area of chromosomal abnormality and its alleged affect on violent behavior.

73.   Smith, W. Lynn, and Arthur Kling, eds.   ISSUES IN BRAIN/ BEHAVIOR CONTROL.   New York: Spectrum, 1976.

Contains items 72 and 75.

74.   Traini, Robert.   MURDER FOR SEX.   London: Kimber, 1960.

Examines motivations in the cases of compulsive "lust murderers."   Valuable as an overview of British thought ten years before the onset of the later "murder epidemic."

75.   Valenstein, Elliot S.   "Brain Stimulation and the Origin of Violent Behavior."   ISSUES IN BRAIN/BEHAVIOR CONTROL. Cited above as item 73.

Discusses Charles Whitman and discounts the sudden, impulsive theory of simultaneous mass murder.

76.   Wilson, Colin.   ORDER OF ASSASSINS.   London: Rupert Hart-Davis, 1972.

The final volume of Wilson's "murder trilogy," concerned primarily with the psychological motives for homicide. Sex crimes and "motiveless" murders receive special attention.

77. Wolfgang, Marvin E., ed. STUDIES IN HOMICIDE. New York:
    Harper and Row, 1967, pp. 170-178.

    Reprints item 83 below.

Articles

78. Campbell, Colin. "Portrait of a Mass Killer." PSYCHOL-
    OGY TODAY 9 (May 1976): 110-111+.

    Cites the California "Skid Row Slasher" case to prove
    that psychological "profiles" of killers still at large
    are "irrelevant and overtouted." An interesting look
    behind the hoopla of publicity.

79. Colligan, D. "Children Who Kill, and Why." SCIENCE
    DIGEST 74 (September 1973): 31-35.

    Examines homicides by juveniles, including parricide.

80. Dorfman, A. "Profiling Serial Killers." SCIENCE DIGEST
    92 (October 1984): 47.

    A brief look at the "science" of preparing profiles
    on serial killers still at large. Dorfman's viewpoint
    is refuted by item 77 above.

81. Evseef, G.F., and W.M. Wisniewski. "A Psychiatric Study
    of a Violent Mass Murderer." JOURNAL OF FORENSIC
    SCIENCE 17 (1972).

    Was there ever a nonviolent mass murderer? The article
    presents an anonymous study of "Bill," a simultaneous
    mass killer who axed his wife and five step-children to
    death. The authors base their theory of "homicidal-
    proneness" on incidents from an abusive childhood, or
    involving sexually provocative parents. Oversimplified.

82. Felthous, Alan R. "Childhood Cruelty to Cats, Dogs, and
    Other Animals." BULLETIN OF THE AMERICAN ACADEMY OF
    PSYCHIATRY AND THE LAW 9 (1981).

    Examines childhood torture of animals as a symptom of
    future violence against humans, with mixed results. It
    is a fact that many mass killers first practiced violence
    on the lower species, but, in turn, the vast majority of

children who are cruel to animals at one time or another
grow to lead "normal" lives. Interesting, but inconclu-
sive.

83. Galvin, James A.V., and John MacDonald. "Psychiatric
     Study of a Mass Murderer." AMERICAN JOURNAL OF PSY-
     CHIATRY 115 (June 1959): 1957-1961.

     Applies MacDonald's "triad" of symptoms—bedwetting,
     arson, and cruelty to animals—to the specific case of
     airline bomber Jack Graham. Interesting.

84. Hellman, Daniel S., and Nathan Blackman. "Enuresis,
     Firesetting, and Cruelty to Animals." AMERICAN JOURNAL
     OF PSYCHIATRY 122 (1966).

     A blanket endorsement of MacDonald's "triad," written
     three years after the fact. The authors go so far as to
     label enuresis (bedwetting) a form of "sadism." Stretching.

85. Herbert, W. "The Case of the Missing Hormones." SCIENCE
     NEWS 122 (October 30, 1982): 282.

     Speculates upon apparent deficits of the homone sero-
     tonin in the brains of certain psychopathic killers.

86. "How to Tell Who Will Kill." NEWSWEEK 81 (June 4, 1973):
     69-70.

     How indeed? Surveys contemporary psychiatric thought,
     in light of Edmund Kemper's homicides in Santa Cruz,
     California.

87. Lunde, Donald T. "Our Murder Boom." PSYCHOLOGY TODAY
     9 (November 1975): 35-40+.

     Excerpts from item 67 above.

88. MacDonald, John M. "The Threat to Kill." AMERICAN
     JOURNAL OF PSYCHIATRY 120 (1963).

     Perhaps the single most influential statement of homi-
     cidal symptoms to date. MacDonald here delineates his
     "triad" of warning signs—childhood bedwetting, arson,
     and cruelty toward animals—which indicate a tendency
     toward homicide in later life. Or do they? Less enthus-
     iastically received today than in the 1960s, this remains
     a seminal work in the field.

89. McBroom, P. "Can Killers Be Predicted?" SCIENCE NEWS
     90 (August 20, 1966): 117.

     Can killers be predicted? Probably not, but in the
     wake of Charles Whitman's murder spree, psychiatrists
     and authors felt obliged to try. This article reviews
     the major theories and the warning signs, including Mac-
     Donald's famous "triad."

90. "The Mind of a Murderer." MEDICAL WORLD NEWS (November
     23, 1973).

     Quotes Dr. Mortimer Gross, and others, on the "close
     link between organic brain disease" and violent acts,
     especially the sudden or impulsive type. Persuasive,
     within limits, but the fact remains that no conclusive
     link has been established.

91. "Mind of the Mass Murderer." TIME 102 (August 27, 1973):
     56-57.

     Examines psychological motives in light of then-recent
     exposure of Dean Corll's Texas homicides. Quotes psy-
     chiatrists on other notorious cases, with a sidebar on
     the problem of teenage runaways (who comprised the bulk
     of Corll's victims).

92. "The Moon and Murder." SKY TELESCOPE 70 (July 1985): 28.

     Contends that there is no evidence of "moon madness"
     as a cause of homicide.

93. Ritts, M. "Why Mass Murderers Kill." MACLEANS 99 (April
     21, 1986): 34-37.

     Interviews Elliott Leyton, author of item 16 above.

94. Simpson, M.L. "Understanding Lethal Violence." INTELLECT
     105 (May 1977): 379-380.

     Searches nebulously for "the motive" in modern homi-
     cides. Foredoomed to failure by the shotgun approach.

95. Zilbauer, A. "Moon Madness." NEWSWEEK 42 (December 14,
     1953): 26+.

     Postulates a link between the phases of the moon and
     violent crime, with "evidence" from contemporary police
     statistics. Refuted by item 91 above.

PART 3
CASE HISTORIES

1. ACQUIN, LORNE (M)

The worst mass murderer in Connecticut history. Acquin was convicted in October 1979 of bludgeoning and stabbing to death a housewife, her seven children, and a neighbor's child before burning the house with their bodies inside. Sentenced to life imprisonment.

* FACTS ON FILE. Volume 39, 1979. Cited above as item 7, p. 819.

    Contemporaneous account of Acquin's trial and conviction.

2. ADORNO, GEORGE (S)

Confessed to triple murder in New York City during 1974, at age 15. Convicted and imprisoned on a lesser charge, he was released in 1977. Nineteen days later he murdered again, and was sent back to prison for life.

* Sifakis, Carl. THE ENCYCLOPEDIA OF AMERICAN CRIME. Cited above as item 29, p. 6.

    Capsule case history presented in an encyclopedic format.

3. ALEXANDER, FRANK and HARALD (M)

Father and son religious fanatics residing at Tenerife, in the Canary Islands, who slaughtered Frank's wife (Harald's mother) and two daughters (Harald's sisters) in December 1970. The victims were battered and grossly mutilated with a hammer and other tools, reputedly as part of a ritual sacrifice. Both father and son were convicted and imprisoned.

* CRIMES AND PUNISHMENT: A PICTORIAL ENCYCLOPEDIA OF ABER-RANT BEHAVIOR, Volume 12. Cited above as item 4, pp. 87-88.

Covers the peculiar case with emphasis on religious mania's impact on violent crime.

* Green, Jonathon. THE GREATEST CRIMINALS OF ALL TIME. Cited above as item 11, p. 248.

Capsule case history presented in encyclopedic format.

4. ALLAWAY, EDWARD (M)

Library janitor at California State University, in Fullerton, who brought a rifle to work in July 1976, killing seven co-workers and wounding two others. Declared not guilty by reason of insanity; admitted to Atascadero State Hospital.

* Levin, Jack, and James Alan Fox. MASS MURDER: AMERICA'S GROWING MENACE. Cited above as item 15.

Brief case history contained in general narrative.

5. ALLEN, JIMMIE LEE (M)

With accomplice Junius Gray, murdered four persons during random burglaries in Bedford Hills, N.Y., on the evening of May 9, 1979. Convicted and imprisoned.

Books

* FACTS ON FILE. Volume 39, 1979. Cited above as item 7, p. 548.

Contemporaneous account of Allen's indictment in July.

Articles

96. "Tucker, Carll. "The End of the Ostrich Option." SATURDAY REVIEW 6 (July 7, 1979): 56.

A Bedford native laments the intrusion of modern-day violence on his idyllic home town. Written prior to the arrest of Allen and Gray.

6. ALLENTOWN, PENN., ARSON (M)

Unsolved firebombing of a nightclub by an angry patron during March 1976. Eight customers were killed, a dozen others injured in the fire.

* Nash, Jay Robert. CRIME CHRONOLOGY, 1900–1983. Cited
  above as item 21, p. 186.

  Capsule case history in time line format.

7. ALTON, ? (S)

First name unavailable, a British "ripper" of the 1880s.
His precise number of victims is uncertain. Mutilation of
victims included excision of female genitalia. A captured
diary described one murder thus: "Killed a young girl today.
It was fine and hot." Hanged for murder in London.

* Masters, R.E.L., and Eduard Lea. PERVERSE CRIMES IN
  HISTORY. Cited above as item 18, p. 93.

  Lamentably brief reference in a chapter dealing with
  "rippers and slashers."

8. ANDERSON, ALLEN LEROY (S)

Departing from Seattle, Wash., in a stolen car, he crossed
some twenty states in 1976, robbing scores of victims, killing
at least eight. Sentenced to life imprisonment.

* Nash, Jay Robert. MURDER, AMERICA. Cited above as item
  23, p. 443.

  Brief case history in time line format.

9. ANDREWS, LOWELL LEE (M)

Obese honor student, fatally shot both parents and his
sister as they watched television in the family home at Wol-
cott, Kansas, in November 1958. First blamed burglars, then
confessed that he had hoped for an inheritance which would
enable him to visit Chicago and become a "hired gun." Hanged
at Leavenworth prison.

* FACTS ON FILE. Volume 18, 1958. Cited above as item 7,
  p. 396.

  Contemporaneous account of the Andrews massacre.

* Nash, Jay Robert. CRIME CHRONOLOGY, 1900–1983. Cited
  above as item 21, p. 157.

  Capsule case history in time line format.

* ————. MURDER, AMERICA. Cited above as item 23, p. 429.

Thumbnail sketch presented in time line format.

10. ANGELOF, ANGEL (M)

Bulgarian refugee-turned-sniper who killed two civilians
and wounded two police officers in New York City, July 1968.
Killed by police at the scene.

* FACTS ON FILE. Volume 28, 1968. Cited above as item 7,
p. 278.

Contemporary report of the shoot-out.

11. ANN ARBOR HOSPITAL MURDERS (S)

Unsolved murders of at least eleven patients at the Veteran's Administration hospital in Ann Arbor, Mich., reported
during August 1975. Patients had been variously killed by
lethal injection and disconnection of respirators. FBI investigation led to the conviction of two hospital nurses in
July 1977. Both won new trials on appeal, and were subsequently
acquitted. No new suspects have been publicly identified.

Books

* FACTS ON FILE. Volume 35, 1975. Cited above as item 7,
p. 859.

Contemporary report of the FBI's continuing probe.

* FACTS ON FILE. Volume 37, 1977. Cited above as item 7,
pp. 568, 999.

Reports the conviction and subsequent successful appeal
of nurses Filipina Narciso and Leonora Perez.

* FACTS ON FILE. Volume 38, 1978. Cited above as item 7,
p. 116.

Reports the dropping of all charges against the suspect
nurses in Ann Arbor.

* Nash, Jay Robert. CRIME CHRONOLOGY, 1900-1983. Cited
above as item 21, p. 188.

Brief synopsis presented in time line format.

97. Wilcox, Robert K. THE MYSTERIOUS DEATHS AT ANN ARBOR.
     New York: Popular Library, 1977.

     Paperback account of the murders and arrests, prepared
     before the charges were dismissed against Narcisso and
     Perez. Wilcox includes the "murder" of an Ann Arbor
     nurse, found dead in her apartment, as one of the unsolved,
     related cases.

                              Articles

98. "Unnatural Causes." NEWSWEEK 86 (September 1, 1975): 19.

     Contemporary report of the continuing investigation.

                     12. ARDISON, VICTOR (S)

     Nineteenth-century French necrophile who slept with the
severed heads of his victims. Executed on the guillotine.

  * CRIMES AND PUNISHMENT: A PICTORIAL ENCYCLOPEDIA OF ABER-
     RANT BEHAVIOR, Volume 7. Cited above as item 4, p. 31.

     Brief case history within a longer chapter devoted to
     human "vampires."

                     13. ARNOLD, LESLIE (M)

     Teenager who killed both parents in an argument about
the family car, October 1958. Both bodies were unearthed
behind the family home in Omaha, Neb., whereupon Arnold confessed.

  * FACTS ON FILE. Volume 18, 1958. Cited above as item 7,
     p. 336.

     Contemporaneous account of Arnold's arrest.

                  14. ARRINGTON, MARIE DEAN (S)

     While free on appeal of a 20-year manslaughter sentence
for killing her husband, Arrington murdered the secretary of
a Florida attorney and was sentenced to death. She escaped
from prison in 1969, and was recaptured by the FBI in 1972.

  * Godwin, John. MURDER USA. Cited above as item 10, p. 131.

     Brief case history in a chapter on female murderers.

15. ATKINS, SUSAN (M)

Female member of the so-called Manson "family," present as a participant or observer in at least eight cult-related homicides in 1969. Sentenced to death in the Tate-LaBianca murders, her sentence was commuted to life imprisonment when California's state supreme court struck down the death penalty as "cruel and unusual" punishment.

99. Atkins, Susan, and Bob Slosser. CHILD OF SATAN, CHILD OF GOD. Plainfield, N.J.: Logos International, 1977.

    Autobiographical account of life with Manson, life in prison, and "rebirth" as a "born-again" Christian. Includes attempts to shift the blame for individual murders to other members of the tribe, along with a bizarre account ot Tex Watson "floating four feet off the ground" at the Tate murder scene, presumably possessed by Satan. Parole authorities remain unimpressed by Atkins's change of heart.

16. ATTERBURY, IRA (M)

Sixty-four-year-old sniper who opened fire on parade spectators in San Antonio, Texas, from his barricaded trailer during April 1979. Atterbury had previously been responsible for the deaths of two women in an auto accident, and while he was absolved of criminal responsibility, family members noted increasing paranoia toward police following the incident. Before he started shooting passers-by, Atterbury was heard to shout, "What kind of society is this? Traitors!" Two persons were killed and 55 wounded during Atterbury's shooting spree. Atterbury shot himself to death after battling police for 45 minutes.

* Tobias, Ronald. THEY SHOOT TO KILL. Cited above as item 31, pp. 64-66.

    Case history within a survey of criminal snipers.

17. AUSTRALIAN SEX MURDERS (S)

Reportedly unsolved homicides of at least seven women around Adelaide, Australia, between 1976 and 1979, "presumably" committed by the same unidentified killer.

* Nash, Jay Robert. CRIME CHRONOLOGY, 1900-1983. Cited above as item 21, p. 196.

The only available reference to this series of crimes.
Based on Nash's reputation, students should proceed with
caution until further documentation is obtained.

18. AVINAIN, CHARLES (S)

Professional butcher and killer for profit who murdered
an uncertain number of victims in France, between 1833 and
the early 1860s. Avinain lured farmers to his shop on the
pretext of buying hay, then murdered them, selling off their
horses, hay, and wagons. On arrest, he led police to two
recent corpses. Executed on the guillotine for double murder.

* Logan, Guy B.H. MASTERS OF CRIME. Cited above as item
   17, pp. 99-109.

   Case history within an anthology of infamous nineteenth-
   century multicides.

* Nash, Jay Robert. ALMANAC OF WORLD CRIME. Cited above
   as item 19, p. 272.

   Brief case history within a chapter on notorious mass
   killers.

19. "AX MAN OF NEW ORLEANS, THE" (S)

Unidentified killer of at least seven persons in New
Orleans between June 1918 and October 1919, so-called because
his favorite weapon was an ax or hatchet. All sources credit
the same killer with other homicides committed in 1911, but
personal research reveals no evidence in media or law enforcement files of any such previous crimes. (The error seemingly
originated with the local press and was perpetuated through
the years by careless authors.) A father and son, convicted
in one of the crimes, were subsequently pardoned when the only
living witness recanted her testimony. Suspect Josef Mumfre
was murdered by the widow of the Ax Man's final victim in
December 1920, but no solid evidence exists to link him with
the crimes.

* Gaute, J.H.H., and Robin Odell. THE MURDERERS' WHO'S
   WHO. Cited above as item 8, pp. 31-32.

   Brief case history contained in an encyclopedic format.

* Nash, Jay Robert. CRIME CHRONOLOGY, 1900-1983. Cited
   above as item21, pp. 45, 48-49.

Reports the Ax Man crimes in time line format, complete with erroneous reference to nonexistent murders in 1911.

* ———. OPEN FILES. Cited above as item 24, pp. 17-21.

Lifts the basic facts (and errors) from item 102 below.

* Purvis, James. GREAT UNSOLVED MYSTERIES. Cited above as item 26, pp. 25-32.

Relies on item 102 below, incorporating the usual facts and mistakes.

100. Reid, Ed. MAFIA. New York: Random House, 1952, pp. 185-186.

Describes the crimes obliquely, and without referring to the Ax Man, as a Mafia vendetta against the Pepitone family, conducted by a hit-man named "Doc" Mumfre. Unfortunately, there is no supporting documentation, and only one of seven known victims—the last—was a member of the Pepitone family. (Several victims were non-Italian.) Unreliable.

101. Saxon, Lyle, Edward Dreyer, and Robert Tallant. GUMBO YA-YA. Boston: WPA Writer's Project, 1945, pp. 75-92.

Predates Tallant's subsequent report in item 102 below, containing identical facts and errors. Interesting primarily for inclusion of other New Orleans phantoms such as "Jack the Clipper."

* Sifakis, Carl. THE ENCYCLOPEDIA OF AMERICAN CRIME. Cited above as item 29, pp. 523-524.

Brief case history in an encyclopedic format.

102. Tallant, Robert. MURDER IN NEW ORLEANS: SEVEN FAMOUS TRIALS. London: William Kimber, 1952, pp. 193-217.

Reworks and expands the report contained in item 101. Obviously the source of subsequent reports, it is unfortunate that Tallant did not look beneath the surface of erroneous newspaper references to alleged Ax Man crimes in 1911.

* Wilson, Colin, and Patricia Putnam. THE ENCYCLOPEDIA OF MURDER. Cited above as item 35, pp. 61-63.

Capsule history contained in an encyclopedic format.

20. "BABYSITTER, THE" (S)

Unidentified killer of at least four children in Oakland County, Mich., during 1976 and '77. (Authorities disagree on inclusion of three other victims in the series.) Children were abducted and killed only during winter months, being smothered or shot after days of captivitiy. Several of the corpses were ritually bathed before abandonment in snow banks adjoining local roads, and two male victims showed evidence of sexual abuse prior to death.

Books

*   Levin, Jack, and James Alan Fox. MASS MURDER: AMERICA'S GROWING MENACE. Cited above as item 15.

    Passing reference as an example of unsolved serial murders.

*   Nash, Jay Robert. CRIME CHRONOLOGY, 1900-1983. Cited above as item 21, p. 189.

    Brief report presented in time line format.

*   ————. OPEN FILES. Cited above as item 24, pp. 60-64.

    Outlines the basic facts of all seven homicides. Better than usual for Nash.

Articles

103. Davidson, Bill. "Town That Lives in Terror." GOOD HOUSEKEEPING 185 (September 1977): 136-137+.

      Reviews the recent homicides and evidence, with emphasis on protective measures undertaken by Oakland County parents and authorities.

104. Montagno, M., and J.C. Jones. "Child Killer." NEWSWEEK 91 (February 13, 1978): 9+.

      Recaps the case, anticipating future crimes which failed to materialize.

105. "They All Trusted Their Killer." TIME 109 (April 4, 1977): 20.

Examines evidence and police theories in the unsolved crimes.

21. BAILEY, SUSAN and ROGER (M)

Sister and brother, aged 15 and 13 respectively, who torched the family home in West Virginia during June 1969, killing both parents and ten siblings, ranging in age from eight months to 17 years. Susan resented her father's threat to have her boyfriend arrested if she continued seeing him, and persuaded her brother to join in the crime.

Books

* FACTS ON FILE. Volume 29, 1969. Cited above as item 7, p. 444.

Contemporaneous report of the crime and arrests.

Articles

106. "Susan and the Elders." NEWSWEEK 73 (June 23, 1969): 37.

Contemporaneous report of the crime and arrests.

22. BALL, JOE (S)

Nightclub proprietor and alligator breeder who murdered two wives and an estimated 20 barmaid/mistresses during the 1920s and '30s, disposing of remains by using them as alligator food. Exposed in 1937 when the family of his latest victim pressed the local sheriff to investigate her sudden disappearance. Ball committed suicide when officers arrived to question him, but evidence was gathered from his neighbors and a simple-minded handyman who helped him feed his five pet alligators.

* Nash, Jay Robert. CRIME CHRONOLOGY, 1900–1983. Cited above as item 21, p. 112.

Capsule summary in time line format.

* ————. MURDER, AMERICA. Cited above as item 23, p. 415.

Brief description of the case in time line format.

* Sifakis, Carl. THE ENCYCLOPEDIA OF AMERICAN CRIME. Cited above as item 29, p. 45.

Brief case history presented in encyclopedic format.

* Wilson, Colin, and Patricia Putnam. THE ENCYCLOPEDIA
  OF MURDER. Cited above as item 35, pp. 64-65.

  The best account of Ball's bizarre career, presented
  in encyclopedic format.

23. BARBARO, ANTHONY F. (M)

Teenaged sniper who killed three persons and wounded
eleven in a 1974 shooting spree at his Olean, N.Y., high
school. The wounded were firemen, attempting to extinguish
fires which Barbaro had set inside the school. Taken into
custody, the suspect hanged himself in jail before he could
be brought to trial.

Books

* Nash, Jay Robert. CRIME CHRONOLOGY, 1900-1983. Cited
  above as item 21, p. 186.

  Brief account presented in time line format.

* Tobias, Ronald. THEY SHOOT TO KILL. Cited above as
  item 31, p. 74.

  Brief case history within a survey of criminal snipers.

Articles

107. "The Pride of Olean." NEWSWEEK 85 (January 13, 1975):
     27.

     Contemporaneous account of the shootings and arrest.

24. BARFIELD, MARGIE VELMA (S)

Sunday school teacher and chronic drug abuser, convicted
of one homicide by poisoning in 1979 and linked to five others
spanning a decade. Victims included her mother, two husbands,
a fiancee, and individuals who hired her as a live-in housekeeper. Executed at Raleigh, N.C., in November 1984, she was
the first woman put to death in the United States since 1962.

Books

* FACTS ON FILE. Volume 44, 1984. Cited above as item 7,
  p. 839.

Contemporaneous report of Barfield's execution.

* Kuncl, Tom, and Paul Einstein. LADIES WHO KILL. Cited
  above as item 14, pp. 134-146.

  Adequate case history extracted from contemporary news
  reports.

Articles

* Darrach, Brad, and Joel Norris. "An American Tragedy."
  Cited above as item 40, pp. 60, 68.

  Relates alleged sexual abuse of Barfield during childhood to her adult homicides.

108. Levin, Eric. "Cunning Prisoner—or Redeemed Christian—
     Velma Barfield Draws Nearer to Her Day of Execution."
     PEOPLE WEEKLY 22 (October 19, 1984): 85-86+.

     Examines Barfield's life in prison and the controversy
     which surrounded her impending death.

109. "Life or Death: A Candidate's Choice." NEWSWEEK 104
     (October 8, 1984): 29.

     Explores the political ramifications of putting a woman
     to death in an election year.

110. Willimon, W.H. "Death in North Carolina." CHRISTIAN
     CENTURY 101 (November 18, 1984): 1116.

     Examines Christian viewpoints on the Barfield execution,
     after the fact.

25. BATES, CLYDE (M)

With companions Oscar Brenhaug, Manuel J. Chavez, and
Manuel J. Hernandez, Bates was forcibly ejected from a Los
Angeles saloon for rowdy conduct during April 1957. The four
returned a short time later and torched the establishment,
killing six persons and injuring three. All were convicted
and jailed.

* FACTS ON FILE. Volume 17, 1957. Cited above as item 7,
  p. 120.

  Contemporaneous report of the crime and arrests.

26. BATHORY, ELISABETH (S)

Hungarian countess obsessed with youth, who sought to halt the aging process by bathing in the blood of murdered virgins. At her trial in 1611, she was accused of personally killing some 650 girls by biting their necks; others had reportedly been tortured to death by Bathory's servants, on her orders. Spared from execution by her royal lineage, the countess was walled up for life in a wing of the family castle, where she died in 1614. Her seven accomplices were put to death.

     * Green, Jonathon. THE GREATEST CRIMINALS OF ALL TIME. Cited above as item 11, p. 268.

       Case history contained in an encyclopedic format.

     * Hurwood, Bernhardt J. VAMPIRES, WEREWOLVES, AND GHOULS. Cited above as item 12, pp. 141-147.

       Surveys the case within a sensational catalogue of "human monsters."

111. Masters, Anthony. THE NATURAL HISTORY OF THE VAMPIRE. New York: G.P. Putnam's Sons, 1972.

       Examines the Bathory case as an outgrowth (and possible origin) of Eastern European vampire legends.

     * Masters, R.E.L., and Eduard Lea. PERVERSE CRIMES IN HISTORY. Cited above as item 18, pp. 12-24.

       Describes the case as an example of sexually-motivated vampirism.

     * Nash, Jay Robert. ALMANAC OF WORLD CRIME. Cited above as item 19, pp. 267-268.

       Presents a brief case summary within a chapter devoted to mass murder.

112. Ronay, Gabriel. THE TRUTH ABOUT DRACULA. New York: Stein & Day, 1972, pp. 94-107.

       Relates the case, and others like it, to the medieval rash of European vampire legends.

27. BAUER, WILLIAM DILWORTH (M)

New Jersey resident who shotgunned his wife, mother, two children and two in-laws before committing suicide in January 1966.

* FACTS ON FILE. Volume 16, 1956. Cited above as item 7, p. 40.

  Contemporaneous account of Bauer's crimes.

28. BAYLY, WILLIAM ALFRED (M)

New Zealander who murdered a neighboring couple in October 1833, following a rancorous dispute over property lines. Hanged in July 1834.

* Gaute, J.H.H., and Robin Odell. THE MURDERERS' WHO'S WHO. Cited above as item 8, p. 37.

  Brief case history presented in encyclopedic format.

* Wilson, Colin, and Patricia Putnam. THE ENCYCLOPEDIA OF MURDER. Cited above as item 35, pp. 71-72.

  Case history presented in an encyclopedic format.

29. BEADLE, WILLIAM (M)

Unstable resident of Weathersfield, Conn., who habitually slept with an ax and knife beside him in bed. Beadle awoke one morning in December 1872, beheaded his wife and four children, then committed suicide by shooting himself with two pistols, one inserted in each ear.

* Green, Jonathon. THE GREATEST CRIMINALS OF ALL TIME. Cited above as item 11, p. 248.

  Brief case history presented in encyclopedic format.

* Nash, Jay Robert. MURDER, AMERICA. Cited above as item 23, p. 312.

  Brief case history in time line format.

* Sifakis, Carl. THE ENCYCLOPEDIA OF AMERICAN CRIME. Cited above as item 29, p. 57.

Capsule case history presented in encyclopedic format.

30. BEANE, SAWNEY (S)

Patriarch of a 15th-century Scottish family which lived
in seaside caves and practiced cannibalism as a life-style.
Incestuous relations produced a brood of 46 children and grand-
children, all of whom participated in the murder and consumption
of unwary travelers. Arrested after one intended victim
managed to escape in 1435, the clan was executed en masse, with
males dismembered and females burned alive.

* CRIMES AND PUNISHMENT: A PICTORIAL ENCYCLOPEDIA OF ABER-
    RANT BEHAVIOR, Volume 5. Cited above as item 4, pp.
    36-37.

  Brief case history within a longer article on cannibals.

* Nash, Jay Robert. ALMANAC OF WORLD CRIME. Cited above
    as item 19, pp. 265-266.

  Presents a brief case hitory within a chapter devoted
  to mass murder.

113. Tannahill, Reay. FLESH AND BLOOD. New York: Stein &
     Day, 1975, pp. 179-180.

  Explores the case of Beane and other "nonconformists"
  within a general history of cannibalism.

* Wilson, Colin. A CASEBOOK OF MURDER. Cited above as
    item 33, pp. 29-32.

  Case history presented within a study of cannibalism.

* ————, and Patricia Putnam. THE ENCYCLOPEDIA OF MURDER.
    Cite above as item 35, pp. 72-73.

  An engaging case history, presented in encyclopedic
  format.

31. BECK, DIETER (S)

West German sex killer who murdered three women between
1961 and 1968. Convicted in 1969 and imprisoned for life.

* Green, Jonathon. THE GREATEST CRIMINALS OF ALL TIME.
    Cited above as item 11, p. 180.

Presents a brief case history in encyclopedic format.

32. BECK, MARTHA (S)

Sadistic nurse who, with lover/accomplice Raymond Fernandez, murdered as estimated 20 women in 1947-49. Known as "The Lonely Hearts Killers," after their method of operation, targeted middle-aged spinsters and widows. Beck posed as Fernandez's sister while he seduced the women, looted their bank accounts, and finally killed them at her instigation. Sentenced to death in New York after confessing to three murders, both were executed in 1951.

* Boar, Roger, and Nigel Blundell. THE WORLD'S MOST INFAMOUS MURDERS. Cited above as item 2, pp. 62-65.

   Brief case history presented in a tabloid-style anthology.

* Brian, Dennis. MURDERERS DIE. Cited above as item 3, pp. 98-105.

   Brief case history within a historic survey of capital punishment.

* CRIMES AND PUNISHMENT: A PICTORIAL ENCYCLOPEDIA OF ABERRANT BEHAVIOR, Volume 4. Cited above as item 4, pp. 63-70.

   Case history illustrating domination of a male criminal by his female accomplice.

* FACTS ON FILE. Volume 9, 1949. Cited above as item 7, p. 280.

   Contemporaneous account of the couple's sentencing.

* Gaute, J.H.H., and Robin Odell. THE MURDERERS' WHO'S WHO. Cited above as item 8, p. 38.

   Capsule case history in an encyclopedic format.

* Green, Jonathon. THE GREATEST CRIMINALS OF ALL TIME. Cited above as item 11, p. 183.

   Brief case history presented in encyclopedic format.

* Nash, Jay Robert. CRIME CHRONOLOGY, 1900–1983. Cited
  above as item 21, p. 137.

  Presents a brief case history in time line format.

* Scott, Sir Harold. THE CONCISE ENCYCLOPEDIA OF CRIME
  AND CRIMINALS. Cited above as item 27, p. 22.

  The British view of Beck and Fernandez.

* Sifakis, Carl. THE ENCYCLOPEDIA OF AMERICAN CRIME.
  Cited above as item 29, p. 60.

  Brief case history presented in encyclopedic format.

* Wilson, Colin. A CRIMINAL HISTORY OF MANKIND. Cited
  above as item 34, pp. 19–20.

  Brief case history contained within a general discussion of human criminality.

* ————, and Patricia Putnam. THE ENCYCLOPEDIA OF MURDER.
  Cited above as item 35, pp. 205–206.

  Case history presented in encyclopedic format.

33. BECKER, MARIE ALEXANDER (S)

Belgian poisoner of the 1930s who used digitalis to
murder her husband, lover, and at least eight female customers
of her dress shop in Liege. The latter homicides were apparently committed for profit, although she obtained only small
sums of money from each of her victims. Sentenced to life,
she died in prison during World War II.

* Nash, Jay Robert. CRIME CHRONOLOGY, 1900–1983. Cited
  above as item 21, p. 107.

  Brief case history presente in time line format.

* ————. LOOK FOR THE WOMAN. Cited above as item 22,
  pp. 22–23.

  Case history within an encyclopedia of female criminals.

34. BEHN, HERMAN (M)

Divorced resident of West Frankfort, Ill., who, on the

day of his scheduled remarriage, murdered his mother and three daughters before committing suicide.

* FACTS ON FILE. Volume 17, 1957. Cited above as item 7, p. 92.

Contemporaneous account of the murders and suicide.

35. BELL, JAMES E. (M)

Paranoid black who ran amok with a shotgun and pistol in Newark, N.J., during March 1929. Shouting that he had been persecuted, Bell killed two complete strangers and wounded three others. Sentenced to life imprisonment.

* Nash, Jay Robert. MURDER, AMERICA. Cited above as item 23, p. 401.

Brief case history presented in time line format.

36. BELL, MARY FLORA (S)

Saidstic eleven-year-old British girl who murdered two boys, ages three and four, during 1968. Suspected or identified in various assaults on other children, including several attempted strangulations. At her trial, she declared, "I like hurting people." Convicted on two counts of manslaughter.

* CRIMES AND PUNISHMENT: A PICTORIAL ENCYCLOPEDIA OF ABER-RANT BEHAVIOR, Volume 13. Cited above as item 4, pp. 41-48.

Case history within a section devoted to homicidal children.

* Nash, Jay Robert. CRIME CHRONOLOGY, 1900-1983. Cited above as item 21, p. 177.

Brief case history presented in time line format.

114. Sereny, Gitta. THE CASE OF MARY BELL. London: Eyre Methuen, 1972.

Relates Mary Bell's behavior to her illegitimate birth, childhood environment, and the neglect of her emotionally unstable mother. Instructive.

* Wilson, Colin. A CASEBOOK OF MURDER. Cited above as
  item 32, p. 223.

  Brief case history within a general discussion of
  modern homicide.

* ————, and Donald Seaman. THE ENCYCLOPEDIA OF MODERN
  MURDER. Cited above as item 36, pp. 16-18.

Capsule case history presented in encyclopedic format.

37. BENDERS, THE (S)

   Homicidal family of four (or five; accounts differ)
which operated a wayside inn near Cherryvale, Kansas, in the
early 1870s. At least eleven guests were robbed and murdered
by the family in 1872-73, before disappearances aroused the
local populace. A posse unearthed bodies on the Bender property, but not before the family had flown. None were ever
apprehended. Rumors of their capture and summary execution by
vigilantes remain unconfirmed.

Books

115. Adelman, Robert H. THE BLOODY BENDERS. New York: Stein
     & Day, 1970.

     A readable attempt to solve one of the West's enduring
     murder mysteries.

* CRIMES AND PUNISHMENT: A PICTORIAL ENCYCLOPEDIA OF ABER-
  RANT BEHAVIOR, Volume 5. Cited above as item 4, pp.
  41-47.

  Case history of a criminal family operating in concert
  to rob and kill.

116. THE FIVE FIENDS, OR THE BENDER HOTEL HORROR IN KANSAS.
     Philadelphia: Old Franklin Publishing Co., 1874.

     The earliest enduring report of the Bender atrocities,
     related in "penny dreadful" style.

* Gaute, J.H.H., and Robin Odell. THE MURDERERS' WHO'S
  WHO. Cited above as item 8, p. 43.

  Capsule case history presented in encyclopedic format.

* Green, Jonathon. THE GREATEST CRIMINALS OF ALL TIME. Cited above as item 11, p. 148.

Brief case history presented in encyclopedic format.

117. Hardy, Allison. KATE BENDER, THE KANSAS MURDERESS. Girard, Kan.: Haldeman-Julius, 1944.

Conjectural biography of the most intriguing Bender. Daughter Kate is generally described, without substantial evidence, as the evil "brains" behind the gang. Author Hardy examines her subject's pretentious posturing as "Professor Kate Bender," allegedly well-versed in mysticism.

118. James, John T. THE BENDERS IN KANSAS. Wichita, Kan.: Kan-Okla Publishing Co., 1913.

An early, sensational description of the crimes and subsequent escape.

* Nash, Jay Robert. ALMANAC OF WORLD CRIME. Cited above as item 19, pp. 6, 277.

Brief, sensational case history within a treatise on mass murder.

* ————. BLOODLETTERS AND BADMEN. Cited above as item 20, pp. 53-54.

Capsule case history presented in encyclopedic format.

* ————. MURDER, AMERICA. Cited above as item 23, p. 354.

Brief case history presented in time line format.

* Sifakis, Carl. THE ENCYCLOPEDIA OF AMERICAN CRIME. Cited above as item 29, pp. 64-65.

Capsule case history presented in encyclopedic format.

* Wilson, Colin, and Patricia Putnam. THE ENCYCLOPEDIA OF MURDER. Cited above as item 35, pp. 74-75.

Case summary presented in encyclopedic format.

119. York, Mary E. THE BENDER TRAGEDY. Mankato, Kan.: G.W.
      Neff, 1875.

      Contemporaneous account of the crimes and escape of
      the suspects.

Articles

120. "The Benders of Kansas." KANSAS MAGAZINE (September 1886).

      An early retrospective, published thirteen years after
      the murderous family absconded.

121. Burkholder, Edwin V. "Those Murdering Benders." TRUE
      WESTERN ADVENTURES (February 1960).

      "Pulp" recitation of the crimes, with speculation on
      the fate of the elusive suspects.

122. Rowe, Fayette. "Kate Bender's Fate Still Mystery of
      Pioneer Kansas." WICHITA EAGLE MAGAZINE (September
      26, 1954).

      Further speculation on the fate and whereabouts of
      the Midwest's most famous murderess.

38. BENOIST, EMILE (M)

Politician's son who opened fire on hikers and joggers
near Hackettstown, N.J., killing six persons in 1977. Benoist
turned his rifle on himself, committing suicide before police
arrived.

   * Tobias, Ronald. THEY SHOOT TO KILL. Cited above as
      item 31, p. 30.

      Brief case history within a survey of criminal snipers.

39. BERKOWTIZ, DAVID RICHARD (S)

New York City's "Son of Sam," the infamous ".44-caliber
Killer." Allegedly stabbed two women, both of whom survived,
on Christmas Eve 1975. Thereafter relied on firearms to de-
personalize homicide, reportedly shooting thirteen victims
and killing six between July 1976 and July 1977. Arrested in
August 1977, Berkowitz initially feigned schizophrenia, blaming
his crimes on the commanding voices of demons—a claim which
he recanted during February 1979. Sentenced to life on the

basis of his confessions as the sole gunman in the "Sam" case,
subsequent interviews and letters from prison indicate that
Berkowitz may have had several accomplices, possibly the members
of a violent Satanic cult.

Books

123. Abrahamsen, David. CONFESSIONS OF SON OF SAM. New York:
      Columbia University Press, 1985.

      Authored by the only one of four psychiatrists who
      pronounced Berkowitz sane and competent for trial.
      Following imprisonment, Berkowitz met with the author
      and corresponded over a six-year period, providing the
      basis for a psychoanalytical biography. With Abrahamsen,
      Berkowitz renounced his claims that murders were in-
      spired by demons, speaking through a neighbor's dog.
      The "Son of Sam" reveals himself as a homicidal exhi-
      bitionist with long-standing urges to "die for a cause."

   * Boar, Roger, and Nigel Blundell. THE WORLD'S MOST IN-
      FAMOUS MURDERS. Cited above as item 2, pp. 8-11.

      Factual, if sensational, account of the case, presented
      in slightly breathless tabloid style.

124. Carpozi, George, Jr. SON OF SAM: THE .44 CALIBER KILLER.
      New York: Manor Books, 1977.

      Quicky paperback examination of the case, prepared
      within days of Berkowitz's arrest by a veteran writer
      for the pulp "detective" magazines.

   * FACTS ON FILE. Volume 37, 1978. Cited above as item 7,
      p. 614, 632m 641-642, 848.

      Contemporaneous reports of New York's greatest manhunt
      to date.

   * FACTS ON FILE. Volume 38, 1978. Cited above as item 7,
      p. 500.

      Reports Berkowitz's plea and sentencing.

   * FACTS ON FILE. Volume 39, 1979. Cited above as item 7,
      p. 156.

      Pre-arrest evidence is revealed by the authorities.

* FACTS ON FILE. Volume 40, 1980. Cited above as item 7, p. 639.

  Berkowtiz recants his spurious insanity plea.

* FACTS ON FILE. Volume 41, 1981. Cited above as item 7, p. 183.

  Reveals Berkowitz's correspondence with a transsexual "lover."

* Green, Jonathon. THE GREATEST CRIMINALS OF ALL TIME. Cited above as item 11, p. 180.

  Brief case history presented in encyclopedic format.

125. Klausner, Lawrence D. SON OF SAM. New York: McGraw-Hill, 1981.

  Readable narrative of the Berkowitz case, based on the killer's recorded interviews with psychiatrists, detectives, and attorneys. Forty pages of Berkowitz's journal are included as an appendix. Critics charge that Klausner was "spoon fed" inaccurate details by police seeking to cover their own negligent handling of certain evidence in the case.

* Levin, Jack, and James Alan Fox. MASS MURDER: AMERICA'S GROWING MENACE. Cited above as item 15.

  Brief case history contained in general narrative.

* Leyton, Elliott. COMPULSIVE KILLERS. Cited above as item 16, pp. 150-187.

  Cannibalizes items 123, 124, 125, and 127 to present a portrait of Berkowitz containing, in Leyton's own words, "nothing new."

* Nash, Jay Robert. CRIME CHRONOLOGY, 1900-1983. Cited above as item 21, p. 189.

  Erroneously places Berkowitz's arrest on the date of the first "Sam" attack, a year before his capture.

* Sifakis, Carl. THE ENCYCLOPEDIA OF AMERICAN CRIME. Cited above as item 29, pp. 674-675.

Brief case history presented in encyclopedic format.

126. Terry, Maury. THE ULTIMATE EVIL. Garden City, N.Y.:
      Doubleday, 1987.

      Rewrites history in the Berkowitz case, revealing per-
      suasive evidence of the killer's involvement with a cult
      of Satanists in New York. Evidence uncovered by Terry
      led to a reopening of the "Sam" investigation, but thus
      far no new suspects have been charged in the case. New
      evidence suggests a possible cult connection between
      the "Son of Sam" shootings, the Manson murders in Calif-
      ornia, and neo-Nazi gunman Fred Cowan. Frightening.

   * Tobias, Ronald. THEY SHOOT TO KILL. Cited above as
      item 31, pp. 178-188.

      Case history within a general survey of criminal snipers.
      Includes material on other gunmen active in New York,
      and still at large today, which meshes neatly with the
      cult activity discussed in item 126 above.

127. Willeford, Charles. OFF THE WALL. Montclair, N.J.:
      Pegasus Rex Press, 1980.

      Examination of the Berkowitz case which is ultimately
      inferior to item 126 above.

   * Wilson, Colin. A CRIMINAL HISTORY OF MANKIND. Cited
      above as item 34, pp. 640-641.

      Brief case history within a general narrative of modern
      violence.

   * ————, and Donald Seaman. THE ENCYCLOPEDIA OF MODERN
      MURDER. Cited above as item 36, pp. 18-21.

      Case history contained in an encyclopedic format.

Articles

128. Abrahamsen, David. "Unmasking 'Son of Sam's' Demons."
      THE NEW YORK TIMES MAGAZINE (July 1, 1979).

      Foreshadows Abrahamsen's subsequent book. See item
      123 above.

129. Alpern, D.M., and S. Agrest. "Will He Stand Trial?"
      NEWSWEEK 90 (August 29, 1977): 27-28.

      Reports Berkowitz's pre-trial insanity plea.

130. Axthelm, P. "City Under Siege." NEWSWEEK 90 (August
      15, 1977): 18+.

      Describes the manhunt's final days.

131. ———. "The Sick World of Son of Sam." NEWSEEK 90
      (August 22, 1977): 16-20+.

      Examines Berkowitz's claim that he was "programmed"
      to murder by demonic voices.

132. ———, and A. Lallande. "Hunting Son of Sam."
      NEWSWEEK 89 (June 20, 1977): 86.

      Reports on the manhunt in progress.

133. "David Berkowitz Story." COMMONWEAL 104 (September 2,
      1977): 547-548.

      Describes the suspect's alleged bizarre life-style.

134. "Man Hunt for Son of Sam Goes On." TIME 110 (August
      15, 1977): 13-15.

      Recounts the final days of terror before Berkowitz's
      arrest.

135. Mathews, T. "Hunting the Son of Sam." NEWSWEEK 90
      (July 11, 1977): 18-21.

      Five weeks before the big arrest, and counting.

136. "Notes and Comments: Press Treatment of Son of Sam Story."
      NEW YORKER 53 (August 15, 1977): 21-22; (September 5,
      1977): 19-22.

      Two-part critique of the media response to the "Sam"
      crime wave and assorted lurid letters to the press.

137. Rosenblatt, R. "Killer Captured." NEW REPUBLIC 177
      (August 20, 1977): 40-41.

      Reports Berkowitz's arrest in New York.

138. "Sam Told Me to Do It ... Sam is the Devil." TIME 110
      (August 22, 1977): 22-23+.

      Recaps Berkowitz's "demon" alibi.

139. "Son of Sam is Not Sleeping." TIME 110 (July 11, 1977):
      61.

      A report from the front as the manhunt nears its climax.

140. "Son of Sam—the Killer Who Terrorized New York."
      READER'S DIGEST 111 (November 1977): 155-160.

      A capsule retrospective on the crimes and manhunt.

141. Tucker, C. "The Night TV Cried Wolf." SATURDAY REVIEW
      5 (October 1, 1977): 56.

      Terse critique of media involvement in the case.

142. Wishengrad, S. "Startling Story of Son of Sam's Real
      Mother." GOOD HOUSEKEEPING 187 (November 1978): 79-82+.

      Relates the facts of Berkowitz's abandonment and
      adoption in infancy.

40. BESNARD, MARIE (S)

      Killer of at least six persons at Loudon, France (and
suspected of another seven), between 1938 and 1952. The victims, including Marie's parents, her husband, and various in-
laws, were generally slain for profit in the form of an inheritance. Husband Leon was suspected, posthumously, in a number
of the early murders. After two mistrials, Marie Besnard was
convicted and imprisoned in 1954.

143. Howard, Toni. "The Queen of Murderers." SATURDAY EVEN-
      ING POST 227 (July 24, 1954): 22-23+.

      An engaging portrait of Besnard's career, published
prior to her ultimate conviction.

41. BIANCHI, KENNETH (S)

      Sadistic slayer, with accomplice Angelo Buono, of ten
young women in Los Angeles during 1977 and 1978. Subsequently
confessed to the slaying of two more women in Bellingham,
Washington. Suspected but never charged in the "Alphabet

Murders" of three young girls in Rochester, N.Y., prior to
joining Buono in California. Bianchi turned state's evidence
against Buono, but thereafter sought to sabotage the trial of
his accomplice with misleading testimony. He was returned to
Washington from California, there to serve a term of life imprisonment without parole. Buono, convicted on nine of ten
premeditated murder charges, received an indentical sentence
in Los Angeles.

Books

* FACTS ON FILE. Volume 39, 1979. Cited above as item 7,
    p. 818.

    Reports Bianchi's sentencing and Buono's indictment.

* FACTS ON FILE. Volume 43, 1983. Cited above as item 7,
    p. 909.

    Contemporaneous report of Buono's conviction and
    sentencing.

* Levin, Jack, and James Alan Fox. MASS MURDER: AMERICA'S
    GROWING MENACE. Cited above as item 15.

    Capsule history presented in the context of a general
    narrative on serial murder.

144. O'Brien, Darcy. TWO OF A KIND: THE HILLSIDE STRANGLERS.
     New York: New American Library, 1985.

     Based on years of study, personal attendance at Buono's
     trial, and interviews with homicide detectives active in
     the case, this volume is definitive. O'Brien has been
     criticized for his fictional "re-creation" of dialogue
     between the killers, both of whom refused to sit for
     interviews, but his portrayal of the stranglers and
     their several victims has the ring of firm, objective
     fact. Unlikely to be equaled or surpassed.

145. Schwarz, Ted. THE HILLSIDE STRANGLER. New York: Double-
     day, 1981.

     The first attempt to capture Ken Bianchi's story in a
     book, prepared while author Schwarz was loosely affili-
     ated with Bianchi's defense. Flawed by Schwarz's credu-
     lous acceptance of Bianchi's "multiple personality"
     charade, later discredited as a complete hoax.

* Wilson, Colin. A CRIMINAL HISTORY OF MANKIND. Cited
   above as item 34, pp. 641-642.

   Case summary within a general history of human criminality.

Articles

146. Farrell, Barry. "Stalking the Hillside Strangler."
     NEW WEST (March 10, 1980): 19-32.

     Scathing review of the case, with particular focus on
     police activity and Bianchi's attempts to emerge as the
     "star" of his own murder prosecution.

147. "Jekyll and Hyde on the Hillside." MACLEANS 92 (May 7,
     1979): 35-36.

     The Canadian view of Bianchi's arrest and insanity plea.

148. "L.A. Strangler." TIME 110 (December 19, 1977): 24.

     Contemporaneous account published while the murders
     were in progress.

149. "Murderous Personality." TIME 113 (May 7, 1979): 26.

     Recounts Bianchi's arrest and insanity plea.

150. "Strangler Suspects." NEWSWEEK 91 (April 10, 1978): 42.

     Includes suspect sketches and an early reference to
     the dreaded possibility of two stranglers working as a
     team.

151. Williams, D.A. "Strangler's Grip." NEWSWEEK 91 (January
     9, 1978): 24-26.

     Contemporaneous account of the murders in progress.

152. ————, and P. Brinkley-Rogers. "Strangler." NEWSWEEK
     90 (December 19, 1977): 36.

     Contemporaneous report of the crimes in progress.

42. BICHEL, ANDREAS (S)

Bavarian "seer" of the early nineteenth century who

stabbed and robbed his female clients while they waited for
their fortunes to be told. Suspected in a minimum of fifty
cases, Bichel was broken on the wheel and beheaded in 1808.

* CRIMES AND PUNISHMENT: A PICTORIAL ENCYCLOPEDIA OF ABER-
  RANT BEHAVIOR, Volume 7. Cited above as item 4, p. 36.

  Brief case history within a chapter on "rippers."

153. Feuerbach, Anselm Ritter Von. NARRATIVES OF REMARKABLE
     CRIMINAL TRIALS. New York: Harper & Brothers, 1846,
     pp. 271-285.

     Contemporaneous examination of the Bichel case.

* Nash, Jay Robert. ALMANAC OF WORLD CRIME. Cited above
  as item 19, pp. 269-270.

  Brief case history within a chapter on mass murder.

* Wilson, Colin. A CASEBOOK OF MURDER. Cited above as
  item 33, pp. 110-111.

  Brief case history examined in the context of murder's
  "social history."

* ————, and Patricia Putnam. THE ENCYCLOPEDIA OF MURDER.
  Cited above as item 35, pp. 82-83.

  Case history presented in encyclopedic format.

43. BIEGENWALD, RICHARD (S)

American killer convicted of one homicide and suspected
in five others. Biegenwald first turned to crime at age five,
setting fire to his own family home. Imprisoned for life.

* Darrach, Brad, and Joel Norris. "An American Tragedy."
  Cited above as item 40, p. 72.

  Passing reference within a general survey of serial
  murder.

44. BINGHAM POISONINGS (S)

Unsolved murders, by poison, of three members of the
Bingham family, historic custodians of Lancaster Castle, in

England. A fourth member of the clan was charged with murder after traces of arsenic were found in all three bodies, but a jury acquitted the suspect after deliberating only 20 minutes.

* Nash, Jay Robert. CRIME CHRONOLOGY, 1900-1983. Cited above as item 21, p. 28.

    Brief case history presented in time line format.

* ————. OPEN FILES. Cited above as item 24, p. 23.

    Fair case history, in an encyclopedia of unsolved crimes.

45. BISHOP, ARTHUR GARY (S)

Former Eagle Scout convicted and sentenced to die for the sex murders of five young boys in Salt Lake City, Utah, committed over a four-year period. Bishop is suspected, but has not been charged, with additional murders in Utah and California.

* Gest, Ted. "On the Trail of America's Serial Killers." Cited above as item 46.

    Brief case history within a survey of the problem.

46. BISHOP, JESSE (S)

Convicted and sentenced to die in Nevada for one homicide, committed during a robbery, Bishop subsequently confessed to eighteen other murders. Put to death in 1979, he was the last man executed in Nevada by means of lethal gas.

* Levin, Jack, and James Alan Fox. MASS MURDER: AMERICA'S GROWING MENACE. Cited above as item 15.

    Brief case history within a general narrative on multi-cide.

47. BITTAKER, LAWRENCE SIGMUND (S)

With accomplice Roy L. Norris, tortured, raped, and strangled at least five young women in the Los Angeles area, operating between June and October 1979. Female hitchhikers were tortured and killed in a panel truck, nicknamed "Murder Mac." The sadists reportedly fantasized killing one female

victim of each "teen" age, from 13 through 19 years old, but
were captured while three victims short of their goal. (Two
of the identified victims were 16 years old.) Both defendants
were sentenced to die.

* Levin, Jack, and James Alan Fox. MASS MURDER: AMERICA'S
  GROWING MENACE. Cited above as item 15.

  Brief case history within a general narrative on
  multicide.

* Nash, Jay Robert. CRIME CHRONOLOGY, 1900-1983. Cited
  above as item 21, pp. 200-201.

  Brief case history presented in time line format.

48. "BLACK DAHLIA" MURDERS (?)

On January 15, 1947, the body of Elizabeth Short was
found in Los Angeles. She had been tortured prior to death,
her body drained of blood and completely bisected at the waist
before it was discarded in a vacant lot. Short had been
nicknamed "the Black Dahlia" after her fondness for black
clothing. The case remains unsolved, although her killer cor-
responded with police and journalists, mailing some of Short's
belongings——including an address book with one page signifi-
cantly missing. Over the next four months, six other California women were slain in various sadistic ways, ranging from
Los Angeles north to Fresno. No striking similarity between
the crimes was discovered, and some of the subsequent cases
were solved, but they remain linked in the public mind and in
the literature as somehow "connected." (In 1982, the son of
a Los Angeles detective claimed Short's killer was alive and
running a saloon in Reno, Nevada; unfortunately, his book on
the subject was never published, and the suspect remains
anonymous.)

154. American Weekly. MY FAVORITE TRUE MYSTERY. New York:
     Coward, McCann, and Geohegan, 1954, pp. 238-242.

     Presents the Dahlia case within an anthology of un-
     solved cases.

155. Anger, Kenneth. HOLLYWOOD BABYLON II. New York: New
     American Library, 1985, pp. 126-132.

     A routine recitation of the case, interesting for its
     first-time publication of police photographs taken at

the crime scene.

* CRIMES AND PUNISHMENT: A PICTORIAL ENCYCLOPEDIA OF ABER-
   RANT BEHAVIOR, Volume 16. Cited above as item 4, pp.
   15-22.

   Case history presented in encyclopedic format.

* FACTS ON FILE. Volume 7, 1947. Cited above as item 7,
   pp. 36, 84, 156.

   Contemporaneous account of the Dahlia case and five
   subsequent murders of California women.

* Gaute, J.H.H., and Robin Odell. THE MURDERERS' WHO'S
   WHO. Cited above as item 8, p. 43.

   British view of the case, in an encyclopedic format.

156. Gribble, Leonard N. THEY HAD A WAY WITH WOMEN. New
    York: Roy Publishers, 1967, pp. 67-80.

    Case history within an anthology of "lady-killers."

* Nash, Jay Robert. ALMANAC OF WORLD CRIME. Cited above
   as item 19, p. 309.

   Brief case history within a survey of sex crimes.

* —————. CRIME CHRONOLOGY, 1900-1983. Cited above as
   item 21, p. 131.

   Capsule case history presented in time line format.

* —————. OPEN FILES. Cited above as item 24, pp. 23-32.

   Case history in an encyclopedia of unsolved crimes.

157. Rice, Craig. 45 MURDERS. New York: Simon & Schuster,
    1952, pp. 269-282.

    Case history contained in an anthology. Rice concludes
    that the Dahlia killer was a mortician or undertaker's
    assistant, with surgical skill and embalming facilities
    readily available.

158. Richardson, James H. FOR THE LIFE OF ME. New York: G.P.
    Putnam's Sons, 1954, pp. 296-312.

A new perspective on the Dahlia case, presented by the
only person known to have conversed with Short's killer
during the investigation. Richardson was city editor
of the newspaper which received correspondence from the
murderer. He describes the killer as a self-styled
"superman" whose "mad ego" would inevitably lead to other
homicides, resulting in his capture. Better luck next
time.

159. Rowan, David. FAMOUS AMERICAN CRIMES. London: Frederick
      Muller, Ltd., 1957, pp. 11-27.

      British view of the Dahlia murders, comparing the
      seven crimes to London's "Jack the Ripper" slayings of
      the nineteenth century. Interesting, but devoid of new
      solutions.

   * Sifakis, Carl. THE ENCYCLOPEDIA OF AMERICAN CRIME.
      Cited above as item 29, pp. 78-79.

      Brief case history presented in encyclopedic format.

160. Sterling, Hank (pseud.). TEN PERFECT CRIMES. New York:
      Stravon Publishers, 1954, pp. 37-51.

      Author Harry Snyder, writing as "Hank Stirling," con-
      cludes that Short's murder was "the result of her deplor-
      able way of life." No surprises.

161. Webb, Jack. THE BADGE. Englewood Cliffs, N.J.: Prentice-
      Hall, 1958, pp. 22-35.

      The star of "Dragnet" and a leading spokesman for Los
      Angeles police reviews the Dahlia case within the context
      of a departmental history. The major theories are explored,
      but Webb declines to pick a favorite of his own.

49. "BLACK DOODLER, THE" (S)

Homosexual slayer of at least six victims, active in San
Francisco during the mid-1970s. The Doodler approached his
white, middle-class victims in gay bars, sketching their por-
traits as a means of introduction, engaging in homosexual acts
before slashing them to death. Psychologists described the
killer as a victim of the "attraction-repulsion complex,"
drawn to gay encounters and simultaneously detesting them.
Still at large.

* Godwin, John. MURDER USA. Cited above as item 10, p. 176.

Brief case history within a chapter on gay homicides.

50. BLACKSTONE, DAVID THOMAS (M): See SMITH, FRED

51. BODEN, WAYNE (S)

Canadian "vampire rapist" and slayer of at least five victims between 1968 and 1970. Boden typically left bite marks on the breasts of his victims, hence the nickname. Confessed to four of the five homicides, strangely balking on the fifth identical case. Sentenced to four life terms in prison.

* CRIMES AND PUNISHMENT: A PICTORIAL ENCYCLOPEDIA OF ABERRANT BEHAVIOR, Volume 17. Cited above as item 4, p. 85.

Case history within an article describing mutilation murders.

* Wilson, Colin, and Donald Seaman. THE ENCYCLOPEDIA OF MODERN MURDER. Cited above as item 36, pp. 21-22.

Engaging case history presented in encyclopedic format.

52. BOGGS, DONALD MELVIN (S)

Perpetrator, with his teenaged accomplice-girlfriend Dixie Radcliff, of a three-state crime spree in August and September 1965. Arrested in Arizona after shooting and bludgeoning four men to death in Texas, Oklahoma, and Utah, Boggs was sentenced to die.

162. "Four Lives to Flagstaff." TIME 86 (September 17, 1965): 40.

Contemporaneous account of the Boggs-Radcliff case.

53. BOLBER, MORRIS (S)

Homicidal phsyician from Philadelphia who murdered between thirty and fifty victims for insurance money between 1932 and 1937. Bolber was assisted by accomplices Carino Favato and the Petrillo cousins, Paul and Herman. Upon conviction, the Petrillos were executed; Bolber and Favato were each sentenced to life imprisonment.

* Sifakis, Carl. THE ENCYCLOPEDIA OF AMERICAN CRIME.
  Cited above as item 29, pp. 83-84.

  Case history presented in encyclopedic format.

54. BOLIN, PATTY (M)

Housewife who went berserk in Columbus, Ohio, during 1976,
shooting her husband and two of her three children to death.
Her weapon jammed, saving the life of her third child, but
Mrs. Bolin repaired it in time to kill herself as police arrived
at the scene.

* Nash, Jay Robert. CRIME CHRONOLOGY, 1900-1983. Cited
  above as item 19, p. 190.

  Brief case history presented in time line format.

* ————. MURDER, AMERICA. Cited above as item 23, p. 444.

  Sketch case history presented in time line format.

55. BONIN, WILLIAM GEORGE (S)

Sadistic mastermind behind Southern California's "Freeway
Murders," which claimed at least 21 male victims in 1979 and
1980. (Some authorities suggest the murders date from 1972,
including a total of 44 young men and boys.) Operating with
at least five accomplices, Bonin molested, tortured, and murdered hitchhikers whom he picked up on the freeways of Los
Angeles and Orange Counties. Convicted on 21 counts of murder,
Bonin was sentenced to die. Accomplice Vernon Robert Butts,
charged with six counts, committed suicide in jail before he
could be tried. Bonin's girlfriend, pleading guilty on two
counts of murder, was sentenced to life imprisonment, as were
accomplices James M. Munro, Gregory Matthew Miley, and Eric
Martin Wijnaendts.

* FACTS ON FILE. Volume 40, 1980. Cited above as item 7,
  pp. 654, 727.

  Contemporaneous report of the Bonin, Butts, Miley, and
  Munro arrests.

* FACTS ON FILE. Volume 41, 1981. Cited above as item 7,
  p. 132.

  Reports the suicide of Butts and arrest of Wijnaendts.

* FACTS ON FILE. Volume 42, 1982. Cited above as item 7, pp. 24, 274.

Reports Bonin's conviction and sentencing.

* Levin, Jack, and James Alan Fox. MASS MURDER: AMERICA'S GROWING MENACE. Cited above as item 15.

Capsule history within a general discussion of serial murder.

56. BOOHER, VERNON (M)

Farmer at Mannville, in the province of Alberta, Canada, who shot and killed his wife, son, and two farm workers in July 1928. Booher then "discovered" the bodies and called police. An Austrian "thought-reader" subsequently identified Booher as the killer, whereupon he confessed and was convicted. Hanged in April 1929.

* Wilson, Colin, and Patricia Putnam. THE ENCYCLOPEDIA OF MURDER. Cited above as item 35, pp. 87-88.

Case history presented in encyclopedic format.

57. BOOST, WERNER (S)

Sexually-motivated "Doubles Killer" of Dusseldorf, Germany, who, with accomplice Franz Lorbach, claimed at least six victims during early 1956. (Further investigations dated back to 1945, producing one of the longest indictments on record in Germany.) Boost's M.O. involved assaults upon couples parked in cars on lover's lanes. The sight of couples parked together made him "see red," and he once declared that, "These sex horrors are the curse of Germany." In early cases, Boost and Lorbach stunned their victims with a chemical prepared by Boost; the men were robbed and women raped, but both were left alive. As Boost degenerated mentally, his violence turned to homicide, with victims variously beaten, drowned, shot, and gassed with cyanide. Ironically, the first attack producing a fatality was mistakenly conducted against two businessmen parked in an automobile, discussing finances. Lorbach turned state's evidence, and Boost received the maximum sentence of life imprisonment.

* Gaute, J.H.H., and Robin Odell. THE MURDERERS' WHO'S WHO. Cited above as item 8, pp. 46-47.

Case history presented in an encyclopedic format.

* Nash, Jay Robert. CRIME CHRONOLOGY, 1900-1983. Cited above as item 21, p. 144.

Brief case history presented in time line format.

* Wilson, Colin. A CRIMINAL HISTORY OF MANKIND. Cited above as item 34, p. 621.

Case history contained within a general narrative on modern sex crimes.

* ————, and Patricia Putnam. THE ENCYCLOPEDIA OF MURDER. Cited above as item 35, pp. 88-89.

Case history presented in an encyclopedic format.

58. BOTKIN, CORDELIA (M)

American murderess who killed her married lover's wife and sister with poisoned chocolates sent through the mail. Sentenced to life imprisonment.

* Gaute, J.H.H., and Robin Odell. THE MURDERERS' WHO'S WHO. Cited above as item 8, p. 49.

Case history presented in an encyclopedic format.

* Pearson, Edmund L. "Rules for Murderesses." Cited above as item 25, p. 17.

Light, facetious recitation of the case within an article on lethal ladies.

* Nash, Jay Robert. BLOODLETTERS AND BADMEN. Cited above as item 20, pp. 78-80.

Case history presented in an encyclopedic format.

* ————. CRIME CHRONOLOGY, 1900-1983. Cited above as item 21, p. 25.

Brief case history presented in time line format.

* Sifakis, Carl. THE ENCYCLOPEDIA OF AMERICAN CRIME. Cited above as item 29, pp. 91-92.

Case history presented in an encyclopedic format.

59. BOWEN, JOSEPH (S)

Imprisoned for the murder of a policeman, Bowen went on
to kill the prison's warden and one of the warden's deputies
in 1975. Sentenced to a double term of life imprisonment for
the latter crimes, he laughed at the court as he was led away
to resume serving his time. In 1981, Bowen led rioting prisoners
who captured 38 hostages. Currently serving his sentence.

* Brian, Dennis. MURDERERS DIE. Cited above as item 3,
   p. 261.

Brief case history within a chapter listing killers
who were "paroled to kill again." Bowen's case, while
possibly an argument in favor of capital punishment,
does not seem to fit the profile, since he committed
his subsequent murders in prison.

60. BRADLEY, JOHN, JR. (M)

Twenty-four-year-old mental patient and suspected drug
abuser who killed both parents at the family home in Dedham,
Mass., during 1974. Following the murders, perpetrated with
a knife and hammer, Bradley attempted suicide by leaping from
a highway overpass. Surviving his injuries, he was committed
to a state hospital for the criminally insane.

163. Russell, Francis. "Murder Strikes Home." NATIONAL
     REVIEW 91 (June 8, 1979): 744-745.

Thoughtful attempt to understand a shocking crime,
written by a close friend of the Bradley family.

61. BRADY, IAN (S)

Perpetrator, with accomplice Myra Hindley, of the British
"Moors Murders" during 1963-65. At least two children and one
teenage youth were murdered in the brutal string of crimes;
the only female victim was molested, photographed in porno-
graphic poses, with her screams recorded for posterity (and
later used in court by Brady's prosecutors). Both defendants
were sentenced to life imprisonment, the death penalty having
been abolished after their crimes, but before their arrests.
(In July 1987, the body of a fourth victim was unearthed, and
a member of Parliament professed to hold evidence of a third
accomplice in the murders, unidentified at this writing.)

Books

* Boar, Roger, and Nigel Blundell. THE WORLD'S MOST IN-
  FAMOUS MURDERS. Cited above as item 2, pp. 24-28.

  Brief case history presented in sensational tabloid
  style.

* CRIMES AND PUNISHMENT: A PICTORIAL ENCYCLOPEDIA OF ABER-
  RANT BEHAVIOR, Volume 1. Cited above as item 4, pp.
  22-30.

  Case history presented in an encyclopedic format.

* FACTS ON FILE. Volume 26, 1966. Cited above as item 7,
  p. 326.

  Contemporaneous report of sentencing in London.

* Gaute, J.H.H., and Robin Odell. THE MURDERERS' WHO'S
  WHO. Cited above as itme 8, pp. 166-167.

  Case history presented in an encyclopedic format.

* Green, Jonathon. THE GREATEST CRIMINALS OF ALL TIME.
  Cited above as item 11, pp. 205-206.

  Brief case history presented in encyclopedic format.

164. Marchbanks, David. THE MOORS MURDERS. London: Frewin,
     1966.

     Contemporary account of the murders, arrests, and
     trial, including excerpts from trial transcripts.

* Nash, Jay Robert. CRIME CHRONOLOGY, 1900-1983. Cited
  above as item 21, p. 170.

  Brief case history presented in time line format.

* ————. LOOK FOR THE WOMAN. Cited above as item 22,
  pp. 199-201.

  Brief report with emphasis on Myra Hindley, contained
  in an encyclopedic format.

165. Potter, John Deane. THE MONSTERS OF THE MOORS. New
     York: Ballantine Books, 1966.

Prepared by a veteran British crime reporter, this
account relies on court transcripts for its contents
and dialogue. Terse and informative.

166. Williams, Emlyn. BEYOND BELIEF. New York: Random House,
      1967.

      The best and most detailed account of the case. Wil-
      liams tentatively links the defendants with a total of
      five murders, an assertion seemingly supported by recent
      evidence.

  *   Wilson, Colin. A CASEBOOK OF MURDER. Cited above as
      item 33, pp. 235-238.

      Case history within a general discussion of modern
      murder.

  *   ————. A CRIMINAL HISTORY OF MANKIND. Cited above as
      item 34, pp. 21-28.

      Case history of classic "thrill killers," presented
      in a general history of human criminality.

  *   ————. ORDER OF ASSASSINS. Cited above as item 76,
      pp. 125-139.

      Examines the moors murders from a psychological per-
      spective.

  *   ————, and Donald Seaman. THE ENCYCLOPEDIA OF MODERN
      MURDER. Cited above as item 36, pp. 26-35.

      Case history presented in an encyclopedic format.

                              Articles

167. "On England's Misty Moors, a Grisly Search." LIFE 56
      (November 12, 1965): 46-47.

      Photo layout on the continuing search for bodies.

                62. BRAM, THOMAS MEAD CHAMBERS (M)

      First mate aboard a ship en route from Boston to South
America in July 1896. Bram used an ax to kill the captain,
his wife, and the second mate, apparently for purposes of robbery. Convicted of murder, Bram served 15 years before his

eventual release.

* Nash, Jay Robert. MURDER, AMERICA. Cited above as item
  23, pp. 14, 137-149.

  Case history within an anthology of "classic" murders.

63. BRAND, SAMUEL (M)

Pennsylvania farmer, "never quite right in the head,"
who torched the family home at Lancaster while his parents
slept, then entered the burning house to shoot his brother.
All three victims died. Hanged in December 1773.

* Nash, Jay Robert. MURDER, AMERICA. Cited above as item
  23, p. 311.

  Brief case history presented in time line format.

64. BRAUN, THOMAS EUGENE (S)

With accomplice Leonard Maine, murdered three persons
and crippled a fourth in a three-state crime spree during
August 1967. Arrested in California, Braun freel confessed
and was sentenced to die; at this writing, he awaits execution.
Maine was sentenced to life imprisonment.

* Green, Jonathon. THE GREATEST CRIMINALS OF ALL TIME.
  Cited above as item 11, p. 249.

  Brief case history in an encyclopedic format.

* Nash, Jay Robert. BLOODLETTERS AND BADMEN. Cited above
  as item 20, pp. 81-83.

  Case history presented in an encyclopedic format.

* ————. CRIME CHRONOLOGY, 1900-1983. Cited above as
  item 21, pp. 174-175.

  Case history presented in time line format.

65. BRESLIN, JOSEPH FRANKLIN (S)

Orphaned as a child, Breslin spent most of his first 25
years in mental institutions, where he murdered a fellow inmate in 1968. Acquitted on grounds of insanity, he was released
as "cured" in 1976. A string of violent incidents followed,

culminating in the murder of a California woman and her daughter in 1982. Breslin left a note at the scene reading: "I don't know why I did it, but I won't be alive for you to get me. You'll have to kill me and I might kill others before I'm dead." Four days later, he was shot to death while trying to steal a car at gunpoint.

168. Beck, Melinda, and Ron LaBrecque. "A Killer Who Slipped Through the System." NEWSWEEK 100 (July 19, 1982): 28.

Contemporaneous account of Breslin's crimes and death, with critical examination of his passage through the loopholes of the mental health system.

66. BRIGGEN, JOSEPH (S)

Murderer of transient workers, on his California ranch, who used remains of victims as food for his prize-winning hogs. Briggen was exposed with the discovery of remains in 1902, and was sentenced to life imprisonment. No estimated body-count is currently available, but at the time, it was believed his crimes had spanned a period of several years.

* Sifakis, Carl. THE ENCYCLOPEDIA OF AMERICAN CRIME. Cited above as item 29, p. 97.

Brief case history in an encyclopedic format.

67. BRINKLEY, RICHARD (M)

Clumsy British poisoner with economic motives who missed his intended victims and killed two others by mistake. Brinkley's amateurish efforts to disguise a forged will cinched the case against him, and he was hanged in August 1907.

* Gaute, J.H.H., and Robin Odell. THE MURDERERS' WHO'S WHO. Cited above as item 8, p. 53.

Case history presented in an encyclopedic format.

* Wilson, Colin, and Patricia Putnam. THE ENCYCLOPEDIA OF MURDER. Cited above as item 35, pp. 101-102.

Case history presented in an encyclopedic format.

68. BRINVILLIERS, MARIE MADELEINE de (S)

French nymphomaniac poisoner for profit whose victims

included her father, two brothers, and her husband. Early in
her career of murder, she "practiced" with poisons on invalid
patients of Parisian hospitals, spiking gifts of fruit with
lethal concoctions in order to see if traces were discovered
during autopsy. Also accused of participation in Black Mass
rituals where children were tortured and killed, Marie was
beheaded in 1676.

* CRIMES AND PUNISHMENT: A PICTORIAL ENCYCLOPEDIA OF ABER-
    RANT BEHAVIOR, Volume 4. Cited above as item 4, pp.
    86-87.

    Brief case history within a longer article on classic
    poisoners.

* Nash, Jay Robert. ALMANAC OF WORLD CRIME. Cited above
    as item 19, pp. 268-269.

    Brief case history within a longer chapter on mass
    murder.

* Wilson, Colin. A CASEBOOK OF MURDER. Cited above as
    item 33, p. 132.

    Brief case history within a "social history" of murder.

* ————. A CRIMINAL HISTORY OF MANKIND. Cited above as
    item 34, pp. 389-392.

    Capsule history of the "Chamber Ardente affair," which
    linked de Brinvilliers and others with Satanism and
    ritual sacrifice of children as well as serial poisoning.

* ————, and Patricia Putnam. THE ENCYCLOPEDIA OF MURDER.
    Cited above as item 35, pp. 102-105.

    Case history presented in encyclopedic format.

69. BRISBON, HENRY (M)

Without apparent motive, Brisbon and three others ran
another car off the highway near Chicago, in June 1973. Brisbon's companions were stunned when he then inexplicably shot
and killed the couple in the other car. At trial, he was
sentenced to a term between 1,000 and 3,000 years.

* Nash, Jay Robert. CRIME CHRONOLOGY, 1900-1983. Cited
    above as item 21, p. 185.

Brief case history presented in time line format.

70. BRENHAUG, OSCAR (M): See BATES, CLYDE

71. BROMLEY, DIANE PRATT (M)

Niece of horror actor Boris Karloff residing in Britain, Bromley killed her two sons, ages ten and thirteen, by slashing their throats in December 1958. The boys had just come home for Christmas recess from their boarding school when they were killed. Bromley was sentenced to prison.

* FACTS ON FILE. Volume 18, 1958. Cited above as item 7, p. 420.

Contemporaneous report of the murders and arrest.

72. BROOKS, DAVID (S): See CORLL, DEAN ARNOLD

73. BROWN, CHARLES NOEL (S)

With accomplice Charles Edwin Kelly, Brown murdered two men during impulsive auto thefts at Council Bluffs, Iowa, in September 1961. Both suspects seemed obsessed with claiming "credit" for the murders. Brown "wasn't sure" about other homicides in Minneapolis and elsewhere. Both defendants were condemned and executed.

* Reinhardt, James Melvin. THE PSYCHOLOGY OF STRANGE KILLERS. Cited above as item 70, pp. 126-145.

Psychological case study, based upon rambling confessions from the killers.

74. "BROWN, JAMES" (M)

Portugese sailor, true name unknown, who killed two shipmates on a fishing boat in 1867. "Brown" was surprised and captured while drinking the blood of his victims. He spent the rest of his life in various lunatic asylums.

* Masters, R.E.L., and Eduard Lea. PERVERSE CRIMES IN HISTORY. Cited above as item 18, p. 109.

Brief case history within a longer chapter on "vampire killers."

75. BRUDOS, JEROME HENRY (S)

Sadistic slayer of at least four women in Oregon. Brudos photographed his victims before and after death, keeping articles of clothing (and sometimes portions of their bodies) as mementos of his crimes. Sentenced to life imprisonment in 1969.

* CRIMES AND PUNISHMENT: A PICTORIAL ENCYCLOPEDIA OF ABER-
  RANT BEHAVIOR, Volume 13. Cited above as item 4, pp.
  86-88.

  Brief case history within a longer article on sex crimes.

169. Stack, Andy (pseud.). LUST KILLER. New York: Signet
     Books, 1983.

     Writing as "Andy Stack," veteran crime reporter Ann
     Rule examines the Brudos case in detail. Interesting.

76. BRUHM, ROBERT (M)

Nineteen-year-old youth who shot and killed his employer, the man's wife, and their ten-year-old daughter, also wounding their seven-year-old son before turning himself in to the marshal at Ft. Pierre, S.D., in March 1958. Sentenced to life.

* Reinhardt, James Melvin. THE PSYCHOLOGY OF STRANGE
  KILLERS. Cited above as item 70, pp. 17-36.

  Psychological case study, based on Bruhm's confessions.

77. "B.T.K. STRANGLER, THE" (S)

Unidentified slayer of at least six persons in Wichita, Kansas, between 1974 and 1977. In his first attack, the slayer wiped out a family of four, the victims trussed up and slaugh-tered in their home. The next two victims were single women, strangled in their apartments. (In the last case, two children of the victim were locked in a closet by the killer, and other-wise unmolested.) Letters to police and local papers claimed a seventh victim, never publicly identified, and authorities concede the possibility of victims yet unknown. The slayer signed his letters "B.T.K.," standing for "Bind, Torture, and Kill," a description of his usual technique. Still at large.

* Tobias, Ronald. THEY SHOOT TO KILL. Cited above as
  item 31, pp. 178-179.

Brief case history within a general survey of modern serial murderers.

78. BULLOCK, DAVID (S)

Thrill-killer of at least six persons in New York City, ranging from a prostitute to his own roommate. At his trial, Bullock told the judge that murder "makes me happy ... It was the Christmas spirit ... something to amuse myself." Sentenced to life imprisonment.

* Levin, Jack, and James Alan Fox. MASS MURDER: AMERICA'S GROWING MENACE. Cited above as item 15.

    Capsule case history within a general discussion of impulse killers.

79. BUNDY, CAROL MARY (S): See CLARK, DOUGLAS DANIEL

80. BUNDY, THEODORE ROBERT (S)

Sentenced to die for three sexually-motivated murders in Florida, Bundy is suspected of killing other women all across America. Body-counts vary from one source to another, but the victims usually named include eight in Washington, four in Utah, five in Colorado, and the three in Florida. Canadian authorities once considered Bundy a suspect in their series of 28 unsolved "Highway Murders," but he was never charged.

Books

* Boar, Roger, and Nigel Blundell. THE WORLD'S MOST IN-FAMOUS MURDERS. Cited above as item 2, pp. 31-33.

    Case history presented in sensational tabloid style.

* Brian, Dennis. MURDERERS DIE. Cited above as item 3, pp. 205-221.

    Examines Bundy as a prime candidate for execution.

* FACTS ON FILE. Volume 39, 1979. Cited above as item 7, p. 604.

    Contemporaneous account of Bundy's death sentence.

* FACTS ON FILE. Volume 40, 1980. Cited above as item 7, p. 136.

Reports Bundy's third Florida death sentence.

170.   Kendall, Elizabeth (pseud.). THE PHANTOM PRINCE: MY
       LIFE WITH TED BUNDY. Seattle: Madrona Publishers, 1981.

       Former Bundy fiancee Liz Kloepfer presents her first-
       person account of life with Bundy, including incidents
       which led her to report him as a suspect in the unsolved
       homicides of several women.

171.   Larsen, Richard W. BUNDY: THE DELIBERATE STRANGER.
       Englewood Cliffs, N.J.: Prentice-Hall, 1980.

       Another "I-knew-Bundy" recitation, this time from a
       journalist in Washington. Larsen emphasizes Bundy's
       strange ability to charm his fellow men—and women—even
       after he had been accused of murder.

   *   Levin, Jack, and James Alan Fox. MASS MURDER: AMERICA'S
       GROWING MENACE. Cited above as item 15.

       Case history within a general discussion of serial
       killers.

   *   Leyton, Elliott. COMPULSIVE KILLERS. Cited above as
       item 16, pp. 73-111.

       Absorbs and "revises" items 170, 171, 172, 173, and
       175, producing, in Leyton's own words, "no new data of
       any kind."

172.   Michaud, Stephen G., and Hugh Aynesworth. THE ONLY
       LIVING WITNESS. New York: Simon & Schuster, 1983.

       Billed as the "confessions" of Ted Bundy, this volume
       falls short of the mark, delivering only the killer's
       cagey "speculations" on a string of unsolved crimes.
       Bundy confesses nothing, and rumors persist that the
       authors duped him into granting interviews by promising
       to prove him innocent in print. (Aynesworth later was
       involved in "exposes" concerning Henry Lucas which were
       likewise tainted by suspicious circumstances.)

   *   Nash, Jay Robert. CRIME CHRONOLOGY, 1900-1983. Cited
       above as item 21, p. 196.

       Brief case history presented in time line format.

173. Rule, Ann. THE STRANGER BESIDE ME. New York: W.W. Norton, 1980.

 The veteran crime reporter drops her "Andy Stack" disguise for this account of her acquaintance with Bundy in Seattle. They worked together on a crisis "hot-line," and despite her long experience with criminals, Rule failed to pierce the Bundy mask. Informative.

174. Wallechinsky, David, and Irving Wallace. THE PEOPLE'S ALMANAC #3. New York: Bantam Books, 1981, pp. 333-337.

 Reviews the Bundy case in a "You be the judge" format, presenting evidence for both sides. An interesting point is made concerning evidence from homicides in Florida: the man who left a semen stain at one crime scene proved to be a "non-secretor" (one whose blood type cannot be determined from examination of his other bodily fluids), whereas Bundy is a known "secretor." Evidence of bite marks on the body, matched to casts of Bundy's teeth, were used to override the seemingly contradictory evidence at his trial.

 * Wilson, Colin. A CRIMINAL HISTORY OF MANKIND. Cited above as item 34, pp. 643-646.

 Case history within a general discussion of modern "motiveless" murder.

 * ————, and Donald Seaman. THE ENCYCLOPEDIA OF MODERN MURDER. Cited above as item 36, pp. 36-41.

 Case history presented in an encyclopedic format.

175. Winn, Steven, and David Merrill. TED BUNDY: THE KILLER NEXT DOOR. New York: Bantam, 1980.

 The first (and possibly the best) account of Bundy's case, replete with details and devoid of first-person intrusions. The authors never knew Bundy, and their distance from the case allows them to present a balanced, readable account in which all sides are represented.

Articles

176. Adams, N.M. "To Catch a Killer: The Search for Ted Bundy." READER'S DIGEST 118 (March 1981): 201-222+.

   Examines the manhunt for Bundy, with all of its false
   starts and set-backs.

177. Daly, M. "Murder! Did Ted Bundy Kill 36 Young Women
      and Will He Go Free?" ROLLING STONE (December 14,
      1978): 55-64+.

      A "hip" examination of the case, published prior to
      Bundy's trial in a magazine more noted for its interviews
      with rock stars. The courts have answered Daly's second
      question; the jury is still out on the first.

178. Lowther, W. "Trail of Blood." MACLEANS 91 (April 3,
      1978): 62.

      Bundy's case from the Canadian perspective.

179. McCall, C. "Enigma of Ted Bundy: Did He Kill 18 Women?
      Or Has He Been Framed?" PEOPLE WEEKLY 13 (January 7,
      1980): 14-19.

      Questions evidence in Bundy's case a month before his
      third death sentence in Florida. Intriguing, but ulti-
      mately unconvincing.

180. Pinsky, M. "Just an Excitable Boy?" NEW TIMES 11 (No-
      vember 27, 1978): 52-53+.

      Another pre-trial look at Bundy's case.

181. "Suppliant Stranger." TIME 104 (September 23, 1974): 30.

      Describes the hunt for a killer of young women in Wash-
      ington, months before Bundy was named as a suspect.

      81. BUONO, ANGELO (S): See BIANCHI, KENNETH

          82. BURKE, WILLIAM (S)

   Operator of a "resurrection" business, with accomplice
William Hare, robbing fresh graves and selling corpses to
Edinburgh physicians as dissection specimens. When grave-
robbing became too tiresome, Burke and Hare turned to murder
as a means of acquiring their "product," dispatching at least
eleven victims during 1828. Hare escaped punishment by turning
state's evidence against his partner, and Burke was hanged in
January 1829. A physician who had purchased the cadavers was
not charged.

* CRIMES AND PUNISHMENT: A PICTORIAL ENCYCLOPEDIA OF ABER-
  RANT BEHAVIOR, Volume 20. Cited above as item 4, pp.
  48-56.

  Examines the "resurrectionists" in detail.

* Douthwaite, L.C. MASS MURDER. Cited above as item 6.

  Capsule case history presented as an example of mass
  murder in nineteenth-century Britain.

* Gaute, J.H.H., and Robin Odell. THE MURDERERS' WHO'S
  WHO. Cited above as item 8, pp. 57-58.

  Case history presented in an encyclopedic format.

* Nash, Jay Robert. ALMANAC OF WORLD CRIME. Cited above
  as item 19, p. 271.

  Brief case history within a general discussion of mass
  murder.

182. Roughead, William. THE MURDERER'S COMPANION. New York:
  W.W. Norton, 1968, pp. 117-174.

  An entertaining look at Burke and Hare, presented in
  an anthology of famous cases.

* Scott, Sir Harold. THE CONCISE ENCYCLOPEDIA OF CRIME
  AND CRIMINALS. Cited above as item 27, pp. 31-32.

  Case history presented in an encyclopedic format.

* Wilson, Colin. A CASEBOOK OF MURDER. Cited above as
  item 33, pp. 114-115.

  Brief case history within a sociological study of murder.

* ———. A CRIMINAL HISTORY OF MANKIND. Cited above as
  item 34, pp. 466-467.

  Case history within a discussion of crime in the Victorian era.

* ———, and Patricia Putnam. THE ENCYCLOPEDIA OF MURDER.
  Cited above as item 35, pp. 117-120.

  Case history presented in an encyclopedic format.

83. BURROWS, ALBERT EDWARD (S)

British laborer who killed his mistress and her two
children in January 1920, dumping their bodies down the air
shaft of a disused coal mine near Glossop. Three years later,
Burrows killed and sexually abused a four-year-old boy, dropping the child's body down the same shaft. Convicted and
hanged in 1923.

*   Nash, Jay Robert. CRIME CHRONOLOGY, 1900-1983. Cited
    above as item 21, p. 51.

    Brief case history presented in time line format.

*   Wilson, Colin, and Patricia Putnam. THE ENCYCLOPEDIA OF
    MURDER. Cited above as item 35, pp. 121-122.

    Case history presented in an encyclopedic format.

84. BURSE, NATHANIEL (S): See DE MAU MAU MURDERS

85. BUTTS, VERNON ROBERT (S): See BONIN, WILLIAM GEORGE

86. CAILLARD, ? (M)

French slayer, aged twenty-seven, who wiped out a family
of five in the village of Nassandres, during March 1898. The
mother, father, and two sons were shot by Caillard, who then
slashed the young daughter's throat. Executed on the guillotine.

*   Logan, Guy B.H. MASTERS OF CRIME. Cited above as item
    17, pp. 172-177.

    Case history within an anthology of 19th-century cases.

87. CAMPBELL, COLIN (S)

Medical doctor and slayer of at least two women in New
Jersey during 1928 and 1929. Campbell met his victims through
a matrimonial agency, shooting each through the head, then
dumping their bodies by the roadside, dousing them with gasoline, and setting them afire. Executed during April 1930.

*   CRIMES AND PUNISHMENT: A PICTORIAL ENCYCLOPEDIA OF ABER-
    RANT BEHAVIOR, Volume 4. Cited above as item 4, pp.
    61-62.

    Case history in a section on "lonely-hearts killers."

88. CAMPBELL, JOHN L. (M)

Half-breed Sioux who slaughtered the Jewett family at
Mankato, Minn., during 1866. Lynched by members of a local
posse.

 *   Nash, Jay Robert. MURDER, AMERICA. Cited above as item
       23, p. 313.

     Sketchy case history presented in time line format.

89. CARAWAN, GEORGE WASHINGTON (S)

Volatile minister in Goose Creek, N.C., who poisoned his
first wife and his second wife's suspected lover. Later, he
shot and killed a parishoner who sued him for slander. At his
trial for that murder, in 1852, Carawan produced two pistols,
bungled an attempt to kill the prosecutor, and then shot himself.

 *   Nash, Jay Robert. MURDER, AMERICA. Cited above as item
       23, pp. 14, 59-62, 340.

     Case history within an anthology of "classic" cases.

90. CARIGNAN, HARVEY LOUIS (S)

Sentenced to hang for the beating death of a woman in
Alaska, during 1949, Carignan was later freed on a legal tech-
nicality. Moving to Seattle, he began a long career of sexual
assault and murder, during which he is known to have slain at
least five women, crushing their skulls with a hammer. Other
victims, who survived in spite of savage beatings, report that
Carignan also rammed the handle of his hammer into their vaginas,
simulating rape. Maps retrieved from Carignan's possession
were marked with 181 ominous red circles; some of these coin-
cided with the location of unsolved homicides, while others
seemed to have no link with any criminal activity. Finally
convicted of murder and assault in Minneapolis, he is serving
forty years in prison, the maximum term allowed by state law.

183. Stack, Andy (pseud.). THE WANT-AD KILLER. New York:
      Signet Books, 1983.

     Ann Rule relates Carignan's case in chilling detail.

91. CARITATIVO, BART (M)

Filipino houseboy who murdered his wealthy employers at

Stimson Beach, Calif., during 1954. Faking a clumsy will which
named himself as beneficiary to their estate, Caritativo was
swiftly arrested and died in the gas chamber four years later.

* Gaute, J.H.H., and Robin Odell. THE MURDERERS' WHO'S
  WHO. Cited above as item 8, p. 63.

  Case history presented in an encyclopedic format.

* Nash, Jay Robert. BLOODLETTERS AND BADMEN. Cited above
  as item 20, pp. 109-111.

  Case history presented in an encyclopedic format.

* ————. CRIME CHRONOLOGY, 1900-1983. Cited above as
  item 21, p. 150.

  Brief case history presented in time line format.

* ————. MURDER, AMERICA. Cited above as item 23, p. 424.

  Sketchy case history presented in time line format.

92. CARNEY, RAYMOND (M)

Escaped convict who murdered a young couple near Pamplico,
S.C., in December 1953. Despite a claim that robbery was the
only motive, Carney's female victim had been raped and then
decapitated; her head was found buried near the shallow grave
which held her boyfriend's body.

* Wilson, Colin. ORDER OF ASSASSINS. Cited above as item
  76, pp. 111-112.

  Case history within a psychological history of murder.

93. CARPENTER, RICHARD (S)

Northern California's "Trailside Killer," responsible
for the ritualistic shooting deaths of at least eight hikers
around San Rafael, between August 1979 and May 1981. Convicted
of multiple murder and sentenced to die.

184. "Death Trail." TIME 116 (December 15, 1980): 24.

  Examines the "trailside" manhunt in progress.

* Gest, Ted, and Douglas C. Lyons. "Behind a Nationwide
  Wave of Unsolved Murders." Cited above as item 47.

Brief case history within a summary of unsolved serial
murder cases, all of which were subsequently broken.

94. CARROLL, FRANCIS M. (M)

New Jersey police officer who, in October 1937, murdered
a North Arlington doctor and the doctor's wife, seeking to con-
ceal the fact of his incestuous relationship with his own
daughter. (The killer's daughter was a patient of the victim.)
Sentenced to life imprisonment; released in September 1950.
Accomplice Paul Nathaniel Dwyer, coerced into hiding the bodies
under threat of death, ironically remained in prison after
Carroll's release.

* Wilson, Colin, and Patricia Putnam. THE ENCYCLOPEDIA OF
  MURDER. Cited above as item 35, pp. 134-136.

Case history presented in an encyclopedic format.

95. CASEY, ANDREW (M)

Fourteen-year-old in Rye, N.Y., who shot his mother and
sister to death in May 1957, following a family argument over
homework from school. Detained as a juvenile.

* FACTS ON FILE. Volume 17, 1957. Cited above as item 7,
  p. 175.

Contemporaneous account of Casey's crime and arrest.

96. CATOE, JARVIS (S)

Rare example of a black serial killer, drawn from the
pre-World War II era. After killing a New York City woman,
in August 1941, Catoe was arrested in Washington, D.C. He
subsequently confessed to that crime, and to an earlier homicide, for which another suspect had already served five years
of a life sentence. In October 1941, Catoe was convicted in
the murder of a third woman, and authorities suspect that there
may have been at least seven murders prior to his arrest.
Executed in the electric chair.

* Godwin, John. MURDER USA. Cited above as item 10, pp.
  10-11.

Passing reference within a tabulation of the century's "worst" multiple murderers.

97. CHALONS, TAILOR OF (S)

Lethal pedophile of the 16th century who molested, murdered, and dismembered children lured to his tailor's shop in Chalons, France. Accused of lycanthropy by clerical authorities upon discovery of his crimes, he was burned alive in Paris, in December 1598.

* Masters, R.E.L., and Eduard Lea. PERVERSE CRIMES IN HISTORY. Cited above as item 18, pp. 60-61.

Brief case history within a survey of "werewolves."

98. CHAPMAN, GEORGE (S)

Real name, Severin Klosovski. Polish native who traveled to England in early 1888, later briefly visiting America before returning "home" to London in 1892 or '93. Employed in the now-extinct trade of "barber-surgeon." Between 1895 and 1902, Chapman poisoned at least three women with whom he was romantically involved; "expert" opinions on motive vary from pure sadism to financial greed. Frequently named as a suspect in the homicides committed by "Jack the Ripper," Chapman's chief "defense" appears to be the argument that a sadistic slasher of prostitutes would be unlikely to change his M.O. after seven years, switching to the relatively "peaceful" poisoning of his own wives and lovers.

185. Adam, H.L. TRIAL OF GEORGE CHAPMAN. London: William Hodge, 1930.

One in a series of volumes on famous British trials, reproducing excerpts from the transcripts of Chapman's case.

* CRIMES AND PUNISHMENT: A PICTORIAL ENCYCLOPEDIA OF ABERRANT BEHAVIOR, Volume 1. Cited above as item 4, pp. 86-87.

Case history within a discussion of "lady-killers."

* Gaute, J.H.H., and Robin Odell. THE MURDERERS' WHO'S WHO. Cited above as item 8, pp. 65-66.

Case history presented in an encyclopedic format.

* Green, Jonathon. THE GREATEST CRIMINALS OF ALL TIME. Cited above as item 11, p. 194.

  Case history presented in an encyclopedic format.

* Nash, Jay Robert. ALMANAC OF WORLD CRIME. Cited above as item 19, pp. 279-281.

  Case history within a general discussion of mass murder.

* ————. CRIME CHRONOLOGY, 1900-1983. Cited above as item 21, pp. 4, 7, 10.

  Traces Chapman's crimes with sketch time line entries.

* Wilson, Colin, and Patricia Putnam. THE ENCYCLOPEDIA OF MURDER. Cited above as item 35, pp. 140-143.

  Case history presented in an encyclopedic format.

99. CHASE, RICHARD TRENTON (S)

Sacramento, Calif., "vampire killer." Known, as an adolescent, to eat live birds, on more than one occasion Chase was found naked in fields, covered with blood from cattle he had slaughtered in a violent frenzy. Killed six persons in a four-day period of January 1978, drinking the blood of at least one victim and taking pieces from some others home to eat. Sentenced to life imprisonment.

Books

* Nash, Jay Robert. CRIME CHRONOLOGY, 1900-1983. Cited above as item 21, p. 194.

  Brief case history presented in time line format.

* ————. MURDER, AMERICA. Cited above as item 23, p. 445.

  Sketchy case history presented in time line format.

Articles

* Darrach, Brad, and Joel Norris. "An American Tragedy." Cited above as item 40.

  Brief case history within a general discussion of serial murder.

100. CHAVEZ, MANUEL J. (M): See BATES, CLYDE

101. CHICAGO CHILD MURDERS (S?)

Unsolved homicides of five Chicago children, committed between October 1955 and December 1956. Brothers John and Anton Schuessler, together with their friend, Robert Peterson, were beaten and strangled to death while walking home from a North Side bowling alley; their nude, mutilated bodies were discovered in some nearby woods after two days of searching. Fourteen months later, in December 1956, sisters Barbara and Patricia Grimes vanished on their way home from a movie. After 25 days of searching, the girls were found—nude, battered, and strangled—in a wooded area fifteen miles from their home. Despite intensive investigation (and an anonymous letter to columnist Ann Landers, purporting to describe the killer and his car), the cases remain open, the killer or killers still at large. Aside from similarity of method in the slayings and disposal of the bodies, no connection between the two sets of murders has been proven.

Books

186.   Browning, Norma Lee. THE PSYCHIC WORLD OF PETER HURKOS. Garden City, N.Y.: Doubleday, 1970, pp. 25-27.

Psychic Hurkos fondles photographs of the Chicago victims as part of a 1960 "test," failing to solve the case. No surprises.

*   FACTS ON FILE. Volume 15, 1955. Cited above as item 7, p. 348.

Contemporaneous account of the Schuessler-Peterson murders.

*   FACTS ON FILE. Volume 17, 1957. Cited above as item 7, p. 36.

Reports the murder of the Grimes sisters.

*   Nash, Jay Robert. CRIME CHRONOLOGY, 1900-1983. Cited above as item 21, pp. 152, 154.

Follows the murders in sketchy time line format.

*   ———. OPEN FILES. Cited above as item 24, pp. 100-101, 219-220.

Reports the various Chicago crimes in an encyclopedia of unsolved cases.

Articles

187. "Who Saw These Three Boys?" LIFE 39 (October 31, 1955): 30-31.

Pictorial spread on the first set of murders.

102. "CHICAGO RIPPER, THE" (S)

Unsolved mutilation murders of approximately twenty women, in which the victims were sexually abused before (or after) death. The series of crimes ended mysteriously in January 1906, leaving police without a clue to the killer's identity.

* Nash, Jay Robert. CRIME CHRONOLOGY, 1900-1983. Cited above as item 21, p. 15.

Brief case history presented in time line format.

103. CHRISTIE, JOHN REGINALD HALLIDAY (S)

Sex-slayer of at least six victims, including his wife, several prostitutes, and a neighbor's female child. The victims were murdered at Christie's home in London, and a number of them were molested after death. A necrophile who shaved the pubic hair of certain victims and retained it as a trophy for the stimulation of his masturbatory fantasies, Christie had been plagued from young adulthood by inadequacy in his intimate relationships with women. Nicknamed "Reggie No-Dick" and "Can't-Do-It Christie" by early female acquaintances, he evnetually reached the point where he could achieve climax only with women who were unconscious or dead. Convicted in the murder of his wife, he was hanged in July 1953.

Books

* Boar, Roger, and Nigel Blundell. THE WORLD'S MOST IN-FAMOUS MURDERS. Cited above as item 2, pp. 39-43.

Case history presented in sensational tabloid style.

* CRIMES AND PUNISHMENT: A PICTORIAL ENCYCLOPEDIA OF ABER-RANT BEHAVIOR, Volume 5. Cited above as item 4, pp. 109-113.

Case history presented in an encyclopedic format.

* FACTS ON FILE. Volume 13, 1953. Cited above as item 7, p. 244.

    Reports Christie's execution.

* Green, Jonathon. THE GREATEST CRIMINALS OF ALL TIME. Cited above as item 11, p. 269.

    Brief case history in an encyclopedic format.

188. Kennedy, Ludovic. 10 RILLINGTON PLACE. London: Gollancz, 1961.

    The definitive study of Christie's case.

* Nash, Jay Robert. CRIME CHRONOLOGY, 1900-1983. Cited above as item 21, p. 145.

    Brief case history presented in time line format.

* Scott, Sir Harold. THE CONCISE ENCYCLOPEDIA OF CRIME AND CRIMINALS. Cited above as item 27, pp. 61-62.

    Case history presented in an encyclopedic format.

* Wilson, Colin. A CRIMINAL HISTORY OF MANKIND. Cited above as item 34, pp. 617-618.

    Case history within a general discussion of modern sex crimes and multiple murder.

* —————. ORDER OF ASSASSINS. Cited above as item 76, pp. 69-71.

    Psychological case history of Christie's crimes.

* —————, and Patricia Putnam. THE ENCYCLOPEDIA OF MURDER. Cited above as item 35, pp. 145-150.

    Case history presented in an encyclopedic format.

Articles

189. "Mild Murderer." NEWSWEEK 42 (July 6, 1953): 30.

    Reports on Christie's crimes and execution.

104. CHRISTOFI, STYLLOU (S)

Cypriot murderess, tried and acquitted in 1925 on charges of killing her mother by ramming a torch down the old woman's throat. In 1953 she went to live with her son and his German wife, in Britain. After arguing repeatedly with her daughter-in-law, Christofi strangled the younger woman to death and attempted to burn her body. Unfortunately for her case this time, a neighbor had observed her feeding the flames, in an attempt to burn what he mistook for a mannequin. Sentenced to death in October 1954, she was hanged after three psychiatrists pronounced her sane.

* CRIMES AND PUNISHMENT: A PICTORIAL ENCYCLOPEDIA OF ABERRANT BEHAVIOR, Volume 12. Cited above as item 4, pp. 115-121.

  Case history presented in an encyclopedic format.

* Gaute, J.H.H., and Robin Odell. THE MURDERERS' WHO'S WHO. Cited above as item 8, p. 68.

  Case history presented in an encyclopedic format.

* Green, Jonathon. THE GREATEST CRIMINALS OF ALL TIME. Cited above as item 11, p. 194.

  Brief case history presented in encyclopedic format.

* Nash, Jay Robert. CRIME CHRONOLOGY, 1900-1983. Cited above as item 21, p. 147.

  Brief case history presented in time line format.

* ————. LOOK FOR THE WOMAN. Cited above as item 22, pp. 78-79.

  Case history presented in an encyclopedic format.

* Wilson, Colin, and Patricia Putnam. THE ENCYCLOPEDIA OF MURDER. Cited above as item 35, pp. 150-151.

  Case history presented in an encyclopedic format.

105. CHRISTOPHER, JOSEPH G. (S)

Mentally unbalanced soldier believed responsible for the

slayings of several black men in Buffalo, N.Y., during 1980.
Four victims were shot to death with a .22-caliber weapon,
while two others, both cab drivers, had their hearts cut out.
Christopher was taken into custody by military police at Fort
Benning, Ga., after he tried to stab a black G.I. and then
attempted suicide. In addition to the shooting deaths in Buffalo, Christopher was also indicted in the murder of a Puerto
Rican victim and the non-fatal stabbing of another black man,
both in New York City. (No suspect has been named in the mutilation murders of the cab drivers.) Christopher pled guilty
to three of the fatal shootings in April 1982, and received a
sentence of 60 years to life. In 1985, his sentence was overturned by an appeals court on the grounds that his attorney
was barred from introducing evidence of mental incompetence.
Awaiting retrial.

Books

* FACTS ON FILE. Volume 40, 1980. Cited above as item 7,
   p. 997.

   Reports the rash of unsolved crimes in Buffalo.

* FACTS ON FILE. Volume 41, 1981. Cited above as item 7,
   pp. 300, 406.

   Reports Christopher's arrest and indictments.

* FACTS ON FILE. Volume 42, 1982. Cited above as item 7,
   p. 428.

   Reports Christopher's guilty plea and sentencing.

* FACTS ON FILE. Volume 45, 1985. Cited above as item 7,
   p. 575.

   Contemporaneous report of Christopher's appeal.

Articles

* Gest, Ted, and Douglas C. Lyons. "Behind a Nationwide
   Wave of Unsolved Murders." Cited above as item 47.

   Includes the Buffalo murders with other open serial
   cases, all of which were subsequently solved.

190. Locklear, J. "Churches in Buffalo Respond to Racial
      Murders with a Rally, Extra Prayer Meetings, and Calls

for Reason." CHRISTIANITY TODAY 24 (November 21, 1980): 52-53.

Describes local reactions to murders of blacks.

106. CHURCH, ELLEN (M)

New Jersey housewife who murdered two of her children and attempted to kill two others in March 1959, believing all of them to be insane. Court psychiatrists disagreed, pronouncing Mrs. Christopher a schizophrenic. Committed to a mental institution.

* FACTS ON FILE. Volume 19, 1959. Cited above as item 7, p. 104.

Reports Church's crimes and arrest.

107. "CINCINNATI STRANGLER, THE" (S): See LASKEY, POSTEAL

108. CIUCCI, VINCENT (M)

Chicago slayer who, in December 1953, chloroformed his wife and three children before shooting all four victims in the head and setting fire to the family apartment. Convicted of quadruple murder, he was executed in 1962.

* Nash, Jay Robert. ALMANAC OF WORLD CRIME. Cited above as item 19, p. 25.

Case history within a general discussion of homicidal arsonists.

109. CLARK, DOUGLAS DANIEL (S)

Los Angeles "Sunset Strip Slayer," responsible, with accomplice Carol Mary Bundy, for the torture-mutilation slayings of at least six women. Clark generally selected prostitutes as victims, "grading" them on their sexual performance under the gun and releasing alive those who "passed." In cases of "failure," he enjoyed shooting victims through the head while they fellated him. A seventh victim was male, an acquaintance of Bundy whom she decapitated after he became suspicious of her relationship with Clark. In custody, awaiting execution, Clark has claimed a body-count of fifty victims, but the claim remains unverified. Carol Bundy received a sentence of 52 years to life, for her role in two murders.

* FACTS ON FILE. Volume 13, 1983. Cited above as item 7,
  pp. 136, 220, 436.

    Traces the arrest, conviction, and sentencing of the
    "Sunset Slayers."

* Levin, Jack, and James Alan Fox. MASS MURDER: AMERICA'S
  GROWING MENACE. Cited above as item 15.

    Case history within a discussion of serial murder.

110. CLARK, MICHAEL ANDREW (M)

Sixteen-year-old freeway sniper at Long Beach, Calif.,
in 1965. Clark killed three passing motorists and wounded
eleven others with random gunfire, committing suicide as the
police arrived.

Books

* Nash, Jay Robert. MURDER, AMERICA. Cited above as item
  23, p. 433.

    Sketchy case history presented in time line format.

Articles

191. "Model Boy." NEWSWEEK 65 (May 10, 1965): 46.

    Reports Clark's crimes and suicide.

111. CLEMENTS, ROBERT GEORGE (S)

British physician known to have murdered his third wife
with an injection of morphine, strongly suspected of killing
her two predecessors as well. Committed suicide, with morphine,
when police began a homicide investigation in the latest death.
A friend and fellow physician, who had wrongly diagnosed the
ailment of the third Mrs. Clements as leukemia, also killed
himself when an autopsy proved the cause of death to be morphine poisoning. His suicide note read: "I have for some time
been aware that I have been making mistakes. I have not
learned from experience."

* Nash, Jay Robert. ALMANAC OF WORLD CRIME. Cited above
  as item 19, p. 325.

    Case history within a discussion of homicidal doctors.

* ————. CRIME CHRONOLOGY, 1900–1983. Cited above as
item 21, pp. 131–132.

Brief case history presented in time line format.

* Wilson, Colin, and Patricia Putnam. THE ENCYCLOPEDIA OF
MURDER. Cited above as item 35, pp. 156–157.

Case history presented in an encyclopedic format.

112. COLE, CARROLL EDWARD (S)

Severely abused as a child by his sadistic, adulterous
mother, forced to dress as a girl for the amusement of her
friends and share the secret of her marital infidelity, Cole
grew up hating "loose" women and homosexuals. At age nine,
he drowned a playmate who made fun of his "sissy" name, progressing in later years to assaults on girls and women. Repeated attempts to seek psychiatric help between 1960 and 1970
were futile, with therapists repeatedly diagnosing Cole as a
malingerer, "no danger to society." Between 1971 and 1981,
Cole murdered at least eleven women in five states. (An interview in 1985 suggested that there may have been two other
victims.) Sentenced to life imprisonment for three murders
in Texas, Cole waived extradition to Nevada in 1984 and was
sentenced to death for an outstanding case in Las Vegas.
Resisting all appeals, while speaking out at every opportunity
against the crime of child abuse, he was executed by lethal
injection in December 1985.

Books

* Brian, Dennis. MURDERERS DIE. Cited above as item 3,
pp. 145–148.

Brief case history within a collection of stories
on killers who were put to death.

Articles

192. Newton, Michael. "Killer." LV, THE MAGAZINE OF LAS
VEGAS 1 (November 1985): 82–89.

Prepared from interviews and correspondence with Cole
on death row, examining his crimes and early life.

193. ————, and Judy Newton. "Death Watch." LV, THE MAGA-
ZINE OF LAS VEGAS 2 (January 1986): 12–13.

Describes Cole's final hours, based upon an interview conducted the afternoon before his execution.

113. COLEMAN, ALTON (S)

Responsible, with accomplice Debra Brown, for at least six homicides committed during a Midwestern crime spree in 1984. Coleman made the FBI's "Most Wanted" list before his arrest in July 1984. At this writing, Coleman has been sentenced to death in Ohio, Indiana, and Illinois, with further trials pending. Brown has been convicted with Coleman in three of the four cases tried, and is serving multiple life sentences.

Books

* FACTS ON FILE. Volume 44, 1984. Cited above as item 7, p. 585.

   Reports Coleman's arrest in Illinois.

* FACTS ON FILE. Volume 45, 1985. Cited above as item 7, p. 391.

   Reports the conviction of Coleman and Brown in Ohio.

Articles

194. "Alton Coleman and Friend Guilty in Ohio Killing." JET 68 (May 27, 1985): 39.

   Report's Coleman's conviction in Cincinnati.

114. COLEMAN, WAYNE (M): See ISSAACS, CARL and BILLY

115. COLLINS, JOHN NORMAN (S)

Sadistic slayer of seven female victims, including several coeds from the University of Michigan at Ypsilanti. Victims were raped and strangled or beaten to death, sometimes mutilated by removal of hands and feet, over a two-year period from 1967 to 1969. Convicted in one of seven "identical" crimes, Collins is also a prime suspect in the murder of a California woman, slain while he was visiting that state. Sentenced to a term of twenty years in prison on his single murder conviction.

Books

* Browning, Norma Lee. THE PSYCHIC WORLD OF PETER HURKOS. Cited above as item 186, pp. 245-253.

  Hurkos reportedly described a killer matching Collins' description in July 1969, before the suspect's arrest, but according to Browning, "Peter's theory is that three or four men comprising a religious cult or blood fraternity are responsible for the eight [?] mutilation slayings of the Michigan coeds." Oops.

* FACTS ON FILE. Volume 29, 1969. Cited above as item 7, pp. 444, 720.

  Reports the last two murders in the series, followed by Collins' arrest.

* Gaute, J.H.H., and Robin Odell. THE MURDERERS' WHO'S WHO. Cited above as item 8, pp. 70-71.

  Case history presented in an encyclopedic format.

* Green, Jonathon. THE GREATEST CRIMINALS OF ALL TIME. Cited above as item 11, p. 181.

  Brief case history presented in encyclopedic format.

195. Keyes, Richard. THE MICHIGAN MURDERS. New York: Reader's Digest Press, 1976.

  The names of innocent and guilty alike are changed in this examination of the Collins case, but Keyes still manages to do a thorough job of studying his subject. Well worth reading.

* Levin, Jack, and James Alan Fox. MASS MURDER: AMERICA'S GROWING MENACE. Cited above as item 15.

  Case history within a discussion of serial murder.

* Nash, Jay Robert. MURDER, AMERICA. Cited above as item 23, p. 436.

  Sketchy case history presented in time line format.

* Wilson, Colin, and Donald Seaman. THE ENCYCLOPEDIA OF MODERN MURDER. Cited above as item 36, pp. 46-50.

  Case history presented in an encyclopedic format.

116. COLLINS, OPAL JUANITA (M)

Hammond, Ind., housewife who shot and killed her husband, her mother-in-law, and two sisters-in-law during a family argument in May 1956. Sentenced to prison.

* FACTS ON FILE. Volume 16, 1956. Cited above as item 7, p. 180.

   Reports Collins' crimes and arrest.

117. CONRAD, FRITZ (M)

German killer who murdered his wife and four children, staging the scene to resemble a murder-suicide committed by his wife. He subsequently "found" the bodies, hanging from hooks in the family apartment, and summoned police to the scene. When Conrad's love affair with a younger woman was discovered by investigators, he confessed the murders and was later executed.

* Wilson, Colin, and Patricia Putnam. THE ENCYCLOPEDIA OF MURDER. Cited above as item 35, pp. 158-159.

   Case history presented in an encyclopedic format.

118. COOK, ROY (M)

North Carolina tenant farmer who, in October 1958, shot and killed his wife, sister-in-law, and a female neighbor. A fourth victim, though wounded, managed to survive. Cook was subsequently shot to death by members of a posse while resisting arrest.

* FACTS ON FILE. Volume 18, 1958. Cited above as item 7, p. 352.

   Reports Cook's crimes and death.

119. COOK, WILLIAM E. (S)

Abducted a family of five near Tulsa, Okla., in 1950, killing all five hostages and the family dog, dropping the bodies into an abandoned well. Cook later killed a traveling salesman and stole the victim's car for his escape. Captured in Mexico, he was returned to the United States for trial and was executed in December 1952.

Books

*   Brian, Dennis. MURDERERS DIE. Cited above as item 3,
    p. 69.

    Case history within an anthology of killers who were
    put to death.

*   FACTS ON FILE. Volume 11, 1951. Cited above as item 7,
    pp. 24, 104, 400.

    Reports the phases of Cook's trial and sentencing.

*   FACTS ON FILE. Volume 12, 1952. Cited above as item 7,
    p. 408.

    Reports Cook's execution.

*   Gaute, J.H.H., and Robin Odell. THE MURDERERS' WHO'S
    WHO. Cited above as item 8, p. 71.

    Case history presented in an encyclopedic format.

*   Green, Jonathon. THE GREATEST CRIMINALS OF ALL TIME.
    Cited above as item 11, p. 251.

    Brief case history in an encyclopedic format.

*   Nash, Jay Robert. BLOODLETTERS AND BADMEN. Cited above
    as item 20, pp. 129-132.

    Case history presented in an encyclopedic format.

*   ————. CRIME CHRONOLOGY, 1900-1983. Cited above as
    item 21, p. 139.

    Brief case history presented in time line format.

*   ————. MURDER, AMERICA. Cited above as item 23, p. 431,

    Sketchy case history presented in time line format.

*   Sifakis, Carl. THE ENCYCLOPEDIA OF AMERICAN CRIME.
    Cited above as item 29, p. 170.

    Case history presented in an encyclopedic format.

* Steiger, Brad. THE MASS MURDERER. Cited above as item 30.

    Brief case history within a general discussion of the
    topic.

Articles

196. "Kid with the Bad Eye." LIFE 30 (January 29, 1951): 17-21.

      Reports Cook's crimes and arrest.

197. "Killer on a Rampage." NEWSWEEK 37 (January 22, 1951): 21.

      Contemporaneous report of Cook's crimes and arrest.

198. "Young Man with a Gun." TIME 57 (January 22, 1951): 19-20.

      Reports on Cook's crimes and arrest.

   120. COOKS, JESSIE LEE (S): See "ZEBRA MURDERS, THE"

121. COOPER, KEVIN (M)

     Escapee from a California prison at Chino who, three days
after his escape in 1983, invaded the home of a local family,
killing four persons and critically wounding a fifth in assaults
committed with a knife and hatchet. Subsequently recaptured,
Cooper was convicted on charges of multiple murder and sentenced to life imprisonment.

Books

* Nash, Jay Robert. CRIME CHRONOLOGY, 1900-1983. Cited
   above as item 21, pp. 204-205.

   Case history presented in time line format.

Articles

199. Alter, J. "Nightmare in California." NEWSWEEK 101 (June
      20, 1983): 28.

      A report of Cooper's crimes, prepared while he was
      still at large.

122. CORLL, DEAN ARNOLD (S)

Homosexual torture-slayer, with accomplices David Brooks

and Elmer Wayne Henley, of at least 27 boys in Houston, Tex.,
between 1971 and 1973. Disappearances of victims from a Houston
neighborhood were unanimously dismissed by the police as "runaways" until August 1973, when Corll was shot to death by
Henley, following a violent argument over the disposition of a
rare female victim. Excavations at Corll's boat shed were
abandoned after homicide investigators topped the body-count
of California's record-holding killer, Juan Corona, even though
a portion of the property was unexplored. Investigations by
reporters raised the possibility that Corll may have murdered
other children, prior to 1971, but with their suspect dead,
detectives showed no interest in the leads. Brooks and Henley
each were subsequently sentenced to a term of life imprisonment
for their roles in the crimes.

Books

* CRIMES AND PUNISHMENT: A PICTORIAL ENCYCLOPEDIA OF ABER-
  RANT BEHAVIOR, Volume 7. Cited above as item 4, p. 79.

  Case history presented in an encyclopedic format.

* FACTS ON FILE. Volume 33, 1973. Cited above as item 7,
  p. 735.

  Reports the shocking discoveries in Houston.

* FACTS ON FILE. Volume 34, 1974. Cited above as item 7,
  p. 720.

  Reports Elmer Henley's murder conviction.

* FACTS ON FILE. Volume 35, 1975. Cited above as item 7,
  p. 425.

  David Brooks receives his life sentence.

* FACTS ON FILE. Volume 37, 1977. Cited above as item 7,
  p. 432.

  Investigation of a child pornography ring links sodomist
  John D. Norman to some of Corll's activities.

* FACTS ON FILE. Volume 38, 1978. Cited above as item 7,
  p. 992.

  Henley's conviction is overturned on the grounds of
  pretrial publicity.

*   FACTS ON FILE. Volume 39, 1979. Cited above as item 7,
     p. 819.

     Reports Henley's second conviction.

*   Gaute, J.H.H., and Robin Odell. THE MURDERERS' WHO'S
     WHO. Cited above as item 8, pp. 72-73.

     Case history presented in encyclopedic format.

*   Godwin, John. MURDER USA. Cited above as item 10, pp.
     161-168.

     Case history within a "chamber of horrors," detailing
     grisly multicides of recent years.

*   Green, Jonathon. THE GREATEST CRIMINALS OF ALL TIME.
     Cited above as item 11, pp. 181-182.

     Case history presented in an encyclopedic format.

200. Gurwell, John K. MASS MURDER IN HOUSTON. Houston: Cor-
     dovan Press, 1974.

     Sensational paperback examination of the case, prepared
     from local interviews and media reports.

*   Nash, Jay Robert. ALMANAC OF WORLD CRIME. Cited above
     as item 19, p. 290.

     Brief case history within a general discussion of mass
     murder.

*   ———. CRIME CHRONOLOGY, 1900-1983. Cited above as
     item 21, p. 185.

     Brief case history presented in time line format.

*   ———. MURDER, AMERICA. Cited above as item 23, p. 441.

     Sketchy case history presented in time line format.

201. Olsen, Jack. THE MAN WITH THE CANDY. New York: Simon
     & Schuster, 1974.

     Informative account of the Houston case, including
     some persuasive evidence that several homicides, at
     least, were overlooked by the authorities, through

negligence and eagerness to close the case once they had "beaten the Corona record."

* Sifakis, Carl. THE ENCYCLOPEDIA OF AMERICAN CRIME. Cited above as item 29, p. 175.

   Case history presented in an encyclopedic format.

* Wilson, Colin. A CRIMINAL HISTORY OF MANKIND. Cited above as item 34, p. 636.

   Brief case history within a general discussion of modern "motiveless" crimes.

* ————, and Donald Seaman. THE ENCYCLOPEDIA OF MODERN MURDER. Cited above as item 36, pp. 53-56.

   Case history presented in an encyclopedic format.

Articles

* Futch, J.D. "Mass Murder, Bourgeois Style." Cited above as item 44.

   Laments the lack of "aristocratic snobbishness" in Corll's "pedestrian" crimes.

202. "Houston Horrors." TIME 102 (August 20, 1973): 24.

   Contemporaneous report of Corll's crimes and death.

203. "Nicest Person." NEWSWEEK 82 (August 20, 1973): 32.

   Reports Corll's death and the exposure of his crimes.

123. CORNWELL, GERRY (M)

Jealous lover in Oakland, Calif., who, in 1955, torched the bedroom occupied by his former mistress and her new lover. A pilot light on the victim's stove prematurely ignited gasoline which Cornwell was pouring around the room, leading him to claim that he was innocent of actually lighting the fire himself. A jury found him guilty on the basis of intent, and he was sentenced to death.

* Wilson, Colin, and Patricia Putnam. THE ENCYCLOPEDIA OF MURDER. Cited above as item 35, pp. 164-165.

Case history presented in an encyclopedic format.

124. CORONA, JUAN VALLEJO (S)

California labor contractor, charged in 1971 with the
bludgeon-and-machete slayings of 25 male migrant workers. The
first corpses were unearthed in orchards near Yuba City, in
May 1971, and evidence recovered from several graves was used
to identify Corona as a suspect. Corona was convicted on all
counts and sentenced to 25 consecutive terms of life imrison-
ment, a verdict subsequently overturned on appeal. Citing
incompetence of Corona's original lawyer, the appeals court
ordered a new trial—at which Corona was again convicted on
all counts. Reports issued in December 1973 tentatively linked
Corona with a twenty-sixth victim, never identified, but no
further charges have been filed. Condition of the bodies,
some with pants pulled down around their ankles, led the prosecution to allege a homosexual motive in the slayings. Defense
attorneys countered that Corona's brother—known for his violent
temper and record of felonious assaults—was a more likely
suspect in the case, but two juries were persuaded by Corona's
handwriting, found on receipt slips recovered from one of the
graves.

Books

204. Cray, Ed. BURDEN OF PROOF. New York: Macmillan, 1973.

Prepared by an ACLU spokesman attached to Corona's
original defense team, the book argues Corona's innocence, based on allegations that the legal "burden of
proof" was shifted from the prosecution to the defense
by unethical sleight-of-hand. An afterword by Corona's
first lawyer—later ruled incompetent by an appeals
court—makes interesting reading. Other sources note
Cray's own alleged unethical behavior during the trial,
in efforts to influence jurors outside the courtroom,
and the author's objectivity is certainly open to
question.

*   FACTS ON FILE. Volume 31, 1971. Cited above as item 7,
    p. 416.

Reports Corona's arrest in Yuba City.

*   FACTS ON FILE. Volume 33, 1973. Cited above as item 7,
    pp. 92, 154.

Reports Corona's conviction and sentencing.

* Gaute, J.H.H., and Robin Odell. THE MURDERERS' WHO'S WHO. Cited above as item 8, p. 73.

    Case history presented in an encyclopedic format.

* Green, Jonathon. THE GREATEST CRIMINALS OF ALL TIME. Cited above as item 11, p. 148.

    Brief case history presented in encyclopedic format.

205. Kidder, Tracy. THE ROAD TO YUBA CITY. Garden City, N.Y.: Doubleday, 1974.

    Notable for its presentation of clumsy errors and apparent incompetence on both sides of the case. Pointing out obvious weaknesses in the prosecution's case, the author avoids any personal judgment of Corona's guilt or innocence.

* Nash, Jay Robert. CRIME CHRONOLOGY, 1900–1983. Cited above as item 21, p. 181.

    Brief case history presented in time line format.

* Sifakis, Carl. THE ENCYCLOPEDIA OF AMERICAN CRIME. Cited above as item 29, pp. 175–176.

    Case history presented in an encyclopedic format.

206. Villasenor, Victor. JURY: THE PEOPLE vs JUAN CORONA. Boston: Little, Brown, 1977.

    Unique and fascinating presentation of Corona's case from the jurors' viewpoint, touching on inconsistencies and incongruities in the evidence advanced by both sides.

* Wilson, Colin. A CRIMINAL HISTORY OF MANKIND. Cited above as item 34, p. 635.

    Case history within a general discussion of modern mass murder.

* ————, and Donald Seaman. THE ENCYCLOPEDIA OF MODERN MURDER. Cited above as item 36, pp. 56–58.

    Case history presented in an encyclopedic format.

Articles

207. "Anatomy of a Murder Suspect." TIME 97 (June 14, 1971):
     24.

     Reports Corona's arrest in Yuba City.

208. "California's Sub-culture." THE NATION 212 (June 14,
     1971): 740.

     Examines the case in light of California's migrant
     labor system.

209. "Case Against Corona." NEWSWEEK 80 (September 25, 1972):
     43-44.

     Summarizes the prosecution's evidence.

210. "Corona in Court." NEWSWEEK 77 (June 14, 1971): 37.

     Reports Corona's indictment on murder charges.

211. "Corona Retrial." TIME 111 (May 22, 1978): 68.

     Describes the appeals court's order for a new trial.

212. "Death in the Orchards." TIME 97 (June 7, 1971): 14.

     Describes the continuing investigation in California.

213. "Grisly Harvest in the Orchard." LIFE 70 (June 11, 1971):
     38-39.

     Photo lay-out of the crime scene, with background.

214. "Mass Murder Mess." TIME 100 (November 13, 1972): 98.

     Describes the prosecution's confused, confusing presen-
     tation of the case against Corona.

215. "Massacre at Yuba City." NEWSWEEK 77 (June 7, 1971):
     28-29.

     Reports the discovery of bodies and the ongoing manhunt.

125. COSTA, ANTONE CHARLES (S)

Sexually-motivated slayer of young women around Province-
town and Cape Cod, Mass., in 1969. Convicted, in 1971, in

two mutilation murders (and suspected of at least two others), Costa was sentenced to a term of life imprisonment without parole. Committed suicide, by hanging, at Walpole state prison in May 1974.

Books

216. Damore, Leo. IN HIS GARDEN. New York: Arbor House, 1981.

    The definitive study of Costa, massive in both size and scope, probing every aspect of the killer's life, death, and psyche. Fascinating.

   * FACTS ON FILE. Volume 29, 1969. Cited above as item 7, p. 444.

    Reports the discovery of bodies at Cape Cod.

   * Leyton, Elliott. COMPULSIVE KILLERS. Cited above as item 16, p. 288.

    Citing item 216 above as his source, Leyton plunges off the proverbial deep end, crediting Costa with 20 murders. Preposterous.

Articles

217. "Graves in the Dunes." TIME 93 (March 14, 1969): 29.

    Reports the discovery of two Cape Cod victims.

218. Vonnegut, Kurt. "There's a Maniac Out There." LIFE 67 (July 25, 1969): 53-54+.

    A celebrity resident surveys his town as the search for an elusive slayer continues.

219. "Weekend on Cape Cod." NEWSWEEK 73 (March 17, 1969): 38.

    Reports the discovery of bodies and the continuing manhunt.

126. COTTINGHAM, RICHARD (S)

Sadistic torture-slayer of young women, convicted and sentenced to 179 years in prison for the murder of two New Jersey victims, subsequently convicted and sentenced to life for the murders of three women in New York City. Cottingham

apparently began assaulting women—mostly prostitutes—in early
1974, killing for the first time in December 1979. All but
one of his known victims were working prostitutes; the sole
exception was a young housewife whom he abducted, raped, and
killed in New Jersey.

220. Leith, Rod. THE PROSTITUTE MURDERS: THE PEOPLE vs RICHARD
      COTTINGHAM. Secaucus, N.J.: Lyle Stuart, 1983.

      Examines Cottingham's case, his background, and the
      emergence of a murderous "Jekyll-and-Hyde" personality
      in young adulthood.

127. COTTON, MARY ANN (S)

Nineteenth-century poisoner, co-holder (with Dennis Nilsen) of the title as Britain's worst multiple murderer to date,
with 15 verified victims and another 21 suspected. Known victims included two of Cotton's four husbands, a sister-in-law,
eight of her own children, and three stepchildren. Most of
Cotton's victims were apparently killed for monetary gain, or
because they stood in the way of her latest impending marriage.
Hanged in 1873.

221. Appleton, Arthur. MARY ANN COTTON: HER STORY AND TRIAL.
      London: Michael Joseph, 1973.

      Credits Cotton with 21 victims, overall.

  * Boar, Roger, and Nigel Blundell. THE WORLD'S MOST IN-
      FAMOUS MURDERS. Cited above as item 2, pp. 34-38.

      Case history presented in sensational tabloid style.

  * Green, Jonathon. THE GREATEST CRIMINALS OF ALL TIME.
      Cited above as item 11, pp. 148-149.

      Brief case history presented in encyclopedic format.

128. COWAN, FREDERICK W. (M)

Neo-Nazi gun enthusiast (and alleged Satanist) in New
Rochelle, N.Y. Suspended from his job following an altercation
with his Jewish boss, Cowan brought a small arsenal with him
on his first day back at work, firing on minority coworkers at
his place of employment. Five persons were killed and two
others wounded before Cowan turned a gun on himself, committing
suicide.

Books

* Godwin, John. MURDER USA. Cited above as item 10, pp. 259-260.

Brief case history within a discussion of mass murder.

* Nash, Jay Robert. CRIME CHRONOLOGY, 1900-1983. Cited above as item 21, p. 191.

Brief case history presented in time line format.

* ————. MURDER, AMERICA. Cited above as item 23, pp. 14, 303-309, 444.

Case history within an anthology of "classic" murders.

* Terry, Maury. THE ULTIMATE EVIL. Cited above as item 126.

Presents theoretical evidence linking Cowan with the same Satanic death cult which allegedly counted David Berkowitz among its active members.

Articles

222. Mathews, T., and S. Agrest. "Nazi of New Rochelle." NEWSWEEK 89 (February 28, 1977): 30.

Reports Cowan's crimes and suicide.

223. "Season of Savagery and Rage." TIME 109 (February 28, 1977): 22-23+.

Reports the New Rochelle massacre.

129. COX, AUSTIN (M)

Deranged resident of Ogden, Utah, who carried guns into a courtroom where his wife had recently won a divorce. Opening fire at random, Cox killed the presiding judge and four other persons before he was subdued. Setnenced to life.

* FACTS ON FILE. Volume 3, 1943. Cited above as item 7, p. 238.

Reports the Utah shootings and Cox's arrest.

130. CRAFT, ELLIS (M)

With accomplices George Ellis and William Neal, Craft invaded a rural home near Ashland, Ken., in 1881, raping two sisters and killing both girls, along with their brother, using crow bars and axes to crush their skulls. The house was burned in an effort to eliminate evidence, but all three killers were cpatured and hanged.

* Nash, Jay Robert. MURDER, AMERICA. Cited above as item 23, p. 364.

  Sketchy case history presented in time line format.

131. CREAM, THOMAS NEILL (S)

Physician and sexual sadist who enjoyed performing abortions, Cream began poisoning victims in 1881. His first four victims were patients, slain before he switched to prostitutes chosen at random. Cream was linked with at least eight deaths prior to his capture in 1892. Considered by some as a prime "Jack the Ripper" suspect, Cream was actually in prison, at Joliet, Ill., when the Whitechapel crimes were committed.

* Boar, Roger, and Nigel Blundell. THE WORLD'S MOST IN-FAMOUS MURDERS. Cited above as item 2, pp. 44-48.

  Sensational case history, presented in tabloid style.

* Douthwaite, L.C. MASS MURDER. Cited above as item 6.

  Brief case history within a general discussion of Victorian multicides.

* Gaute, J.H.H., and Robin Odell. THE MURDERERS' WHO'S WHO. Cited above as item 8, pp. 75-76.

  Case history presented in an encyclopedic format.

* Green, Jonathon. THE GREATEST CRIMINALS OF ALL TIME. Cited above as item 11, p. 182.

  Case history presented in an encyclopedic format.

* Gribble, Leonard. THEY HAD A WAY WITH WOMEN. Cited above as item 154.

Case history presented in an anthology of "lady-killers."

* Nash, Jay Robert. ALMANAC OF WORLD CRIME. Cited above
  as item 19, pp. 318-319.

  Brief case history within a general discussion of mass
  murder.

* ————. MURDER, AMERICA. Cited above as item 23, pp.
  14, 94-118, 132, 363.

  Case history in an anthology of "classic" murders.

224. Shore, W. Teignmouth (ed.). TRIAL OF THOMAS NEIL CREAM.
  London: William Hodge & Co., 1923.

  Presents excerpts from the transcript of Cream's
  murder trial as one in a series of "notable British
  trials." Interesting as a primary source and a slice
  of criminal history.

* Wilson, Colin. A CASEBOOK OF MURDER. Cited above as
  item 33, pp. 126-131.

  Case history within a general discussion of murder's
  sociological roots.

* ————, and Patricia Putnam. THE ENCYCLOPEDIA OF MURDER.
  Cited above as item 35, pp. 165-168.

  Case history presented in an encyclopedic format.

132. CREIGHTON, JOHN and MARY FRANCIS (S)

Husband and wife in New York, responsible for at least
three poison murders in the 1920s and 1930s, including Mary's
brother and John's mother. John died before the crimes were
exposed; Mary was convicted and executed in July 1936.

* CRIMES AND PUNISHMENT: A PICTORIAL ENCYCLOPEDIA OF ABER-
  RANT BEHAVIOR, Volume 12. Cited above as item 4, pp.
  83-86.

  Case history within a general discussion of murderous
  married couples.

* Nash, Jay Robert. MURDER, AMERICA. Cited above as item
  23, p. 410.

Sketchy case history presented in time line format.

133. CRIMMINS, ALICE (M)

Promiscuous New York divorcee who murdered her two children in 1965 and tried to make the crimes appear to be a
bungled kidnapping. Convicted of first-degree manslaughter in
the death of her daughter only, Crimmins appealed, and her sentence was overturned. At her second trial, the defendant was
convicted again in the death of her daughter, and of first-
degree murder in the death of her son. The latter conviction
was overturned on appeal in 1975, and Crimmins was released on
parole a year later.

*   FACTS ON FILE. Volume 28, 1968. Cited above as item 7,
    p. 476.

    Contemporaneous account of conviction and sentencing.

*   FACTS ON FILE. Volume 31, 1971. Cited above as item 7,
    p. 575.

    Reports Crimmins's second conviction and sentencing.

*   FACTS ON FILE. Volume 35, 1975. Cited above as item 7,
    p. 150.

    Reports the affirmation of Crimmins's manslaughter
    conviction on appeal.

*   Gaute, J.H.H., and Robin Odell. THE MURDERERS' WHO'S
    WHO. Cited above as item 8, pp. 76-77.

    Case history presented in an encyclopedic format.

225. Gross, Kenneth. THE ALICE CRIMMINS CASE. New York:
      Alfred A. Knopf, 1975.

      Finds Crimmins innocent, a victim of ambitious, sexist
      prosecutors and "a society cold to liberated women."
      More controversial than convincing.

*   Nash, Jay Robert. CRIME CHRONOLOGY, 1900-1983. Cited
    above as item 21, p. 171.

    Brief case history presented in time line format.

* Sifakis, Carl. THE ENCYCLOPEDIA OF AMERICAN CRIME. Cited above as item 29, p. 186.

    Case history presented in an encyclopedic format.

* Wilson, Colin, and Donald Seaman. THE ENCYCLOPEDIA OF MODERN MURDER. Cited above as item 36, pp. 58-59.

    Case history presented in an encyclopedic format.

134. CROSSLEY, WAYNE LEE (M)

Unemployed carpenter and gun enthusiast, fond of boasting: "I'm going to die in a shoot-out with the police." In July 1984, while heavily intoxicated, Crossley killed three persons and wounded two others in Hot Springs, Ark., finally shooting himself to death at the crime scene.

226. "Masssacre in Hot Springs." NEWSWEEK 104 (August 6, 1984): 21.

    Contemporaneous account of Crossley's crimes and death.

135. CROYDON MURDERS, THE (S)

Unsolved poisoning deaths involving two interrelated families in South Croydon, England, between 1928 and 1929. Three members of the Sydney and Duff families died from arsenic poisoning during the inexplicable attacks, but no suspect was ever discovered.

* Wilson, Colin, and Patricia Putnam. THE ENCYCLOPEDIA OF MURDER. Cited above as item 35, pp. 170-171.

    Case history presented in an encyclopedic format.

136. CULOMBE, ARTHUR (S)

With accomplice Joseph Taborsky, Culombe robbed and murdered six persons in Hartford, Conn., in the three months ending February 1957. In custody, Taborsky confessed to the murder of another man, in 1951, also in Hartford. Both were sentenced to life imprisonment.

* Brian, Dennis. MURDERERS DIE. Cited above as item 3, p. 260.

    Brief case history on Taborsky, in an anthology of capital cases.

* FACTS ON FILE. Volume 17, 1957. Cited above as item 7,
   p. 76.

   Contemporaneous account of the arrests and confessions.

   137. CUMMINS, GORDON FREDERICK (S)

   London's "Blackout Ripper," convicted of slaying four
women during as many days in February 1942. A gas mask dropped
at the scene of one crime identified the killer, an RAF cadet,
and Cummins confessed to the crimes, which were apparently
motivated as much by cash as by sex. Sentenced to die for his
crimes, Cummins was executed in June 1942—ironically, while
a German air raid was in progress.

* CRIMES AND PUNISHMENT: A PICTORIAL ENCYCLOPEDIA OF ABER-
   RANT BEHAVIOR, Volume 17. Cited above as item 4, pp.
   45-52.

   Case history presented in a segment devoted to "ripper"
   slayings.

* Gaute, J.H.H., and Robin Odell. THE MURDERERS' WHO'S
   WHO. Cited above as item 8, p. 80.

   Case history presented in an encyclopedic format.

* Gribble, Leonard. THEY HAD A WAY WITH WOMEN. Cited
   above as item 156.

   Case history in an anthology of "lady-killers."

* Nash, Jay Robert. CRIME CHRONOLOGY, 1900-1983. Cited
   above as item 21, pp. 119-120.

   Brief case history presented in time line format.

* Tullett, Tom. STRICTLY MURDER. Cited above as item 32.

   Case history in an anthology of Scotland Yard's cases.

* Wilson, Colin, and Patricia Putnam. THE ENCYCLOPEDIA OF
   MURDER. Cited above as item 35, pp. 171-172.

   Case history presented in an encyclopedic format.

138. CURGENVEN, ROBERT (M)

Eleven-year-old arrested at Mansfield, Conn., in April 1956, for the shotgun slayings of his mother and brother. The boy was reportedly angry over recent spankings and family arguments at the time of the shootings. Committed to a mental institution for observation.

* FACTS ON FILE. Volume 16, 1956. Cited above as item 7, p. 140.

  Contemporaneous report of the shootings and arrest.

139. DAHMEN, JOHN (S)

Convicted of two robbery-murders at Albany, Ind., in 1820, Dahmen confessed to three murders in Europe and a minimum of six more in the United States. Sentenced to death and hanged in Indiana.

* Nash, Jay Robert. MURDER, AMERICA. Cited above as item 23, p. 323.

  Brief case history presented in time line format.

140. DAKIN, JANE (M)

Seventeen-year-old who killed both her parents in Wisconsin, during 1958. Held for psychiatric observation.

* FACTS ON FILE. Volume 18, 1958. Cited above as item 7, p. 420.

  Contemporaneous report of the crimes and arrest.

141. D'ARCY, PATRICK (M)

Murdered his two mistresses, mother and daughter, in May 1967. The older woman's body was never found, but her daughter's corpse was discovered by beachcombers on the western coast of Ireland. D'Arcy committed suicide when he came under suspicion for the crimes.

* CRIMES AND PUNISHMENT: A PICTORIAL ENCYCLOPEDIA OF ABERRANT BEHAVIOR, Volume 4. Cited above as item 4, p. 62.

  Brief case history within a general discussion of "lonely-hearts killers."

142. DAVEY, MARGARET (S)

British cook and mass-poisoner, suspected in numerous
cases with no final body-count established. Boiled alive in
1542.

* Green, Jonathon. THE GREATEST CRIMINALS OF ALL TIME.
  Cited above as item 11, p. 155.

  Brief case history presented in encyclopedic format.

143. DAVIES, GEORGE J. (S)

Paroled sex offender who confessed, in May 1957, to the
murders of two Connecticut girls, ages eight and sixteen,
killed at different times. The younger victim had been strangled with her own sweater, then stabbed at least 22 times.
Returned to prison.

* FACTS ON FILE. Volume 17, 1957. Cited above as item 7,
  pp. 160, 168.

  Contemporaneous account of the murders and arrest.

144. DAVIS, BRUCE A. (S)

Arrested on murder charges in Illinois, Davis confessed
to slaying 33 men in more than a dozen American cities. Still
not charged in the majority of cases which he has admitted,
Davis is serving a life sentence in prison.

* Levin, Jack, and James Alan Fox. MASS MURDER: AMERICA'S
  GROWING MENACE. Cited above as item 15.

  Brief case history within a general discussion of
  serial murder.

145. DAVIS, MURL (S)

With accomplice John Coulter West, murdered at least six
persons in a two-week Ohio crime spree during 1948. Three
victims—the superintendent of a reformatory, his wife and
daughter—were abducted and murdered to settle a grudge; the
other victims were slain during robberies. West was killed
by a posse, which also captured Davis, in July 1948. Convicted
of multiple murder charges, Davis was executed in 1949.

* FACTS ON FILE. Volume 8, 1948. Cited above as item 7, p. 240.

    Contemporaneous report of the crimes and arrest.

* Sifakis, Carl. THE ENCYCLOPEDIA OF AMERICAN CRIME. Cited above as item 29, pp. 193-194.

    Case history presented in an encyclopedic format.

146. DEEMING, ALFRED (S)

Australian swindler and serial wife-killer, credited with the murders of "no less than 20" women in Australia and Britain. Hanged in 1892, upon conviction for his latest homicide.

* Douthwaite, L.C. MASS MURDER. Cited above as item 6.

    Case history presented in a general discussion of Victorian murderers.

* Green, Jonathon. THE GREATEST CRIMINALS OF ALL TIME. Cited above as item 11, p. 195.

    Brief case history presented in encyclopedic format.

* Nash, Jay Robert. ALMANAC OF WORLD CRIME. Cited above as item 19, pp. 278-279.

    Brief case history in a discussion of mass murder.

147. DEEMING, FREDERICK BAILEY (S)

Confidence man and slayer of at least six persons in Australia, generally women whose remains were bricked up in the hearths of homes Deeming owned. Convicted and condemned to die, Deeming also confessed to being "Jack the Ripper"—an impossibility, since he had been imprisoned on other charges during the crucial period of 1888. Hanged in May 1892.

* CRIMES AND PUNISHMENT: A PICTORIAL ENCYCLOPEDIA OF ABERRANT BEHAVIOR, Volume 1. Cited above as item 4, p. 88.

    Brief case history in a discussion of "lady-killers."

* Gaute, J.H.H., and Robin Odell. THE MURDERERS' WHO'S WHO. Cited above as item 8, p. 83.

Case history presented in an encyclopedic format.

* Logan, Guy B.H. MASTERS OF CRIME. Cited above as item
   17, pp. 198-204.

   Case history within an anthology of 19th-century multicides.

* Wilson, Colin, and Patricia Putnam. THE ENCYCLOPEDIA OF
   MURDER. Cite above as item 35, pp. 175-178.

   Case history presented in an encyclopedic format.

148. DeFEO, RONALD, Jr. (M)

Drug abuser and petty criminal who, in November 1974,
shot his parents and four siblings to death at the family home
in Amityville, N.Y. Suspected, but never charged, in the
drowning death of another victim during 1972. Sentenced to
life imprisonment despite a bizarre insanity defense. The
DeFeo home has subsequently become the central object of novels
and films in the "Amityville Horror" series, alleging that
Ronald was possessed by demons.

Books

227. Holzer, Hans. MURDER IN AMITYVILLE. New York: Belmont
      Tower Books, 1979.

      "Ghost hunter" Holzer concludes that DeFeo was "used
      by forces beyond our physical world to do their bidding"
      on the night of the murders. No other-worldly motive
      for the massacre is suggested.

* Levin, Jack, and James Alan Fox. MASS MURDER: AMERICA'S
   GROWING MENACE. Cited above as item 15.

   Case history within a general discussion of mass
   murder.

* Sifakis, Carl. THE ENCYCLOPEDIA OF AMERICAN CRIME.
   Cited above as item 29, p. 198.

   Case history presented in an encyclopedic format.

228. Sullivan, Gerard, and Harvey Aronson. HIGH HOPES: THE
      AMITYVILLE MURDERS. New York: Coward, McCann, 1981.

Presents the DeFeo case from the prosecutor's point of view. Especially revealing in regard to the suspect's lame insanity defense.

Articles

229. Hoffman, P. "Our Dream House Was Haunted." GOOD HOUSE-KEEPING 184 (April 1977): 119+.

    The Lutz family tell their ghost story for the record, subsequently expanded into three books and three feature films dealing with the "supernatural aura" of their home.

230. "Rich Kid." NEWSWEEK 84 (November 25, 1974): 43.

    Contemporaneous report of the case, sans spooks.

149. De La ROCHE, HARRY, Jr. (M)

Firearms enthusiast, habitually belittled by his father, who murdered his parents and two siblings at their Montvale, N.J., home in November 1976. De La Roche received four concurrent terms of life imprisonment.

* Levin, Jack, and James Alan Fox. MASS MURDER: AMERICA'S GROWING MENACE. Cited above as item 15.

    Case history within a discussion of mass murder in the family.

231. Roesche, Roberta, and Harry De La Rocher, Jr. ANYONE'S SON. Kansas City: Andrews & McMeel, 1979.

    The killer's first-person views are intercut with author Roesche's narrative in this attempt to understand a family tragedy. Perhaps predictably, the manuscript reveals more sympathy for De La Roche than was displayed by members of his jury. An interesting look at multicide committed by "the boy next door."

150. DE MAU MAU MURDERS (S)

Random, racially-motivated murders of nine white persons, committed by members of a gang, "De Mau Mau," which existed for the sole purpose of terrorizing whites in Chicago. Eight members of the group, mostly black veterans of Vietnam, were arrested on murder charges in October 1972 and eventually convicted. The defendants included: brothers Donald and Reuben

Taylor; Nathaniel Burse; Edward Moran, Jr.; Robert Wilson;
Darrell Peatry; and Garland Jackson. All are presently in
prison.

* FACTS ON FILE. Volume 32, 1972. Cited above as item 7,
    p. 942.

    Contemporaneous report of the murders and arrests.

151. DENKE, KARL (S)

    Cannibalistic slayer of at least 30 persons in a three-
year period of German famine. Denke was caught in the act of
an attempted murder, in December 1924, and the subsequent
search of his home turned up damning evidence: tubs of pickled
meat, with quantities of fat and bone, were calculated to include the remains of 30 victims, while a ledger dating back
to 1921 recorded details of each murder Denke had committed.
Transients, tramps, and beggars were his usual victims, persons
who would not be missed in the upheaval of the post-war years.
Shortly after his arrest, Denke committed suicide in his cell
by hanging himself with his suspenders.

* Green, Jonathon. THE GREATEST CRIMINALS OF ALL TIME.
    Cited above as item 11, p. 270.

    Brief case history presetned in encyclopedic format.

* Hurwood, Bernhardt. VAMPIRES, WEREWOLVES, AND GHOULS.
    Cited above as item 12, pp. 74-76.

    Sensational case history within an anthology of "human
    monsters."

* Nash, Jay Robert. ALMANAC OF WORLD CRIME. Cited above
    as item 19, p. 285.

    Brief case history in a general discussion of mass
    murder.

* ————. CRIME CHRONOLOGY, 1900-1983. Cited above as
    item 21, p. 64.

    Brief case history presented in time line format.

* Wilson, Colin. A CRIMINAL HISTORY OF MANKIND. Cited
    above as item 34, p. 607.

Brief case history in a disucssion of modern mass murder.

* ————, and Patricia Putnam. THE ENCYCLOPEDIA OF MURDER.
Cited above as item 35, pp. 179-180.

Case history presented in an encyclopedic format.

152. DeSALVO, ALBERT HENRY (S)

Confessed slayer of thirteen women in Boston during an 18-month period beginning in mid-1962. Eleven of the victims were strangled with silk stockings, one was stabbed, and the thirteenth—connected to the murder series only by DeSalvo's confession—allegedly died of a heart attack when the killer tried to enter her apartment. Nine of the Boston victims were elderly women; four others broke the pattern, ranging in age from 19 to 25 years. These age discrepancies, and the different mode of death in at least two cases, have led some authorities to question the veracity of DeSalvo's confessions. In custody on other charges at the time of his decision to confess, DeSalvo struck a bargain with the prosecution: in return for full confession, he received a life sentence on outstanding charges, and was never indicted for the slayings. The case was briefly "reopened" in February 1968, based on alleged "new information," and was then "closed permanently" two months later. DeSalvo spent six years in Walpole prison, and was stabbed to death by a fellow inmate there in 1973.

Books

232. Bailey, F. Lee, and Harvey Aronson. THE DEFENSE NEVER RESTS. New York: Stein & Day, 1971, pp. 143-186.

An account of the DeSalvo case prepared by his attorney. Bailey describes the maneuvers which kept DeSalvo from standing trial for murder and closes by asking: "Did the system work? Not on your life."

233. Banks, Harold K. THE STRANGLER! New York: Avon Books, 1967.

Sensational paperback account of the Boston case, based primarily on media reports.

* Boar, Roger, and Nigel Blundell. THE WORLD'S MOST IN-FAMOUS MURDERS. Cited above as item 2, pp. 58-61.

Case history presented in sensational tabloid style.

* Browning, Norma Lee. THE PSYCHIC WORLD OF PETER HURKOS.
  Cited above as item 186, pp. 113-160.

  Psychic Hurkos fingers suspect "Charles O'Brien," who
  voluntarily committed himself to a mental institution
  in February 1964. "O'Brien" was allegedly a fellow inmate
  of DeSalvo's, presumably coaching him on details of his
  persuasive confessions, which Hurkos describes as
  "phony baloney." Interesting primarily since other in-
  dependent sources have reached similar conclusions in
  recent years.

* Brussel, James A. CASEBOOK OF A CRIME PSYCHIATRIST.
  Cited above as item 63, pp. 136-196.

  Includes two chapters by the psychiatrist who prepared
  "profiles" of the strangler prior to his capture, and
  who subsequently interviews DeSalvo in custody.

* CRIMES AND PUNISHMENT: A PICTORIAL ENCYCLOPEDIA OF ABER-
  RANT BEHAVIOR, Volume 14. Cited above as item 4, pp.
  37-44.

  Case history presented in an encyclopedic format.

* FACTS ON FILE. Volume 33, 1973. Cited above as item 7,
  p. 1068.

  Reports DeSalvo's murder by another prison inmate.

234. Frank, Gerold. THE BOSTON STRANGLER. New York: New
     American Library, 1966.

  Controversial best-seller which traces the Strangler
  manhunt, pointing out various "prime suspects" before
  coming down solidly on the prosecution's side of the
  case. Critics charge, with reason, that Frank has been
  too swift (in this and other books) to buy the state's
  official line on complex cases. Interesting ... but not
  necessarily the last word on DeSalvo.

* Gaute, J.H.H., and Robin Odell. THE MURDERERS' WHO'S
  WHO. Cited above as item 8, pp. 48-49.

  Case history presented in an encyclopedic format.

* Godwin, John. MURDER USA. Cited above as item 10,
  pp. 275-276.

Capsule summary of DeSalvo's alleged motives for murder.

* Green, Jonathon. THE GREATEST CRIMINALS OF ALL TIME. Cited above as item 11, p. 188.

Brief case history presented in encyclopedic format.

* Levin, Jack, and James Alan Fox. MASS MURDER: AMERICA'S GROWING MENACE. Cited above as item 15.

Brief case history in a discussion of serial murder.

* Leyton, Elliott. COMPULSIVE KILLERS. Cited above as item 16, pp. 112-149.

"Revises" published material from items 63, 233, 234, and 235, coming up with "no new data of any kind."

* Nash, Jay Robert. CRIME CHRONOLOGY, 1900-1983. Cited above as item 21, p. 164.

Sketchy case history presented in time line format.

235. Rae, George William. CONFESSIONS OF THE BOSTON STRANGLER. New York: Pyramid Books, 1967.

Paperback compilation of excerpts from DeSalvo's recorded confessions, collected by a former Boston newsman. Rae's presentation of DeSalvo's statements is more complete than Gerold Frank's later, more commercially successful work in item 234 above.

* Sifakis, Carl. THE ENCYCLOPEDIA OF AMERICAN CRIME. Cited above as item 29, pp. 203-204.

Case history presented in an encyclopedic format.

* Wilson, Colin. A CRIMINAL HISTORY OF MANKIND. Cited above as item 34, pp. 623-625.

Case history within a discussion of modern sexual murders.

* ————, and Donald Seaman. THE ENCYCLOPEDIA OF MODERN MURDER. Cited above as item 36, pp. 60-66.

Case history presented in an encyclopedic format.

Articles

236. "Bailey and the Boston Strangler." TIME 89 (January 27,
      1967): 40.

      Reports the legal maneuvers in DeSalvo's case.

237. Byers, M. "Fear Walks Home with the Women." LIFE 54
      (February 15, 1963): 16-21.

      Describes the Strangler hysteria in Boston with murders
      still in progress, prior to DeSalvo's confession.

238. Frank, Gerold. "The Boston Strangler." LADIES' HOME
      JOURNAL 83 (August 1966): 65-72+; (September 1966):
      91-98+.

      Two-part condensation of item 234 above.

239. Gardner, Earle Stanley. "Mad Strangler of Boston."
      ATLANTIC MONTHLY 213 (May 1964): 49-56.

      The creator of fictional attorney Perry Mason examines
      the murders in Boston.

240. Iams, J. "Search for the Strangler." SATURDAY EVENING
      POST 236 (May 18, 1963): 28+.

      An examination of the manhunt, prior to DeSalvo's arrest.

241. Schmidt, S. "The Boston Strangler." NEWSWEEK 68 (October
      31, 1966): 118+.

      Critical review of item 234 above, taking author Frank
      to task for his heavy reliance on media reports and
      prosecution statements, as well as his failure to inde-
      pendently corroborate crucial statements in the DeSalvo
      confessions.

153. DEVEUREUX, ARTHUR (M)

British chemist's assistant who murdered his wife and
twin sons in April 1905, storing their bodies in a steamer
trunk. Deveureux was approached by detectives of Scotland
Yard, but before they could begin to question him, he blurted
out: "You have made a mistake. I don't know anything about a
tin trunk." He subsequently confessed the crimes, was convicted and sentenced to hang.

* CRIMES AND PUNISHMENT: A PICTORIAL ENCYCLOPEDIA OF ABER-
  RANT BEHAVIOR, Volume 10. Cited above as item 4, pp.
  110-114.

  Case history presented in an encyclopedic format.

* Wilson, Colin, and Patricia Putnam. THE ENCYCLOPEDIA OF
  MURDER. Cited above as item 35, pp. 181-182.

  Case history presented in an encyclopedic format.

154. DICKINSON, TEXAS, MURDERS (M)

Unsolved slaying of Ruby McPherson, her son George, and
her mother, Zola Norman, at the family home on June 26, 1955.
Police broadcast a bulletin describing an unidentified house
guest of the victims, last seen wearing a uniform of the United
States Air Force. At this writing, the killer has not been
publicly identified.

* FACTS ON FILE. Volume 15, 1955. Cited above as item 7,
  p. 220.

  Contemporaneous report of the murders and manhunt.

155. DINGUM (S)

Australian "bushranger," active around Port Phillip in
1837. With accomplice Cornerford, killed seven fellow outlaws
when food ran short, devouring their remains. Cornerford was
lynched shortly after his arrest. With no other witnesses
against him, Dingum was sentenced to life imprisonment.

* Wilson, Colin. A CASEBOOK OF MURDER. Cited above as
  item 33, p. 92.

  Brief case history within a sociological history of
  murder.

156. DOBBERT, ERNEST (S)

Florida slayer convicted, in 1972, of beating and strangling to death his nine-year-old daughter. During the police
investigation, it was proved that Dobbert had also killed his
son (age seven), that he had cruelly tortured an 11-year-old,
and that he had abused another of his daughters, aged five.
Executed in 1984.

* Brian, Dennis. MURDERERS DIE. Cited above as item 3,
  p. 253.

  Case history within an anthology of killers who were
  put to death.

157. DOMINICI, GASTON (M)

Murdered a tourist family of three in France during August 1952. When questioned by police, Dominici confessed and
was sentenced to death in November 1954. In 1960, his sentence was commuted to life imprisonment on grounds of his
advanced age; Dominici was then 83 years old. Subsequent to
sentencing, Dominici recanted his confession, accusing his
son, Gustave, of the murders, but no further charges were
filed in the case.

Books

* CRIMES AND PUNISHMENT: A PICTORIAL ENCYCLOPEDIA OF ABER-
  RANT BEHAVIOR, Volume 2. Cited above as item 4, pp.
  114-122.

  Case history presented in an encyclopedic format.

* Scott, Sir Harold. THE CONCISE ENCYCLOPEDIA OF CRIME
  AND CRIMINALS. Cited above as item 27, p. 132.

  Case history presented in an encyclopedic format.

* Wilson, Colin, and Patricia Putnam. THE ENCYCLOPEDIA
  OF MURDER. Cited above as item 35, pp. 184-185.

  Case history presented in an encyclopedic format.

Articles

242. O'Donnell, James P. "Who Murdered the Tourists?" SAT-
     URDAY EVENING POST 227 (June 4, 1955): 38-39+.

     A post-trial examination of the evidence in Dominici's
     case, suggesting that the suspect may have covered for
     his guilty sons.

158. DOSS, NANNIE HAZEL (S)

Prolific poisoner of Tulsa, Okla., specializing in the
murder of husbands and other relatives. Questioned by police

regarding the suspicious death of her latest husband, in 1954, Doss confessed to poisoning eleven victims: included in the body-count were four husbands, two sisters, and two of her own children. Sentenced to life, she died in prison, of leukemia, a short time after her conviction.

* CRIMES AND PUNISHMENT: A PICTORIAL ENCYCLOPEDIA OF ABER-RANT BEHAVIOR, Volume 4. Cited above as item 4, pp. 87-88.

  Brief case history in a general discussion of murders by poison.

* Green, Jonathon. THE GREATEST CRIMINALS OF ALL TIME. Cited above as item 11, p. 149.

  Brief case history in an encyclopedic format.

* Nash, Jay Robert. LOOK FOR THE WOMAN. Cited above as item 22, p. 132.

  Nash's encyclopedic entry mistakenly lists the date of Doss's arrest as 1964, this despite a published mug shot which is clearly dated ten years earlier. Typical care-lessness from an author more concerned with quantity than quality.

* —————. MURDER, AMERICA. Cited above as item 23, pp. 14, 285-287, 425.

  Brief case history in an anthology of "classic" murders.

* Reinhardy, James Melvin. THE PSYCHOLOGY OF STRANGE KILLERS. Cited above as item 70, pp. 37-51.

  Psychological case study based on Doss's confessions.

159. DRABING, MICHAEL EDWARD (M)

Stabbed to death a family of three in Lincoln, Neb., during 1976. Drabing's stated goal was to "kill the rich"; his roster of potential victims included the governor of Illinois and other politicians. Arrested prior to putting any further stages of his plan in operation, Drabing was sentenced to a term of life imprisonment.

* Nash, Jay Robert. CRIME CHRONOLOGY, 1900-1983. Cited above as item 21, p. 189.

Brief case history presented in time line format.

* ————. MURDER, AMERICA. Cited above as item 23, pp. 443-444.

Sketchy case history presented in time line format.

160. DRENTH, HERMAN (S)

Sadistic slayer of an estimated fifty victims in the decade after 1921. Drenth traveled the United States, marrying wealthy women and subsequently gassing them in his "scientific laboratory" at Clarksburg, West Virginia, achieving orgasm while watching their death throes. In one particularly brutal case, he used a hammer to kill three children of his latest murdered wife. Indicted on five murder charges in which remains were found, he refused to reveal the whereabouts of other corpses, telling detectives: "You've got me on five. What good would fifty do?" Hanged in March 1932.

* Nash, Jay Robert. CRIME CHRONOLOGY, 1900-1983. Cited above as item 21, p. 88.

Brief case history presented in time line format.

* ————. MURDER, AMERICA. Cited above as item 23, pp. 401-402.

Sketchy case history presented in time line format.

161. DUDLEY, KENNETH E. and IRENE GWYN (S)

Homicidal husband and wife who murdered five of their six children during a three-year trek across the United States, 1958 to 1961. Bodies were discovered in Florida, Kentucky, Louisiana, and Virginia. Finally arrested in Virginia, the couple was sentenced to life imprisonment.

* Reinhardt, James Melvin. THE PSYCHOLOGY OF STRANGE KILLERS. Cited above as item 70, pp. 52-87.

Psychological case study based on the confessions of the Dudleys and the recollections of their surviving children.

162. DUMOLLARD, MARTIN and MARIE (S)

Convicted slayers of at least ten young women in the

vicinity of Lyons, France, circa 1855-1861. Martin way-laid victims on the district's country roads, murdered them and stripped them naked, bringing home the clothing and possessions to his wife, who washed and wore the stolen dresses. Several intended victims managed to escape his clutches prior to 1861, when he was finally arrested. The clothing of ten victims was displayed in court at the Dumollards' trial, and evidence was introduced to the effect that one of Martin's victims had been buried while alive. Martin was beheaded in March 1862; Marie, convicted as an accessory, was sentenced to 20 years in prison.

* Logan, Guy B.H. MASTERS OF CRIME. Cited above as item 17, pp. 97-99.

  Case history in an anthology of 19th-century murders.

* Nash, Jay Robert. LOOK FOR THE WOMAN. Cited above as item 22, pp. 133-134.

  Case history presented in an encyclopedic format.

* Wilson, Colin. A CASEBOOK OF MURDER. Cited above as item 33, pp. 111-112.

  Brief case history within a general discussion of murder's sociological history.

* ————, and Patricia Putnam. THE ENCYCLOPEDIA OF MURDER. Cited above as item 35, pp. 189-191.

  Case history presented in an encyclopedic format.

163. DUNGEE, GEORGE (M): See ISSACS, BILLY and CARL

164. DUNN, LISA (M): See WALTER, MARK

165. DURRANT, WILLIAM HENRY THEODORE (S)

Medical student, assistant Sunday school superintendent, and slayer of two young women in San Francisco during April 1895. After strangling his first victim, Durrant concealed her body in the belfry of his church, there engaging in acts of necrophilia with the corpse. His second victim was raped and mutilated after death, her body left in a closet of the church library, where it was quickly discovered. Convicted and sentenced to hang in 1895, Durrant managed to delay his execution for three years with appeals to higher courts. He was put to death in Jaunary 1898.

* CRIMES AND PUNISHMENT: A PICTORIAL ENCYCLOPEDIA OF ABER-
  RANT BEHAVIOR, Volume 7. Cited above as item 4, p. 61.

    Case history presented in an encyclopedic format.

* Gaute, J.H.H., and Robin Odell. THE MURDERERS' WHO'S
  WHO. Cited above as item 8, pp. 90-92.

    Case history presented in an encyclopedic format.

* Green, Jonathon. THE GREATEST CRIMINALS OF ALL TIME.
  Cited above as item 11, p. 270.

    Brief case history in an encyclopedic format.

* Nash, Jay Robert. BLOODLETTERS AND BADMEN. Cited above
  as item 20, pp. 185-187.

    Case history presented in an encyclopedic format.

* ————. MURDER, AMERICA. Cited above as item 23.

    Case history in an anthology of "classic" murders.

* Wilson, Colin. A CASEBOOK OF MURDER. Cited above as
  item 33, p. 217.

    Brief case history, in sociological context.

166. DYER, ALBERT (S)

    Slayer of three children in Los Angeles during 1938.
Dyer lured his victims to a secluded ravine, there molesting
and killing each in turn. After each murder, he ritually
cleaned the bodies, tidied up the victims' clothing, and
lingered to pray over the corpses. Captured during an attempt
to seize his fourth victim, Dyer confessed his murders and was
hanged.

* Nash, Jay Robert. MURDER, AMERICA. Cited above as item
  23, p. 414.

    Sketchy case history presented in time line format.

167. DYER, AMELIA ELIZABETH (S)

    British "baby farmer" who collected boarding fees from
parents who were tired of dealing with their children, then

strangled her charges and dumped their tiny corpses into a
canal near Reading, England. Accused of slaying fifteen victims, no final body-count was ever determined for the decade
during which Amelia plied her lethal trade. Convicted in May
1896, despite a weak insanity defense, she was hanged a month
later. During the search for victims, Dyer told detectives:
"You'll know all mine by the tape around their necks."

* Green, Jonathon. THE GREATEST CRIMINALS OF ALL TIME.
  Cited above as item 11, p. 207.

  Brief case history in an encyclopedic format.

* Nash, Jay Robert. LOOK FOR THE WOMAN. Cited above as
  item 22, p. 134.

  Case history presented in an encyclopedic format.

168. EDEL, FREDERICK W. (S)

Suspected of "several" murders, including two at Meriden,
Conn., in 1925, Edel was convicted for the slaying of a New
York City woman two years later. Sentenced to death in 1928.

* Nash, Jay Robert. MURDER, AMERICA. Cited above as item
  23, p. 400.

  Sketchy case history presented in time line format.

169. EDER, CARL A. (M)

Sixteen-year-old charged in December 1958 with shooting
a woman to death and then killing her four children, ages two
through nine, with a knife in San Diego, California. Ruled
competent for trial, Eder was sentenced to life imprisonment.

* FACTS ON FILE. Volume 18, 1958. Cited above as item 7,
  p. 412.

  Reports Eder's crimes and arrest.

170. EDWARDS, EDGAR (M)

Pretending interest in the purchase of a shop, in Camber-
well, England, Edwards murdered the shopkeeper, his wife and
infant child, in December 1902, aftwerward looting the establishment. Captured following a subsequent attack upon another
merchant, he was convicted and hanged in 1903.

* Nash, Jay Robert. CRIME CHRONOLOGY, 1900-1983. Cited
above as item 21, p. 7.

Brief case history presented in time line format.

171. EDWARDS, MACK (S)

Slayer of several children in and around Los Angeles,
California. Edwards surrendered voluntarily to homicide
detectives in 1970, confessing his guilt in two series of
killings, commmitted from 1953 to 1956, and again from 1968
to 1970. Estimated body-counts vary widely, from a minimum
of six to a maximum of 22. Convicted on the basis of his own
confession, Edwards was sentenced to die. He told the court:
"My lawyer told me there are a hundred men to die in the chair.
I'm asking the judge if I can have the first man's place.
He's sitting there sweating right now. I'm not sweating. I'm
ready for it." Still awaiting execution.

* Green, Jonathon. THE GREATEST CRIMINALS OF ALL TIME.
Cited above as item 11, p. 149.

Brief case history in an encyclopedic format, crediting Edwards with 22 murders.

* Wilson, Colin. ORDER OF ASSASSINS. Cited above as item
76, pp. 81-82.

Brief case history crediting Edwards with six victims.

172. ESSEX, MARK JAMES ROBERT (M)

Black military veteran who ran amok with a rifle at a
Howard Johnson's hotel in New Orleans during January 1973,
setting fires and shooting passers-by at random. Essex killed
six persons and wounded another fifteen, all of them white,
before he was himself killed by police sharpshooters. Ballis-
tics evidence proved that he had also killed two police
officers the previous day.

Books

* FACTS ON FILE. Volume 33, 1973. Cited above as item 7,
p. 40.

Contemporaneous report of the New Orleans shootout.

243. Hernon, Peter. A TERRIBLE THUNDER. Garden City, N.Y.: Doubleday, 1978.

   The definitive study of Essex, including his family background adn motives for his murder spree.

* Leyton, Elliott. COMPULSIVE KILLERS. Cited above as item 16, pp. 189-221.

   Cannibalizes items 31 and 243 above, still managing to place Essex's rampage in the wrong year (1975), with an incorrect body-count. Sloppy.

* Nash, Jay Robert. CRIME CHRONOLOGY, 1900-1983. Cited above as item 21, p. 184.

   Brief case history presented in time line format.

* ————. MURDER, AMERICA. Cited above as item 23, pp. 440-441.

   Sketchy case history presented in time line format.

* Tobias, Ronald. THEY SHOOT TO KILL. Cited above as item 31, pp. 79-117.

   Examines Essex as a classic example of the "hit-and-run" criminal sniper.

Articles

244. "Battle of New Orleans." NEWSWEEK 81 (January 22, 1973): 26-27.

   Contemporaneous report of the shootout.

245. "Death in New Orleans." TIME 101 (January 22, 1973): 20-21.

   Reports the shootout and Essex's death.

173. ELLIS, GEORGE (M): See CRAFT, ELLIS

174. EMORY, JOSEPH (S)

   Los Angeles physician, convicted of second-degree murder in 1962, following the death of a patient in an illegal abortion.

While free on appeal, in 1963, Emory was convicted of performing another abortion, sentenced to three years in prison, with his medical license revoked. Shortly after restoration of his license, in 1974, Emory opened a cut-rate "medical center," catering to impoverished Mexican aliens. Twenty-five new-born infants died at Emory's clinic over the next two years, and in 1976 he was charged with murder in ten of those cases. According to the prosecution, the infant deaths stemmed from Emory's "wanton and reckless disregard for life."

246. "The Cut-Rate Osteopath." TIME 107 (June 21, 1976): 45.

    Reports Emory's arrest, with a review of his career.

175. ESPINOZA BROTHERS, THE (S)

    Mexican nationals Felipe, Julian, and Victorio Espinoza entered the United States in 1863, bent on murdering "600 Anglos" to avenge the losses suffered by their family during the Mexican War. They managed to kill 26 persons before they were hunted down and killed by a posse of bounty hunters, their heads removed as trophies of the hunt.

   * Sifakis, Carl. THE ENCYCLOPEDIA OF AMERICAN CRIME.
      Cited above as item 29, pp. 233-234.

    Case history presented in an encyclopedic format.

176. EVANGELISTA MURDERS, THE (M)

    Unsolved mutilation murders of Detroit car salesman Benjamino Evangelista, his wife and four children during 1929. Benjamino was found decapitated, the other members of his family dismembered in the family home, slain by persons unknown. The slayings were tentatively linked to a voodoo cult led by Benjamino. Police kept tabs on several suspects, but each died, committed suicide, or was murdered before charges could be filed. The puzzling case remains open today.

   * Nash, Jay Robert. CRIME CHRONOLOGY, 1900-1983. Cited
      above as item 21, p. 78.

    Brief case history presented in time line format.

   * ————. OPEN FILES. Cited above as item 24, pp. 70-73.

    Case history presented in an encyclopedic format.

177. FALLING, CHRISTINE (S)

Homicidal Florida babysitter, charged in 1982 with murdering five children who died in her care over a two-year period.
Falling eventually confessed to slaying three of the children,
claiming innocence in the other two suspicious cases, and was
sentenced to life imprisonment.

Books

* FACTS ON FILE. Volume 42, 1982. Cited above as item 7,
    pp. 577, 924.

  Reports Falling's arrest and confession.

* Nash, Jay Robert. CRIME CHRONOLOGY, 1900–1983. Cited
    above as item 21, p. 202.

  Brief case history presented in time line format.

Articles

247. Chandler, David. "Real–Life Dr. Quincy Tracks Down a
     Murder Suspect." PEOPLE WEEKLY 18 (October 11, 1982):
     139–140.

  Reviews the scientific search for evidence of murder
  in the Falling case.

178. FAVATO, CARINO (S): See BOLBER, MORRIS

179. FERNANDEZ, RAYMOND (S): See BECK, MARTHA

180. FIELD, FREDERICK HERBERT CHARLES (S)

British slayer of two prostitutes in 1931 and 1936.
Arrested and tried for the first homicide, Field was acquitted
by a jury. He subsequently confessed not only to that slaying,
but also the murder of a second woman five years later.
Hanged in 1936.

* Wilson, Colin, and Patricia Putnam. THE ENCYCLOPEDIA OF
    MURDER. Cited above as item 35, pp. 207–208.

  Case history presented in an encyclopedic format.

181. FITZGERALD, MARK (M)

Following an unsuccessful attempt to poison members of his family, Fitzgerald killed his parents and brother with a hatchet as they slept in the family home at Sterling, N.Y. Tried, convicted, and executed in 1855.

* Nash, Jay Robert. MURDER, AMERICA. Cited above as item 23, p. 343.

   Sketchy case history presented in time line format.

182. FISH, ALBERT (S)

Sadomasochistic pedophile and cannibal, apprehended in 1935 for the slaying of a young girl seven years earlier. In his rambling, obscene confessions, Fish admitted murdering a man in Delaware in 1910, with "over 400" children slain in the next quarter-century. Despite admissions by psychiatrists that Fish had lived a life of "unparalleled perversity," he was found to be sane and sentenced to die in the electric chair. Ironically, the countless needles which he had implanted in his body during masochistic orgies caused the chair to function poorly, and a second application was required to kill Fish in January 1936.

248.   Angelella, Michael. TRAIL OF BLOOD. New York: New American Library, 1979.

   Modern paperback examination of the Fish case.

* Brian, Dennis. MURDERERS DIE. Cited above as item 3, pp. 64-69.

   Case history in an anthology of killers who were put to death.

* CRIMES AND PUNISHMENT: A PICTORIAL ENCYCLOPEDIA OF ABERRANT BEHAVIOR, Volume 17. Cited above as item 4, pp. 96-104.

   Case history within a section on cannibals and "human vampires."

* Gaute, J.H.H., and Robin Odell. THE MURDERERS' WHO'S WHO. Cited above as item 8, pp. 101-102.

   Case history presented in an encyclopedic format.

* Green, Jonathon. THE GREATEST CRIMINALS OF ALL TIME. Cited above as item 11, p. 270.

  Brief case history in an encyclopedic format.

249. Heimer, Mel. THE CANNIBAL: THE CASE OF ALBERT FISH. New York: Lyle Stuart, 1971.

  Modern, detailed study of the case, with emphasis on psychiatric explanations of Fish's bizarre behavior.

* Levin, Jack, and James Alan Fox. MASS MURDER: AMERICA'S GROWING MENACE. Cited above as item 15.

  Brief case history within a general discussion of serial murder.

* Masters, R.E.L., and Eduard Lea. PERVERSE CRIMES IN HISTORY. Cited above as item 18, pp. x–xi, 105–107.

  Credits Fish with eight to fifteen victims. Interesting for inclusion of a preface by Dr. John Cassity, one of several psychiatrists who examined Fish in 1935.

* Nash, Jay Robert. ALMANAC OF WORLD CRIME. Cited above as item 19, pp. 9, 209–211.

  Case history within a general discussion of mass murder.

* ————. BLOODLETTERS AND BADMEN. Cited above as item 20, pp. 195–199.

  Case history presented in an encyclopedic format.

* ————. CRIME CHRONOLOGY, 1900–1983. Cited above as item 21, pp. 71, 75, 106.

  Traces Fish's career through time line entries.

* ————. MURDER, AMERICA. Cited above as item 23, pp. 387–388.

  Brief case history presented in time line format.

* Scott, Sir Harold. THE CONCISE ENCYCLOPEDIA OF CRIME AND CRIMINALS. Cited above as item 27, pp. 146–147.

  Case history presented in an encyclopedic format.

  * Sifakis, Carl. THE ENCYCLOPEDIA OF AMERICAN CRIME.
    Cited above as item 29, p. 251.

    Case history presented in an encyclopedic format.

  * Wilson, Colin. A CRIMINAL HISTORY OF MANKIND. Cited
    above as item 34, pp. 608-609.

    Brief case history within a discussion of modern sex
    crimes.

  * ————, and Patricia Putnam. THE ENCYCLOPEDIA OF MURDER.
    Cited above as item 35, pp. 211-213.

    Case history presented in an encyclopedic format.

183. FITZSIMMONS, GEORGE (S)

Following the murder of his parents, Fitzsimmons was
acquitted on grounds of insanity and confined to an asylum.
Upon his release, years later, he went to live with an aunt
and uncle, informing psychiatrists that he loved the couple
as if they were his parents. A short time later, Fitzsimmons
stabbed his latest benefactors to death, and police determined
that insurance money had been the motivation in all four
murders. Sentenced to life imprisonment.

  * Brian, Dennis. MURDERERS DIE. Cited above as item 3,
    p. 260.

    Case history presented as an argument in favor of
    capital punishment.

184. FLOYD, CHARLES (S)

Moronic "peeping Tom," with an obsession for redheads,
who killed five victims and injured three others in Dallas,
Tex., between 1942 and 1948. Despite eyewitness testimony
from survivors at the final crime scene, Floyd was not
arrested until 1949. His low intelligence and obvious dis-
orientation under questioning led to commitment for life in
a mental institution.

  * Wilson, Colin, and Patricia Putnam. THE ENCYCLOPEDIA OF
    MURDER. Cited above as item 35, pp. 213-214.

    Case history presented in an encyclopedic format.

185. FOOSE, NORMAN (M)

Shot and killed two Mexican children as they stood beside their mother, in Cuba, N.M., during July 1958. Under questioning by detectives, Foose explained that he was trying to curb the population explosion. Sentenced to life imprisonment.

* Wilson, Colin. A CRIMINAL HISTORY OF MANKIND. Cited above as item 34, p. 12.

    Brief case history within a discussion of "motiveless" murders.

* ————. ORDER OF ASSASSINS. Cited above as item 76, p. 27.

    Brief psychological case study.

186. FORD, ARTHUR KENDRICK (S)

British slayer of two women, poisoned on separate occasions with doses of the reputed aphrodisiac "Spanish fly." Convicted of manslaughter and sentenced to five years in jail.

* CRIMES AND PUNISHMENT: A PICTORIAL ENCYCLOPEDIA OF ABERRANT BEHAVIOR, Volume 14. Cited above as item 4, pp. 23-30.

    Case history presented in an encyclopedic format.

187. FORD, PRISCILLA (M)

Religious fanatic with a history of apparent mental illness who drove her car along a crowded sidewalk in Reno, Nev., on Thanksgiving Day, 1980, killing five persons and injuring another 23. Convicted on five counts of first-degree murder and sentenced to death.

* Kuncl, Tom, and Paul Einstein. LADIES WHO KILL. Cited above as item 14, pp. 70-95.

    Sensational case history prepared from media reports.

188. FORTMEYER, JULIA (S)

Nineteenth-century abortionist who turned to murder in St. Louis, Mo. Upon her arrest in 1875, three corpses were

found in her home, with dozens of other bones inside her stove.
Convicted of manslaughter only, she was sentenced to a term of
five years.

250.   LIFE, CRIMES AND CONFESSION OF MRS. JULIA FORTMEYER.
       Philadelphia: Barclay and Co., 1875.

       Contemporaneous report, drawing upon court transcripts.

  *   Nash, Jay Robert. MURDER, AMERICA. Cited above as item
       23, p. 358.

       Sketchy case history presented in time line format.

                189. FORT WORTH, TEXAS, MURDERS (S)

       Unsolved slayings of five young women, apparently by the
same killer, between October 1984 and January 1985. The early
victims disappeared under mysterious circumstances, but by the
end of January 1985, skeletal remains of all five victims had
been recovered in the Fort Worth area. At this writing, no
further slayings have been reported, and no suspect has been
identified.

  *   FACTS ON FILE. Volume 45, 1985. Cited above as item 7,
       p. 70.

       Reports the murders and discovery of remains.

               190. FRANKLIN, JOSEPH PAUL (S)

       Racist murderer who found the Ku Klux Klan and similar
hate groups "too tame," launching a one-man campaign against
American Jews and blacks in the late 1970s. Convicted of
first-degree murder in the sniper slaying of two black joggers
in Salt Lake City, Utah, during August 1980, and suspected in
at least eight other homicides. Convicted in 1984 of bombing
a Tennessee synagogue seven years earlier. Tried and acquitted in the non-fatal shooting of civil rights leader Vernon
Jordan; suspected, but never charged, in the shooting of
soft-porn publisher Larry Flynt. Convicted in 1986 for the
murder of an interracial couple; sentenced to life in prison.

                            Books

  *   FACTS ON FILE. Volume 40, 1980. Cited above as item 7,
       pp. 410, 442.

Reports the shooting of Vernon Jordan, for which Franklin was later tried and acquitted.

* FACTS ON FILE. Volume 41, 1981. Cited above as item 7, pp. 208, 704.

Reports Franklin's conviction in the slaying of two Utah blacks.

* FACTS ON FILE. Volume 42, 1982. Cited above as item 7, pp. 428, 692.

Reports Franklin's acquittal in the Jordan case.

Articles

251. Gaines, John R. "On the Trail of a Murderous Sniper Suspect." PEOPLE WEEKLY 14 (November 24, 1980): 30-35.

Reports Franklin's arrest, with brief biography and a tally of his suspected crimes.

252. "Racist Joseph P. Franklin Linked to 13 More Killings." JET 66 (April 23, 1984): 30.

Brief, sensational report listing crimes to which Franklin is tentatively linked. Most have not been charged against him, and probably never will be.

253. "Racist Killer Convicted of Slaying Interracial Couple." JET 69 (March 10, 1986): 16.

Reports Franklin's most recent murder conviction.

254. "Racist Rifleman." TIME 116 (November 10, 1980): 22.

Reports Franklin's arrest.

255. "Tracing a Pattern of Racial Murder." NEWSWEEK 96 (November 10, 1980): 45.

Reports Franklin's arrest.

191. FRAZIER, JOHN LINLEY (M)

Paranoid schizophrenic, drug abuser, and practicing occultist who imagined that the voice of God had instructed him to "rid the world of materialism." To that end, Frazier invaded the home of a physician at Santa Cruz, Calif., in 1970, killing the doctor, his wife and two children, as well as his secretary. The bodies were dumped in a swimming pool, and Frazier left behind a cryptic message containing references to Tarot cards. Sentenced to life imprisonment.

Books

* CRIMES AND PUNISHMENT: A PICTORIAL ENCYCLOPEDIA OF ABER-RANT BEHAVIOR, Volume 2. Cited above as item 4, p. 113.

   Brief case history within a general discussion of "motiveless" murder.

* FACTS ON FILE. Volume 30, 1970. Cited above as item 7, pp. 779-780.

   Reports the Santa Cruz massacre and Frazier's arrest.

* FACTS ON FILE. Volume 31, 1971. Cited above as item 7, pp. 960, 1038.

   Reports Frazier's conviction and sentencing.

* Green, Jonathon. THE GREATEST CRIMINALS OF ALL TIME. Cited above as item 11, pp. 149-150.

   Brief case history in an encyclopedic format.

* Levin, Jack, and James Alan Fox. MASS MURDER: AMERICA'S GROWING MENACE. Cited above as item 15.

   Brief case history in a discussion of mass murder.

* Lunde, Donald T. MURDER AND MADNESS. Cited above as item 68, pp. 49-52.

   Case history presented by one of the psychiatrists who examined Frazier in custody.

* Wilson, Colin. A CRIMINAL HISTORY OF MANKIND. Cited above as item 34, p. 16.

   Case history cited as an example of modern "motive-less" crime.

* ————. ORDER OF ASSASSINS. Cited above as item 76, pp. 202-205.

Psychological case history of a mass killer.

* ————, and Donald Seaman. THE ENCYCLOPEDIA OF MODERN MURDER. Cited above as item 36, pp. 68-70.

Case history presented in an encyclopedic format.

Articles

256. "Mass Murder in Soquel." TIME 96 (November 2, 1970): 10-11.

Reports the California massacre before Frazier's arrest.

257. "Tarot Murders." NEWSWEEK 76 (November 2, 1970): 32+.

Contemporaneous report of the murders and manhunt.

192. FREEMAN, JENNACE (M)

Lesbian man-hater, embittered by a rape suffered during childhood, who murdered the young son and daughter of her lover, Gertrude Jackson, in Oregon during 1961. Because the double slaying was committed with Jackson's full cooperation, both were convicted and sentenced to die. The sentences were commuted to life imprisonment three years later.

* Green, Jonathon. THE GREATEST CRIMINALS OF ALL TIME. Cited above as item 11, pp. 252-253.

Brief case history in an encyclopedic format.

* Wilson, Colin. A CASEBOOK OF MURDER. Cited above as item 33, pp. 223-226.

Case history within a study of murder's sociological roots.

193. FREEMAN, JOHN GILBERT (M)

Arizona's worst mass murderer to date. Suspecting a neighbor of running away with his wife, Freeman armed himself with two pistols and invaded the neighbor's Phoenix home, killing seven persons. Held to be incompetent at a preliminary hearing in 1971, Freeman spent four years in a mental hospital before he was finally brought to trial, receiving seven consecutive life terms.

*   Nash, Jay Robert. CRIME CHRONOLOGY, 1900–1983. Cited
    above as item 21, p. 182.

    Brief case history presented in time line format.

*   ———. MURDER, AMERICA. Cited above as item 23, pp.
    439–440.

    Sketchy case history presented in time line format.

194. FRENCH, JAMES DONALD (S)

    Hitchhiker who hijacked a Texas motorist in 1958, murder-
ing his hostage near Stroud, Okla. Following arrest, French
strangled his cellmate in jail, and was subsequently executed.

*   Nash, Jay Robert. MURDER, AMERICA. Cited above as item
    23, p. 429.

    Sketchy case history presented in time line format.

195. FRONTIER COUNTY, NEB., MURDERS (M)

    Unsolved slaying of Edwin and Wilma Hoyt, committed in
September 1973. Dismembered remains of the victims were found
floating in Strunk Lake a week later, creating local panic.
The murdered couple's daughter reported an anonymous campaign
of harassment against the family prior to the slayings, including defoliant chemicals sprayed on their shrubbery and
lawn, but no suspects have been identified.

258. "Nebraska Gothic." NEWSWEEK 82 (November 26, 1973): 37.

    Reports the murders and resultant investigation.

196. FROST, SAMUEL (S)

    Acquitted of driving a stake through his father's head
in 1783, Frost murdered his Princeton, Mass., landlord with
a hoe ten years later and was this time convicted of murder.
Hanged in October 1793.

*   Nash, Jay Robert. MURDER, AMERICA. Cited above as item
    23, p. 313.

    Sketchy case history presented in time line format.

197. FUGATE, CARIL (S): See STARKWEATHER, CHARLES

198. GACY, JOHN WAYNE, Jr. (S)

Homosexual torture-slayer of 33 young men and boys in
Chicago, Ill. Gacy holds the American record for murder convictions. Victims were selected mainly from the ranks of runaways and male prostitutes abounding in Chicago's gay district,
although Gacy sometimes preyed on male employees of his own
construction firm. Most of the bodies were buried in a crawl-
space under Gacy's suburban home, producing noxious odors
which neighbors managed to ignore from 1973 to 1978, when
Gacy was finally arrested. A weak insanity defense, with
feigned multiple personalities, failed to impress the court
and Gacy was sentenced to die. Awaiting execution.

Books

* Boar, Roger, and Nigel Blundell. THE WORLD'S MOST IN-
   FAMOUS MURDERS. Cited above as item 2, pp. 66-70.

   Sensational case history presented in tabloid style.

259. Cahill, Tim. BURIED DREAMS. New York: Bantam, 1985.

   Produced with the cooperation of investigative journalists who covered Gacy's case, Cahill's volume seeks
   the roots of violence in Gacy's relationship with his
   abusive, alcoholic father. Cahill ultimately begs the
   question of Gacy's sanity, refusing to decide whether
   the killer was mad, or "merely evil."

* FACTS ON FILE. Volume 39, 1979. Cited above as item 7,
   p. 24.

   Reports Gacy's murder indictment.

* FACTS ON FILE. Volume 40, 1980. Cited above as item 7,
   p. 214.

   Reports Gacy's conviction in Chicago.

* Levin, Jack, and James Alan Fox. MASS MURDER: AMERICA'S
   GROWING MENACE. Cited above as item 15.

   Brief case history within a discussion of serial murder.

260. Linedecker, Clifford L. THE MAN WHO KILLED BOYS. New
     York: St. Martin's Pres, 1980.

     Written before Gacy's conviction, the book presumes
     his guilt on all charges and closes with a thinly-veiled
     plea for the death penalty. A paperback edition, re-
     leased in 1985 with the verdict a fait accompli, brings
     events in the case more immediately up to date.

*   Nash, Jay Robert. ALMANAC OF WORLD CRIME. Cited above
     as item 19, pp. 290-291.

     Brief case history in a discussion of mass murder.

*   ———. CRIME CHRONOLOGY, 1900-1983. Cited above as
     item 21, p. 194.

     Brief case history presented in time line format.

*   ———. MURDER, AMERICA. Cited above as item 23, p. 446.

     Sketchy case history presented in time line format.

*   Sifakis, Carl. THE ENCYCLOPEDIA OF AMERICAN CRIME.
     Cited above as item 29, p. 269.

     Case history presented in an encyclopedic format.

261. Sullivan, Terry, and Peter T. Maiken. KILLER CLOWN.
     New York: Grosset & Dunlap, 1983.

     An "inside" examination of the case, prepared by the
     prosecuting attorney who won the record-breaking murder
     conviction. Detailed and instructive.

*   Wilson, Colin. A CRIMINAL HISTORY OF MANKIND. Cited
     above as item 34, p. 642.

     Brief case history within a discussion of mass murder.

*   ———, and Donald Seaman. THE ENCYCLOPEDIA OF MODERN
     MURDER. Cited above as item 36, pp. 71-73.

     Case history presented in an encyclopedic format.

                            Articles

262. "I Do Rotten, Horrible Things." TIME 113 (January 8, 1979): 23.

> Reports Gacy's arrest and early confessions.

263. Mathews, T., and F. Maier. "Double Life of a Clown." NEWSWEEK 93 (January 8, 1979): 24+.

> Reports Gacy's arrest and indictment.

199. GALLEGO, GERALD (S)

Convicted of murdering a man and his fiancee near Sacramento, Calif., in November 1980, sexual sadist Gallego was sentenced to die. Authorities in Nevada, mistrusting the California death sentence, fought for the killer's extradition on one of four Nevada murders in which he is suspected. Money for the trial was raised through unprecedented public donations, and Gallego was again sentenced to die, this time in a state where the sentence seemed more likely to be carried out. Suspected in a total of eleven murders, spanning three states, Gallego is known to have occasionally buried his female victims alive.

264. "Making Sure." TIME 123 (February 27, 1984): 27.

> Reports the grass roots effort to finance Gallego's trial.

200. GALLOWAY, ROBERT M. (M)

Portland, Ore., construction executive who shot to death his wife, two children, and the family dog in November 1983. A third child was wounded but escaped before Galloway turned his weapon on himself, committing suicide.

Books

* Levin, Jack, and James Alan Fox. MASS MURDER: AMERICA'S GROWING MENACE. Cited above as item 15.

> Brief case history within a discussion of mass murder.

Articles

265. Alter, Jonathan. "Oregon: Deaths in the Family." NEWSWEEK 102 (December 5, 1983): 73.

Contemporaneous report of the Galloway massacre.

201. GARNIER, GILLES (S)

French slayer of at least four children, two of each sex, in the late 16th century. Three of the victims were mutilated and partially devoured, leading religious authorities to charge Garnier as a "werewolf." Burned at the stake for lycanthropy in 1573, after being forced to pay the costs of his own prosecution.

266.   Aylesworth, Thomas G. WEREWOLVES AND OTHER MONSTERS. Boston: G.K. Hall & Co., 1973, pp. 56-57.

Case history within a discussion of werewolf lore.

267.   Garden, Nancy. WEREWOLVES. New York: J.B. Lippincott Co., 1973, pp. 66-68.

Case history in a discussion of historic "werewolves."

268.   McHargue, Georgess. MEET THE WEREWOLF. Philadelphia: J.B. Lippincott Co., 1976, pp. 46-50.

Arbitrarily changes Garnier's name to "Jean" and dates his trial from 1603, 30 years after his execution.

*   Masters, R.E.L., and Eduard Lea. PERVERSE CRIMES IN HISTORY. Cited above as item 18, pp. 58-60.

Brief case history in a discussion of human "werewolves."

202. GARCIA, JOSEPH (M)

Transient who stabbed a family of five to death at Monmouthshire, England, during July 1878, setting the house afire in an effort to cover his crime. Suspicion fell on Garcia when he was found near the scene, with bloody clothes and scratches on his arms. Convicted and hanged.

*   Logan, Guy B.H. MASTERS OF CRIME. Cited above as item 17, pp. 161-172.

Case history in an anthology of 19th-century murders.

203. GARY, CARLTON (S)

Convicted in one of seven "identical" rape-murders of

elderly women which terrorized Columbus, Ga., in 1977 and 1978. Gary was not apprehended until 1984, spending five of the intervening years in prison on other charges. With his conviction in a single case, detectives consider the other six "silk stocking" murders to be solved.

Books

* FACTS ON FILE. Volume 38, 1978. Cited above as item 7, p. 232.

  Reports the discovery of a sixth "silk stocking" victime in Columbus, with a retrospective look at previous crimes in the series.

* Levin, Jack, and James Alan Fox. MASS MURDER: AMERICA'S GROWING MENACE. Cited above as item 15.

  Brief case history in a discussion of serial murder.

Articles

* Gest, Ted, and D.C. Lyons. "Behind a Nationwide Wave of Unsolved Murders." Cited above as item 47.

  Examines the Columbus stranglings in conjunction with other on-going serial crimes, all subsequently solved.

* Sonnenschein, Allan. "Serial Killers." Cited above as item 55, p. 32.

  Brief case history in a discussion of serial murder.

204. GARVIE, MAX (M)

Wealthy English farmer, age 33, who killed his wife and her 22-year-old lover in 1968. Evidence produced at trial proved that Garvie had originally connived to arrange the affair through a "swinger's" organization, afterward becoming jealous. Setnenced to life imprisonment.

* Wilson, Colin. A CASEBOOK OF MURDER. Cited above as item 33, pp. 42-43.

  Brief case history within a sociological study of murder.

205. GBRUREK, TILLIE (S)

Poisoner of at least eight husbands between 1914 and
1921, surviving on insurance money and the proceeds from successive wills. Arrested in Chicago after number eight and
sentenced to a term of life imprisonment.

* Nash, Jay Robert. MURDER, AMERICA. Cited above as item
  23, pp. 14, 189-191, 396.

  Case history in an anthology of "classic" murders.

206. GECHT, ROBIN (S): See KOKORALEIS, ANDREW and THOMAS

207. GEIN, EDWARD (S)

Wisconsin necrophile, grave robber, and cannibal who
skinned and disemboweled his female victims, using parts of
their bodies as clothing and decorations for his home near
Plainfield.   Nurturing a secret desire for transsexual surgery
but lacking the requisite courage and funds, Gein made do by
wearing female "vests" and death masks made from human skin.
When thefts of body parts from recent graves no longer met
his needs, he turned to homicide, slaying victims at Plainfield in 1954 and 1957. Careless in the latter case, Gein was
traced by deputies who discovered a veritable chamber of
horrors in his farm house. Obviously insane, Gein was committed
to a state institution for life, and died there in 1984.
Comparison of the recovered body parts with funeral records
demonstrates that Gein was clearly guilty of at least two
other homicides; conjecture links him with three additional
deaths or disappearances in the Plainfield area, including
the "accidental" death of his brother in the late 1940s.

Books

* CRIMES AND PUNISHMENT: A PICTORIAL ENCYCLOPEDIA OF ABER-
  RANT BEHAVIOR, Volume 5. Cited above as item 4, p. 113.

  Case history presented in an encyclopedic format.

* FACTS ON FILE. Volume 17, 1957. Cited above as item 7,
  p. 384.

  Contemporaneous account of Gein's arrest.

* Gaute, J.H.H., and Robin Odell. THE MURDERERS' WHO'S
  WHO. Cited above as item 8, pp. 107-108.

Case history presented in an encyclopedic format.

269. Gollmar, Robert H. EDWARD GEIN. New York: Charles
     Hallberg & Co., 1981.

     The best account of Gein's case, prepared by the judge
     who presided at his trial. Gollmar presents evidence
     linking Gein with five homicides other than the two
     with which he was formally charged, publishing previously
     censored photographs of Gein's house and bizarre
     "furnishings." Well worth reading.

 * Green, Jonathon. THE GREATEST CRIMINALS OF ALL TIME.
    Cited above as item 11, p. 271.

    Brief case history in an encyclopedic format.

 * Levin, Jack, and James Alan Fox. MASS MURDER: AMERICA'S
    GROWING MENACE. Cited above as item 15.

    Case history presented as a graphic lead-in to the
    problem of modern multicide.

 * Masters, R.E.L., and Eduard Lea. PERVERSE CRIMES IN
    HISTORY. Cited above as item 18, pp. 170-172.

    Case history presented in a general discussion of
    "ghouls" and necrophilia.

 * Nash, Jay Robert. BLOODLETTERS AND BADMEN. Cited
    above as item 20, pp. 206-208.

    Case history presented in an encyclopedic format.

 * Sifakis, Carl. THE ENCYCLOPEDIA OF AMERICAN CRIME.
    Cited above as item 29, pp. 277-278.

    Case history presented in an encyclopedic format.

 * Wilson, Colin. A CASEBOOK OF MURDER. Cited above as
    item 33, pp. 226-229.

    Case history within a sociological study of homicide.

 * ————. ORDER OF ASSASSINS. Cited above as item 76,
    p. 78.

    Brief psychological case history on Gein.

Articles

270. "House of Horror Stuns the Nation." LIFE 43 (December
      2, 1957): 24–31.

      Photo spread and article recounting local reactions to
      the discovery of Gein's "hobby."

271. "Portrait of a Killer." TIME 70 (December 2, 1957):
      38–40.

      Contemporaneous report of Gein's arrest.

272. "Secrets of the Farm." NEWSWEEK 50 (December 2, 1957):
      30+.

      Reports Gein's arrest and indictment.

208. GIBBS, JANIE LOU (S)

Active church member in Cordele, Ga., who poisoned her
husband, three sons, and infant grandson over a two-year
period, apparently for insurance benefits (one-tenth of which
were immediately donated to her church). Autopsies in the
latter cases led to exhumation of earlier bodies, and a discovery that all five victims died of arsenic poisoning. Gibbs
was arrested on Christmas Eve, 1967, but eight years passed
before she was ruled competent to stand trial, receiving five
consecutive life sentences.

   * Godwin, John. MURDER USA. Cited above as item 10,
      pp. 124–125.

      Brief case history in a discussion of female killers.

209. GIBSON, HUGH (M)

With fellow inmates Clinton Grate and James Raymond,
Gibson set a fire at the Ohio penitentiary in April 1930,
hoping that the flames and resultant confusion would help
them all escape. The would-be escapees were unsuccessful,
but 322 other inmates died in the fire they had set. All
three were convicted of second-degree murder; Gibson continued
serving his sentence, while his two accomplices committed
suicide in their cells.

   * Nash, Jay Robert. ALMANAC OF WORLD CRIME. Cited above
      as item 19, p. 24.

Brief case history in a general discussion of arson.

210. GIFFARD, MILES (M)

Welsh parricide who beat his father and mother to death with a length of pipe at Cornwall, in 1952. The bodies were carried by wheelbarrow and dumped over a cliff at the end of the family garden. Upon discovery of the remains, Giffard was swiftly arrested, tried, and executed.

* CRIMES AND PUNISHMENT: A PICTORIAL ENCYCLOPEDIA OF ABER-
  RANT BEHAVIOR, Volume 7. Cited above as item 4, p. 105.

  Brief case history in a discussion of parent-killers.

* Wilson, Colin. A CASEBOOK OF MURDER. Cited above as
  item 33, pp. 194-200.

  Case history within a sociological study of murder.

* ————, and Patricia Putnam. THE ENCYCLOPEDIA OF MURDER.
  Cited above as item 35, pp. 229-231.

  Case history presented in an encyclopedic format.

211. GILLIGAN, AMY (S)

Homicidal nurse who ran a home for the elderly in Hart-ford, Conn., during the early 20th century. The sudden death of a patient in June 1914 made relatives suspicious, whereupon police were called. Detectives found the home to have an average death rate of twelve patients per year over the past four years—with only fourteen residents at any given time. The deaths ceased for several months following the infiltra-tion of a policewoman, posing as a patient, but resumed in late 1914. Gilligan's late husband and three other victims were exhumed, all bearing traces of arsenic poisoning. Gilli-gan was sentenced to life, but was subsequently found insane by court psychiatrists who reexamined her in 1923.

* Wilson, Colin, and Patricia Putnam. THE ENCYCLOPEDIA
  OF MURDER. Cited above as item 35, pp. 231-232.

  Case history presented in an encyclopedic format.

212. GIRARD, HENRI (S)

French murderer for profit who poisoned his victims with

germ cultures, collecting their insurance benefits. Charged
with two homicides, committed in 1912 and 1918, respectively,
Girard was awaiting grial in 1921 when he committed suicide
by swallowing a germ culture.

*   Gaute, J.H.H., and Robin Odell. THE MURDERERS' WHO'S
    WHO. Cited above as item 8, p. 109.

    Case history presented in an encyclopedic format.

213. GIRARDI, JAMES A. (M)

Despondent over recent unemployment, Griardi killed his
four children as they slept in the family home at Briarcliff
Manor, N.Y., then shot himself to death.

*   Levin, Jack, and James Alan Fox. MASS MURDER: AMERICA'S
    GROWING MENACE. Cited above as item 15.

    Brief case history in a discussion of family murders.

214. GLATMAN, HARVEY MURRAY (S)

Bondage fetishist and sadomasochist who raped and murdered three women in Los Angeles during 1957 and 1958. Posing
as a professional photographer, Glatman convinced his victims
to pose for "jeopardy" photos, presumably sold to pulp detective magazines. Once the models were securely bound, Glatman
would rape them repeatedly, photograph them in various stages
of undress, and strangle them with his favorite piece of rope.
A fourth potential victim managed to wrestle Glatman's pistol
away from him, holding the killer at bay until police arrived.
Glatman freely confessed his crimes and refused to appeal his
death sentence. He was executed in August 1959.

*   CRIMES AND PUNISHMENT: A PICTORIAL ENCYCLOPEDIA OF ABER-
    RANT BEHAVIOR, Volume 16. Cited above as item 4, pp.
    113-114.

    Case history presented in an encyclopedic format.

*   Gaute, J.H.H., and Robin Odell. THE MURDERERS' WHO'S
    WHO. Cited above as item 8, p. 110.

    Case history presented in an encyclopedic format.

*   Nash, Jay Robert. ALMANAC OF WORLD CRIME. Cited above
    as item 19, p. 101.

Brief case history in a discussion of mass murder.

* ———. BLOODLETTERS AND BADMEN. Cited above as item 20, pp. 219-221.

Case history presented in an encyclopedic format.

* ———. CRIME CHRONOLOGY, 1900-1983. Cited above as item 21, p. 155.

Brief case history presented in time line format.

* Sifakis, Carl. THE ENCYCLOPEDIA OF AMERICAN CRIME. Cited above as item 29, pp. 284-285.

Case history presented in an encyclopedic format.

* Wilson, Colin. ORDER OF ASSASSINS. Cited above as item 76, pp. 80-81.

Brief psychological survey of Glatman's case.

215. GODFRIDA, SISTER (S)

Belgian nun, addicted to morphine, who in 1978 confessed to murdering three patients at the geriatric hospital where she was employed as a nurse. Her victims, all killed with insulin injections, were robbed to support her narcotics habit. Co-workers denounced Sister Godfrida to administrators, charging that she tortured elderly patients, pointing out that 21 of 38 patients assigned to her care had died within a single year. In the wake of her confession, hospital spokesmen announced that the death toll "could just as well be 30 people as three."

273. "The Nun's Story." TIME 111 (March 13, 1978): 51.

Reports Sister Godfrida's arrest and confessions.

216. GOHL, BILLY (S)

As an officer with the seaman's union hiring office in Aberdeen, Wash., Gohl was assigned to recruit sailors. During the quarter-century between 1903 and 1928, he murdered an estimated minimum of 40 seamen, presumably robbing them after death. Convicted on two murder charges, Gohl was sentenced to life imprisonment.

  * Sifakis, Carl. THE ENCYCLOPEDIA OF AMERICAN CRIME.
    Cited above as item 29, pp. 285-286.

    Case history presented in an encyclopedic format.

217. GONZALES, FRANCISCO PAULA (M)

Warehouse worker, plagued by mental and financial problems, who produced a pistol on a flight from Reno to San Francisco in May 1964. Shooting the pilot and first officer, he
thereby caused the plane to crash, killing all 44 persons on
board.

274. "Death Wish." TIME 22 (November 6, 1964): 22+.

    Reports the findings of an investigation into the
    crash of Pacific Airlines Flight 773.

218. GONZALEZ, DELFINA and MARIA (S)

Mexican sisters believed responsible for the murders of
more than 100 persons in Guadalajara during the early 1960s.
The sisters ran a white slave operation, abducting young women
or purchasing them from others, forcibly addicting them to
narcotics, and putting them to work as prostitutes. Girls
who lost their looks or who "made trouble" were routinely
murdered and buried at a ranch belonging to the sisters. Police
excavations at the ranch unearthed 80 female corpses, along
with the remains of "numerous" new-born infants. Also discovered were the skeletal remains of eleven men, believed to
be migratory workers robbed and murdered in the sisters'
several brothels. Convicted of murder, Delfina and Maria
each received terms of 40 years in prison; their considerable
fortune was confiscated by the state, for division among the
families of their victims. A two-year investigation landed
various accomplices in jail for lesser terms.

Books

  * Wilson, Colin, and Donald Seaman. THE ENCYCLOPEDIA OF
    MODERN MURDER. Cited above as item 36, pp. 83-85.

    Case history presented in an encyclopedic format.

Articles

275. "Murdering Madams." NEWSWEEK 64 (November 2, 1964): 60.

Contemporaneous report of the investigation and arrests.

219. GOODE, ARTHUR FREDERICK III (S)

Homosexual pedophile and slayer of two boys during March 1976. Goode's first victim was strangled in Florida, the second in Virginia, with fifteen days separating the crimes. Goode was sentenced to life imprisonment in Virginia, then extradited to Florida, where he was sentenced to death. While awaiting trial in Florida, Goode confided to visitors: "If I ever get my hands on another boy—a sexy little boy—he will never make it home."

* Godwin, John. MURDER USA. Cited above as item 10, pp. 321-323.

   Case history in a discussion of sadistic sex crimes.

220. GOSSMAN, KLAUS (S)

Random sniper in his native Germany who killed two victims in 1960, with one each in 1962, 1963, and 1966. Sentenced to life imprisonment at his trial in 1967. As Gossman told the court, "People are no more than things to me. Inanimate. Ciphers. I am a pragmatist."

* Green, Jonathon. THE GREATEST CRIMINALS OF ALL TIME. Cited above as item 11, p. 240.

   Brief case history in an encyclopedic format.

* Nash, Jay Robert. ALMANAC OF WORLD CRIME. Cited above as item 19, p. 290.

   Case history in a discussion of mass murder.

* ————. CRIME CHRONOLOGY, 1900-1983. Cited above as item 21, p. 167.

   Brief case history presented in time line format.

* Wilson, Colin. A CASEBOOK OF MURDER. Cited above as item 33, pp. 247-250.

   Case history in a sociological survey of murder.

* ————. A CRIMINAL HISTORY OF MANKIND. Cited above as item 34, pp. 128-129.

Case history in a discussion of "motiveless" murder.

221. GOTTFRIED, GESINA MARGARETHA (S)

German poisoner of at least 20 persons between 1815 and 1828. Her victims included her own parents, a brother, three husbands, and her own children. Captured when her latest husband became suspicious of the white powder sprinkled over every meal, Gesina confessed to more than thirty murders spanning thirteen years. A number of the crimes had romantic or financial motivations, but Gottfried also confessed to achieving climax as she watched her victims die. Beheaded in 1828.

* Green, Jonathon. THE GREATEST CRIMINALS OF ALL TIME. Cited above as item 11, pp. 240-241.

  Brief case history in an encyclopedic format.

* Nash, Jay Robert. ALMANAC OF WORLD CRIME. Cited above as item 21, p. 271.

  Case history in a general discussion of mass murder.

* ————. LOOK FOR THE WOMAN. Cited above as item 22, pp. 170-172.

  Case history presented in an encyclopedic format.

222. GRACE, EDWIN JAMES (M)

Bearing a grudge against the staff of an employment agency in Cherry Hill, N.J., Grace entered the agency's office building in June 1972 and began shooting persons at random. Two of the six dead were agency employees; six other persons were wounded by Grace before he turned the gun on himself, committing suicide at the scene.

* FACTS ON FILE. Volume 32, 1972. Cited above as item 7, p. 795.

  Contemporaneous report of the New Jersey shootings.

223. GRACE, JAMES WILLIE (S)

Habitual criminal, diagnosed as a paranoid schizophrenic in 1974. Grace killed two persons and wounded three others in sniper attacks around Durham, N.C., in December 1976.

* Tobias, Ronald. THEY SHOOT TO KILL. Cited above as
   item 31, pp. 136-140.

   Case history in a survey of criminal snipers.

224. GRAHAM, ERIC STANLEY GEORGE (M)

Multiple murderer and the object of New Zealand's most
sensational manhunt. Following a violent incident with neighbors, Graham was sought by police in October 1941. When
officers arrived to question him at home, Graham shot and
killed four of them in a blazing gun battle. Wounded several
times during an eight-day search, Graham killed two members of
the posse before he was finally shot to death.

* Gaute, J.H.H., and Robin Odell. THE MURDERERS' WHO'S
   WHO. Cited above as item 8, p. 112.

   Case history presented in an encyclopedic format.

* Green, Jonathon. THE GREATEST CRIMINALS OF ALL TIME.
   Cited above as item 11, p. 254.

   Brief case history in an encyclopedic format.

* Nash, Jay Robert. CRIME CHRONOLOGY, 1900-1983. Cited
   above as item 21, pp. 117-118.

   Brief case history presented in time line format.

225. GRAHAM, JOHN GILBERT (M)

Planted a bomb aboard United Air Lines Flight 629, from
Denver, in November 1955, killing his mother and 43 others
in the resultant explosion. Graham sought to collect flight
insurance on his mother, in addition to a sizeable inheritance,
but agents of the FBI discovered his involvement in the crime.
Convicted of murder in 1956; executed in January 1957.

Books

* CRIMES AND PUNISHMENT: A PICTORIAL ENCYCLOPEDIA OF ABER-
   RANT BEHAVIOR, Volume 7. Cited above as item 4, p. 105.

   Case history in a discussion of parricide.

* FACTS ON FILE. Volume 15, 1955. Cited above as item 7,
   pp. 372, 388, 412.

Reports the crime, Graham's arrest, and his insanity plea.

* FACTS ON FILE. Volume 16, 1956. Cited above as item 7, p. 156.

Reports Graham's conviction.

* FACTS ON FILE. Volume 17, 1957. Cited above as item 7, p. 16.

Reports Graham's execution in Colorado.

* Green, Jonathon. THE GREATEST CRIMINALS OF ALL TIME. Cited above as item 11, p. 254.

Brief case history in an encyclopedic format.

* Nash, Jay Robert. ALMANAC OF WORLD CRIME. Cited above as item 19, p. 84.

Case history in a discussion of mass murder.

* ————. BLOODLETTERS AND BADMEN. Cited above as item 20, pp. 225–227.

Case history presented in an encyclopedic format.

* ————. CRIME CHRONOLOGY, 1900–1983. Cited above as item 21, p. 152.

Brief case history presented in time line format.

* Sifakis, Carl. THE ENCYCLOPEDIA OF AMERICAN CRIME. Cited above as item 29, pp. 293–294.

Case history presented in an encyclopedic format.

276. Whitehead, Don. THE FBI STORY. New York: Random House, 1956, pp. 3–11.

Case history of Graham's arrest and conviction.

* Wilson, Colin. A CRIMINAL HISTORY OF MANKIND. Cited above as item 34, p. 605.

Case history in a general discussion of mass murder.

* Wolfgang, Marvin E. STUDIES IN HOMICIDE. Cited above
  as item 77, pp. 170-178.

  Reprints item 83 above, dealing with Graham's case.

Articles

* Galvin, James A.V., and John M. MacDonald. "A Psychiatric Study of a Mass Murderer." Cited above as item 83.

  Examines Graham's childhood for symptoms of MacDonald's
  "triad."

  226. GRANS, HANS (S): See HAARMAN, FRITZ

  227. GRATE, CLINTON (M): See GIBSON, HUGH

228. "THE GRAVE" (M)

Unsolved arson fire which claimed seven lives in May 1968.
After being ejected for rowdy behavior, an unidentified patron
of The Grave, an aptly-named nightclub in Ft. Worth, Tex.,
returned with a gasoline bomb and hurled it into the crowded
establishment. Seven customers died in the fire, with another
half-dozen sustaining critical injuries.

* Nash, Jay Robert. ALMANAC OF WORLD CRIME. Cited above
  as item 19, p. 86.

  Case history in a general discussion of arson.

* ————. CRIME CHRONOLOGY, 1900-1983. Cited above as
  item 21, p. 176.

  Brief case history presented in time line format.

  229. GRAY, JUNIUS (M): See ALLEN, JIMMIE LEE

  230. GREEN, LARRY C. (S): See "ZEBRA MURDERS"

231. GREEN, NAPOLEON (M)

American airman, awaiting court martial on charges of
theft, who went berserk on the U.S. Air Force base at Manston,
England, in August 1955. Green shot and killed three persons,
wounding nine others before he committed suicide.

*   FACTS ON FILE. Volume 15, 1955. Cited above as item 7,
    p. 292.

    Contemporaneous report of the Manston shootings.

232. "GREEN RIVER KILLER, THE" (S)

    Unidentified killer of at least 37 women in Kings County,
Wash., since July 1982. As many as eleven other missing women
are presumed to be victims of the same killer, but their cases
cannot be officially connected prior to the discovery of remains which verify their deaths. Most of the victims have
been prostitutes or runaways, picked up along the "Sea-Tac
Strip," between Seattle and Tacoma. Many of the corpses have
been found in or near the Green River, hence the killer's
public nickname. Still at large, with no new crimes reported
since the early part of 1985.

Books

*   FACTS ON FILE. Volume 44, 1984. Cited above as item 7,
    p. 979.

    Reports the lapse of a limited-time reward offer in
    the case.

*   Levin, Jack, and James Alan Fox. MASS MURDER: AMERICA'S
    GROWING MENACE. Cited above as item 15.

    Case history in a general discussion of serial murder.

Articles

277. Penn, R. "The Green River Flows Red." PROGRESSIVE 48
      (October 1984): 17.

      Brief examination of the continuing manhunt.

278. "River of Blood." TIME 123 (April 16, 1984): 26.

      Examines the manhunt after two years.

279. Starr, M. "Washington's Green River Killer." NEWSWEEK
      103 (January 9, 1984): 25.

      Contemporaneous examination of the case.

233. GREEN, SAMUEL (S)

Severely abused by his parents, who thought him "possessed," Green committed acts of arson and attempted murder as a child, also killing family pets and livestock. As a young man, he embarked on a life of major crime with an accomplice named Ash, committing "numerous" murders, rapes, and robberies throughout New England. Finally apprehended in Massachusetts, Green was hanged in April 1822.

* Nash, Jay Robert. MURDER, AMERICA. Cited above as item 23, pp. 14, 34-38, 320.

  Case history in an anthology of "classic" murders.

234. GREENWALT, RANDY (M): See TISON, GARY

235. GREENWOOD, VAUGHN ORRIN (S)

Self-styled Satanist and "Skid Row Slasher," held responsible for the slayings of 11 tramps in Los Angeles. Nine victims were killed in "ritual" style during December 1974 and January 1975, their throats slit, shoes removed, with quantities of salt scattered around each corpse. Greenwood became a suspect in late 1975, after an attempted burglary of actor Burt Reynolds' home. In January 1976, he was indicted for the nine recent slayings, as well as two similar murders committed in 1964. Prosecutors alleged that Greenwood drank the blood of several victims, presumably as part of some Satanic ritual. Sentenced to die, he awaits execution.

Books

* FACTS ON FILE. Volume 35, 1975. Cited above as item 7, p. 150.

  Reports on the "Slasher" manhunt in progress.

* Levin, Jack, and James Alan Fox. MASS MURDER: AMERICA'S GROWING MENACE. Cited above as item 15.

  Brief case history in a discussion of serial murder.

* Nash, Jay Robert. CRIME CHRONOLOGY, 1900-1983. Cited above as item 21, p. 186.

  Presenting a brief case history in time line format, Nash perpetuates his published error from item 24 above

by describing the Slasher case as "unsolved." (This
nine years after Greenwood's conviction made headlines
from coast to coast.)

*   ————. OPEN FILES. Cited above as item 24, pp. 157-158.

Another "open" case which actually closed without the
author noticing, in this instance seven years before his
book was published. Nash describes the slayings as "an
orgy of murder that has yet to be explained," perpetrated
by "an unknown maniac." He also reproduces sketches of
a Caucasian "suspect" which were instantly retracted by
police with the arrest of Greenwood (a black) in 1975.

*   Campbell, Colin. "Portrait of a Mass Killer." Cited
    above as item 78.

Critically examines the "science" of preparing psychiatric profiles for unidentified criminals. In the
Slasher case, a "profile" described the elusive killer
as a homosexual Caucasian in his late 20s or early 30s,
six feet tall and 190 pounds, with shoulder-length,
stringy blond hair. In fact, the killer was a black
man who apparently performed the ritualistic murders as
a form of sacrifice to Satan.

280. "Skid Row Slasher." TIME 105 (February 10, 1975): 18.

Reports on the crimes prior to Greenwood's arrest.

236. GRETZLER, DOUGLAS (S)

With accomplice William Steelman, Gretzler invaded a
home in Victor, Calif., in November 1973, killing all seven
persons present before looting the house. Evidence discovered
at the scene linked the pair with a similar double slaying
committed the previous month. With the arrest of both suspects
in mid-November, Arizona authorities declared that Gretzler
and Steelman were linked with five other slayings and four
disappearances in that state. Sentenced to life in California,
the pair was subsequently extradited to Arizona, and there
sentenced to die.

Books

*   FACTS ON FILE. Volume 33, 1973. Cited above as item 7,
    p. 1023.

Reports the arrests of Gretzler and Steelman.

* FACTS ON FILE. Volume 34, 1974. Cited above as item 7, p. 907.

Reports the imposition of sentences in California.

* Godwin, John. MURDER USA. Cited above as item 10, pp. 305-308.

Case history within a "chamber of horrors" reserved for gruesome multicides.

* Nash, Jay Robert. MURDER, AMERICA. Cited above as item 23, p. 441.

Sketchy case history presented in time line format.

Articles

281. "Murder in California." TIME 102 (November 19, 1973): 41.

Reports the arrests, with a summary of suspected crimes.

237. GROSSMAN, GEORGE KARL (S)

Professional butcher and convicted child molester in Berlin, Germany, who was also known to practice bestiality. Arrested in August 1921, when his landlord heard sounds of a struggle emanating from Grossman's kitchen and called police; the officers found a recently-killed girl in the kitchen, bound as if ready for butchering. Evidence found in the butcher shop indicated that at least three women had been killed within as many weeks. No final body-count was ever established, but Grossman had been "doing business" at the same address since 1913, and the total may have been substantial. Sentenced to die, Grossman hanged himself in jail before he could be executed by the state.

* Green, Jonathon. THE GREATEST CRIMINALS OF ALL TIME. Cited above as item 11, p. 272.

Brief case history in an encyclopedic format.

* Hurwood, Bernhardt J. VAMPIRES, WEREWOLVES, AND GHOULS. Cited above as item 12, pp. 79-80.

Sensational case history within a catalogue of "human monsters."

* Masters, R.E.L., and Eduard Lea. PERVERSE CRIMES IN HISTORY. Cited above as item 18, pp. 101-102, 169-170.

Case history in a general discussion of cannibalism.

* Nash, Jay Robert. CRIME CHRONOLOGY, 1900-1983. Cited above as item 21, p. 52.

Brief case history presented in time line format.

* Wilson, Colin. A CRIMINAL HISTORY OF MANKIND. Cited above as item 34, p. 607.

Case history in a discussion of modern mass murder.

* ————, and Patricia Putnam. THE ENCYCLOPEDIA OF MURDER. Cited above as item 35, pp. 243-244.

Case history presented in an encyclopedic format.

238. GROSSO, SANTO (M)

Frenchman who took a woman and her son hostage in September 1973, raped the woman, then shot both hostages to death. Grosso committed suicide as police stormed his hideout.

* Green, Jonathon. THE GREATEST CRIMINALS OF ALL TIME. Cited above as item 11, p. 254.

Brief case history in an encyclopedic format.

239. GUAY, JOSEPH ALBERT (M)

Canada's worst mass murderer to date. Guay planted a bomb aboard a Canadian Pacific Airlines flight in September 1949, killing his wife and 22 others. Guay allegedly murdered his wife to clear the way for his marriage to a teenaged girl. Former lover Marie Petri and her brother were indicted as accessories to murder for purchasing explosives on Guay's behalf, and for carrying the bomb—disguised as a "religious statuette"—to the airport. All three were convicted and executed during 1950.

* Green, Jonathon. THE GREATEST CRIMINALS OF ALL TIME. Cited above as item 11, p. 255.

Brief case history in an encyclopedic format.

*   Nash, Jay Robert. ALMANAC OF WORLD CRIME. Cited above
     as item 19, pp. 83-84.

Case history in a general discussion of mass murder.

*   ————. CRIME CHRONOLOGY, 1900-1983. Cited above as
     item 21, p. 137.

Brief case history presented in time line format.

*   Wilson, Colin. A CRIMINAL HISTORY OF MANKIND. Cited
     above as item 34, pp. 604-605.

Case history in a discussion of modern mass murder.

*   ————, and Patricia Putnam. THE ENCYCLOPEDIA OF MURDER.
     Cited above as item 35, pp. 244-245.

Case history presented in an encyclopedic format.

240. GUFLER, MAX (S)

Austrian "bluebeard" who suffered a head injury at age
nine and thereafter was subject to unpredictable fits of
violence. Further head injuries in World War II apparently
worsened his condition. Suspected by police of murdering at
least 18 persons between 1952 and 1958, most of them women
lured by offers of marriage. Convicted on eight counts of
homicide, Gufler was sentenced to life in May 1961.

*   Wilson, Colin, and Patricia Putnam. THE ENCYCLOPEDIA
     OF MURDER. Cited above as item 35, pp. 246-247.

Case history presented in an encyclopedic format.

241. GUIBOURG, ABBE (S)

Corrupt Catholic priest and closet Satanist, accused in
1680, with Madame de Montespan, of sacrificing 140 infants
in an occult conspiracy to make her the next queen of France.
At Guibourg's trial, it was alleged that participants in the
so-called black masses were required to drink the blood of
murdered children, as well as engaging in various acts of
blasphemy and perversion. Upon conviction, the priest was
sentenced to death and beheaded.

282. Hoeller, Stephen A. "The Real Black Mass." THE WORLD'S
      WEIRDEST CULTS. Edited by Martin Ebon. New York:
      New American Library, 1979, pp. 176-186.

      Case history of the trials conducted under Louis XIV,
      with details of the testimony elicited from participants.

  *   Masters, R.E.L., and Eduard Lea. PERVERSE CRIMES IN
      HISTORY. Cited above as item 18, pp. 9-10.

      Case history in a discussion of sexually-motivated
      murders.

      242. GUNNESS, BELLA POULSDATTER SORENSON (S)

      Acquitted of killing her second husband with a hatchet
at La Porte, Ind., Gunness began to advertise for future matrimonial prospects in the Chicago newspapers. (A previous
husband had also died mysteriously, in Chicago.) Billing herself as a "rich, good-looking widow," she attracted several
would-be husbands in the first decade of the 20th century.
Victims were invariably drugged, robbed, strangled, and dismembered, their remains fed to pigs or buried on the Gunness
farm. In April 1908, the Gunness home burned down; the
bodies of Belle's three children were recovered from the rubble,
along with a corpse believed to be hers. Searchers inadvert-
ently discovered the remains of numerous male victims at the
same time; published body-counts range from 13 to 28. It was
subsequently claimed, but never proved, that Gunness faked
her own death, murdering her children and substituting
another woman's body for her own, escaping with the proceeds
of her robberies to parts unknown. (Belle had a knack for
arson; a rooming house she owned in Chicago had also burned
down, improving her financial outlook with insurance payments.)
A local handyman was charged with arson in the case, but never
with the deaths of Gunness of her children.

                            Books

  *   CRIMES AND PUNISHMENT: A PICTORIAL ENCYCLOPEDIA OF ABER-
      RANT BEHAVIOR, Volume 4. Cited above as item 4, pp.
      58-60.

      Case history in a chapter on "lonely-hearts" killers.

  *   Jones, Ann. WOMEN WHO KILL. Cited above as item 13,
      pp. 129-139.

A feminist perspective on the Gunness case.

283. Langlois, Janet L.   BELLE GUNNESS: THE LADY BLUEBEARD.
     Bloomington, Ind.: Indiana University Press, 1985.

     A local scholar examines the case from a modern
     perspective.

  * Nash, Jay Robert.   ALMANAC OF WORLD CRIME.   Cited above
     as item 19, pp. 281-282.

     Case history in a general discussion of mass murder.

  * ————.   LOOK FOR THE WOMAN.   Cited above as item 22,
     pp. 176-177.

     Case history presented in an encyclopedic format,
     listing 13 victims.

  * ————.   MURDER, AMERICA.   Cited above as item 23, p. 379.

     Sketchy case history presented in time line format.

  * Scott, Sir Harold.   THE CONCISE ENCYCLOPEDIA OF CRIME
     AND CRIMINALS.   Cited above as item 27, p. 160.

     Case history presented in an encyclopedic format.

  * Sifakis, Carl.   THE ENCYCLOPEDIA OF AMERICAN CRIME.
     Cited above as item 29, pp. 304-305.

     Case history presented in an encyclopedic format.

284. Torre, Lillian de la.   THE TRUTH ABOUT BELLE GUNNESS.
     New York: Gold Medal, 1955.

     Paperback examination of the case.   Its "truth" re-
     mains subject to question.

  * Wilson, Colin, and Patricia Putnam.   THE ENCYCLOPEDIA
     OF MURDER.   Cited above as item 35, pp. 247-249.

     Case history presented in an encyclopedic format.

                              Articles

285. Hynd, A.   "Madame Bluebeard."   GOOD HOUSEKEEPING 119
     (December 1944): 42+.

Historical retrospective on the Gunness case.

243. HAARMANN, FRITZ (S)

"The Hanover Vampire," homosexual slayer of at least 28
German youths between 1918 and 1924. Haarmann sexually molested his victims, killed them by biting their throats, and then
dismembered their bodies, frequently selling the flesh as
black market "beef" in war-torn Hanover. Many of the killings
were planned by accomplice Hans Grans, who kept the victims'
clothing for himself. The typical victims were male transients and runaways, between the ages of thirteen and twenty.
Haarmann ultimately confessed to 28 murders, but police
believed his total body-count may have been closer to 50.
Detectives asserted that Grans and Haarmann averaged two victims a week during their last eighteen months together; the
media was quick to note that some 600 boys were missing from
Hanover during Haarmann's heyday. Haarmann was put to death;
Grans, already jailed on other charges when the case was
broken, never came to trial.

* Boar, Roger, and Nigel Blundell. THE WORLD'S MOST IN-
    FAMOUS MURDERS. Cited above as item 2, pp. 78-79.

    Sensational case history presented in tabloid style.

* Douthwaite, L.C. MASS MURDER. Cited above as item 6.

    Then-recent case history of Haarmann's crimes.

* Gaute, J.H.H., and Robin Odell. THE MURDERERS' WHO'S
    WHO. Cited above as item 8, p. 118.

    Case history presented in an encyclopedic format.

* Green, Jonathon. THE GREATEST CRIMINALS OF ALL TIME.
    Cited above as item 11, p. 272.

    Brief case history in an encyclopedic format.

* Hurwood, Bernhardt J. VAMPIRES, WEREWOLVES, AND GHOULS.
    Cited above as item 12, pp. 109-114.

    Sensational case history in an anthology of "human
    monsters."

* Masters, R.E.L., and Eduard Lea. PERVERSE CRIMES IN
    HISTORY. Cited above as item 18, pp. 102-105, 169, 172.

Case history in a general discussion of vampirism.

* Nash, Jay Robert. ALMANAC OF WORLD CRIME. Cited above
  as item 19, pp. 285-287.

Case history in a discussion of mass murder.

* ————. CRIME CHRONOLOGY, 1900-1983. Cited above as
  item 21, p. 63.

Brief case history presented in time line format.

* Wilson, Colin. A CRIMINAL HISTORY OF MANKIND. Cited
  above as item 34, p. 607.

Case history in a discussion of modern mass murder.

* ————, and Patricia Putnam. THE ENCYCLOPEDIA OF MURDER.
  Cited above as item 35, pp. 249-251.

Case history presented in an encyclopedic format.

244. HAHN, ANNA MARIE (S)

Poisoner of at least six elderly men who enticed her
lonely victims with romance, then killed them and looted their
bank accounts. Her luck ran out when she failed in an attempt
to poison her husband during 1937. Convicted on two counts
of murder in 1938, Hahn became the first woman to be executed
in Ohio's history.

* Nash, Jay Robert. CRIME CHRONOLOGY, 1900-1983. Cited
  above as item 21, p. 109.

Brief case history presented in time line format.

* Sifakis, Carl. THE ENCYCLOPEDIA OF AMERICAN CRIME.
  Cited above as item 29, p. 307.

Case history presented in an encyclopedic format.

245. HAIGH, JOHN GEORGE (S)

British slayer of at least nine persons in the 1940s.
While not averse to robbing his victims, living off the proceeds of his crimes, Haigh also confessed an uncontrollable
desire to drink human blood. His chosen victims were bludgeoned to death, their bodies dissolved in a vat of acid after Haigh

had slaked his thirst. Documents and physical remains found at his home substantiated Haigh's confession, and he was executed in August 1949.

* Boar, Roager, and Nigel Blundell. THE WORLD'S MOST IN-FAMOUS MURDERS. Cited above as item 2, pp. 71-73.

    Sensational case history presented in tabloid style.

* CRIMES AND PUNISHMENT: A PICTORIAL ENCYCLOPEDIA OF ABER-RANT BEHAVIOR, Volume 7. Cited above as item 4, p. 37.

    Case history presented in an encyclopedic format.

* Gaute, J.H.H., and Robin Odell. THE MURDERERS' WHO'S WHO. Cited above as item 8, pp. 118-120.

    Case history presented in an encyclopedic format.

* Green, Jonathon. THE GREATEST CRIMINALS OF ALL TIME. Cited above as item 11, p. 255.

    Brief case history in an encyclopedic format.

* Masters, R.E.L., and Eduard Lea. PERVERSE CRIMES IN HISTORY. Cited above as item 18, pp. 107-109, 173-174.

    Case history in a general discussion of vampirism.

* Nash, Jay Robert. CRIME CHRONOLOGY, 1900-1983. Cited above as item 21, p. 136.

    Brief case history presented in time line format.

* Tullet, Tom. STRICTLY MURDER. Cited above as item 32.

    Case history in an anthology of Scotland Yard's cases.

* Wilson, Colin. A CRIMINAL HISTORY OF MANKIND. Cited above as item 34, p. 85.

    Case history in a discussion of sexually-motivated murders.

* ———, and Patricia Putnam. THE ENCYCLOPEDIA OF MURDER. Cited above as item 35, pp. 252-255.

    Case history presented in an encyclopedic format.

246. HAIGHT, EDWARD (M)

Seventeen-year-old who murdered his two sisters during a family dispute, in September 1942. Put to death in the electric chair at Sing Sing, ten months later.

* FACTS ON FILE. Volume 3, 1943. Cited above as item 7, p. 222.

Reports Haight's execution in New York.

247. HALL, ARCHIBALD (S)

British jewel thief and swindler, guilty, with accomplice Michael Kitto, of at least five murders. Victims included Hall's brother and female partner in crime, as well as targets of various confidence schemes gone wrong. Arrested in 1978, both men confessed their crimes. Kitto received a sentence of fifteen years, while Hall was imprisoned for life without parole.

286. Lucas, Norman, and Phil Davies. THE MONSTER BUTLER. London: Arthur Barker, 1979.

The only book-length account of Hall's case. Instructive.

* Wilson, Colin, and Donald Seaman. THE ENCYCLOPEDIA OF MODERN MURDER. Cited above as item 36, pp. 87-91.

Case history presented in an encyclopedic format.

248. HALL, LEO (M)

With a female accomplice, Hall entered a rural cottage near Erland Point, Wash., in March 1934, with the intention of committing robbery. The six adult residents were bound, then bludgeoned with a hammer, after which Hall shot each victim in the head "to make sure." Hanged in 1935.

* Nash, Jay Robert. CRIME CHRONOLOGY, 1900-1983. Cited above as item 21, p. 98.

Brief case history presented in time line format.

* ———. MURDER, AMERICA. Cited above as item 23, p. 409.

Sketchy case history presented in time line format.

249. HANSEN, ROBERT (S)

Pled guilty in 1984 to charges of murdering four women
in Anchorage, Alaska. Upon his arrest, Hansen confessed to
the murders of seventeen women, mostly prostitutes, over a
ten-year period. His usual method involved abduction of
streetwalkers, who were then flown to remote areas and released for Hansen to stalk, rape, and murder in a sort of
"hunting expedition." Sentenced to 461 years in prison.

* FACTS ON FILE. Volume 44, 1984. Cited above as item 7,
  p. 978.

  Reports Hansen's confession and sentencing.

* Levin, Jack, and James Alan Fox. MASS MURDER: AMERICA'S
  GROWING MENACE. Cited above as item 15.

  Case history in a general discussion of serial murder.

250. HARE, WILLIAM (S): See BURKE, WILLIAM

251. HARPE, WILLIAM MICAJAH and WILEY (S)

Tory guerillas in their native North Carolina, the Harpe
brothers moved west after Britain's defeat in the American
Revolution, becoming the scourge of travelers along the Wilderness Trail. Robbery and brutal murder were a form of sport
for "Big" and "Little" Harpe. In the 1790s, a series of
particularly vicious murders were attributed to the Harpes,
with victims disemboweled, weighted internally with stones,
and dumped into rivers as a means of disposal. Several dozen
homicides were credited to the brothers before they were
finally cornered by a posse in the Ohio Territory, during 1799.
Wiley escaped, but his older brother was wounded, captured,
and decapitated on the spot by vengeful members of the posse,
his skull nailed to a roadside tree as a permanent warning to
highwaymen. There were no further incidents with Wiley Harpe—
or, at least none where witnesses survived to tell the tale—
and he is presumed to have died in the trackless frontier
wilderness sometime in early 1800.

* Demaris, Ovid. AMERICA THE VIOLENT. Cited above as
  item 5, pp. 29-32.

  Brief case history in a survey of American violence.

* Nash, Jay Robert. BLOODLETTERS AND BADMEN. Cited
  above as item 20, pp. 246-247.

  Case history presented in an encyclopedic format.

252. HARPER, ROBERT (S)

Escapee from a Michigan prison who killed two persons
in 1931. Upon his recapture, Harper murdered the prison's
warden and the warden's deputy. Sentenced to die.

* Brian, Denis. MURDERERS DIE. Cited above as item 3,
  p. 259.

  Case history in an anthology of killers who were put
  to death.

253. HARPER, STEVEN ROY (M)

Nebraska slayer who poisoned three victims with a cancer-
causing rocket fuel additive in September 1978. Two victims—
the man who had married Harper's former girlfriend and the
man's infant nephew—died; a third victims, the dead man's
two-year-old daughter, survived. Harper was sentenced to
death in November 1979.

* FACTS ON FILE. Volume 39, 1979. Cited above as item 7,
  p. 891.

  Contemporaneous report of Harper's sentencing.

254. HARRIES, THOMAS RONALD (M)

British murderer who killed his aunt and uncle at their
farm, near Carmarthenshire, England, in October 1953, burying
the bodies in a nearby field. Detectives disbelieved his
story of a sudden trip to London, and staged a disturbance
outside the farmhouse several nights later. When Harries
rushed to check the secret graves, he was arrested. Convicted
of murder and hanged.

* Nash, Jay Robert. CRIME CHRONOLOGY, 1900-1983. Cited
  above as item 21, pp. 147-148.

  Brief case history presented in time line format.

255. HARVEY, JULIAN (M)

American sea captain who massacred all but one of his passengers and crew in 1961, while trying to "get rid of his wife." Upon learning that his infant daughter had survived the massacre, Harvey killed himself.

* Reinhardt, James Melvin. THE PSYCHOLOGY OF STRANGE
  KILLERS. Cited above as item 70, pp. 5-7.

  Brief psychological case study.

* Sifakis, Carl. THE ENCYCLOPEDIA OF AMERICAN CRIME.
  Cited above as item 29, p. 318.

  Case history presented in an encyclopedic format.

256. HART, GENE LEROY (M)

Escaped convict suspected as the sex-slayer of three young girls at a Girl Scout camp in Oklahoma, during June 1977. Hart, a Cherokee Indian, was arrested in April 1978 and was acquitted of murder charges in early 1979. Several of Hart's alibi witnesses were subsequently charged with perjury, and police remain convinced of his guilt, despite the acquittal. Returned to prison as an escapee, Hart died in June 1979, while exercising in the prison yard.

* FACTS ON FILE. Volume 37, 1977. Cited above as item 7,
  pp. 492, 711.

  Reports the Oklahoma crimes and manhunt.

* FACTS ON FILE. Volume 38, 1978. Cited above as item 7,
  p. 380.

  Reports Hart's arrest on murder charges.

* FACTS ON FILE. Volume 39, 1979. Cited above as item 7,
  pp. 291, 508.

  Reports Hart's acquittal and subsequent death.

287. Wilderson, Michael and Dick. SOMEONE CRY FOR THE
     CHILDREN. New York: Dial Press, 1981.

     Detailed examination of the case which concurs with
     police in finding Hart guilty as charged.

257. HASTINGS, JEFFREY (M)

Convicted of murdering his wife in 1973, Hastings escaped from prison and was still at large in 1980, when he drowned a Haitian woman and her five children during an abortive smuggling attempt. Convicted of manslaughter in April 1980, he was sentenced to an additional 180 years in prison.

* FACTS ON FILE. Volume 40, 1980. Cited above as item 7, p. 503.

    Reports Hastings' manslaughter conviction.

258. HEATH, NEVILLE GEORGE CLEVELY (S)

Sadistic slayer of at least five London women during 1946. A practitioner of bondage and flagellation, Heath was several times arrested prior to the commission of his first homicide. Convicted in that case, despite a lame insanity defense, he waived appeal and was hanged in October 1946.

* Boar, Roger, and Nigel Blundell. THE WORLD'S MOST IN-FAMOUS MURDERS. Cited above as item 2, pp. 84-89.

    Sensational case history presented in tabloid style.

* CRIMES AND PUNISHMENT: A PICTORIAL ENCYCLOPEDIA OF ABERRANT BEHAVIOR, Volume 1. Cited above as item 4, pp. 89-96.

    Case history presented in an encyclopedic format.

* FACTS ON FILE. Volume 6, 1946. Cited above as item 7, p. 311.

    Reports Heath's conviction and sentencing.

* Green, Jonathon. THE GREATEST CRIMINALS OF ALL TIME. Cited above as item 11, pp. 255-256.

    Brief case history in an encyclopedic format.

* Nash, Jay Robert. CRIME CHRONOLOGY, 1900-1983. Cited above as item 21, p. 128.

    Brief case history presented in time line format.

*   Scott, Sir Harold. THE CONCISE ENCYCLOPEDIA OF CRIME
     AND CRIMINALS. Cited above as item 27, p. 181.

     Case history presented in an encyclopedic format.

*   Wilson, Colin. A CRIMINAL HISTORY OF MANKIND. Cited
     above as item 34, p. 617.

     Case history in a discussion of modern mass murder.

*   ————, and Patricia Putnam. THE ENCYCLOPEDIA OF MURDER.
     Cited above as item 35, pp. 272-274.

     Case history presented in an encyclopedic format.

259. HEIRENS, WILLIAM (S)

     Teenaged Chicago burglar who murdered two women and a
six-year-old girl during a four-month period of 1945-1946.
Heirens committed scores of other burglaries, with at least
one more assault, achieving orgasm while looting the homes of
strangers. At one crime scene, he left a message scrawled in
lipstick: "For heaven's sake catch me before I kill more. I
cannot control myself." Arrested during a June 1946 break-in,
Heirens was eventually sentenced to three consecutive terms
of life imprisonment. To the end, he steadfastly protested
his innocence, blaming the murders on an alter-ego called
"George Murman" (short for "Murder Man").

*   CRIMES AND PUNISHMENT: A PICTORIAL ENCYCLOPEDIA OF ABER-
     RANT BEHAVIOR, Volume 20. Cited above as item 4, pp.
     91-92.

     Case history presented in an encyclopedic format.

288. Downs, Thomas. MURDER MAN. New York: Dell, 1984.

     Paperback case history, including lengthy excerpts
     from Heirens' confessions.

*   FACTS ON FILE. Volume 6, 1946. Cited above as item 7,
     pp. 16, 258.

     Reports Heirens' arrest and confession.

289. Freeman, Lucy. "BEFORE I KILL MORE..." New York:
      Crown Publishers, 1955.

Detailed examination of the case, flawed by the
author's eagerness to accept the killer's insanity plea
at face value. Includes Herins' complete confession.

*   Gaute, J.H.H., and Robin Odell. THE MURDERERS' WHO'S
    WHO. Cited above as item 8, pp. 124-125.

    Case history presented in an encyclopedic format.

*   Green, Jonathon. THE GREATEST CRIMINALS OF ALL TIME.
    Cited above as item 11, p. 184.

    Brief case history in an encyclopedic format.

*   Nash, Jay Robert. ALMANAC OF WORLD CRIME. Cited above
    as item 19, p. 220.

    Brief case history in a discussion of mass murder.

*   ————. BLOODLETTERS AND BADMEN. Cited above as item
    20, pp. 253-255.

    Case history presented in an encyclopedic format.

*   ————. CRIME CHRONOLOGY, 1900-1983. Cited above as
    item 21, pp. 126-127.

    Brief case history presented in time line format.

*   ————. MURDER, AMERICA. Cited above as item 23, p. 419.

    Sketchy case history presented in time line format.

*   Scott, Sir Harold. THE CONCISE ENCYCLOPEDIA OF CRIME
    AND CRIMINALS. Cited above as item 27, p. 182.

    Case history presented in an encyclopedic format.

*   Sifakis, Carl. THE ENCYCLOPEDIA OF AMERICAN CRIME.
    Cited above as item 29, pp. 326-327.

    Case history presented in an encyclopedic format.

*   Wilson, Colin. A CRIMINAL HISTORY OF MANKIND. Cited
    above as item 34, pp. 613-614.

    Case history in a discussion of modern lust murder.

* ———, and Patricia Putnam. THE ENCYCLOPEDIA OF MURDER.
   Cited above as item 35, pp. 274-276.

Case history presented in an encyclopedic format.

260. HELLIER, THOMAS (M)

Virginia laborer who axed his man-and-wife employers to
death, along with their maid, in 1678. Convicted and hanged.

* Green, Jonathon. THE GREATEST CRIMINALS OF ALL TIME.
   Cited above as item 11, p. 256.

Case history presented in an encyclopedic format.

261. HENLEY, ELMER WAYNE (S): See CORLL, DEAN ARNOLD

262. HERNANDEZ, MANUEL J. (M): See BATES, CLYDE

263. HICKOCK, RICHARD E. (M)

With accomplice Perry Smith, murdered four members of
the Clutter family following a bungled robbery attempt in
Kansas, during November 1959. Traced to Las Vegas, the killers
were returned for trial and sentenced to death. Hanged in
April 1965.

Books

* Brian, Denis. MURDERERS DIE. Cited above as item 3,
   pp. 105-118.

Case history in an anthology of killers who were put
to death.

290. Capote, Truman. IN COLD BLOOD. New York: New American
      Library, 1965.

Over-rated "nonfiction novel" which set the standard
for subsequent works in the true-crime genre. Capote's
book, and the Hollywood film it inspired, are heavily
laced with anti-death penalty propaganda. An entertaining read, if taken as the novel that it is.

* FACTS ON FILE. Volume 20, 1960. Cited above as item 7,
   p. 8.

Reports confessions in the Clutter case.

* FACTS ON FILE. Volume 25, 1965. Cited above as item 7, p. 508.

  Reports the hanging of Hickock and Smith.

* Green, Jonathon. THE GREATEST CRIMINALS OF ALL TIME. Cited above as item 11, p. 151.

  Brief case history in an encyclopedic format.

* Nash, Jay Robert. CRIME CHRONOLOGY, 1900–1983. Cited above as item 21, p. 159.

  Brief case history presented in time line format.

* Sifakis, Carl. THE ENCYCLOPEDIA OF AMERICAN CRIME. Cited above as item 29, pp. 154–155.

  Case history presented in an encyclopedic format.

* Wilson, Colin, and Donald Seaman. THE ENCYCLOPEDIA OF MODERN MURDER. Cited above as item 36, pp. 210–211.

  Case history presented in an encyclopedic format.

Articles

291. Greene, T. "In Cold Blood." NEWSWEEK 67 (January 24, 1966): 59–63.

     Reviews item 290 above.

292. Howard, J. "Horror Spawns a Masterpiece." LIFE 60 (January 7, 1966): 72+.

     Pictorial retrospective of the case and Capote's involvement with the killers.

264. HICKS, ALBERT E. (M)

Seaman who murdered his captain and two fellow sailors on an oyster boat bound from Virginia to New York, during March 1860. Robbery was the apparent motive, and Hicks confessed his crimes. Hanged in July 1860.

* Logan, Guy B.H. MASTERS OF CRIME. Cited above as item 17, pp. 178–179.

Case history in an anthology of 19th-century murders.

265. HICKS, RICHARD HAROLD (M)

Deranged motorist who, in 1974, spent six hours driving along Interstate 10 from Los Angeles to Phoenix, shooting other drivers from his car. Hicks killed three persons and wounded another six before he was finally apprehended by police.

* Tobias, Ronald. THEY SHOOT TO KILL. Cited above as item 31, p. 134.

Brief case history in a discussion of criminal snipers.

266. "HIGHWAY MURDERS, THE" (S)

Unsolved sex murders of 28 young women in the western provinces of Canada during the 1970s and early 1980s. Victims were raped, then stabbed or strangled by their killer(s). Police efforts to connect killers Ted Bundy, Harvey Carignan, and Henry Lucas with the crimes have thus far produced no viable results.

293. Gray, M. "Hunting the Highway Murderer(s)." MACLEANS 94 (November 20, 1981): 27-28.

Surveys the murder series, with a partial list of victims.

267. HILL, DAVID (S): See KEARNEY, PATRICK

268. HILL, HAROLD (M)

British soldier and pedophile who abducted, stabbed, and strangled two young girls near Penn, Buckinghamshire, in November 1941. Hill was traced through laundry marks on a handkerchief dropped at the crime scene, and finally identified from fingerprints found on a gas mask, discarded nearby. Convicted of murder and hanged in 1942.

* Nash, Jay Robert. CRIME CHRONOLOGY, 1900-1983. Cited above as item 21, p. 118.

Sketchy case history presented in time line format.

269. HINDLEY, MYRA (S): See BRADY, IAN

270. HOBBS, N.M., MURDERS (M)

Trucker J.D. Cantrell was shot and killed near Hobbs, in July 1957, when he stopped to help two women change a tire on their car. The women, Dorothy Gibson and Barbara Lemmons, were abducted by the unknown gunman, subsequently murdered, and their bodies dumped 35 miles away from the original crime scene. Unsolved at this writing.

* FACTS ON FILE. Volume 17, 1957. Cited above as item 7, p. 240.

    Reports the Hobbs murders and manhunt.

271. HOCH, JOHANN OTTO (S)

Born John Schmidt, in Germany, this "bluebeard: moved to the United States and there began a long career of marrying— and murdering—for money. Between 1887 and 1898, Hoch wed and subsequently poisoned at least a dozen women; approximately fifteen more were slain between 1900 and 1905. Finally apprehended and convicted of a single murder charge, Hoch was hanged in New York during February 1906.

Books

* Boar, Roger, and Nigel Blundell. THE WORLD'S MOST IN-FAMOUS MURDERS. Cited above as item 2, pp. 90-91.

    Sensational case history presented in tabloid style.

* Gaute, J.H.H., and Robin Odell. THE MURDERERS' WHO'S WHO. Cited above as item 8, pp. 127-128.

    Case history presented in an encyclopedic format.

* Nash, Jay Robert. ALMANAC OF WORLD CRIME. Cited above as item 19, p. 281.

    Brief case history in a discussion of mass murder.

* ————. CRIME CHRONOLOGY, 1900-1983. Cited above as item 21, p. 15.

    Sketchy case history presented in time line format.

* ————. MURDER, AMERICA. Cited above as item 23, pp. 14, 125-129, 367, 447.

Case history in an anthology of "classic" homicides.

294. Schutzer, A.I. "The Lady Killer." STORIES OF GREAT
      CRIMES AND TRIALS, FROM AMERICAN HERITAGE MAGAZINE.
      New York: McGraw Hill, 1965.

      Reprints item 295 below.

   * Sifakis, Carl. THE ENCYCLOPEDIA OF AMERICAN CRIME.
      Cited above as item 28, pp. 337-338.

      Case history presented in an encyclopedic format.

                            Articles

295. Schutzer, A.I. "The Lady Killer." AMERICAN HERITAGE
      15 (October 1964): 36-39+.

      Presents an engaging portrait of Hoch's career in
      matrimonial murder.

                    `272. HOFFMAN, KUNO (S)

German necrophile in the pattern of Wisconsin's Ed Gein.
Hoffman was known to exhume corpses by moonlight, gnawing on
the remains, until such activities no longer provided the
necessary stimulation. Slayer of at least three victims,
each of whom was bitten and raped after death. Sentenced to
life imprisonment.

   * Green, Jonathon. THE GREATEST CRIMINALS OF ALL TIME.
      Cited above as item 11, p. 272.

      Brief case history in an encyclopedic format.

                    273. HOLMAN, GEORGE (S)

Pyromaniac active in the San Francisco-Oakland area
during March 1944. Holman set eleven fires during a three-day
period, claiming 22 lives. Upon arrest and conviction, he
was sentenced to 22 consecutive terms of life imprisonment.

   * Nash, Jay Robert. ALMANAC OF WORLD CRIME. Cited above
      as item 19, pp. 24-25.

      Brief case history in a discussion of arson.

274.   Deleted.

275. HONKA, FRITZ (S)

German necrophile and murderer, arrested in January 1975.
Police recovered mummified remains of several women in Honka's
apartment, but the final number of his victims is uncertain,
due to advanced decomposition of remains and Honka's faulty
memory. Sentenced to life.

* Green, Jonathon. THE GREATEST CRIMINALS OF ALL TIME.
  Cited above as item 11, pp. 272-273.

   Brief case history in an encyclopedic format.

276. HOOIJAIJERS, FRANS (S)

Former monk, later a nursing home attendant in the
Netherlands, convicted in 1971 of murdering five patients with
overdoses of insulin. Sentenced to thirteen years in prison
on those counts, Hooijaijers is suspected in as many as 259
other "suspicious" deaths spanning a five-year period.

* Nash, Jay Robert. ALMANAC OF WORLD CRIME. Cited above
  as item 19, p. 264.

   Brief case history in a discussion of mass murder.

277. HUBERTY, JAMES OLIVER (M)

Deranged gunman who opened fire on a crowd of diners at
McDonald's restaurant at San Ysidro, Calif., in July 1984.
Before he was slain by police snipers, Huberty killed 21 persons and wounded another 19, breaking the previous American
record for simultaneous mass murder. Following the massacre,
McDonald's razed their restaurant, in response to minority
damands (most of the victims were Hispanic), establishing a
"people's park" on the sight of the shootout.

                         Books

* FACTS ON FILE. Volume 44, 1984. Cited above as item 7,
  pp. 548, 979.

   Contemporaneous report of the San Ysidro massacre.

* Levin, Jack, and James Alan Fox. MASS MURDER: AMERICA'S
  GROWING MENACE. Cited above as item 15.

   Brief history in a discussion of mass murderers.

* Leyton, Elliott. COMPULSIVE KILLERS. Cited above as
  item 16, pp. 18-19.

  Brief case history lifted from newspaper clippings.

Articles

296. Burns, R.E. "Dressed to Kill." U.S. CATHOLIC 49 (Oc-
     tober 1984): 2.

     Examines the case from a religious viewpoint.

297. Gomez, L. "Ninety Minutes at McDonalds." LIFE 8 (Jan-
     uary 1985): 76-84+.

     Pictorial spread on the massacre.

298. Granberry, M., and B. Weinhouse. "The Children of San
     Ysidro." LADIES HOME JOURNAL 102 (January 1985): 59-60+.

     Examines the psychological aftermath of the shootout.

299. Leo, J. "Sudden Death." TIME 124 (July 30, 1984): 90-91.

     Contemporaneous report of the massacre.

300. O'Hara, J., and M. Posner. "The Massacre at McDonald's."
     MACLEANS 97 (July 30, 1984): 23-27.

     Canadian perspective on the shootout.

301. Strasser, S. "Murder at McDonald's." NEWSWEEK 104
     (July 30, 1984): 30-31.

     Contemporaneous report of the massacre.

302. "When Rage Turns Into Mass Murder." U.S. NEWS & WORLD
     REPORT 97 (July 30, 1984): 14.

     Contemporaneous report of the San Ysidro massacre.

278. HUNTER, MARK (M): See WALTER, MARK

279. HUNTER, RICHARD (S)

Convicted forger and drug abuser charged with the
strangulation murders of four elderly black women in Atlanta,
Ga., during March and April 1986. Disposition of the case

is pending, although media reports indicate that Hunter has pled guilty to at least one of the four "identical" crimes.

303. "A Lady Killer Stalks Atlanta." TIME 127 (April 28, 1986): 38.

    Reports on the murders, prior to Hunter's arrest.

280. HUTCHINSON, JOHN JAMES (M)

    Chemist's assistant in Dalkeith, Englang, who poisoned 17 persons at his parents' silver anniversary party, lacing their coffee with arsenic in an attempt to hasten his inheritance. Sentenced to life imprisonment, Hutchinson committed suicide by poison in February 1911.

  * Nash, Jay Robert. CRIME CHRONOLOGY, 1900-1983. Cited above as item 21, p. 28.

    Case history presented in time line format.

281. HYDE, BENNETT CLARKE (S)

    Homicidal doctor indicted during February 1910, in Kansas City, for poisoning several rich in-laws. Despite persuasive evidence of guilt, Hyde was freed after three marathon trials, in which jurors were allegedly bribed to assure a "hung" jury.

  * Nash, Jay Robert. CRIME CHRONOLOGY, 1900-1983. Cited above as item 21, p. 25.

    Sketchy case history presented in time line format.

282. HUSSEY, CHARLES (M)

    Slayer of a wealthy man and his houskeeper at Greenwich, England, during 1818. Both victims were bludgeoned to death, and the house looted. Hussey called attention to himself by paying off substantial debts a short time later. Upon arrest, he quickly confessed and was hanged.

  * Logan, Guy B.H. MASTERS OF CRIME. Cited above as item 17, pp. 225-226.

    Brief case history in an anthology of 19th-century multicides.

283. INGENITO, ERNEST (M)

Angered by an argument with his wife, Ingenito went berserk in Minotola, N.J., during 1950, shooting her and eight
other persons, only one of whom survived. Found to be insane
by court-appointed psychiatrists, he was committed to the
state hospital for life.

* FACTS ON FILE. Volume 10, 1950. Cited above as item 7,
    p. 380.

    Reports Ingenito's crimes and arrest.

* FACTS ON FILE. Volume 11, 1951. Cited above as item 7,
    p. 40.

    Reports Ingenito's sentencing.

* Gaute, J.H.H., and Robin Odell. THE MURDERERS' WHO'S
    WHO. Cited above as item 8, p. 132.

    Case history presented in an encyclopedic format.

* Green, Jonathon. THE GREATEST CRIMINALS OF ALL TIME.
    Cited above as item 11, p. 151.

    Brief case history in an encyclopedic format.

* Nash, Jay Robert. ALMANAC OF WORLD CRIME. Cited above
    as item 19, pp. 288-289.

    Brief case history in a discussion of mass murder.

* ————. BLOODLETTERS AND BADMEN. Cited above as item
    20, pp. 261-263.

    Case history presented in an encyclopedic format.

* ————. CRIME CHRONOLOGY, 1900-1983. Cited above as
    item 21, p. 139.

    Brief case history presented in time line format.

* ————. MURDER, AMERICA. Cited above as item 23, p. 421.

    Sketchy case history presented in time line format.

* Steiger, Brad. THE MASS MURDERER. Cited above as item
  30.

    Brief case history in a quicky paperback treatment of
    the general subject.

284. IRWIN, ROBERT (M)

Deranged New York sculptor who once attempted self-
castration in an effort to help himself concentrate on art.
Despondent over unemployment, Irwin went to the home of his
lover in March 1937, there strangling the woman, her mother,
and her sister. In a subsequent attack, he killed a next-door
neighbor with an ice pick, apparently seeking to eliminate
potential witnesses. Sentenced to life.

* CRIMES AND PUNISHMENT: A PICTORIAL ENCYCLOPEDIA OF ABER-
  RANT BEHAVIOR, Volume 20. Cited above as item 4, pp.
  92-93.

    Case history presented in an encyclopedic format.

* Nash, Jay Robert. CRIME CHRONOLOGY, 1900-1983. Cited
  above as item 21, p. 109.

    Brief case history presented in time line format.

* ————. MURDER, AMERICA. Cited above as item 23, pp.
  412-413.

    Sketchy case history presented in time line format.

* Wilson, Colin. A CASEBOOK OF MURDER. Cited above as
  item 33, p. 12.

    Brief psychological case study of Irwin.

285. ISSACS, CARL and BILLY (M)

Brothers and escaped convicts who, with half-brother
Wayne Coleman and black accomplice George Dungee, murdered six
members of the Alday family in rural Georgia during May 1973.
All members of the family were shot execution-style, with the
only female member being raped and sodomized repeatedly prior
to death. Billy Issacs turned state's evidence against the
other three, receiving a life sentence while the rest were
sentenced to die. In 1986, an appeals court overturned the
death sentences of Coleman and Carl Issacs, citing pretrial

publicity as an impediment to fair trial. Presently awaiting
retrial with a change of venue.

* Godwin, John. MURDER USA. Cited above as item 10, pp.
  297-299.

     Case history within a general discussion of mass murder.

304. Howard, Clark. BROTHERS IN BLOOD. New York: St. Martin's
     Press, 1983.

     An excellent and engrossing study of the Alday mass-
     acre, providing insight into lives of both the killers
     and victims. Well worth reading.

* Nash, Jay Robert. CRIME CHRONOLOGY, 1900-1983. Cited
  above as item 21, pp. 184-185.

     Brief case history presented in time line format.

286. "IVAN THE RIPPER" (S)

     Unidentified slayer of several women in Moscow, USSR,
during October 1974. According to rumors, never confirmed,
the killer chose his victims on the subway, followed them to
nearby darkened streets, and there killed them with a cobbler's
knife. The arrest of a suspect was "unofficially" announced
in early November 1974, but deliberate confusion still sur-
rounds this case of serial murder behind the Iron Curtain.

305. "Ivan the Ripper." NEWSWEEK 84 (November 11, 1974): 55.

     Contemporaneous report of the rumor-ridden case.

287. "JACK THE RIPPER" (S)

     Unidentified slayer of five prostitutes in the White-
chapel district of London during autumn, 1888. The Ripper
taunted police with mocking letters, and on one occasion mailed
a portion of one victim's kidney to authorities. Suspects in
the tantalizing case have ranged from Jewish slaughtermen and
barber surgeons to members of the British royal family, but
no conclusive evidence against any suspect has yet been produced. Some authorities regard the Ripper case as the "father"
of modern sex crimes, although Jack was neither the first nor
most prolific of the early serial killers. Curiously, during
1885-1888, other unsolved "ripper" homicides were reported in
Moscow, in the state of Texas, and in Nicaragua, suggesting

that the slayer may have traveled widely in his search for victims.

Books

306. Barnard, Allan (ed.). THE HARLOT KILLER. New York: Dodd, Mead, & Co., 1953.

An anthology of Ripper material, inlcuding both factual pieces and works of fiction based on the case.

*   Boar, Roger, and Nigel Blundell. THE WORLD'S MOST IN-FAMOUS MURDERS. Cited above as item 2, pp. 92-97.

Case history presented in sensational tabloid style.

*   CRIMES AND PUNISHMENT: A PICTORIAL ENCYCLOPEDIA OF ABER-RANT BEHAVIOR, Volume 20. Cited above as item 4, pp. 15-30.

Case history presented in an encyclopedic format.

307. Cullen, Tom A. WHEN LONDON WALKED IN TERROR. New York: Houghton Mifflin, 1965.

Names the Ripper as a London barrister, Montague John Druitt, who reputedly committed suicide shortly after the last genuine ripper slaying. Druitt was one of three prime suspects named in notes prepared by an officer in charge of the Ripper case, but the evidence against him remains entirely circumstantial, totally devoid of motive or any solid evidence that he participated in the murders.

308. Farson, Daniel. JACK THE RIPPER. London: Michael Joseph, 1972.

Reviews various "solutions" to the case, finally settling on suspect M.J. Druitt. Entertaining, but the same material was covered earlier—and better—in item 307 above.

*   Gaute, J.H.H., and Robin Odell. THE MURDERERS' WHO'S WHO. Cited above as item 8, pp. 133-134.

Case history presented in an encyclopedic format.

309. Harrison, Michael. CLARENCE. London: W.H. Allen, 1972.

      Despite the title, Harrison exonerates the Duke of
      Clarence as a Ripper suspect, naming the Duke's tutor
      and alleged homosexual lover, James Stephen, as the
      killer. Based primarily on handwriting comparisons and
      Stephen's apparent hatred of women, Harrison's analysis
      breaks down with the inclusion of several victims who
      were plainly killed by a Ripper copycat.

  *   Hurwood, Bernhardt J. VAMPIRES, WEREWOLVES, AND GHOULS.
      Cited above as item 12, pp. 95-100.

      Sensational case history in a catalogue of "human
      monsters."

310. Kelly, Alexander. JACK THE RIPPER: A BIBLIOGRAPHY AND
      REVIEW OF THE LITERATURE. London: Association of
      Assistant Librarians, 1973.

      A listing and examination of Ripper material.

311. Knight, Stephen. JACK THE RIPPER: THE FINAL SOLUTION.
      New York: Granada, 1977.

      Advances an elaborate conspiracy in which the British
      government and members of the Masonic lodge commit the
      Ripper murders to protect the Duke of Clarence from a
      scandal surrounding his secret marriage to a Catholic.
      In Knight's theory, there were three killers: Sir William
      Gull, Physician in Ordinary to the royal family; Gull's
      coachman, John Netley; and artist William Sickert, en-
      listed by the plotters for no apparent reason other than
      his loyalty to the lodge. Mutilations suffered by the
      victims are related to Masonic ritual and legend, but
      the overall account is flawed by Knight's reliance on
      the thoroughly discredited "Protocols of the Elders of
      Zion" as "proof" of the Masonic plot. Originally forged
      by Czarist agents as an antisemitic document, the
      "Protocols" are carelessly accepted by Knight as a
      "secret" Masonic plan for domination of the Christian
      world.

  *   Logan, Guy B.H. MASTERS OF CRIME. Cited above as item
      17, pp. 15-34.

      Suggests that the Ripper was a victim of veneral dis-
      ease, employing his convenient surgical skills to seek

revenge on London prostitutes.

312. McCormick, Donald. THE IDENTITY OF JACK THE RIPPER.
London: Arrow Books, 1970.

Names one Alexander Pedachenko, a Russian, as the
killer. Unfortunately, McCormick's case is based primarily on the memoirs of a gossip columnist and pathological liar, William Le Queux, which in turn allege
the "proof" of Pedachenko's guilt to be the writings of
Rasputin. Distinctly unreliable.

* Masters, R.E.L., and Eduard Lea. PERVERSE CRIMES IN
HISTORY. Cited above as item 18, pp. 82-88.

Generously credits the Ripper with "no more than 20
victims," when, in fact, he claimed only five.

313. Matters, Leonard. THE MYSTERY OF JACK THE RIPPER.
London: W.H. Allen, 1948.

Heavily fictionalized account of the case, naming a
British surgeon, one "Dr. Stanley," as the killer,
allegedly based on Stanley's own deathbed confessions.
Venereal disease is the culprit again, but this time
Stanley's son was the victim, inspiring his father to
embark on a homicidal course of revenge. Although
Matters could find no such Dr. Stanley in the medical
registers of Britain, he accepts the story anyway, inserting melodramatic dialogue and probing the minds of
his characters in a style more commonly associated with
pulp fiction.

* Nash, Jay Robert. ALMANAC OF WORLD CRIME. Cited above
as item 19, pp. 291-293.

Case history within a discussion of mass murder.

* ———. OPEN FILES. Cited above as item 24, pp. 120-
146.

Case history presented in an encyclopedic format.

314. Odell, Robin. JACK THE RIPPER IN FACT AND FICTION.
London: Harrap & Co., 1965.

Suggests, without a shred of evidence, that the Ripper
was a deranged Jewish slaughterman, employed at a kosher

slaughterhouse in Whitechapel. In the absence of a
specific suspect, Odell's colorful descriptions of the
killer's thought processes have no apparent validity.

315. Rumbelow, Donald. THE COMPLETE JACK THE RIPPER. Boston:
     New York Graphic Society, 1975.

     True to its title, Rumbelow's delightful reference
     work examines each and every suspect, theory, and bit
     of evidence revealed prior to 1975. Unique in his re-
     fusal to support a "pet" theory, Rumbelow, a former
     London police officer, reviews the strengths and weak-
     nesses of other theories with perfect objectivity. By
     far the best work on the Ripper case to date.

   * Scott, Sir Harold. THE CONCISE ENCYCLOPEDIA OF CRIME
     AND CRIMINALS. Cited above as item 27, pp. 197-198.

     Case history presented in an encyclopedic format.

316. Spiering, Frank. PRINCE JACK. Garden City, N.Y.:
     Doubleday, 1978.

     While passing by a London slaughterhouse one night, the
     Duke of Clarence suddenly goes insane, steals a knife,
     and begins attacking prostitutes for no apparent reason,
     while detectives cover up his crimes to spare the Queen
     embarrassment. Sadly lacking in motivation or evidence
     of any sort.

317. Stewart, William. JACK THE RIPPER. London: Quality
     Press, 1939.

     Opts for "Jill the Ripper," suggesting that the killer
     was a midwife and abortionist, seeking revenge on women
     in general after she was sent to prison on the testimony
     of a married "patient." The fanciful—and absolutely
     unsupported—theory is further weakened by the fact
     that only one Ripper victim, the last, was pregnant at
     the time of death, apparently eliminating any access
     by the lethal midwife to four preceding victims.

   * Wilson, Colin. A CASEBOOK OF MURDER. Cited above as
     item 33, pp. 133-148.

     Case history in a sociological survey of murder.

*   ————. A CRIMINAL HISTORY OF MANKIND. Cited above as
        item 34, pp. 483-486.

        Case history in a discussion of Victorian sex crimes.

*   ————. ORDER OF ASSASSINS. Cited above as item 76,
        pp. 229-235.

        Psychological examination of the Ripper case.

*   ————, and Patricia Putnam. THE ENCYCLOPEDIA OF MURDER.
        Cited above as item 35, pp. 209-305.

        Case history presented in an encyclopedic format.

Articles

318. Hubler, R.G. "Stunning Explanation of the Jack the
        Ripper Riddle." CORONET 41 (November 1956): 100-106.

        An early examination of the "case" against the Duke
of Clarence, heir to the British throne.

319. Hynd, A. "Murder Unlimited." GOOD HOUSEKEEPING 120
        (February 1945): 29+.

        A survey of the case, sans solutions.

288. "JACK THE STRIPPER" (S)

        Slayer of at least six British prostitutes, whose nude
bodies were dumped in or near the Thames during 1964 and 1965.
(As with Jack the Ripper, there is disagreement over the final
body-count. Some sources include two other victims, slain in
1959 and 1963, respectively.) In several cases, the victims'
front teeth were removed by the killer, apparently to facilitate oral sex. Particles of paint on several bodies indicated
they had lain in a paint shop for some time after death.
Despite continuing controversy over his identity (never published), most sources agree with Scotland Yard detectives
that the killer committed suicide in 1965.

Books

320. DuRose, John. MURDER WAS MY BUSINESS. London: W.H.
        Allen, 1971, pp. 92-107.

        The memoirs of a ranking homicide detective include a

chapter on the Stripper slayings. DuRose credits the killer
with six victims, claiming that a prime suspect committed
suicide within a month of the final murder. Even so, the
officer admits that "no positive evidence was available to
prove or disprove our belief that he was in fact the man we
were seeking. Because he was never arrested, or stood trial,
he must be considered innocent and will therefore never be
named."

*   Gaute, J.H.H., and Robin Odell. THE MURDERERS' WHO'S
    WHO. Cited above as item 8, p. 121.

    Case history presented in an encyclopedic format,
    suggesting a deceased heavy-weight boxer as the killer.

*   Green, Jonathon. THE GREATEST CRIMINALS OF ALL TIME.
    Cited above as item 11, p. 185.

    Brief case history in an encyclopedic format.

321. McConnell, Brian. FOUND NAKED AND DEAD. London: New
      English Library, 1974.

      Persuasively connects the Stripper with eight murders,
      rather than the "accepted" six. McConnell describes the
      slayer as an alcoholic ex-policeman, dubbed "Big John,"
      who took his own life in 1965. Easily the best account
      of the case ... but still devoid of any real conclusion.

*   Nash, Jay Robert. CRIME CHRONOLOGY, 1900-1983. Cited
    above as item 21, p. 169.

    Sketchy case history presented in time line format.

*   ————. OPEN FILES. Cited above as item 24, pp. 146-
    147.

    Brief case history in an encyclopedic format.

*   Purvis, James. GREAT UNSOLVED MYSTERIES. Cited above
    as item 26, pp. 40-46.

    Case history in an anthology of unsolved crimes.

*   Rumbelow, Donald. THE COMPLETE JACK THE RIPPER.
    Cited above as item 315, pp. 250-257.

    Compares the Stripper with London's gaslight ghoul.

* Wilson, Colin. ORDER OF ASSASSINS. Cited above as item 76, pp. 71-75.

   Psychological case study of the crimes.

* ————, and Donald Seaman. THE ENCYCLOPEDIA OF MODERN MURDER. Cited above as item 36, pp. 113-115.

   Case history presented in an encyclopedic format.

Articles

322. "Killer." NEWSWEEK 64 (December 24, 1964): 38.

   Reports the murders and manhunt in progress.

289. JACKSON, CALVIN (S)

While employed as a porter at New York's Park Plaza Hotel, between April 1973 and August 1974, Jackson raped, robbed, and murdered eight elderly female guests. Arrested following a ninth rape-murder, committed in an apartment building adjoining the hotel, Jackson received eighteen sentences of life imprisonment.

* Godwin, John. MURDER USA. Cited above as item 10, pp. 262-265.

   Case history in a discussion of multiple murder.

* Levin, Jack, and James Alan Fox. MASS MURDER: AMERICA'S GROWING MENACE. Cited above as item 15.

   Brief case history in a discussion of serial murder.

* Nash, Jay Robert. CRIME CHRONOLOGY, 1900-1983. Cited above as item 21, p. 184.

   Brief case history presented in time line format.

* ————. MURDER, AMERICA. Cited above as item 23, pp. 14, 301-303, 442.

   Case history in an anthology of "classic" homicides.

290. JACKSON, GARLAND (S): See "DE MAU MAU MURDERS"

291. Deleted.

292. JACKSON, GERTRUDE (M): See FREEMAN, JENNACE

293. JACKSON, RICHARD HILLIARD (S)

Violent alcoholic who was sentenced to ten years in prison for killing his infant stepson, in Maryland, during 1972. Paroled to a half-way house after serving only 20 months, Jackson was such an incorrigible drinker that authorities gave up on him and set him free to roam the streets without supervision. In July 1977, he was convicted of strangling an elderly woman to death and was returned to prison for life.

* Godwin, John. MURDER USA. Cited above as item 10, pp. 268-269.

  Case history in a survey of mentally-unbalanced killers.

294. JARRETTE, HENRY (S)

Escapee from a Georgia prison, where he was serving time for two murders. While free, Jarrette stabbed a young man to death in the course of stealing his car. Recaptured and returned to prison, with an additional life sentence.

* Brian, Dennis. MURDERERS DIE. Cited above as item 3, p. 261.

  Case history employed as an argument in favor of capital punishment.

295. JAYNE, JOHN (M)

Teenager in Moravia, N.Y., who shotgunned his parents, a brother and sister to death in January 1959. According to police, the slaughter was occasioned by Jayne's "resentment over a spanking last summer." Sentenced to life.

* FACTS ON FILE. Volume 19, 1959. Cited above as item 7, p. 48.

  Contemporaneous report of the crime and arrest.

296. "JEFFRIES THE MONSTER" (S)

Australian convict, rapist, and cannibal who claimed "several" victims in the 19th century. Killed by a posse when he resisted arrest.

* Green, Jonathon. THE GREATEST CRIMINALS OF ALL TIME. Cited above as item 11, p. 273.

Brief case history in an encyclopedic format.

297. JEGADO, HELENE (S)

French cook who poisoned an estimated 60 victims during her 20-year career, for the simple enjoyment of watching them suffer and die. Convicted and put to death in 1851.

* Green, Jonathon. THE GREATEST CRIMINALS OF ALL TIME. Cited above as item 11, p. 151.

   Brief case history in an encyclopedic format.

* Nash, Jay Robert. ALMANAC OF WORLD CRIME. Cited above as item 19, p. 272.

   Case history in a discussion of mass murder.

298. JOHNSON, JOEY (M)

Perpetrator, with accomplices Monty Landers and David Maxwell, of the October 1983 robbery-massacre at a Kentucky Fried Chicken restaurant in Kilgore, Texas. Five employees, including three men and two women, were shot to death as they stood with hands raised, after surrendering their money. All three killers were sentenced to die.

323. "Texas Massacre." TIME 122 (October 10, 1983): 27.

   Contemporaneous report of the murders and manhunt.

299. JOHNSON, POWELL (M)

New York ex-convict and aspiring artist who shot and killed two female coworkers, in Febraury 1959, after they "laughed at [his] paintings." Sentenced to life.

* FACTS ON FILE. Volume 19, 1959. Cited above as item 7, p. 56.

   Reports the murders and Johnson's arrest.

300. JOLIET, ILL., "WEEKEND MURDERS" (S?)

Unsolved series of 17 murders, committed on weekends, which terrorized Joliet, Ill., during the summer of 1983. Suspect Donald R. Lego, 51, was charged in one of the crimes, committed in September, but eyewitnesses describe a group of

younger men, still unidentified, as participants in the
murders committed between June and August. Killers still at
large.

Books

*   FACTS ON FILE. Volume 43, 1983. Cited above as item 7,
        p. 965.

    Reports the arrest of Lego, and police announcements
    that his case is unrelated to the other crimes.

*   Nash, Jay Robert. CRIME CHRONOLOGY, 1900-1983. Cited
        above as item 21, p. 205.

    Sketchy case history presented in time line format.

Articles

324. Beck, M. "The Weekend Murders Case." NEWSWEEK 102
        (September 5, 1983): 24.

    Reports the continuing investigation in progress.

301. JONES, GENENE (S)

    Texas "Death Nurse," linked with murders of six children
in Kerrville and "over a dozen" in San Antonio. All of the
victims were patients, injected with drugs as a form of "mercy"
killing. In other cases, Jones seemingly changed her mind,
appearing "euphoric" when she managed to revive a dying child
whom she had earlier poisoned. Sentenced to life in 1982.

*   Levin, Jack, and James Alan Fox. MASS MURDER: AMERICA'S
        GROWING MENACE. Cited above as item 15.

    Case history in a discussion of medical multicides.

302. JONES, GEORGE (M)

    Eleven-year-old boy who, in March 1958, confessed that
he had drowned two playmates, a four-year-old girl and a
seven-year-old boy, in the Hudson River because he was "angry."
Remanded to the custody of juvenile authorities.

*   FACTS ON FILE. Volume 18, 1958. Cited above as item 7,
        p. 76.

Reports the crimes and Jones' confession.

303. JONES, HAROLD (S)

Teenaged slayer of two children in separate incidents. Acquitted of killing an eight-year-old girl in February 1921, Jones fell under suspicion in the disappearance of an eleven-year-old girl two weeks after his trial. After the second victim's body was found in his attic, he confessed to both crimes and received a life sentence for the second slaying.

* Nash, Jay Robert. CRIME CHRONOLOGY, 1900-1983. Cited above as item 21, p. 55.

  Brief case history presented in time line format.

304. JORDAN, ROBERT WILLIAM (M)

Resident of Elizabeth City, N.C., who went berserk on learning he was to be drafted into military service. Jordan shot four coworkers, three of them fatally, during his 1954 rampage. Sentenced to life.

* Nash, Jay Robert. CRIME CHRONOLOGY, 1900-1983. Cited above as item 21, p. 150.

  Brief case history presented in time line format.

* ————. MURDER, AMERICA. Cited above as item 23, p. 424.

  Sketchy case history presented in time line format.

305. JOYNER, ANTHONY (S)

Former kitchen employee at a Philadelphia home for the elderly, charged in September 1983 with raping and murdering six women at the home in recent months. His victims ranged in age from 83 to 92 years. Joyner's case is still before the courts at this writing.

* Nash, Jay Robert. CRIME CHRONOLOGY, 1900-1983. Cited above as item 21, p. 205.

  Brief case history presented in time line format.

306. JUDY, STEPHEN T. (S?)

Stopping "to help" an Indiana motorist change her tire

in April 1979, Judy abducted the woman and her three small
children, driving them to a rural location where the woman
was raped and murdered. Judy then drowned all three children,
to eliminate witnesses. Previously convicted of brutal
assaults on women in Indianapolis and Chicago, Judy told the
jury at his trial: "You had better put me to death, because
next time it might be you or your daughter." The jury complied,
and he was sentenced to death in February 1980. Fending off
appeals and vocally asserting his desire to die, Judy referred
to "a string of bodies" in Texas, Florida, Louisiana, Illinois,
and Indiana. Claiming to have raped and murdered "more women
than he could remember," Judy offered up his vague confessions
in defense of others who might subsequently be charged with
"his" crimes. None of the other cases were corroborated prior
to his execution in 1981.

* FACTS ON FILE. Volume 41, 1981. Cited above as item 7,
  pp. 158-159.

  Reports Judy's execution.

* Levin, Jack, and James Alan Fox. MASS MURDER: AMERICA'S
  GROWING MENACE. Cited above as item 15.

  Passing reference in a discussion of multicide.

* Nash, Jay Robert. CRIME CHRONOLOGY, 19-0-1983. Cited
  above as item 21, p. 196.

  Sketchy case history presented in time line format.

* Wilson, Colin. A CRIMINAL HISTORY OF MANKIND. Cited
  above as item 34, p. 87.

  Case history in a discussion of "motiveless" murder.

* ————, and Donald Seaman. THE ENCYCLOPEDIA OF MODERN
  MURDER. Cited above as item 36, pp. 116-117.

  Case history presented in an encyclopedic format.

307. JUSTICE, JOHN, Jr. (M)

Seventeen-year-old who murdered his parents and younger
brother at the family home in Kenmore, N.Y., before a bungled
suicide attempt in September 1985. After slashing his wrists,
Justice drove off in the family car, crashing into another
vehicle and killing its driver instantly. Held for psychiatric
study prior to trial.

325. Hammer, Joshua. "Driven By His Long-Buried Rage, a
      17-Year-Old Honor Student Lethally Lashes Out at His
      Family." PEOPLE WEEKLY 24 (November 18, 1985): 127-130.

      Profiles Justice and his victims, seeking answers.

308. KALLINGER, JOSEPH (S)

      A product of abuse in childhood, Kallinger, a shoemaker,
would be convicted, in adulthood, of torturing his own children
as a form of "discipline." He also practiced homicide and
arson in the 1970s, claiming victims in Pennsylvania and New
Jersey. One of three known murder victims was his own son.
Ironically, another son sometimes accompanied Kallinger on
his felonious expeditions, participating in acts of torture
and homicide. Attempts to paint himself as suffering from a
"split personality" failed to impress a jury, and Kallinger
was sentenced to life.

Books

326. Schreiber, Flor Rheta. THE SHOEMAKER. New York: Simon
      & Schuster, 1983.

      The best-selling author of SYBIL finds another multi-
personality in Kallinger, providing a belated brief for
his insanity defense. Undoubtedly well-meaning, Schreiber swallows Kallinger's reports of floating heads and
disembodied voices calling out for blood with absolute
faith in the killer's veracity. So touched was Kallinger by his biogarpher's apparent trust that he composed
a sheaf of poems to her from his prison cell. Best
taken with a grain of salt.

Articles

327. Bell, A. "Wife of the Accused." ESQUIRE 84 (November
      1975): 132-135+.

      Examines Kallinger's home life, and his wife's
apparent tendency to overlook his strange behavior.

328. "Bizarre Case of Father and Son." TIME 105 (February
      3, 1975): 13-14.

      Contemporaneous report of Kallinger's crimes and
arrest.

309. KEARNEY, PATRICK (S)

Former aerospace worker and avowed homosexual, linked, with accomplice David D. Hill, to 28 "trash bag murders" in Southern California. So-called because dismembered victims had been dumped in plastic bags and trash cans from Los Angeles to Newport Beach, the murders claimed male victims exclusively. In December 1977, Kearney pled guilty to 21 counts of murder, receiving two concurrent life sentences. Prosecutors opted to dismiss seven other cases in return for Kearney's guilty plea. In February 1978, Kearney confessed to additional murders, bringing his total to 32, but no new prosecutions have reulsted at this writing.

Books

*   FACTS ON FILE. Volume 37, 1977. Cited above as item 7, p. 991.

    Reports Kearney's sentencing.

*   FACTS ON FILE. Volume 38, 1978. Cited above as item 7, p. 232.

    Details Kearney's new confessions.

*   Godwin, John. MURDER USA. Cited above as item 10, pp. 159-160.

    Brief case history in a discussion of "gay" murders.

*   Sifakis, Carl. THE ENCYCLOPEDIA OF AMERICAN CRIME. Cited above as item 29, p. 722.

    Case history presented in an encyclopedic format.

Articles

329. "Twenty-eight and Counting." TIME 110 (July 18, 1977): 49.

     Reports the arrests of Kearney and Hill.

330. Williams, D.A., and J. Huck. "Trash-bag Murders." NEWSWEEK 90 (July 18, 1977): 22.

     Contemporaneous report on the crimes and arrests.

310. KELBACH, WALTER (S)

With fellow ex-convict and homosexual Myron Lance, killed and raped two Salt Lake City, Utah, men on successive nights in 1966. The brutal crime spree climaxed with a barroom massacre, in which three additional victims were shot to death. Both killers were sentenced to die, their sentences later commuted to life imprisonment.

* Green, Jonathon. THE GREATEST CRIMINALS OF ALL TIME. Cited above as item 11, p. 151.

  Brief case history in an encyclopedic format.

* Nash, Jay Robert. MURDER, AMERICA. Cited above as item 23, pp. 14., 294-297, 436.

  Case history in an anthology of "classic" murders.

* Wilson, Colin. A CASEBOOK OF MURDER. Cited above as item 33, pp. 261-262.

  Case history in a sociological survey of homicide.

311. KEMPER, EDMUND EMIL III (S)

Classic sadist and necrophile, convicted in a string of brutal mutilation murders around Santa Cruz, Calif., in the early 1970s. As a child, Kemper mutilated his sister's dolls and slaughtered family pets, progressing to the murder of his maternal grandparents at age 14. Remanded to a state hospital for treatment, Kemper was paroled to his mother's care in 1969, against the advice of psychiatrists. Between May 1972 and February 1973, he murdered five co-eds from the local university, mutilating their bodies and enjoying sex with the remains. Tiring of the "sport," he turned on his family again in April 1973, killing his mother and one of her female friends. Kemper decapitated his mother's body, after which he raped it, pushed her larynx down the garbage disposal, and propped her head on the mantle to use it as a dart board. Finally satisfied, he voluntarily surrendered to police and was subsequently sentenced to life.

Books

331. Cheney, Margaret. THE CO-ED KILLER. New York: Walker, 1976.

The best and most detailed account of Kemper's case.

332. Damio, Ward. URGE TO KILL. New York: Pinnacle, 1974.

   Quicky paperback examination of the case, along with
   other homicides committed by Santa Cruz killers John
   Frazier and Herbert Mullin around the same time. (Kemper
   openly despised Frazier and Mullin for their inefficien-
   cy and "lack of legitimacy.") An adequate presentation
   of the facts, with little insight into motives.

* FACTS ON FILE. Volume 33, 1973. Cited above as item 7,
   p. 999.

   Reports Kemper's conviction.

* Gaute, J.H.H., and Robin Odell. THE MURDERERS' WHO'S
   WHO. Cited above as item 8, p. 138.

   Case history presented in an encyclopedic format.

* Godwin, John. MURDER USA. Cited above as item 10, pp.
   312-317.

   Case history in a "chamber of horrors" reserved for
   especially repulsive multicides.

* Green, Jonathon. THE GREATEST CRIMINALS OF ALL TIME.
   Cited above as item 11, pp. 257-258.

   Brief case history in an encyclopedic format.

* Levin, Jack, and James Alan Fox. MASS MURDER: AMERICA'S
   GROWING MENACE. Citeg above as item 15.

   Case history in a discussion of modern serial murder.

* Leyton, Elliott. COMPULSIVE KILLERS. Cited above as
   item 16, pp. 36-72.

   Cannibalizes items 68, 331, and 332, coming up with
   "no new data of any kind."

* Lunde, Donald. MURDER AND MADNESS. Cited above as
   item 68, pp. 53-56.

   Describes Kemper as a "sadistic sociopath," deriving
   sexual release from mutilation of lifeless victims.

* Nash, Jay Robert. CRIME CHRONOLOGY, 1900–1983. Cited above as item 21, p. 170.

   Brief case history presented in time line format.

* ————. MURDER, AMERICA. Cited above as item 23, p. 438.

   Sketchy case history presented in time line format.

* Sifakis, Carl. THE ENCYCLOPEDIA OF AMERICAN CRIME. Cited above as item 29, p. 392.

   Case history presented in an encyclopedic format.

333. West, Donald. SACRIFICE UNTO ME. New York: Pyramid Books, 1974.

   Paperback examination of the case, providing little insight into Kemper's motivations.

* Wilson, Colin. A CRIMINAL HISTORY OF MANKIND. Cited above as item 34, pp. 636–637.

   Case history in a discussion of "motiveless" murder.

* ————, and Donald Seaman. THE ENCYCLOPEDIA OF MODERN MURDER. Cited above as item 36, pp. 119–122.

   Case history presented in an encyclopedic format.

Articles

* "How to Tell Who Will Kill." Cited above as item 86.

   Examines Kemper's case for symptoms of potential violence overlooked in childhood.

312. KENOSHA, WIS., MURDERS (?)

   Series of seven brutal murders perpetrated over a period of fourteen years, in or adjacent to an unpaved alley running between 64th and 67th Streets in Kenosha. The first victim, a seventeen-year-old girl, was abducted from the alleyway and slain in February 1967. Her killer was never identified. Six other victims were killed, in or near their homes along the alley, between January 1978 and January 1981. Two of the cases have been cleared by conviction of suspects at this writing, but Coroner Thomas J. Dorff, of Kenosha, views the circumstances of all seven crimes with suspicion. "There is something strange out by that alley," he declared in 1981. "Sort of a 'Bermuda Triangle of Murder,' I'd say. What seems to be going on is unexplainable." Ooo-ee-ooo.

* Nash, Jay Robert. CRIME CHRONOLOGY, 1900-1983. Cited above as item 21, p. 174.

    Brief case history presented in time line format.

* ———. OPEN FILES. Cited above as item 24, p. 149.

    Case history presented in an encyclopedic format.

313. KIGER, JO ANN (M)

Sixteen-year-old girl who shot her parents and brother while "walking in her sleep," at their Kentucky home, on August 16, 1943. According to Kiger's defense, she dreamed that a huge madman with wild eyes was breaking into the house, endangering her family. Rising from bed, she took her father's two loaded revolvers and first "rescued" her six-year-old brother, shooting him once in the head and twice in the abdomen, killing him instantly. Moving on to her parents' room, Jo Ann blazed away with both guns, killing her father and wounding her mother in the hip, whereupon she "woke up" and declared, "There's a crazy man here who's going to kill all of us." A trial jury accepted the sleep-walking defense, and Kiger was acquitted on all counts.

* CRIME AND PUNISHMENT: A PICTORIAL ENCYCLOPEDIA OF ABERRANT BEHAVIOR, Volume 5. Cited above as item 4, pp. 62-63.

    Case history presented in an encyclopedic format.

314. KING, ALVIN LEE III (M)

Former high school teacher who invaded a crowded church in Daingerfield, Tex., during June 1980, and opened fire on the worshippers, killing five persons and wounding ten. King then shot himself in the head, but survived the wound to stand trial. Previously charged with incest by his daughter, King is also a prime suspect in the stabbing death of a local minister who persuaded the girl to contact police. Hanged himself in jail during January 1982.

Books

* FACTS ON FILE. Volume 40, 1980. Cited above as item 7,
    p. 568.

    Contemporaneous report of the Daingerfield shootings.

Articles

334. "This is War!" TIME 116 (July 7, 1980): 18.

    Reports the massacre and King's arrest.

315. KING, MRS. CHARLES L. (M)

A housewife in Xenia, Ohio, undergoing psychiatric treatment for depression, who attacked and killed her three small
children with a hammer during April 1958. Committed to a
mental institution for further treatment.

* FACTS ON FILE. Volume 18, 1958. Cited above as item 7,
    p. 124.

    Reports the murders and arrest of Mrs. King.

316. KINMAN, DONALD (S)

Transient and psychopath who confessed to the rape-murders
of two Los Angeles nursing orderlies in April 1958 and November 1959. Kinman turned himself in to police a month after
the second slaying, remarking that, "I guess I should get the
gas chamber. I think I deserve it, don't you?" A jury con-
curred, and Kinman was subsequently executed.

* Wilson, Colin, and Patricia Putnam. THE ENCYCLOPEDIA OF
    MURDER. Cited above as item 35, pp. 319-320.

    Case history presented in an encyclopedic format.

317. KINNE, SHARON (S)

Kansas City housewife who shot and killed her husband
for insurance money during March 1960. Three years later,
she was acquitted in the murder of her married lover's spouse,
but Missouri authorities held her for trial in the death of
her husband, beginning a protracted series of trials and
appeals. Free on bond in 1964, she traveled to Mexico with
another boyfriend, and was arrested by Mexican authorities

after he was murdered in their hotel room. Returned to the
United States, she was convicted of her husband's murder and
imprisoned in Missouri.

335.   Hamill, Pete, and David Weber. "I'm Just an Ordinary
        Girl." SATURDAY EVENING POST 238 (September 25, 1965):
        91-97.

        Readable case history, including details of Kinne's
        various trials.

                    318. KISS, BELA (S)

        Hungarian amateur astrologer and slayer of at least 24
persons, all of whom were strangled, then preserved in drums
of alcohol at Kiss's home, in the village of Czinkota. The
killer's first victims were his wife and her adulterous lover,
apparently slain in a jealous rage. The others were all lonely
women who delivered their savings to Kiss, receiving promises
of marriage in return, and who subsequently disappeared. Con-
scripted into military service in November 1914, Kiss was reportedly killed in action during May of 1916. Soldiers who
arrived a month thereafter, searching for his rumored cache
of "oil," were horrified to find, instead, two dozen pickled
corpses. After Kiss was seen, alive, in 1919, the authorities
discovered that he had deserted from the military, switching
identification with a battlefield casualty. In 1924, he was
traced to the French Foreign Legion, using the name "Hoffmann,"
but he again deserted before the arrival of Hungarian police.
In 1932, a New York homicide detective told superiors that he
had sighted Kiss, emerging from a Times Square subway station,
but the murderer was never apprehended.

    *   Boar, Roger, and Nigel Blundell. THE WORLD'S MOST IN-
        FAMOUS MURDERS. Cited above as item 2, pp. 98-99.

        Brief case history presented in tabloid style.

    *   CRIMES AND PUNISHMENT: A PICTORIAL ENCYCLOPEDIA OF ABER-
        RANT BEHAVIOR, Volume 1. Cited above as item 4, p. 88.

        Brief case history in a chapter on "lady-killers."

    *   Nash, Jay Robert. ALMANAC OF WORLD CRIME. Cited above
        as item 19, p. 282.

        Brief case history in a discussion of mass murder.

* Wilson, Colin. A CRIMINAL HISTORY OF MANKIND. Cited
  above as item 34, p. 606.

  Case history in a discussion of modern mass murder.

* ————, and Patricia Putnam. THE ENCYCLOEPDIA OF MURDER.
  Cited above as item 35, pp. 320-321.

  Case history presented in an encyclopedic format.

319. Deleted.

320. KLIMEK, TILLIE (S)

Polish immigrant who settled in Chicago, indicted and
convicted during 1922 for poisoning four husbands, one lover,
"several" of her own children, and "some cousins." In addition
to her own murders, perpetrated largely for financial gain,
it was alleged that Klimek helped a cousin, Nellie Koulik,
dispose of one or two husbands on the side. Sentenced to life.

* Jones, Ann. WOMEN WHO KILL. Cited above as item 13,
  p. 128.

  Brief case history, from a feminist perspective.

321. KNOPPA, ANTHONY MICHAEL (M): See LANHAM, HARRY

322. KNOWLES, JOHN PAUL (S)

Habitual criminal and escapee from a Florida jail who,
by his own estimate, murdered 35 persons during a four-month
rampage in 1974. (Police confirmed his link with 18 homicides
and several other felonies, including the attempted rape of a
teenaged girl.) Between July 26, 1974, when he robbed and
murdered an elderly woman, and his capture on November 17,
Knowles traveled in stolen cars from Florida to California
and back again, picking off victims en route. Before his
capture, Knowles murdered at least five persons in Florida,
at least five in Georgia, two in Connecticut, two in Nevada,
and one each in Ohio, Texas, Alabama, and Virginia. Most of
his victims were women, invariable raped before they were
killed. The day after his arrest in Florida, Knowles picked
the lock on his handcuffs and attempted to disarm the local
sheriff, whereupon he was shot and killed by an FBI agent.

336. Fawkes, Sandy. KILLING TIME. London: Hamlyn, 1978.

A British journalist describes three days she spent
with Knowles after he picked her up in an Atlanta, Georgia,

nightclub on November 8, 1974. Their "tender" relationship ended on November 11, after Knowles attempted to
rape a friend of Fawkes at gunpoint. The intended victim, another British newswoman, managed to escape and
flagged a passing squad car down, but Knowles eluded his
pursuers after brandishing a sawed-off shotgun.

* Wilson, Colin. A CRIMINAL HISTORY OF MANKIND. Cited
   above as item 34, pp. 638-639.

   Brief case history in a discussion of multiple murder.

* ————, and Donald Seaman. THE ENCYCLOPEDIA OF MODERN
   MURDER. Cited above as item 36, pp. 724-728.

   Case history presented in an encyclopedic format.

   323. KOKORALEIS, ANDREW and THOMAS (S)

   Self-styled Satanists and cannibals who, with accomplices
Robin Gecht and Edward Spreitzer, stand convicted of six murders
in Chicago and environs during 1981 and 1982. Five of the six
victims were young women, abducted as sacrificial victims for
Satanic ceremonies held in Gecht's home. As part of the cult's
ritual, one or both breasts of a victim were severed with loops
of piano wire, then sectioned and devoured by the "worshippers." Victims were strangled and raped, their mutilated
bodies discarded around the Chicago suburbs over a period of
months. (As many as ten other women are believed to have
been murdered by the cult, but no charges have been filed in
those cases.) A sixth conviction arose from the sniper slaying
of a Latin drug dealer who had "burned" the cultists on a dope
transaction. Under questioning, Andrew Kokoraleis confessed
to the ritual slaying of a sixth woman, leading police to a
field where remains were allegedly buried, but no body was
found. According to the brothers' confessions, Gecht accumu-
lated "ten or fifteen" severed breasts at one point in their
grim careet. Sentenced to life without parole.

337. Newton, Michael. "Killer Cults." CHIC 10 (January 1986):
   82.

   Brief case history in a discussion of American Satanic
   cults.

338. ————. "Something Wicked." LV, THE MAGAZINE OF LAS
   VEGAS 2 (December 1986): 76

Brief case history in a general discussion of Satanic
cults in America, primarily focusing on Nevada.

324. KRAUS, KIRK (M)

Despondent over long-term unemployment, this Connecticut
resident strangled his sister and her three children, then
committed suicide by slashing his own wrists and throat in
April 1959.

* FACTS ON FILE. Volum 19, 1959. Cited above as item 7,
  p. 123.

Reports Kraus's crimes and suicide.

325. KRENWINKLE, PATRICIA (M): See MANSON, CHARLES

326. KROLL, JOACHIM (S)

The "Ruhr Hunter," a rapist and cannibal responsible for
at least 14 murders, committed in Germany between February 1955
and July 1976. In the majority of cases, victims were found
mutilated by removal of their buttocks or other fleshy portions
of their bodies, which were carried away by the killer. A
mental defective employed as a lavatory attendant, Kroll (like
Britain's Dennis Nilsen, some years later) was betrayed by
plumbing when he sought to flush remains of victims down his
toilet. Plumbers found the organs of a small child, including
the lungs, when they tried to clear his pipes, and officers
were summoned to the scene. On entering Kroll's flat, they
found parcels of human flesh in the freezer, and a child's
hand boiling on the stove, with carrots and potatoes. Readily
confessing to a string of crimes—the ones he could remember—
Kroll was sentenced to life.

* Wilson, Colin, and Donald Seaman. THE ENCYCLOPEDIA OF
  MODERN MURDER. Cited above as item 36, pp. 132-135.

Case history presented in an encyclopedic format.

327. KULAK, FRANK (M)

Marine Corps veteran of World War II who detonated several
bombs around Chicago during 1967 and 1968, attempting to halt
the sale of war toys and show citizens "what the war in Vietnam
was like." When police approached him at his home, in April
1969, to question him about the bombings, Kulak opened fire
with several weapons, hurling hand grenades and home-made bombs

during a three-hour siege. Two officers were killed in the
exchange; the toll from bombings brought Kulak's toll to four
dead and 20 wounded. Arrested at the scene, he was eventually
jailed for life.

339. "The Marine's Last Battle." NEWSWEEK 73 (April 28, 1969):
      44-45.

      Contemporaneous report of the Chicago shootout.

328. KURTEN, PETER (S)

        Sadistic "Monster of Dusseldorf," whose crimes included
arson, murder, rape, and vampirism. One of 13 children raised
in an abusive, sexually-charged environment, Kurten grew up
with incest and violence, torturing animals and committing
his first murder—of a playmate—around age nine. In his early
teens, Kurten ran away from home to become a vagabond, practicing bestiality with livestock and discovering the "thrill"
of stabbing a sheep to death during intercourse. He often
drank the blood of slaughtered animals, sometimes ripping out
their throats with his teeth, and would later repeat this act
with human victims. Beginning at age 15, he was sentenced to
prison on 17 separate occasions, serving a total of 27 years
behind bars, on charges ranging from theft and fraud to
attempted murder. His first sexual murder, of a 13-year-old
girl, was committed in May 1913. After that, his crimes in-
creased in frequency and violence, with Kurten reaching climax
in the midst of an assault on either male or female victims,
often brandishing a hammer, knife, or hatchet. Settling in
Dusseldorf, in 1925, he launched a four-year reign of terror
which included 23 arson fires, at least 18 attempted murders,
and a minimum of nine homicides. His murdered victims, in
this period, included five women, one man, and three children.
In May 1929, Kurten attacked his final victim, a young woman,
inexplicably allowing her to live when she convinced him that
she had forgotten his address. With detectives closing in,
Kurten persuaded his wife to denounce him, for the outstanding
reward. Guillotined in July 1931, Kurten's final wish was
that he might survive decapitation long enough to hear his
own blood spurting from his severed arteries. In his opinion,
it was bound to be the greatest thrill of all.

340. Berg, Karl. THE SADIST. London: Heinemann, 1932.

        The best account of Kurten's strange career, prepared
      by a psychiatrist who came to know the killer well dur-
      ing Kurten's two years of final captivity. A classic.

* Boar, Roger, and Nigel Blundell. THE WORLD'S MOST IN-
  FAMOUS MURDERS. Cited above as item 2, pp. 100-106.

  Case history presented in sensational tabloid style.

* CRIMES AND PUNISHMENT: A PICTORIAL ENCYCLOPEDIA OF ABER-
  RANT BEHAVIOR, Volume 7. Cited above as item 4, p. 45.

  Case history in a section on "vampire" killers.

* CRIMES AND PUNISHMENT: A PICTORIAL ENCYCLOPEDIA OF ABER-
  RANT BEHAVIOR, Volume 13. Cited above as item 4, pp.
  36-37.

  Revisits the case in a survey of sexual murders.

* Gaute, J.H.H., and Robin Odell. THE MURDERERS' WHO'S
  WHO. Cited above as item 8, pp. 141-142.

  Case history presented in an encyclopedic format.

341. Godwin, George. PETER KURTEN: A STUDY IN SADISM. London:
  Acorn Press, 1938.

  Instructive, but inferior to item 340 above.

* Hurwood, Bernhardt J. VAMPIRES, WEREWOLVES, AND GHOULS.
  Cited above as item 12, pp. 130-141.

  Sensational case history in a catalogue of "human
  monsters."

* Masters, R.E.L., and Eduard Lea. PERVERSE CRIMES IN
  HISTORY. Cited above as item 18, pp. 143-154.

  Case history in a survey of "vampire" killers.

* Nash, Jay Robert. ALMANAC OF WORLD CRIME. Cited above
  as item 19, pp. 23, 163, 211-212.

  Case history in a general discussion of mass murder.

* ————. CRIME CHRONOLOGY, 1900-1983. Cited above as
  item 21, pp. 4, 84-85.

  Sketchy case history presented in time line format.

* Rumbelow, Donald. THE COMPLETE JACK THE RIPPER. Cited
  above as item 315, pp. 257-274.

  Compares Kurten to the Ripper, after whom the Dusseldorf killer consciously patterned his crimes.

* Scott, Sir Harold. THE CONCISE ENCYCLOPEDIA OF CRIME
  AND CRIMINALS. Cited above as item 27, pp. 210-211.

  Case history presented in an encyclopedic format.

342. Wagner, Margaret Seaton. THE MONSTER OF DUSSELDORF.
     London: Faber & Faber, 1932.

  A readable account, lacking the clinical insight
  of item 340 above, which was published simultaneously.

* Wilson, Colin. A CASEBOOK OF MURDER. Cited above as
  item 33, pp. 19-20.

  Case history in a sociological survey of murder.

* ————. A CRIMINAL HISTORY OF MANKIND. Cited above as
  item 34, p. 607.

  Case history in a discussion of modern multicide.

* ————, and Patricia Putnam. THE ENCYCLOPEDIA OF MURDER.
  Cited above as item 35, pp. 326-335.

  Case history presented in an encyclopedic format.

329. LACENAIRE, GEORGES (S)

French slayer of at least four persons, at Lyons, in
1834. His first victim was an intoxicated "gentleman,"
throttled and tossed in a river to drown on a whim, after a
late night of drinking. Two others, a widow and her son,
were stabbed to death in their home by Lacenaire and an accomplice, named Avril, in December 1834. Twelve days later,
with an accomplice named Francois, Lacenaire murdered a bank
employee for purposes of robbery. Upon his arrest, Lacenaire
confessed his murders, and was subsequently executed.

* Logan, Guy B.H. MASTERS OF CRIME. Cited above as item
  17, pp. 127-143.

  Case history in an anthology of 19th-century murders.

* Wilson, Colin, and Patricia Putnam. THE ENCYCLOPEDIA
  OF MURDER. Cited above as item 35, pp. 238-240.

  Case history presented in an encyclopedic format.

330. LADD, GLORIA (M)

California housewife who committed herself voluntarily
to Napa State Hospital following an attempt to murder her two
young sons. Later, after her release as "cured," she succeeded
in killing both children but failed in her attempt at suicide.
Sentenced to life.

* Godwin, John. MURDER USA. Cited above as item 10, p. 272.

  Case history in a chapter on mentally-unbalanced
  killers.

331. LAKE, LEONARD (S)

Self-styled "survivalist" from northern California, suspected, with accomplice Charles Chitat Ng, in the disappearances and deaths of more than 20 victims from the San Francisco
area. The murders were exposed in June 1985, after an off-duty
policeman saw Ng shoplifting at a hardware store. Ng escaped,
but Lake was apprehended with the stolen merchandise in his
car, still parked at the scene. In custody, Lake committed
suicide by swallowing a cyanide capsule. Police sent to
search his home for other stolen goods found mutilated bodies,
skeletal remains, torture devises, and video tapes of women
being used by Lake and Ng as "sex slaves." Estimates of a
final body-count for the murderous duo range as high as 25,
with many of the decomposed remains still unidentified.
According to reports, the victims included Lake's younger
brother, as well as various neighbors, friends, and chance
acquaintances. Charles Ng, an ex-Marine, ex-convict, and
fugitive from justice when he met Lake in 1981, escaped to
Canada, where he was captured following another shoplifting
incident in July 1985. Because he faced the death penalty
if convicted of multiple murder in California, extradition
to the United States was denied. Convicted of theft and
attempted murder in Calgary, Alberta, Ng is currently serving
a prison sentence in Canda.

Books

* FACTS ON FILE. Volume 45, 1985. Cited above as item 7,
  p. 610.

Follows the investigation through Ng's arrest.

Articles

343.   Starr, M.   "The Wilseyville Horror."   NEWSWEEK 105
       (June 24, 1985): 36.

       Reports the discoveries at Lake's rural home, with Ng
       still at large.

332. LAKEY, SAMUEL PENDER (M)

Slayer of his neighbors—a farmer and his wife—60 miles
from Auckland, New Zealand, in October 1933.   Lakey first
blamed the woman's death on her missing husband, but police
found hair, bone, and bits of flesh in Lakey's house, along
with the missing man's watch and cigarette lighter.   Hanged
in July 1934.

*   Nash, Jay Robert.   CRIME CHRONOLOGY, 1900-1983.   Cited
        above as item 21, p. 92.

        Case history presented in time line format.

333. LAMBRIGHT, DONALD M. (M)

Son of black comedian "Stepin Fetchit," who killed his
wife in April 1969 and then opened fire on motorists along
the Pennsylvania Turnpike near Harrisburg, killing three other
persons and wounding seventeen before committing suicide.

*   FACTS ON FILE.   Volume 29, 1969.   Cited above as item 7,
        p. 444.

        Reports the Harrisburg shootings.

*   Tobias, Ronald.   THEY SHOOT TO KILL.   Cited above as
        item 31, pp. 133-134.

        Case history within a discussion of criminal snipers.

334. LANCE, MYRON (S): See KELBACH, WALTER

335. LANDERS, MONTY (M): See JOHNSON, JOEY

336. LANHAM, HARRY (S)

Linked, with accomplice Anthony Michael Knoppa, to the

sex murders of two Texas women during November 1971. Acting
alone, Lanham was "made" for a third homicide, committed a
month after the other two. In each case, the victims were
abducted, raped, then slain by shotgun blasts. Both killers
were sentenced to life.

* Wilson, Colin, and Donald Seaman. THE ENCYCLOPEDIA OF
  MODERN MURDER. Cited above as item 36, pp. 137-138.

  Case history presented in an encyclopedic format.

337. LANDRU, HENRI DESIRE (S)

French "Bluebeard" suspected in the disappearance and
death of at least nine women, all of whom accepted his marriage
proposals between 1914 and 1919, bestowing their worldly goods
on Landru prior to vanishing. In the case of his first lethal
engagement, a child also disappeared along with Landru's
fiancée, bringing the body-count to a minimum of ten victims.
No trace of Landru's victims was ever found, and he remained
convinced that he could never be convicted without at least
one body to be used in evidence against him. A judge and jury
disagreed, finding him guilty on the basis of circumstantial
evidence and sentencing him to die. Silent to the end, he
qas guillotined in February 1922.

* Boar, Roger, and Nigel Blundell. THE WORLD'S MOST IN-
  FAMOUS MURDERS. Cited above as item 2, pp. 107-115.

  Case history presented in sensational tabloid style.

* Brian, Dennis. MURDERERS DIE. Cited above as item 3,
  pp. 84-89.

  Case history in an anthology of killers who were put
  to death.

* CRIMES AND PUNISHMENT: A PICTORIAL ENCYCLOPEDI OF ABER-
  RANT BEHAVIOR, Volume 1. Cited above as item 4, pp.
  85-86, 97-104.

  Case history presented in an encyclopedic format.

* Douthwaite, L.C. MASS MURDER. Cited above as item 6.

  Case history in a general survey of multicide.

* Gaute, J.H.H., and Robin Odell. THE MURDERERS' WHO'S
  WHO. Cited above as item 8, pp. 145-147.

  Case history presented in an encyclopedic format.

* Nash, Jay Robert. ALMANAC OF WORLD CRIME. Cited above
  as item 19, pp. 163, 282-285.

  Case history in a general discussion of mass murder.

* ————. CRIME CHRONOLOGY, 1900-1983. Cited above as
  item 21, pp. 38, 43, 45, 48, 58.

  Traces Landru's career through time line entries.

* Scott, Sir Harold. THE CONCISE ENCYCLOPEDIA OF CRIME
  AND CRIMINALS. Cited above as item 27, p. 212.

  Case history presented in an encyclopedic format.

* Wilson, Colin, and Patricia Putnam. THE ENCYCLOPEDIA
  OF MURDER. Cited above as itme 35, pp. 346-351.

  Case history presented in an encyclopedic format.

338. LASHER, FRANK H. (M)

Physician of Garden City, N.Y., who, dejected over his
son's recent illness, shot the boy, his wife, his mother, and
himself in October 1946. Ironically, Lasher's son was the sole
survivor of the massacre.

* FACTS ON FILE. Volume 6, 1946. Cited above as item 7,
  p. 346.

  Reports the Garden City shootings,

339. LASKEY, POSTEAL (S)

Cincinnati resident convicted and sentenced to life for
one of seven "identical" rape-slayings committed during 1965
and 1966. In each case, middle-aged or elderly women were
raped and strangled in their homes. While the first six slayings remain officially "unsolved," investigators are convinced
of Laskey's guilt in all seven crimes.

344. "Strangler." NEWSWEEK 68 (October 31, 1966): 46.

Reports the investigation after six murders, published more than a month before Laskey's arrest in a seventh case.

340. LA VOISIN, CATHERINE (S)

Seventeenth-century "witch" and associate of King Louis XIV, who in 1680 confessed to participating in ritual black masses with Abbe Guibourg, Madame de Montespan, and other highly-placed members of French society. Children were apparently sacrificed to Satan in perverted rituals which spanned a period of years. While no two versions of the case agree upon a final body-count, reports alleging 2,500 infant victims have been published without reliable contradiction.

* Hoeller, Stephen A. "The Real Black Mass." Cited above as item 282.

Case history of the "Chamber Ardente Affair," recounting details of the alleged black mass rituals, confessions, and estimates of the sacrificial body-count.

* Masters, R.E.L., and Eduard Lea. PERVERSE CRIMES IN HISTORY. Cited above as item 18, pp. 9-10.

Places La Voisin's body-count in the general neighborhood of 1,500 victims, 1,000 below item 282 above.

341. LEE, BRUCE (S)

British arsonist, whose several fires claimed the lives of 26 persons between 1973 and 1980. Committed to a mental institution with an indeterminate, no-time-limit sentence.

* Wilson, Colin, and Donald Seaman. THE ENCYCLOPEDIA OF MODERN MURDER. Cited above as item 36, pp. 138-139.

Case history presented in an encyclopedic format.

342. LEE, LUDWIG (S)

Demented slayer who, in 1927, murdered his landlady and a female neighbor, cutting up their bodies and scattering the pieces around New York City. Sentenced to death.

* Nash, Jay Robert. MURDER, AMERICA. Cited above as item 23, pp. 224-227, 399.

Case history in an anthology of "classic" murders.

343. LEHMAN, CHRISTA (M)

German housewife who fatally poisoned three of her neighbors, without apparent motive, in February 1954. Sentenced to
life.

*   Nash, Jay Robert. CRIME CHRONOLOGY, 1900-1983. Cited
    above as item 21, p. 149.

    Brief case history presented in time line format.

344. LELIEVRE, ANDRE and YVETTE (S)

French married couple, arrested in 1969 for murdering
seven of their own new-born children over a period of years.
In lieu of practicing birth control, the defendants drowned
each successive infant, shortly after birth, and buried the
remains in a garden near their home. Sentenced to life
imprisonment.

*   CRIMES AND PUNISHMENT: A PICTORIAL ENCYCLOPEDIA OF ABER-
    RANT BEHAVIOR, Volume 12. Cited above as item 4, p. 110.

    Case history presented in an encyclopedic format.

345. LEONOSKI, EDWARD JOSEPH (S)

American soldier, stationed in Australia during World
War II. Leonoski strangled three Melbourne women in a period
of sixteen days, in May 1942. Although the murders were considered sexually-motivated, none of the victims were molested.
In his confession, Leonoski said he killed the women "to get
their voices," hence his popular nickname of "the Singing
Strangler." Hanged by order of a court martial, in November
1942.

*   CRIMES AND PUNISHMENT: A PICTORIAL ENCYCLOPEDIA OF ABER-
    RANT BEHAVIOR, Volume 7. Cited above as item 4, p. 53.

    Case history presented in an encyclopedic format.

*   Gaute, J.H.H., and Robin Odell. THE MURDERERS' WHO'S
    WHO. Cited above as item 8, p. 150.

    Case history presented in an encyclopedic format.

346. LEWINGDON, GARY JAMES and THADDEUS CHARLES (S)

Brothers and perpetrators of the Columbus, Ohio, ".22-
caliber murders," which claimed ten lives in 1978. Robbery
appeared to be the motive in each case, but the killers repeatedly "lost control," firing multiple bullets into each
unresisting victim after their demands were met. Gary Lewingdon was convicted in eight of the murders, receiving eight
consecutive life sentences in May 1979. His brother, charged
with only three slayings, was convicted on all counts; he
received three consecutive life sentences, plus a sentence of
seven to 25 years for aggravated robbery.

345. Keyes, Daniel. UNVEILING CLAUDIA. New York: Bantam, 1986.

Reviews the case in a fascinating psychological portrait of Claudia Yasko, an early suspect who confessed
to the crimes in amazing detail, despite the fact that
she was innocent. Keyes unravels the mysteries of
Claudia's disordered mind, revealing the source of her
uncanny confessions, which nearly permitted two serial
killers to escape justice.

347. LIGHTBOURNE, WENDELL (S)

Golf caddy in Bermuda, who raped and murdered three
women between March and September 1959. Upon his capture
and confession, Lightbourne received a life sentence, which
he is currently serving in Britain.

*   Nash, Jay Robert. CRIME CHRONOLOGY, 1900-1983. Cited
     above as item 21, p. 159.

Case history presented in time line format.

348. LINEVELDT, GAMAT SALIE (S)

Sexual sadist who murdered four women in Cape Town,
South Africa, during October and November 1940. Lineveldt
idolized Jack the Ripper, and is said to have been impotent
with women unless their bodies were smeared with blood. Each
victim was brutally beaten and mutilated, after which Lineveldt raped their corpses, carrying away an item of under-
clothing from each as a souvenir. In early November, when
a newspaper reported the discovery of a thumbprint at the
latest crime scene, Lineveldt cut off the tip of his thumb to
prevent identification. The effort was wasted, and following
his arrest, he made a full confession. Hanged.

* CRIMES AND PUNISHMENT: A PICTORIAL ENCYCLOPEDIA OF ABER-
  RANT BEHAVIOR, Volume 20. Cited above as item 4, pp.
  88-91.

  Case history in a chapter on sadistic sex killers.

349. LISEMBA, MAJOR RAYMOND (S)

Slayer for profit who drowned at least two wives for
their insurance payments, subsequently staging a car "accident"
which killed a male friend, for identical motives. Active in
Colorado and California over a decade or more, Lisemba was
also a practicing masochist. Hanged, at San Quentin, in May
1942.

* Nash, Jay Robert. MURDER, AMERICA. Cited above as item
  23, pp. 234-245.

  Case history in an anthology of "classic" murders.

350. LIST, JOHN E. (M)

Affluent Westfield, N.J., accountant and Sunday-school
teacher who shot his wife, three children, and mother-in-law
to death in December 1971. Sentenced to life.

346. "Ballroom Murders." NEWSWEEK 78 (December 20, 1971): 30+.

  Reports the massacre and manhunt for List.

351. LOCKHART, JAMES (S)

After murdering a fellow tenant of a state-subsidized
home for former mental patients, in Georgia, Lockhart was
found innocent by reason of insanity. Released from the
asylum after four years, he immediately killed again, and
was sentenced to life imprisonment.

* Brian, Dennis. MURDERERS DIE. Cited above as item 3,
  p. 263.

  Case history used as an argument in favor of capital
  punishment.

352. LOPEZ, PEDRO ALONZO (S)

The "Monster of the Andes," imprisoned in Ecuador following hif confession to the murders of 163 young girls. Lopez

led authorities to 53 hidden corpses in 1980, causing them to accept his confessions in other cases where bodies were not recovered. Sexually molested as a child, and again as a teen-ager in prison, Lopez grew up determined to "steal the innocence" of as many children as possible. In addition to his crimes in Ecuador, Lopez also admitted murdering 100 girls in Colombia and "many more than 100" in neighboring Peru. Authorities in Ecuador are on record as believing that "the estimate of 300 is very low." If true, Lopex may be the most prolific serial murderer of the century.

* Boar, Roger, and Nigel Blundell. THE WORLD'S MOST IN-FAMOUS MURDERS. Cited above as item 2, pp. 116-118.

Case history presented in sensational tabloid style. This appears to be the only English-language reference to the Lopez case in book form.

353. LORBACH, FRANZ (S): See BOOST, WERNER

354. LORTIE, DENIS (M)

Corporal in the Canadian armed forces who, in May 1984, killed three persons and wounded 13 with submachine gun fire in the Quebec national assembly. An anoymous tape sent to the news media by Lortie, prior to the shootings, denounced the government "for doing much wrong to the French-language people of Quebec and the rest of Canada." Convicted of murder and sentenced to prison.

347. Canine, C. "Murder in the Assembly." NEWSWEEK 103 (May 21, 1984): 49.

Reports the massacre and Lortie's arrest.

348. Wilson-Smith, Anthony. "A Deadly Siege in Quebec." MACLEANS 97 (May 21, 1984): 14-16.

Contemporaneous report of the shootings and arrest.

355. LUCAS, HENRY LEE (S)

Bisexual sadist and transient convicted of eleven murders spanning the United States, suspected in more than 200 other homicides. Lucas murdered his alcoholic mother in 1960, serv-ing ten years in prison, and was subsequently reimprisoned for attempting to abduct two girls, in the early 1970s. Arrested

for illegal handgun possession in Texas, during June 1983, he
confessed to an eight-year series of murders across North
America. Often traveling with sidekick (and cannibal) Ottis
Elwood Toole, Lucas variously confessed to 175, 360, and "way
over 500" homicides. Some of the confessions were obviously
fanciful, but police in more than twenty states declared that
Lucas and/or Toole had "cleared the books" on 219 unsolved
deaths, usually characterized by sadistic "overkill" and gross
mutilation of the victims. In early 1985, Lucas began "recanting" the confessions which had earned him a death sentence,
and Dallas newsman Hugh Aynesworth "exposed" a long-running
"Lucas hoax," allegedly designed to embarrass police. More
than 100 "Lucas cases" were subsequently reopened by authorities, although there were significant problems with Aynesworth's
story. Despite his claim that Lucas revealed the "hoax" in
October 1983, Aynesworth was still touting Lucas as the "greatest mass murderer in history"—and working on a Lucas biography
—as late as February 1985. In fact, the motivation for the
belated "expose" appears to be a case of "sour grapes," inspired by Aynesworth's discovering that his publishing contract
with Lucas was null and void. Since recanting his confessions,
Lucas has smuggled letters out of jail to other reporters,
insisting that his change of tune had been the product of
coercion. The investigation of Lucas and Toole continues.

Books

349. Call, Max. HAND OF DEATH: THE HENRY LEE LUCAS STORY.
      Lafayette, La.: Prescott Press, 1985.

      A curious, highly-fictionalized account of Lucas and
      Toole, produced by the Chrstian author of such works as
      AL CAPONE'S DEVIL DRIVER. Call flirts with libel in de-
      scribing one of Lucas's victims—an 80-year-old Texas
      woman—as a member of a Satanic death cult, "capable of
      any crime," and lapses into the absurb by naming other
      alleged cultists such as Lee Harvey Oswald. The more
      bizarre assertions have Lucas participating in the
      (unreported) murder of Texas billionaires, assassinating
      military officers in Spain, and flying to Guyana with a
      shipment of poison for Rev. Jim Jones's final Kool-Aid
      party. Recalled from circulation after Lucas recanted
      his confessions, the book was subsequently reissued with
      new advertising—and no other changes—as a possible
      "solution" to the Lucas controversy.

  *   FACTS ON FILE. Volume 44, 1984. Cited above as item 7,
      pp. 283, 694.

Reports Lucas's April 1984 conviction in a Texas murder, and his August tour of California which "cleared" 13 unsolved cases.

* Levin, Jack, and James Alan Fox. MASS MURDER: AMERICA'S GROWING MENACE. Cited above as item 15.

  Brief references in a general discussion of serial murder.

* Leyton, Elliott. COMPULSIVE KILLERS. Cited above as item 16, pp. 16-18.

  Brief case history, reflecting the author's apparent ignorance of subsequent controversy in the case.

* Nash, Jay Robert. CRIME CHRONOLOGY, 1900-1983. Cited above as item 21, p. 206.

  Garbled case history, presented in time line format. Nash incorrectly "credits" Ottis Toole with matricide, a crime which was, in fact, committed by Lucas.

Articles

* Darrach, Brad, and Joel Norris. "An American Tragedy." Cited above as item 40.

  Includes profiles of Lucas and Toole in a general discussion of serial murder.

350. Nocers, Joseph. "True Confessions?" TEXAS MONTHLY (September 1984): 112-119.

  Casts doubts upon certain "Lucas cases," six months before Aynesworth's "startling expose."

* Sonnenschein, Allen. "Serial Killers." Cited above as item 55.

  Includes an interview with Lucas, conducted by newsman Hugh Aynesworth, published 16 months after Lucas allegedly confessed his "hoax" to Aynesworth. In the interview, Aynesworth coaxes Lucas to describe his "many" crimes with leading comments, such as: "According to the numbers, you started killing furiously after that [e.g., after 1975]." This, from a journalist who claims to have "known the truth" since early October, 1983.

* Stanley, A. "Catching a New Breed of Killer." Cited above as item 56.

Spotlights Lucas and Toole in a survey of modern serial killers.

* Starr, Mark. "The Random Killers." Cited above as item 57.

Includes a brief interview with Lucas and his captors, in a general overview of serial murder.

356. LUDKE, BRUNO (S)

Mentally defective German murderer who began killing at age eighteen, claiming numerous victims during World War II. A petty thief and sadist, who enjoyed torturing animals, Ludke was charged with sexual assault and sterilized by the SS under Hitler's regime. The surgery failed to inhibit his perverse desires, and rape remained the driving motive in his later crimes. Arrested on a murder charge in 1943, Ludke confessed to killing 85 women in the past fifteen years. He sought to avoid indictment on grounds of insanity, but Nazi officials were so embarrassed by his case that they "buried" him without a trial. Ludke was sent to Vienna, as a human guinea pig for medical experiments, and there died from a chemical injection during April 1944.

* Nash, Jay Robert. ALMANAC OF WORLD CRIME. Cited above as item 19, p. 288.

Brief case history in a discussion of mass murder.

* ————. CRIME CHRONOLOGY, 1900–1983. Cited above as item 21, pp. 121–122.

Sketchy case history presented in time line format.

* Wilson, Colin. A CRIMINAL HISTORY OF MANKIND. Cited above as item 34, p. 609.

Brief case history in a discussion of mass murder.

* ————, and Patricia Putnam. THE ENCYCLOPEDIA OF MURDER. Cited above as item 35, pp. 363–364.

Case history presented in an encyclopedic format.

357. LYLES, ANJETTE (S)

Practitioner of black magic and voodoo who poisoned two
husbands, her mother-in-law, and one of her own daughters.
Police in Macon, Ga., were alerted, in 1958, by an anonymous
letter, hinting that the death of Lyles's daughter, Marcia,
might have been "suspicious." Investigation revealed traces
of arsenic in the exhumed bodies of all four victims, and
Lyles was sentenced to die. State psychiatrists subsequently
pronounced her insane, and she was transferred to a mental
institution for life.

* Nash, Jay Robert. LOOK FOR THE WOMAN. Cited above as
  item 22, pp. 253-254.

  Case history presented in an encyclopedic format.

358. MacDONALD, JEFFREY ROBERT (M)

Army officer and surgeon who murdered his wife and two
young daughters at Ft. Bragg, N.C., in February 1970. Following the murders, MacDonald stabbed himself and called the
authorities, reporting that a group of "hippies" had invaded
his home, attacking his family. Messages written on the walls
in blood were similar to evidence in the Manson Family murders,
in Southern California, then making daily headlines nationwide.
Physical evidence and contradictory statements from MacDonald
led to his indictment in 1975, and after numerous delays, he
was convicted, in 1979, on all three murder charges. In 1980,
a federal appeals court set the conviction aside, on consti-
tutional grounds. That decision was overturned, and Mac-
Donald's sentence reinstated, by the United States Supreme
Court in 1982. Currently serving three consecutive life
sentences.

Books

* FACTS ON FILE. Volume 39, 1979. Cited above as item 7,
  pp. 203, 817.

  Reports pretrial maneuvers and MacDonald's conviction.

* FACTS ON FILE. Volume 40, 1980. Cited above as item 7,
  p. 654.

  Reports MacDonald's successful federal appeal.

   * FACTS ON FILE. Volume 41, 1981. Cited above as item 7,
     p. 930.

   The Supreme Court reviews MacDonald's case.

   * FACTS ON FILE. Volume 42, 1982. Cited above as item 7,
     pp. 246, 692.

   Updates MacDonald's continuing appeals.

   * FACTS ON FILE. Volume 43, 1983. Cited above as item 7,
     p. 13.

   The Supreme Court rejects MacDonald's latest appeal.

   * FACTS ON FILE. Volume 44, 1984. Cited above as item 7,
     p. 910.

   Announces the airing of a TV movie based on the case.

351. McGinniss, Joe. FATAL VISION. New York: G.P. Putnam's
     Sons, 1983.

     The definitive study of MacDonald's case, prepared by
     an author whom MacDonald personally selected (and later
     sued, on grounds that McGinniss had not produced a book
     painting MacDonald as innocent). Expecting to clear
     MacDonald's name in print, McGinniss wound up convinced
     of the defendant's guilt, and builds a damning case
     against MacDonald in this exemplary report.

                              Articles

352. Bruning, F. "A Bloody, Made-for-TV Murder." MACLEANS
     97 (December 17, 1984): 9.

     Reviews the case in light of an upcoming television
     "docudrama."

353. Jennes, G. "A Grisly Triple Murder from 13 Years Ago
     Yields a Best-Seller—and Controversy—for Joe Mc-
     Ginniss." PEOPLE WEEKLY 20 (October 10, 1983): 73-74+.

     Profiles McGinniss and his involvement in the case.

354. McGinniss, Joe. "Fatal Vision." ROLLING STONE (Septem-
     ber 29, 1983): 30-31+.

Excerpts from item 351 above.

359. MacDONALD, WILLIAM (S)

The "Sydney Mutilator," homosexual sadist and slayer of at least four "down-and-outs" around Sydney, Australia, in the early 1960s. Traumatized and mentally unbalanced by his own homosexual rape as a teenager, MacDonald went on, in later life, to victimize others. Sentenced to life.

* CRIMES AND PUNISHMENT: A PICTORIAL ENCYCLOPEDIA OF ABER-
   RANT BEHAVIOR, Volume 17. Cited above as item 4, p. 84.

   Case history in a discussion of sadistic slayers.

360. MacGREGOR, JOHN (S)

Homicidal physician of Bad Axe, Michigan. Between 1909 and 1911, MacGregor poisoned the husband and three sons of his mistress, sharing substantial insurance benefits with the be-reaved widow. Sentence to life in 1912, he was released four years later in an act of gubernatorial clemency. A scandal erupted when MacGregor was appointed prison physician at the same insitution where he had been previously caged, but he maintained the post until his death, in 1928.

* Nash, Jay Robert. ALMANAC OF WORLD CRIME. Cited above
   as item 19, p. 322.

   Brief case history in a chapter on lethal physicians.

361. MacKAY, PATRICK DAVID (S)

Young British psychopath, convicted of three murders and questioned in eight others. As a child, MacKay tortured ani-mals and displayed preoccupation with death. He had attempted two murders by age 15, and police believe he succeeded in killing at least six persons in the next seven years. Finally sentenced to life for three slayings, including that of a priest who was killed with an ax.

355. Clark, Tim, and John Penycate. PSYCHOPATH. London:
   Routledge & Kegan Paul, 1976.

   Examines MacKay's childhood and adolescence for clues to his bizarre, sadistic behavior as an adult.

* Gaute, J.H.H., and Robin Odell. THE MURDERERS' WHO'S
  WHO. Cited above as item 8, p. 155.

  Case history presented in an encyclopedic format.

* Green, Jonathon. THE GREATEST CRIMINALS FO ALL TIME.
  Cited above as item 11, p. 258.

  Case history presented in an encyclopedic format.

* Nash, Jay Robert. CRIME CHRONOLOGY, 1900-1983. Cited
  above as item 21, p. 186.

  Brief case history presented in time line format.

* Wilson, Colin, and Donald Seaman. THE ENCYCLOPEDIA OF
  MODERN MURDER. Cited above as item 36, pp. 146-147.

  Case history presented in an encyclopedic format.

362. McCABE, MICHAEL (M): See REID, PATRICK

363. McCLURE, LESLIE EDWARD (M)

Debt-ridden cancer patient in Miami, Fla., who shot his
wife and two infant children to death on Christmas Day, 1956.
McClures attempt to kill himself was foiled by the arrival of
police, and he subsequently died in prison.

* FACTS ON FILE. Volume 16, 1956. Cited above as item 7,
  p. 432.

  Reports the Miami murders and arrest.

364. McMANUS, FRED EUGENE (S)

Marine Corps private who murdered five persons during a
three-day crime spree in Rochester, N.Y., in March 1953. All
five victims were shot with a .45-caliber pistol, during the
course of petty robberies. Arrested a month after the killings,
McManus was found to be sane and was sentenced to life.

* FACTS ON FILE. Volume 13, 1953. Cited above as item 7,
  pp. 112, 176, 328.

  Follows the case from arrest, through sentencing.

365. McRAE, DAVID, Jr. (M)

Police cadet in Norfolk, Va., who became obsessed with the need to "eliminate crime" through direct, personal action. Entering a local bar, in May 1976, McRae shot and killed four persons he suspected of being pimps or prostitutes. Before police arrived, he turned his weapon on himself, committing suicide.

* Nash, Jay Robert. MURDER, AMERICA. Cited above as item 23, p. 443.

   Sketchy case history presented in time line format.

366. McRAE, JOEL P. (M)

Enraged husband who shot his wife and her lover to death, in November 1950, after finding them nude in a lakeside cabin near Palatka, Fla. McRae was released without any charges being filed against him.

* FACTS ON FILE. Volume 10, 1950. Cited above as item 7, p. 380.

   Reports the shootings and McRae's eventual release.

367. McCRARY FAMILY, THE (S)

Sherman McCrary, his wife Carolyn, their teenaged son Danny, daughter Ginger, and son-in-law Raymond Carl Taylor, cut a swath of murder, rape, and robbery across America in 1971 and 1972. Investigators linked the homicidal nomads with 22 slayings, from Florida to California, in a two-year period. Many of the victims were young women, abducted, raped, and murdered execution-style. Most of the abductions and murders were apparently incidental to robberies, through which the brutal family supported itself on the road. All were subsequently convicted on various charges, ranging from check fraud to kidnapping, sexual assault, and murder.

* Green, Jonathon. THE GREATEST CRIMINALS OF ALL TIME. Cited above as item 11, p. 153.

   Brief case history in an encyclopedic format.

* Wilson, Colin. A CRIMINAL HISTORY OF MANKIND. Cited above as item 34, pp. 635-636.

Case history in a general discussion of modern crime.

*   ————, and Donald Seaman. THE ENCYCLOPEDIA OF MODERN
    MURDER. Cited above as item 36, pp. 143-144.

    Case history presented in an encyclopedic format.

368. MACEK, RICHARD (S)

Wisconsin's "Mad Biter," so called for the teeth marks
he left on the bodies of his victims. Convicted of two murders
and suspected in six others, Macek accepted his sentence of
200 to 400 years with the comment that, "I don't have any
remorse for what I did."

*   Starr, Mark. "The Random Killers." Cited above as item
    57, p. 104.

    Brief case history in a general discussion of serial
    murder.

369. "MAD BUTCHER OF KINGSBURY RUN, THE" (S)

Unidentified mutilation-slayer of at least 16 persons
in the 1930s. Nicknamed for a gully, in Cleveland, where many
of his victims were discarded, the elusive slayer was also
dubbed the "Torso Killer," since his victims were invariably
decapitated, with their arms and legs severed. (Some torsos
were further mutilated through bisection, emasculation, or
removal of internal organs, and at least two were treated with
chemical preservatives by the killer.) Thirteen victims were
discovered in Cleveland between September 1934 and August 1938;
another three, discovered in obsolete box cars at McKees Rocks,
Pa., in May 1940, had actually been killed months earlier,
when the cars were on a siding near Youngstown, Ohio. Speculation links the Butcher with several unsolved murders near
New Castle, Pa., during the same period, but no positive connection was ever demonstrated, and the number of New Castle
victims has been widely exaggerated by careless reporters.
Likewise, a "torso" case from Cleveland, discovered in July
1950, was never officially linked with the Butcher, although
the coroner described it as "virtually identical." Peter
Merylo, a homicide detective who pursued the killer into re-
tirement, believed the Butcher was responsible for more than
50 slayings, including the "Black Dahlia" murders in California (although none of the victims were decapitated, and none
of those crimes were ever connected by Western authorities).

A letter, purportedly from the Butcher, was mailed from Los
Angeles to Cleveland police in 1939; the author linked the
unsolved crimes with on-going "medical research," asserting
that his latest "operations," in the West, had been "successful." So proficient was the Butcher in his work, that only
three of 16 proven victims were ever identified; in eleven
cases, the severed heads were never found.

Books

* CRIMES AND PUNISHMENT: A PICTORIAL ENCYCLOPEDIA OF ABER-
    RANT BEHAVIOR, Volume 5. Cited above as item 4, pp.
    13-14.

    Brief case history in a discussion of mutilation murders.

356. Martin, John Bartlow. BUTCHER'S DOZEN. New York:
     Harper & Brothers, 1950, pp. 55-99, 233-235.

     The best published summary of the case, despite several
     glaring errors. A review of newspaper files in New
     Castle, Pa., demonstrates that some of the "torso" crimes
     attributed by Martin to that city did not, in fact,
     take place. The same is true of Martin's reference to
     corpses found "in Pittsburgh."

* Nash, Jay Robert. CRIME CHRONOLOGY, 1900-1983. Cited
    above as item 21, p. 104.

    Brief case history presented in time line format.

* ————. OPEN FILES. Cited above as item 24, pp. 163-165.

    Report flawed by careless errors, including the non-
    existent "discovery" of "two more mutilated corpses in
    Pittsburgh, in 1942," a circumstance of which Pittsburgh
    newsmen and police remain ignorant to this day.

* Purvis, James. GREAT UNSOLVED MYSTERIES. Cited above
    as item 26, pp. 15-24.

    Case history in an anthology of unsolved crimes.

357. Ritt, William. "The Head Hunter of Kingsbury Run."
     CLEVELAND MURDERS. Edited by Howard Beaufait. New
     York: Duell, Sloan & Pearce, 1947.

An adequate review of the case, including the usual
references to New Castle murders which never occurred.
Includes the full text of the January 1939 letter to
Cleveland police.

*   Wilson, Colin. A CRIMINAL HISTORY OF MANKIND. Cited
    above as item 34, p. 609.

    Brief case history in a discussion of sadistic murder.

Articles

358. Deleted.

359. Beaufait, Howard. "Kingsbury Run Murders." HOMESPUN
     (November 1955): 32-33+.

     Unremarkable survey of the case, by the editor of item
     357 above.

360. Lamb, Michael. "Torso Murders: 40 Years Unsolved."
     PLAIN DEALER MAGAZINE (October 12, 1975).

     A readable review of the case, following the deaths
     of all major (known) participants.

361. "The Mad Butcher." NEWSWEEK 36 (August 7, 1950): 30-31.

     Reports the discovery of an "identical" Cleveland torso
     victim, eleven years after the murders reportedly ceased.

362. Martin, John Bartlow. "Butcher's Dozen." HARPER'S 199
     (November 1949): 56-69.

     Serialization of item 356 above.

363. Miller, William. "Cleveland's Rue Morgue." KEN MAGA-
     ZINE (January 12, 1939): 14-15.

     Contemporaneous report of the manhunt in progress.

364. "Torso Murders." CLEVELAND MAGAZINE (October 1977):
     88-89.

     Historical retrospective on the case.

370. MAINE, LEONARD (S): See BRAUN, THOMAS EUGENE

371. MAJIK, ALI (S)

Confessed rape-murderer of three young boys in Damascus, Syria. Alleged to be "the first such case in Syrian history." Hanged in Marhc 1977.

* Nash, Jay Robert. CRIME CHRONOLOGY, 1900-1983. Cited above as item 21, p. 192.

Sketchy case history presented in time line format.

372. MANGUM, RICHARD (M)

Escaped convict who, with accomplices Dalton Williams and Jerry Ben Ulmer, launched a vicious crime spree in Colorado, in August 1974. Before they were tracked down by police, the three fugitives murdered two persons, shot and wounded five others, and raped two women. Mangum was killed by police, while resisting arrest; his cohorts were captured alive and returned to prison.

* FACTS ON FILE. Volume 34, 1974. Cited above as item 7, p. 907.

Reports the crime spree and recapture of the fugitives.

373. MANN, EDWARD THOMAS (M)

Embittered former employee of IBM, who entered the company's Bethesda, Md., offices with four guns in May 1982. Mann killed two persons and wounded another seven before he was captured, unharmed. Sentenced to life.

* FACTS ON FILE. Volume 42, 1982. Cited above as item 7, p. 446.

374. MANSON, CHARLES MILLES (M/S)

Habitual criminal and Satanic death-cult leader who controlled a troop of mostly-teenaged followers with drugs and sex, expounding "Biblical messages" which he found "hidden" in popular music of the 1960s. From a Beatles song, Manson developed the concept of "Helter Skelter," defined as an apocalyptic race war which would wipe out most Caucasians. The only survivors, according to Manson, would be himself and his loyal followers, who planned to escape the holocaust by hiding in a "bottomless pit," theoretically located in the California desert. Following Helter Skelter, the Manson tribe

would emerge and find themselves in great demand as leaders,
since the "inferior" nonwhite victors of the race war were
incompetent to rule themselves. Manson reportedly sought to
precipitate Helter Skelter through a series of grisly murders,
aimed at wealthy whites and blamed on blacks. To that end,
he dispatched teams of his disciples to slaughter specific
individuals, leaving "witchy" or "political" clues at the
scene (including slogans written on the walls, in blood). In
August 1969, four Manson acolytes—Charles Watson, Susan Atkins,
Patricia Krenwinkel, and Linda Kasabian (who later turned
state's evidence)—entered the Los Angeles home of film director
Roman Polanski, and there brutally murdered five persons (including Polanski's wife, actess Sharon Tate). The following
night, Manson's hit team—with the addition of Leslie Van Houten
—invaded another home, killing Leno and Posemary LaBianca.
Other homicides appear to have been drug-related, or commis-
sioned by Manson in an effort to silence witnesses. "Family"
members Robert Beausoleil, Susan Atkins, Bruce Davis, and
Steven Grogan were convicted of murdering musician Gary Hinman,
on Manson's orders, in an apparent dispute over money and/or
drugs. Davis and Grogan were subsequently convicted of killing
Donald Shea, a potential prosecution witness who disappeared
during Manson's first trial. Manson, himself, stands convicted of nine murders, and is suspected of committing—or com-
missioning—several others. All defendants were sentenced to
die, their penalties commuted to life imprisonment following
a Supreme Court ruling which briefly banned capital punishment.
Remnants of the Manson "family" still survive and occasionally
make headlines, as when alumnus Lynette "Squeaky" Fromme tried
to assassinate President Gerald Ford, in 1975.

Books

*   Atkins, Susan, and Bob Slosser. CHILD OF SATAN, CHILD
    OF GOD. Cited above as item 99.

    Self-serving attempt to portray Atkins as a Manson
    "victim," thereby hastening her own hoped-for parole.

364A. Bishop, George. WITNESS TO EVIL. Los Angeles: Nash
       Publishing, 1971.

    A journalist presents excerpts from the transcript of
    Manson's trial, with personal observations.

*   Boar, Rober, and Nigel Blundell. THE WORLD'S MOST IN-
    FAMOUS MURDERS. Cited above as item 2, pp. 119-121.

Brief case history, presented in sensational tabloid
style.

* Browning, Norma Lee. THE PSYCHIC WORLD OF PETER HURKOS.
  Cited above as item 186, pp. 253-255.

Details of the psychic's "incredible" performance were
withheld pending Manson's trial. According to the
author, "we're saving them for our next book"—which
has yet to be published. (It is revealed that Hurkos
named "a man called Charlie" as a suspect, no great feat
after the arrest of two separate Charlie's in the case.)

365. Bugliosi, Vincent, and Curt Gentry. HELTER SKELTER. New
     York: W.W. Norton, 1974.

Inside view of the Manson investigation and trial, from
the prosecuting attorney who broke the family.

* CRIMES AND PUNISHMENT: A PICTORIAL ENCYCLOPEDIA OF ABER-
  RANT BEHAVIOR, Volume 5. Cited above as item 4, pp.
  49-57.

Case history presented in an encyclopedic format.

366. Emmons, Nuel, and Charles Manson. MANSON IN HIS OWN
     WORDS. New York: Grove Press, 1986.

Long-awaited first-person account of the Manson family
from its founder and leader. Manson, through Emmons,
predictably struggles to lay off blame for his predica-
ment on virtually everyone except himself, primarily
"middle-class" families who "forced" their sons and
daughters to join his nomadic clan. Side-steps the
persistent and persuasive allegations of Satanic cult
involvement raised by items 126 above and 368 below.

* FACTS ON FILE. Volume 29, 1969. Cited above as item 7,
  pp. 720, 862.

Reports the Los Angeles murders and indictments.

* FACTS ON FILE. Volume 30, 1970. Cited above as item 7,
  pp. 448, 548, 575, 909.

Reports the events of Manson's trial.

* FACTS ON FILE. Volume 31, 1971. Cited above as item 7, pp. 59, 239, 724, 1037-1038.

    Continues coverage of the Manson and Watson trials.

* FACTS ON FILE. Volume 37, 1977. Cited above as item 7, p. 342.

    An appeals court refuses to review Manson's verdict.

* FACTS ON FILE. Volume 38, 1978. Cited above as item 7, p. 824.

    Leslie Van Houten's third trial results in a triple life sentence.

* FACTS ON FILE. Volume 44, 1984. Cited above as item 7, p. 960.

    A fellow inmate sets Manson on fire, inflicting minor injuries.

* Gaute, J.H.H., and Robin Odell. THE MURDERERS' WHO'S WHO. Cited above as item 8, pp. 158-159.

    Case history presented in an encyclopedic format.

* Green, Jonathon. THE GREATEST CRIMINALS OF ALL TIME. Cited above as item 11, pp. 153-154.

    Brief case history in an encyclopedic format.

* Levin, Jack, and James Alan Fox. MASS MURDER: AMERICA'S GROWING MENACE. Cited above as item 15.

    Profiles the "family" in a discussion of mass murder.

367. Livsey, Clara. THE MANSON WOMEN: A "FAMILY" PORTRAIT. New York: Richard Marek, 1980.

    Examines certain female members of the tribe, including family background and psychological profiles.

* Nash, Jay Robert. BLOODLETTERS AND BADMEN. Cited above as item 20, pp. 361-362.

    Case history presented in an encyclopedic format.

* ————. CRIME CHRONOLOGY, 1900–1983. Cited above as item 21, p. 178.

Sketchy case history presented in time line format.

368. Sanders, Ed. THE FAMILY. New York: E.P. Dutton, 1971.

Fascinating profile of Manson and his disciples, with heavy emphasis on occult "sleazo inputs" which influenced the group's tendency toward ritualistic murder. Material on California's death cults in general is superior to the coverage of Manson himself, although lawsuits intimidated the publisher into dropping a chapter on Manson's links with one Satanic cult, the Process Church of Final Judgment, from later editions. Thought-provoking and frightening.

369. Schiller, Lawrence. THE KILLING OF SHARON TATE. New York: New American Library, 1970.

Sensational paperback examination of the case.

* Sifakis, Carl. THE ENCYCLOPEDIA OF AMERICAN CRIME. Cited above as item 29, pp. 471–472.

Case history presented in an encyclopedic format.

* Terry, Maury. THE ULTIMATE EVIL. Cited above as item 126.

Presents new evidence linking Manson and some of his followers, still at large, with a series of Satanic murders continuing into the 1980s. An excellent companion volume to item 368 above.

370. Watkins, Paul, and Guillermo Soledad. MY LIFE WITH CHARLES MANSON. New York: Bantam, 1979.

Manson's self-proclaimed "number two man" laments the perversion of "communal love" by a man he once idolized. Interesting for its insider's perspective, and refreshing, as the only Manson family memoir from a member who has not been "born again" in an effort to get out of jail free.

371. Watson, Charles "Tex". WILL YOU DIE FOR ME? Dallas, Tex.: Cross Roads Publications, 1978.

Yet another religious broadside from a convicted murderer, this time Tex Watson, leader of the hit team that slaughtered seven California residents in two nights of mayhem. Again, parole boards remain prudently unimpressed.

*   Wilson, Colin. A CRIMINAL HISTORY OF MANKIND. Cited above as item 34, pp. 628-630.

Case history in a general discussion of modern, irrational crimes.

*   ————, and Donald Seaman. THE ENCYCLOPEDIA OF MODERN MURDER. Cited above as item 36, pp. 148-155.

Case history presented in an encyclopedic format.

Articles

372. Adelson, S. "Emerging from Her Grief, Gwen Tate Crusades to Keep Sharon's Murderers in Jail." PEOPLE WEEKLY 18 (September 20, 1982): 80+.

Recounts the struggle of a victim's mother to avert parole for members of the Manson tribe.

373. "Case of the Hypnotic Hippie." NEWSWEEK 74 (December 15, 1969): 30-32+.

Background on Manson and company.

374. Conroy, F. "Manson Wins! A Fantasy." HARPER'S 241 (November 1970): 53-59.

Tongue-in-cheek appraisal of the consequences of a Manson acquittal.

375. Coyne, J.R. "Helter Skelter." NATIONAL REVIEW 27 (January 31, 1975): 119.

Reviews item 365 above.

376. "Demon of Death Valley." TIME 94 (December 12, 1969): 22+.

Background on Manson and his followers.

377. Farrell, B. "In Hollywood, the Dead Keep Right on Dying." LIFE 67 (November 7, 1969): 4.

Continuing coverage of the Manson case.

378. "Helter Skelter." NEWSWEEK 84 (October 28, 1974): 32.

    Reviews item 365 above.

379. "Helter Skelter." TIME 104 (November 4, 1974): 112+.

    Reviews item 365 above.

380. "Hollywood Murders." NEWSWEEK 74 (August 18, 1969): 28.

    Reports the Tate-La Bianca homicides.

381. Maas, Peter. "Sharon Tate Murders." LADIES' HOME JOURNAL 87 (April 1970): 52+.

    Examines the crimes and perpetrators.

382. Muggeridge, Malcol. "Helter Skelter." ESQUIRE 84 (July 1975): 22+.

    Reviews item 365 above.

383. "Night of Horror." TIME 94 (August 22, 1969): 16-17.

    Further reports on the Hollywood crimes.

384. "Nothing but Bodies." TIME 94 (August 15, 1969): 24.

    Original report of the Tate murders.

385. O'Neil, P. "Monstrous Manson Family." LIFE 67 (December 19, 1969): 2A, 20-31.

    Pictorial examination of the Manson tribe.

386. Roberts, S.V. "Charlie Manson: One Man's Family." NEW YORK TIMES MAGAZINE (January 4, 1970): 10-11+.

    Examines life with Manson from an outsider's viewpoint.

387. Sanders, Ed. "Charlie and the Devil." ESQUIRE 76 (November 1971): 105-112+.

    Excerpts from item 368 above, dealing with the occult connections of Manson and company.

388. Singer, M. "Fragments from the Shooting Gallery."
      RAMPARTS MAGAZINE 8 (April 1970): 16-18.

      "Radical" view of the family, police procedures, and
      the Tate murders.

389. "Tate Set." NEWSWEEK 74 (August 25, 1969): 24-25.

      Examines the murder and on-going manhunt.

390. Thompson, T. "Tragic House on the Hill." LIFE 67
      (August 29, 1969): 42-46+.

      Pictorial examination of the Tate murders.

391. "Where Have All the Flowers Gone?" NATIONAL REVIEW
      21 (December 16, 1969): 1257.

      Conservative assessment of the "flower generation's"
      decline, using Manson as a prime example of degeneration.

392. Woods, W.C. "Helter Skelter." NEW REPUBLIC 172 (Janu-
      ary 4, 1975): 112+.

      Reviews item 365 above.

               375. MANUEL, PETER THOMAS ANTHONY (S)

      Scottish habitual criminal and slayer of at least eleven
persons between 1954 and 1958. Roughly half of Manuel's victims were homeowners slain in their beds during burglaries;
the rest were girls and young women, strangled or beaten to
death in the course of abortive sexual assaults. (Although
clothing was removed from the victims in each case, Manuel
never succeeded in raping any of them.) Hanged in 1958.

   * Boar, Roger, and Nigel Blundell. THE WORLD'S MOST IN-
      FAMOUS MURDERS. Cited above as item 2, pp. 122-126.

      Case history presented in sensational tabloid style.

   * CRIMES AND PUNISHMENT: A PICTORIAL ENCYCLOPEDIA OF ABER-
      RANT BEHAVIOR, Volume 7. Cited above as item 4, p. 79.

      Case history presented in an encyclopedic format.

   * Nash, Jay Robert. CRIME CHRONOLOGY, 1900-1983. Cited
      above as item 21, p. 157.

Brief case history presented in time line format.

* Wilson, Colin, and Patricia Putnam. THE ENCYCLOEPDIA OF
MURDER . Cited above as item 35, pp. 372-375.

Case history presented in an encyclopedic format.

376. MARQUETTE, RICHARD (S)

Oregon sex slayer who raped, strangled, and dismembered
his first female victim in 1961. Sentenced to life imprisonment, he was paroled after serving twelve years. Shortly after
his release, Marquette murdered and dissected another woman,
whereupon he was returned to prison.

* Brian, Dennis. MURDERERS DIE. Cited above as item 3,
p. 261.

Uses Marquette's case as an argument in favor of capital punishment.

* Nash, Jay Robert. MURDER, AMERICA. Cited above as item
23, p. 431.

Sketchy case history presented in time line format.

377. MARTIN, RHONDA BELL (S)

Homicidal housewife who confessed, in 1956, to poisoning
her mother , three of her five husbands, and three of her own
children. The six murders (one husband survive, though paralyzed) spanned a period of 19 years, beginning in 1937. Sentenced to life.

* CRIMES AND PUNISHMENT: A PICTORIAL ENCYCLOPEDIA OF ABER-
RANT BEHAVIOR, Volume 12. Cited above as item 4, p. 110.

Case history in a section on female murderers.

* FACTS ON FILE. Volume 16, 1956. Cited above as item 7,
p. 88.

Reports Martin's arrest and confession.

378. MATTHEWS, J.B. Jr. (M)

Virginia resident who beat his three children to death
with a baseball bat, in April 1959. After attacking and

injuring his wife with the same weapon, Matthews committed
suicide by stabbing himself.

* FACTS ON FILE. Volume 19, 1959. Cited above as item 7,
  p. 123.

   Contemporaneous report of the Matthews massacre.

379. MATUSHKA, SYLVESTRE (M)

   Hungarian sexual deviate, capable of achieving orgasm
only while watching train wrecks. In the pursuit of gratifi-
cation, he made several attempts to derail trains around Buda-
pest, finally succeeding with a dynamite charge which claimed
22 lives in September 1931. Seeking to cash in on the tragedy,
Matushka joined passengers of the train in filing damage suits
against the railroad. Official curiosity was aroused when he
could not prove that he had been a passenger. Subsequent investigation led to his arrest and swift confession. A sentence of death was commuted to life imprisonment. Matushka
was subsequently freed by Soviet authorities, who put him to
work as an explosives expert.

* CRIMES AND PUNISHMENT: A PICTORIAL ENCYCLOPEDIA OF ABER-
  RANT BEHAVIOR, Volume 20. Cited above as tiem 4, p. 10.

   Case history presented in an encyclopedic format.

* Wilson, Colin. A CRIMINAL HISTORY OF MANKIND. Cited
  above as item 34, p. 608.

   Brief case history in a discussion of sexually-inspired
   crimes.

380. MAXWELL, BOBBY JOE (S)

   The Los Angeles "Skid Row Stabber," one of several random
slayers who have preyed upon homeless transients in recent
years. Maxwell's crime spree followed, and in some ways emu-
lated, that of "Skid Row Slasher" Vaughn Greenwood, although
the two men were apparently unacquainted. Ten male victims
were stabbed to death, apparently by the same assailant,
during 1978 and 1979. Maxwell was convicted in two of the
cases, in 1984, and police consider the eight other "identical" crimes to be solved with his imprisonment.

* FACTS ON FILE. Volume 44, 1984. Cited above as item 7,
  p. 978.

* Levin, Jack, and James Alan Fox. MASS MURDER: AMERICA'S
  GROWING MENACE. Cited above as item 15.

  Brief case history in a discussion of serial murder.

381. MAXWELL, DAVID (M): See JOHNSON, JOEY

382. MAYBERRY, FRANK (M)

Resident of Evergreen, Va., who settled a rancorous family
argument by shooting his brother-in-law in 1955. When a doctor
arrived to treat the dying man, Mayberry killed him, as well.
Cornered and wounded by police at his home, Mayberry was subsequently sentenced to life.

* FACTS ON FILE. Volume 15, 1955. Cited above as item 7,
  p. 72.

  Reports the shootings and Mayberry's arrest.

383. MEADOWS, JOHNNY (S)

Convicted of murdering one woman near Odessa, Tex.,
Meadows signed confessions to three other sexually-motivated
slayings, but he was never prosecuted in those cases. His
sentence of 99 years in prison ended a series of stranglings
in Ector County and environs. Various stabbing deaths of other
women in the vicinity, between 1968 and 1972 (when Meadows was
convicted) are considered to be unrelated.

* Nash, Jay Robert. CRIME CHRONOLOGY, 1900-1983. Cited
  above as item 21, p. 182.

  Erroneous case history presented in time line format.
  A year after being advised of the Meadows conviction,
  Nash still credits eleven victims to "the so-called
  Texas Strangler," whom he describes as still at large.

* ————. OPEN FILES. Cited above as item 24, pp. 246-247.

  Carelessly includes two of Meadows's known victims in
  a list of twelve killings attributed to "the Texas
  Strangler." Eleven years after Meadows was convicted
  in Odessa, Nash reports that the killer "has not been
  apprehended."

384. MEEK, GLYDE EARL (M)

Ex-wrestler and con man who murdered his lover's parents
and burned their home in Jackson, N.H., during 1985. Twelve
days later, police near Gainesville, Fla., discovered the
charred bodies of a man and woman in a burned-out rural shack.
A suicide note nearby indicated that Meek had strangled his
lover, then committed suicide by burning the shack with himself
inside. Neither body has been positively identified, and New
Hampshire State Police believe that Meek, at least, is still
alive.

393. Wadler, Joyce. "Playing with Fire." PEOPLE WEEKLY 25
      (April 28, 1986): 76-83.

      An intriguing examination of the case, sans solutions.

385. MERRETT, JOHN DONALD (S)

Born in New Zealand, Merrett grew up in Scotland, and there
shot his mother to death in 1926. The jury at his trial returned
a verdict of "not proven," and Merrett was released. More than
a quarter-century later, in 1954, Merrett murdered his wife and
mother-in-law, shooting himself to death before police could
track him down.

 * CRIMES AND PUNISHMENT: A PICTORIAL ENCYCLOPEDIA OF ABER-
    RANT BEHAVIOR, Volume 6. Cited above as item 4, pp.
    59-60.

    Brief case history in an encyclopedic format.

 * Wilson, Colin, and Patricia Putnam. THE ENCYCLOPEDIA
    OF MURDER. Cited above as item 35, pp. 388-391.

    Case history presented in an encyclopedic format.

386. MERILL, HENRY BURTON (S)

Hermit and fur trapper, arrested in 1982 on murder
charges, with associate Jerry Van Pendley, after police found
skeletal remains of two (or three) men in an abandoned well
near Blum, Texas.

394. "Body Count." TIME 120 (August 23, 1982): 12.

      Composite article recounting recent mass slayings in
      Texas.

387. MILEY, GREGORY MATTHEW (S): See BONIN, WILLIAM GEORGE

388. MILLER, ROBERT (M)

Hawaiian sniper, confined to a mental institution after the unprovoked wounding of a tourist. Released as "cured" after six years, Miller returned to a beach in Waikiki, in 1979, and shot seven more people with a rifle.

* Brian, Dennis. MURDERERS DIE. Cited above as item 3, p. 261.

   Another case used as an argument in favor of capital punishment.

389. MILLER, WALTER (S)

Slayer of two elderly victims at Chelsea, England, during May 1870. Both victims were attacked in their homes, which were looted following the murders. Miller's first victim was an old man, beaten to death with a shovel. He subsequently strangled an elderly woman, and was found out when a porter, called to remove the second body in a crate, noticed blood leaking out. Upon his confession, Miller was hanged.

* Logan, Guy B.H. MASTERS OF CRIME. Cited above as item 17, pp. 209-215.

   Case history in an anthology of 19th-century murders.

390. "MONSTER OF FLORENCE, THE" (S)

Unidentified Italian serial slayer who has claimed at least 16 victims in the countryside surrounding Florence, in the past 19 years. The first casualties were an adulterous wife and her lover, shot to death in a car, during August 1968. (The woman's young son, lying in the back seat, slept through the murder.) The woman's husband was convicted and sentenced to prison, serving six years before another couple was killed with the same gun, in 1974. Another lull in the murders followed, until 1981, when two separate couples were slain, again with the same pistol. In each year since 1981, the unknown killer has murdered one couple, parked or camped within a 19-mile radius of Florence. Each murder has occurred on moonless summer nights, between 10 p.m. and midnight, with the killer making only one tactical "mistake": in 1983, two men were shot, police believing that one's long hair deceived

the killer into thinking his target was a woman. With the
exception of the 1968 and 1983 attacks, police believe the
male victims were shot first, after which the women were shot
and sexually mutilated with a knife. (The female victim in
1985 was slashed 100 times, with one of her breasts hacked off;
next day, police received a portion of her genitalia in the
mail.) At this writing, police have no suspects in the case.

395.   Moody, John. "The Monster of Florence." TIME 127 (March
        24, 1986): 54.

        Reviews the case, anticipating future murders.

            391. "MOONLIGHT MURDERER, THE" (S)

        Texarkana gunman who attacked eight victims, killing
five, between February and May 1946. Preying normally on
couples parked in lover's lanes, the hooded sadist allowed his
first victims to live, pistol-whipping the boy and "raping"
the girl with his gun barrel. In two subsequent attacks, both
victims were shot to death, and neither girl was apparently
raped. (Sources disagree on whether the female victims were
tortured prior to death or mutilated afterward, but the more
substantial accounts seem to indicate they were not.) The
final attack, in May, broke the killer's pattern when he invaded a rural home, shooting a farmer to death and wounding
the dead man's wife before she managed to escape in the dark-
ness. The discovery of a man's mutilated body on nearby railroad tracks, days later, raised initial hopes that the killer
had committed suicide, but an autopsy revealed that the man
had been stabbed to death, then thrown on the tracks. Some
authorities now consider the man another victim of the "Texarkana Phantom." Texas Rangers in charge of the case regard
the murders as an unsolved mystery, while some local authorities maintain the killer was identified, but never prosecuted
due to lack of evidence.

                          Books

    *   Wilson, Colin. A CASEBOOK OF MURDER. Cited above as
        item 33, p. 152.

        Brief case history in a sociological study of murder.

    *   ————. ORDER OF ASSASSINS. Cited above as item 76,
        p. 80.

        Sketches a psychological profile of the killer.

* ————, and Patricia Putnam. THE ENCYCLOPEDIA OF MURDER.
  Cited above as item 35, pp. 401-402.

  Case history presented in an encyclopedic format.

Articles

396. "Texarkana Terror." LIFE 20 (June 10, 1946): 40-41.

     Pictorial spread on precatuions taken by frightened
     locals, unaware that the killer had already "retired."

392. MONTESPAN, MADAME DE (S)

Chief mistress of French King Louis XIV, who sought to
hold his affections through resort to black magic and Satanism.
With Abbe Guibourg, Catherine La Voisin, and others, she participated in numerous black mass ceremonies, at which infants
were sacrificed during incantations to various demons. Estimates of the final infant body-count range from a minimum of
1,500 to a maximum of some 3,000 victims. Released without
prosecution, by royal decree.

* Hoeller, Stephen A. "The Real Black Mass." Cited above
  as item 282.

  Recaps the notorious "black chamber" scandal of Louis's
  reign, detailing prosecution evidence.

* Masters, R.E.L., and Eduard Lea. PERVERSE CRIMES IN
  HISTORY. Cited above as item 18, pp. 9-10.

  Brief recap of the black mass investigations, included
  in a general discussion of sexually perverse crimes.

393. MONTREAL CHILD MURDERS (S)

Unsolved slayings of at least five children, ages five
through twelve, taking place in Montreal, Canada, between November 1984 and July 1985. All of the victims were male, and
at least two were sexually abused. Methods of murder included
beating, stabbing, and drowning, with the bodies discarded in
rural areas near the city. At this writing, police have
"officially" linked only two of the crimes with a single, unidentified killer, and the investigation is continuing.

397. "The Montreal Murderer." MACLEANS 98 (July 1, 1985): 56.

     Reports the murders and manhunt in progress.

394. MOONEY, ALLAN (M)

Convicted, in a sensational trial, for the brutal murders
of two women at Saranac Lake, N.Y. Executed in May 1904.

* Nash, Jay Robert. CRIME CHRONOLOGY, 1900-1983. Cited
  above as item 21, p. 12.

  Case history presented in time line format.

395. MOORE, MANUEL (S): See "ZEBRA MURDERS"

396. MORAN, EDWARD, Jr. (S): See "DE MAU MAU MURDERS"

397. MORS, FRDERICK (S)

Austrian immigrant to New York City, who took a job as
a nurse's aide at a Bronx home for the elderly. Between August 1914 and January 1915, Mors killed 17 patients with arsenic
and chloroform. Following his arrest, he was declared insane
by state psychiatrists and confined to a mental institution
for life. Mors escaped from the hospital after serving ten
years, and was never recaptured.

* Nash, Jay Robert. MURDER, AMERICA. Cited above as item
  23, p. 390.

  Sketchy case history presented in time line format.

398. MORRIS, RAYMOND LESLIE (S)

British sadist and rape-slayer of at least five children
in the mid-1960s. Between 1965 and 1967, Morris is known to
have abducted five girls, ages six through ten, whom he sexually abused before strangling or smothering them. Capital
punishment having been abolished in England, Morris was sentenced to life.

* Wilson, Colin. A CASEBOOK OF MURDER. Cited above as
  item 33, pp. 14-17.

  Case history in a sociological survey of murder.

* ———. ORDER OF ASSASSINS. Cited above as item 76,
  pp. 101-103.

  Sketches a psychological profile of Morris.

* ————, and Donald Seaman. THE ENCYCLOPEDIA OF MODERN
MURDER. Cited above as item 36, pp. 161-164.

Case history presented in an encyclopedic format.

399. MORSE, JOSEPH (S)

California slayer who murdered his own mother and his
crippled sister. While awaiting trial for those crimes, he
killed a third victim, apparently selected at random. Following receipt of his death sentence, Morse told an interviewer:
"I can't change because I can't benefit by experience. If I
get out of here, I'd probably kill again."

* Brian, Dennis. MURDERERS DIE. Cited above as item 3,
p. 261.

Another case used as an argument in favor of capital
punishment.

400. "MOSCOW RIPPER, THE" (S)

Unidentified slayer who mutilated several Russian women
during 1885, escaping detection. Some students of the 19th-
century "Ripper" phenomenon consider this killer's appearance
—and sudden disappearance—three years before Jack the Ripper's crimes in London as more than coincidental.

* Masters, R.E.L., and Eduard Lea. PERVERSE CRIMES IN
HISTORY. Cited above as item 18, p. 93.

Lamentably brief case history in a general discussion
of sadistic mutilation murders.

401. MOSCOW SEX MURDERS (S)

Apparently unsolved decapitation slayings of several
Moscow women during 1979. Refusal of Soviet authorities to
admit the existence of major crime in their capital city makes
the case difficult to pursue. A possibility remains that the
killer was identified and disposed of without publicity, as
was alleged in the case of "Ivan the Ripper."

* Nash, Jay Robert. CRIME CHRONOLOGY, 1900-1983. Cited
above as item 21, p. 196.

Brief case history presented in time line format.

402. MUDGETT, HERMAN WEBSTER (S)

Medical student, bigamist, swindler, and sadistic slayer who worked as a druggist in Chicago during the Chicago Fair of 1893. As "H.H. Holmes," Mudgett also ran a rooming house, later dubbed the "murder castle," in which various tenants were slain and robbed. Investigation of an attempted insurance fraud finally led to exposure of Mudgett's more lethal acitivities, in 1894, and a search of his "castle" revealed sumps, lime pits, gas chambers, a makeshift crematorium, and many secret passageways. After his conviction in one murder, Mudgett confessed to killing 27 other victims, mainly young women attracted to Chicago by the fair. Students of his case are unanimous in their agreement that there were, undoubtedly, more victims, but in the absence of physical evidence, no firm body-count is available. (Estimates range from 50 victims to "over 200.") Hanged in May 1896.

Books

398. Boswell, Charles, and Lewis Thompson. "Nightmare Castle."
      THE CHICAGO CRIME BOOK. Cleveland, Ohio: World Pub-
      lishing Co., 1967, pp. 217-237.

      Reviews the case in an anthology of famous trials.

   * CRIMES AND PUNISHMENT: A PICTORIAL ENCYCLOPEDIA OF ABER-
      RANT BEHAVIOR, Volume 5. Cited above as item 4, pp.
      116-122.

      Case history presented in an encyclopedic format.

399. Eckert, Allan W. THE SCARLET MANSION. Boston: Little,
      Brown, 1985.

      Speculative novelization of Mudgett's career, billed
      erroneously as "true crime" by the publisher. Despite
      a foundation in solid research, this should not be con-
      fused with nonfiction.

400. Franke, David. THE TORTURE DOCTOR. New York: Hawthorn
      Books, 1975.

      A detailed examination of the Mudgett case, Franke's
      volume includes contemporary illustrations and excerpts
      from Chicago press reports which give the book an inter-
      esting 19th-century flavor. Valuable.

401. HOLMES, THE ARCH FIEND, OR A CARNIVAL OF CRIME, THE LIFE,
      TRIAL, CONFESSION AND EXECUTION OF H.H. HOLMES. Cin-
      cinnati: Barclay and Co., 1895.

      If the registered copyright date is correct, this sen-
      sational effort had the distinction of covering Mudgett's
      hanging a year before the actual event!

402. HOLMES' OWN STORY. Philadelphia: Burke & McFeteridge, 1895.

      Draws upon Mudgett's confessions to compile another
      sensational, contemporaneous account.

   * Nash, Jay Robert. ALMANAC OF WORLD CRIME. Cited above
      as item 19, p. 22.

      Brief case history of Mudgett's sideline career as an
      arsonist-for-profit in Chicago.

   * ————. BLOODLETTERS AND BADMEN. Cited above as item
      20, pp. 382-387.

      Case history presented in an encyclopedic format.

   * ————. MURDER, AMERICA. Cited above as item 23, pp.
      188-189, 255. 368, 372, 447.

      Various references in an anthology of "classic" murders.

   * Scott, Sir Harold. THE CONCISE ENCYCLOPEDIA OF CRIME
      AND CRIMINALS. Cited above as item 27, pp. 184-185.

      Case history presented in an encyclopedic format.

   * Sifakis, Carl. THE ENCYCLOPEDIA OF AMERICAN CRIME.
      Cited above as item 29, p. 343.

      Brief case history presented in encyclopedic format.

403. TRIAL OF HERMAN WEBSTER MUDGETT, ALIAS H.H. HOLMES.
      Philadelphia: George T. Bisel, 1897.

      Contemporaneous account of Mudgett's case, published
      soon after his execution.

   * Wilson, Colin. A CRIMINAL HISTORY OF MANKIND. Cited
      above as item 34, pp. 486-491.

Case history in a discussion of 19th-century murder.

* ————, and Patricia Putnam. THE ENCYCLOPEDIA OF MURDER. Cited above as item 35, pp. 286-289.

Case history presented in an encyclopedic format.

Articles

404. Hynd, A. "House on Sixty-third Street." GOOD HOUSE-KEEPING 120 (January 1945): 24+.

Historical retrospective on Mudgett's case.

405. Martin, John Bartlow. "Killer's Castle." AMERICAN MERCURY 83 (October 1956): 116-124.

Thirteen years after item 406 below, author Martin revisits the Mudgett case.

406. ————. "Master of the Murder Castle." HARPER'S WEEKLY. 188 (December 1943): 76-85.

Reviews the case from a historical perspective.

403. MULLIN, HERBERT WILLIAM (S)

Paranoid schizophrenic who claimed 13 victims around Santa Cruz, Calif., at the same time another serial killer, Edmund Kemper, was active in the area. Mullin heard "voices" of potential victims, begging him to kill them, and professed to believe that his "human sacrifices" had averted natural disasters, such as catastrophic earthquakes. Ten of his victims were shot, two were stabbed, (including a priest, killed in his confessional), and one was beaten to death with a base-ball bat. Considered sane by legal standards, Mullin was charged with ten of the slayings, convicted in August 1973, and sentenced to life.

Books

* Damio, Ward. URGE TO KILL. Cited above as item 332.

Quicky paperback examination of the Santa Cruz "murder epidemic." Factual reporting of the crimes, but with little insight into motives of the killers.

* FACTS ON FILE. Volume 33, 1973. Cited above as item 7,
  p. 796.

  Reports Mullin's conviction.

* Godwin, John. MURDER USA. Cited above as item 10,
  pp. 260–261.

  Brief case history in a discussion of multiple murder.

* Levin, Jack, and James Alan Fox. MASS MURDER: AMERICA'S
  GROWING MENACE. Cited above as item 15.

  Brief case history in a discussion of serial murder.

* Lunde, Donald T. MURDER AND MADNESS. Cited above as
  item 68, pp. 63–81.

  The psychiatrist who examined Mullin prior to trial
  relates his findings. Lunde blames the crimes, in part,
  on budget cuts which closed numerous mental institutions
  in California, denying treatment to patients like Mullin,
  with a potential for violence.

407. ————, and Jefferson Morgan. THE DIE SONG. New York:
  W.W. Norton, 1980.

  Lunde enlists a co-author to produce a more detailed
  examination of the Mullin case. Instructive.

* Nash, Jay Robert. ALMANAC OF WORLD CRIME. Cited above
  as item 19, p. 290.

  Brief case history in a discussion of mass murder.

* Sifakis, Carl. THE ENCYCLOPEDIA OF AMERICAN CRIME.
  Cited above as item 29, p. 506.

  Brief case history in an encyclopedic format.

* West, Don. SACRIFICE UNTO ME. Cited above as item 333.

  Sensational overview of the Santa Cruz murders, with
  no serious attempt to analyze motives.

* Wilson, Colin. A CRIMINAL HISTORY OF MANKIND. Cited
  above as item 34, p. 637.

Case history in a discussion of modern serial murder.

* ———, and Donald Seaman. THE ENCYCLOPEDIA OF MODERN
  MURDER. Cited above as item 36, pp. 165-167.

Case history presented in an encyclopedic format.

Articles

408. "Murderville, U.S.A." NEWSWEEK 81 (March 5, 1973): 30.

Reports the continuing search for multiple maniacs in
Santa Cruz.

404. MURREL, JOHN A. (S)

Enigmatic Tennesseean who served ten years in prison for
his role as the alleged organizer of an abortive slave revolt.
Also linked with the unpunished murders of numerous blacks,
with one estimate placing his body-count near the 500 mark.

* Sifakis, Carl. THE ENCYCLOPEDIA OF AMERICAN CRIME.
  Cited above as item 29, pp. 512-513.

Case history presented in an encyclopedic format.

405. NASH, STEPHEN A. (S)

Convicted, in 1957, of stabbing two men to death in Los
Angeles, Nash subsequently confessed to nine other murders,
committed at random. He was never charged in the other cases,
having already been sentenced to die.

* FACTS ON FILE. Volume 17, 1957. Cited above as item 7,
  p. 76.

Reports Nash's confession and sentencing.

406. NEAL, JAMES LEROY (M)

Resident of El Reno, Okla., who raped and killed three
women in a drunken spree on Christmas Eve, 1956. Armed with
a gun as he fled the scene of his crime, Neal accidentally
shot and killed himself when his car slid into a ditch.

* FACTS ON FILE. Volume 16, 1956. Cited above as item 7,
  p. 432.

Reports Neal's crimes and subsequent accidental death.

407. NEAL, WILLIAM (M): See CRAFT, ELLIS

408. NELSON, DALE MERLE (M)

Canadian logger, reportedly under the influence of LSD, who murdered eight of his neighbors—including one man, two women, and five children—in a wild crime spree during September 1970. Bizarre acts of mutilation, necrophilia, and cannibalism were inflicted upon the bodies of two young female victims before Nelson was captured. (In one case, he opened the victim's stomach with a knife, thrust his face inside, and devoured recently-ingested food.) Deemed sane by state psychiatrists, Nelson was convicted on two counts of murder in 1971 and was sentenced to life.

* FACTS ON FILE. Volume 30, 1970. Cited above as item 7, p. 648.

   Reports Nelson's crimes and arrest.

* Gaute, J.H.H., and Robin Odell. THE MURDERERS' WHO'S WHO. Cited above as item 8, p. 173.

   Case history presented in an encyclopedic format.

* Green, Jonathon. THE GREATEST CRIMINALS OF ALL TIME. Cited above as item 11, pp. 260-261.

   Brief case history in an encyclopedic format.

* Nash, Jay Robert. CRIME CHRONOLOGY, 1900-1983. Cited above as item 21, p. 180.

   Sketchy case histroy presented in time line format.

409. Still, Larry. THE LIMITS OF SANITY. New York: St. Martin's Press, 1973.

   Attacks the standards for judging legal sanity and condemns the court system for handling Nelson as a rational and competent defendant.

409. NELSON, EARLE LEONARD (S)

Notorious "Gorilla Murderer" of the 1920s, credited with the rape-slayings of at least 22 female victims in 1926 and

1927. (He was also suspected in at least three other deaths, but without substantial evidence.) Most of Nelson's victims were also his landladies, although one was a child, eight months old. Nelson began to exhibit perverse, violent tendencies in childhood, following an accident in which he was struck and dragged by a trolley car, sustaining critical head injuries which left him comatose for nearly a week. (Another potential source of Nelson's mental instability may lie in the fact that his mother died of venereal disease complications, shortly after his birth.) Sentenced to prison for a Philadelphia rape, Nelson escape twice, and was a hunted fugitive when he began his killing spree. Finally arrested and convicted for one of three Canadian murders, Nelson was hanged in January 1928. His nickname derived from his short stature and brutish, simian appearance.

* CRIMES AND PUNISHMENT: A PICTORIAL ENCYCLOPEDIA OF ABERRANT BEHAVIOR, Volume 7. Cited above as item 4, p. 79.

   Case history presented in an encyclopedic format.

* Douthwaite, L.C. MASS MURDER. Cited above as item 6.

   Case history of then-recent murders, in a general discourse on multiple slayings.

* Gaute, J.H.H., and Robin Odell. THE MURDERERS' WHO'S WHO. Cited above as item 8, pp. 173-174.

   Case history presented in an encyclopedic format.

* Nash, Jay Robert. ALMANAC OF WORLD CRIME. Cited above as item 19, p. 263.

   Brief case history in a general discussion of mass murder

* ————. BLOODLETTERS AND BADMEN. Cited above as item 20, pp. 397-402.

   Case history presented in an encyclopedic format.

* ————. CRIME CHRONOLOGY, 1900-1983. Cited above as item 21, pp. 45, 68, 71-72.

   Follows Nelson's crime spree with time line entries.

* Sifakis, Carl. THE ENCYCLOPEDIA OF AMERICAN CRIME. Cited above as item 29, pp. 519-520.

Case history presented in an encyclopedic format.

* Wilson, Colin. A CRIMINAL HISTORY OF MANKIND. Cited above as item 34, p. 607.

Brief case history in a discussion of mass murder.

* ————, and Patricia Putnam. THE ENCYCLOPEDIA OF MURDER. Cited above as item 35, pp. 411-414.

Case history presented in an encyclopedic format.

410. NELSON, SIMON PETER (M)

Illinois resident who fatally stabbed his six children, in January 1978, to "get even" with his estranged wife, who was planning a divorce. Convicted in May 1978, Nelson was sentenced to life.

* FACTS ON FILE. Volume 38, 1978. Cited above as item 7, p. 396.

Reports Nelson's conviction, with a recap of the case.

411. NESSETT, ARNFINN (S)

Director of the Orkdal Valley Nursing Home, in Norway, and holder of the title as Scandinavia's most prolific murderer. Convicted of slaying 22 patients between 1977 and 1980, Nessett is a prime suspect in the deaths of some 62 others who died unexpectedly, over a 20-year period, at three hospitals where the killer was employed. Most of Nessett's victims were dispatched with poison, a curare derivative. During police interrogations, prior to his trial, Nessett remarked that, "I've killed so many, I'm unable to remember them all." He received the maximum sentence possible under Norwegian law: 21 years in prison, with a possible ten years preventive detention tack on, for good measure.

* Levin, Jack, and James Alan Fox. MASS MURDER: AMERICA'S GROWING MENACE. Cited above as item 15.

Brief case history in a discussion of serial murder.

* Wilson, Colin, and Donald Seaman. THE ENCYCLOPEDIA OF MODERN MURDER. Cited above as item 36, pp. 172-173.

Case history presented in an encyclopedic format.

412. NEW HAMPSHIRE INFANT MURDERS (S)

In early April 1983, homeowner Ruth Davis, of Somersworth, N.H., was cleaning her basement when she decided to open an old steamer trunk which she had been storing for a friend the past 20 years. Inside, she found the mummified remains of five infants, each wrapped in local newspapers spanning the period from 1949 to 1952. Police announced that the previous owner of the trunk——Shirley Thomas, of Rochester, N.H.——would not be indicted, based on evidence that she, in turn, had received the trunk from a third party, since deceased. No final solution to the gothic case has been made public at this writing.

410. Shapiro, Walter, and Marsha Zabarsky. "New England
        Gothic: Skeletons in a Trunk." NEWSWEEK 101 (May 16,
        1983): 42.

Contemporaneous report of the unfolding case.

413. NEW JERSEY HOSPITAL MURDERS (S)

Sudden, unexplained deaths of 13 patients at Riverdell Hospital, in Oradell, N.J., over a ten-month period beginning in December 1965. Patients, ranging from a four-year-old girl to a woman of eighty, expired during otherwise uneventful re-cuperation, following routine surgical procedures. Suspicion fell upon a hospital surgeon, dubbed "Dr. X" by the press, after empty vials of curare were found in his locker. Despite "strong circumstantial evidence," the investigation was drop-ped by police after only two weeks, then reopened ten years later, after mysterious deaths in an Ann Arbor, Mich., hospital attracted national attention. Dr. Mario E. Jascalevich was indicted in 1976, on a charge of murdering five patients at Riverdell; he was acquitted on all counts at his trial, in October 1978, and the case remains unsolved.

Books

 * FACTS ON FILE. Volume 36, 1976. Cited above as item 7,
        p. 384.

Reports the indictment of Dr. Jascalevich.

Articles

411. Clark, Matt, and Dan Shapiro. "The Strange Case of Dr.
        X." NEWSWEEK 87 (March 22, 1976): 85-86.

Reports the reopening of the Riverdell investigation.

* "Death Follows Art." Cited above as item 41.

Reports the hospital deaths in Michigan and New Jersey.

414. NEWMAN, SARAH JANE (S)

Classic "black widow," credited with the murder-for-profit of at least four husbands in Texas, spanning a period of years. Never apprehended, she disappeared on a trip to Mexico, with her fifth husband, and is "believed dead."

* Sifakis, Carl. THE ENCYCLOPEDIA OF AMERICAN CRIME. Cited above as item 29, p. 663.

Case history presented in an encyclopedic format.

415. "NICARAGUAN RIPPER, THE" (S)

Unidentified mutilation-slayer of "several" Central American prostitutes in 1889, roughly a year after the more famous Ripper ceased operations in London. Considering the relative rarity of such crimes in the 19th century, some students of the case suspect a connection with London's Jack, the Moscow Ripper of 1885, and a similar series of crimes, in Texas, during 1887.

* Masters, R.E.L., and Eduard Lea. PERVERSE CRIMES IN HISTORY. Cited above as item 18, p. 93.

Damnably short and vague account, within a general discussion of sadistic mutilation murders.

416. NICHOLSON, PHILIP (M)

British valet who slit the throats of his employers on a whim, confessing his crime after a bungled suicide attempt. Hanged in August 1813.

* Logan, Guy B.H. MASTERS OF CRIME. Cited above as item 17, pp. 219-225.

Case history in an anthology of 19th-century murders.

417. NICOLAUS, ROBERT (M)

On the day after his wife left him, in 1964, Nicolaus

took their daughter, with two children of his own from a prior marriage, and shot all three to death in a rural California field. Nicolaus explained to police that he "thought it was the best way to send them to heaven." Sentenced to die, Nicolaus had his sentence reduced, by the state supreme court, to a term of five years to life. Paroled in 1977, Nicolaus waited seven years before launching a campaign of harassment and threats against his ex-wife. In 1985, he blocked her car in a Sacramento alleyway and shot her to death, whereupon he was returned to prison.

* Brian, Denis. MURDERERS DIE. Cited above as item 3, pp. 261-262.

Case history employed as an argument in favor of capital punishment.

418. NILSEN, DENNIS ANDREW (S)

Ex-policeman and homosexual slayer who holds Britain's 20th-century record for individual murders. Between December 1978 and February 1983, Nilsen murdered 15 men, concealing the remains of several victims in and around his London apartment. Like Joachim Kroll in Germany, seven years earlier, Nilsen was finally betrayed by plumbing. Pieces of his latest victim, flushed down the toilet, caused a blockage of communal drains in his apartment building. Plumbers, summoned by neighbors, grew suspicious at the quantities of rotting meat which they recovered from the drains and called police. Other remains were discovered in closets, cupboards, and beneath the floor of Nilsen's flat. Based on Nilsen's confessions, it appears the murders were motivated by a combination of loneliness (with the bodies being kept around as "company") and a long-standing, morbid fascination with death. Asked about his motives, by psychiatrists, Nilsen responded that "enjoying it is as good a reason as any." While awaiting trial, Nilsen described himself as "an irresponsible selfish bastard who deserves everything that is coming to him." In fact, he received a term of life imprisonment, with a recommended minimum of 25 years.

412. Masters, Brian. KILLING FOR COMPANY. London: Jonathan Cape, 1985.

The definitive study of Nilsen, prepared with the killer's full cooperation. Masters's excellent account draws heavily on Nilsen's voluminous confessions (collected in 30-odd notebooks), his poetry, and sketches of the murder scenes. Invaluable.

* Wilson, Colin, and Donald Seaman. THE ENCYCLOPEDIA OF
MODERN MURDER. Cited above as item 36, pp. 173-181.

Case history presented in an encyclopedic format.

419. NORRIS, ROY L. (S): See BITTAKER, LAWRENCE, SIGMUND

420. NORTHCOTT, GORDON STEWART (S)

Pedophile and sexual sadist whose adult crimes, at least
in part, seem to have been conditioned by ancestry: Northcott's
father died in an asylum, while a maternal uncle was sentenced
to life imprisonment on conviction for one of his three known
murders. Around 1928, Northcott began abducting children,
sometimes in groups, and sexually abusing them for days or
weeks before killing them and dismembering their bodies. From
the testimony of part-time accomplices Sanford Clark and Clarence Robinson, it is apparent that some of Northcott's victims
were kidnapped for "sale" to wealthy Southern California child
molesters. Northcott eventually confessed to the murders of
17 children, although police suspected there were other victims
unaccounted for. He was executed in October 1930. Northcott's
mother, convicted of helping him murder a nine-year-old boy,
was confined to prison for life.

* Brian, Dennis. MURDERERS DIE. Cited above as item 3,
pp. 37-46.

Case history within an anthology of killers who were
put to death.

* Nash, Jay Robert. CRIME CHRONOLOGY, 1900-1983. Cited
above as item 21, p. 75.

Brief case history presented in time line format.

* ————. MURDER, AMERICA. Cited above as item 23, pp.
213, 400-401.

Sketchy case history presented in time line format.

421. OGORZOV, PAUL (S)

German "S Bahn murderer," a railway worker and member of
the Nazi party who raped and killed at least eight women between

1939 and 1941.   A sadist who enjoyed terrorizing his victims,
Ogorzov normally killed on board a train, or near the railway
at Rummelsburg, on the Berlin line.   His one-day trial, in July
1941, was conducted in secrecy to spare the Nazi party from
public embarrassment.   Two days later, Ogorzov was quietly put
to death.

*   Wilson, Colin, and Patricia Putnam.   THE ENCYCLOPEDIA OF
     MURDER.   Cited above as item 35, p. 422.

     Case history presented in an encyclopedic format.

422. OHLSON, RAYMOND R. (M)

     Recent parolee on a charge of attempted murder, resulting
from the near-strangulation of a youth in 1950, Ohlson attacked
two brothers, ages ten and twelve, stabbing them to death in
July 1957, at Stoughton, Mass.   Returned to prison for life.

*   FACTS ON FILE.   Volume 17, 1957.   Cited above as item 7,
     p. 248.

     Reports Ohlson's crimes and arrest.

423. OLAH, SUSANNE (S)

     Hungarian "seeress," famous as "the White Witch of Nag-
zrev," who convinced residents of her native village that she
could predict the deaths of local undesirables, ranging from
crippled children to adulterous husbands and wives.   In fact,
her self-fulfilling "prophecies" were helped along with poison
and the assistance of three "spiritual aides."   Well-paid in
advance for her timely "predictions," it is estimated that
Olah murdered at least 100 persons between 1909 and her arrest,
20 years later.   Her three accomplices were convicted and executed, while Olah escaped justice by committing suicide prior
to her trial.

*   CRIMES AND PUNISHMENT: A PICTORIAL ENCYCLOPEDIA OF ABER-
     RANT BEHAVIOR, Volume 12.   Cited above as item 4, pp.
     110-111.

     Case history presented in an encyclopedic format.

*   Nash, Jay Robert.   ALMANAC OF WORLD CRIME.   Cited above
     as item 19, p. 287.

     Brief case history in a discussion of mass murder.

424. OLDEN, JOSEPH (S)

American "Bluebeard" who married an estimated 15 women
during 1918 and 1919, collecting brides in Canada and the
western United States. Using the name James B. Watson in his
travels, Olden murdered at least eight of his wives before he
was arrested by Los Angeles police, in January 1920. His ultimate confession was hazy on the exact number of victims; in
fact, he had forgotten the names of two women he married and
subsequently killed. A sadistic motive was evident in most
of the killings, with the breasts and genitalia of several
victims being stabbed and slashed. Olden took jewelry from
the corpses to delay identification, but informed detectives
that, "The money part never did occur to me." Executed at
San Quentin.

* Reinhardt, James Melvin. THE PSYCHOLOGY OF STRANGE
  KILLERS. Cited above as item 70, pp. 146-164.

  Case history in an anthology of multiple murders.

425. OLIVER, FRANK (M): See SMITH, FRED

426. OLSON, CLIFFORD ROBERT (S)

Canadian habitual criminal and sadistic child killer who
beat, strangled, and stabbed to death eleven children, ages
nine to eighteen, during a nine-month period in 1980 and 1981.
(Police suspect Olson in "as many as eight more" deaths around
Vancouver in the same period.) Several of the victims were
sexually molested, before or after death. Based upon Olson's
relatively advanced age, authorities remain convinced that
there were doubtless other victims, still unknown, before the
final murder spree which led to his arrest. (Most serial
killers begin their "careers" around age 23 or 24, whereas
Olson was 42 years old at the time of his guilty plea, in
January 1982. By this reckoning, he may have been killing for
two decades prior to his eventual arrest.) Before entering
his guilty plea, Olson negotiated a controversial bargain for
the "sale" of his victims, whereby his family received a
payment of $10,000 for each corpse recovered through Olson's
confessions. By January 1982, his wife had received $90,000,
whereupon Olson accepted a sentence of eleven concurrent life
terms. He will be technically eligible for parole in the
year 2007.

Books

* Levin, Jack, and James Alan Fox. MASS MURDER: AMERICA'S
  GROWING MENACE. Cited above as item 15.

  Brief case history in a discussion of serial murder.

413. Murdock, Derrick. DISAPPEARANCES: TRUE ACCOUNTS OF
     CANADIANS WHO HAVE VANISHED. Toronto: Doubleday of
     Canada, Ltd., 1983, pp. 48-53.

     Case history examining the role of serial slayers in
     some modern disappearances.

* Nash, Jay Robert. CRIME CHRONOLOGY, 1900-1983. Cited
  above as item 21, p. 201.

  Brief, inaccurate case history presented in time line
  format. Three years after Olson's arrest, Nash reports
  the Vancouver child murders as "unsolved."

* ————. OPEN FILES. Cited above as item 24, p. 256.

  Bungling nearly every fact of the case, Nash omits at
  least three victims, placing the "Vancouver Teen Killer's"
  body-count at eight, rather than eleven. Again, despite
  the passage of two years since Olson's arrest and confession, Nash reports that "[p]olice are still searching
  for the Vancouver teen killer." Nash was informed of
  this error in 1983, but went on to repeat it in item
  21 above, the following year.

Articles

414. Gray, M. "Most Difficult Deaths of All." MACLEANS 94
     (September 14, 1981): 35.

     Reports Olson's indictment in Vancouver.

415. ————. "Olson's Fast Trip to the Coast." MACLEANS 95
     (December 13, 1982): 15.

     Recounts the search for bodies of Olson's victims.

416. Maitland, A. "Rhythm of Accusations." MACLEANS 94
     (August 31, 1981): 33.

     Reports Olson's arrest in the Vancouver crimes.

427. OMAHA, NEBRASKA, MURDERS (M)

Unsolved shootings in an Omaha nightclub, during late 1977. An unidentified black man entered the crowded bar with a shotgun and opened fire on patrons, killing two and wounding another 26 before he fled into the night. At this writing, police still have no solid suspects.

* Tobias, Ronald. THEY SHOOT TO KILL. Cited above as item 31, p. 140.

Brief case history in a survey of criminal snipers.

428. ORGERON, PAUL HAROLD (M)

Demented ex-convict who carried a suitcase filled with explosives onto a Houston, Tex., schoolyard in September 1959. Detonation of the bomb killed Orgeron, his young son, and four other persons, while wounding another nineteen.

* FACTS ON FILE. Volume 19, 1959. Cited above as item 7, p. 300.

Reports the Houston bombing and its aftermath.

429. OSBORNE FAMILY MURDERS (M)

Unsolved massacre of a Fort Wayne, Ind., family, committed by persons unknown in late September 1983. Dan and Jane Osborne, their 11-year-old son, and the family dog were found beaten to death in their fashionable home. A two-year-old daughter, though raped, was allowed to survive. A black suspect, named Perry, was arrested by police several months later, and died—the victim of a hanging—while in police custody, awaiting trial. A federal investigation confirmed the death as suicide, a verdict which failed to pacify minority groups in Fort Wayne.

Books

* Nash, Jay Robert. CRIME CHRONOLOGY, 1900-1983. Cited above as item 21, p. 206.

Brief case history presented in time line format.

Articles

417.   "Blacks Await Federal Probe Findings in Hanging Death
       of Accused Killer Perry." JET 65 (February 6, 1984):
       15.

       Describes minority unrest in Ft. Wayne, with the probe
       of Perry's death in progress.

418.   Strasser, Steven, and David Haynes. "Terror on a Gentle
       Street." NEWSWEEK 102 (October 3, 1983): 52.

       Describes the crime and manhunt in progress.

430. OWEN, JOHN (M)

       British ex-convict who invaded the home of a blacksmith
in Denham, England, during the week of his release, in May 1870.
Using a sledge hammer, Owen killed the smith, his wife, his
mother, and four children, for a total of seven victims in all.
Following the massacre, he robbed the house, but was quickly
apprehended, whereupon he made a full confession. Hanged.

   *   Logan, Guy B.H. MASTERS OF CRIME. Cited above as item
       17, pp. 53-65.

       Case history in an anthology of 19th-century murders.

431. PACKER, ALFRED (M)

       Colorado mountain man and cannibal, employed to serve
as a guide for five gold prospectors in 1873. When food ran
out, Packer killed and devoured his five companions. Upon his
arrest and conviction, he was sentenced to 40 years in prison.

Books

419.   Fenwick, Robert. ALFRED PACKER. Denver: Denver Post,
       1963.

       Historical review of Colorado's most notorious mass
       murderer.

420.   Gantt, Paul H. THE CASE OF ALFRED PACKER, THE MAN EATER.
       Denver: University of Denver, 1952.

       Scholarly approach to an historic murder case.

   *   Green, Jonathon. THE GREATEST CRIMINALS OF ALL TIME.
       Cited above as item 11, pp. 273-274.

Case history presented in an encyclopedic format.

* Hurwood, Bernhardt J. VAMPIRES, WEREWOLVES, AND GHOULS. Cited above as item 12, pp. 117-125.

    Sensational case history in an anthology of "human monsters."

* Nash, Jay Robert. BLOODLETTERS AND BADMEN. Cited above as item 20, pp. 433-435.

    Case history presented in an encyclopedic format. Unaccountably omitted from a later paperback edition, published by Warner Books.

* ————. MURDER, AMERICA. Cited above as item 23, pp. 356-357.

    Sketchy case history presented in time line format.

* Sifakis, Carl. THE ENCYCLOPEDIA OF AMERICAN CRIME. Cited above as item 29, p. 551.

    Case history presented in an encyclopedic format.

Articles

421. Randolph, John. "Alfred Packer, Cannibal." HARPER'S WEEKLY (October 17, 1874).

    Contemporaneous report of the crimes and Packer's trial.

432. PALMER, WILLIAM (S)

Degenerate British physician and poisoner-for-profit. During his five years as an apprentice physician, Palmer operated an illegal abortion clinic, while fathering 14 illegitimate children of his own, on the side, several of whom he later killed. His first victim was a male acquaintance, poisoned merely so that Palmer could observe the actions of strychnine. Subsequent murders were usually motivated by greed, or by Palmer's desire to eliminate "troublesome" relatives. The precise number of victims is unknown, but there seem to have been at least 16: in addition to his first, experimental victims, Palmer also poisoned his wife, his mother-in-law, his brother, an uncle, four legitimate children and "several" illegitimate ones, two creditors, a rival doctor, and at least one male friend. Despite the peculiar circumstances

of an autopsy on his final victim—at which Palmer was allowed
to abscond with the internal organs—circumstantial evidence
led to his conviction, and he was hanged in 1856.

* Boar, Roger, and Nigel Blundell. THE WORLD'S MOST IN-
  FAMOUS MURDERS. Cited above as item 2, pp. 127-136.

  Case history presented in sensational tabloid style.

* CRIMES AND PUNISHMENT: A PICTORIAL ENCYCLOPEDIA OF ABER-
  RANT BEHAVIOR, Volume 4. Cited above as item 4, pp.
  89-96.

  Case history presented in an encyclopedic format.

* Nash, Jay Robert. ALMANAC OF WORLD CRIME. Cited above
  as item 19, pp. 315-316.

  Case history in a general discussion of homicidal
  physicians.

* Wilson, Colin, and Patricia Putnam. THE ENCYCLOPEDIA OF
  MURDER. Cited above as item 35, pp. 428-430.

  Case history presented in an encyclopedic format.

433. PANCHENKO, DEMITRI (S)

Russian physician who gained a reputation for disposing
of unwanted relatives—for a price. His downfall occurred in
1911, when an impoverished noble employed him to dispose of
several wealthy in-laws. Panchenko succeeded in poisoning
his client's brother-in-law, inserting cholera and diptheria
cultures into the victim's food, but authorities discovered
the poisons, and Panchenko's mistress was induced to testify
against him. The doctor received a sentence of 15 years for
his part in the murder, while his employer was jailed for
life. Several other murders were suspected, but Panchenko was
never prosecuted.

* Nash, Jay Robert. ALMANAC OF WORLD CRIME. Cited above
  as item 19, p. 322.

  Brief case history in a discussion of homicidal doctors.

434. PANZRAM, CARL (S)

Habitual criminal and sexual sadist, whose adult crimes

were undoubtedly conditioned by the physical and sexual brutal-
ity he experienced as an adolescent, while confined to a state
reformatory. An American, who committed murders both in the
United States and in various parts of Africa, Panzram was
sentenced to die, in 1930, for the slaying of a Leavenworth
prison employee. While awaiting execution, Panzram kept a
journal, which contained his complete confessions. "In my
lifetime," he wrote, "I have murdered 21 human beings. I have
committed thousands of burglaries, larcenies, arsons, and last
but not least I have committed sodomy on more than 1,000 male
human beings. I have no conscience so that does not worry me.
I don't believe in men, God nor Devil. I hate the whole
damned race, including myself." Panzram's case became a rallying point for opponents of capital punishment, but as the
September 1930 execution date approached, the killer resisted
all efforts on his behalf. Asked for any last words, as he
stood on the gallows, Panzram replied, "Hurry it up! I could
hang a dozen men while you're fooling around."

422. Gaddis, Thomas E., and James O. Long. KILLER: A JOURNAL
      OF MURDER. New York: Macmillan, 1970.

      Draws on Panzram's diary to produce a fascinating
      psychological portrait of the classic misanthrope.

  *   Gaute, J.H.H., and Robin Odell. THE MURDERERS' WHO'S
      WHO. Cited above as item 8, p. 180.

      Case history presented in an encyclopedic format.

  *   Green, Jonathon. THE GREATEST CRIMINALS OF ALL TIME.
      Cited above as item 11, pp. 261-262.

      Brief case history in an encyclopedic format.

  *   Leyton, Elliott. COMPULSIVE KILLERS. Cited above as
      item 16, pp. 282-286.

      Cannibalizes item 422 above, with no new material.

  *   Nash, Jay Robert. ALMANAC OF WORLD CRIME. Cited above
      as item 19, pp. 23, 101-102.

      Brief case history in a discussion of capital punishment.

  *   ————. BLOODLETTERS AND BADMEN. Cited above as item
      20, pp. 435-440.

Case history presented in an encyclopedic format.

* ———. CRIME CHRONOLOGY, 1900-1983. Cited above as
    item 21, pp. 60, 77.

    Brief case history presented in time line format.

* ———. MURDER, AMERICA. Cited above as item 23, pp.
    393-394.

    Sketchy case history presented in time line format.

* Sifakis, Carl. THE ENCYCLOPEDIA OF AMERICAN CRIME.
    Cited above as item 29, p. 553.

    Case history presented in an encyclopedic format.

* Wilson, Colin. A CRIMINAL HISTORY OF MANKIND. Cited
    above as item 34, pp. 78-86.

    Case history of an extreme antisocial personality.

435. PAPE, GORDON (M)

Cincinnati youth who shot and killed his girlfriend and
her father, in December 1956. Pape also shot the girl's mother,
who survived her wounds, before turning the gun on himself and
committing suicide.

* FACTS ON FILE. Volume 16, 1956. Cited above as item 7,
    p. 432.

    Contemporaneous report of the Cincinnati shootings.

436. PAPIN, CHRISTINE and LEA (M)

French sisters, employed as household maids, who brutally
murdered their employers, without apparent motive, in 1933.
The victims were stabbed and slashed, their eyes gouged out
with knives, their corpses battered almost beyond recognition
with a hammer and a pewter pot. Blood was splattered on the
walls of the death chamber to a height of seven feet. Instead
of fleeing the scene, Christine and Lea remained in the house,
where they were discovered together, naked, in the bed they
shared. Death sentences for both sisters were later commuted
to prison terms. Christine was ruled insane, while still in
prison, and committed to a state asylum; Lea served her time,
and was released to a life of obscurity.

* CRIMES AND PUNISHMENT: A PICTORIAL ENCYCLOPEDIA OF ABER-
  RANT BEHAVIOR, Volume 7. Cited above as item 4, p. 66.

Case history presented in an encyclopedic format.

437. PARIS, RICHARD JAMES (M)

Two-time army deserter who married an unsuspecting young
woman in January 1967, driving to Las Vegas for the honeymoon.
Once inside their room, at the Orbit Inn, Paris produced a
pistol and a homemade bomb, firing a bullet into the explosive
device. The resultant blast demolished two floors of the hotel-
casino, instantly killing Paris, his bride, and five other
tourists.

* Nash, Jay Robert. ALMANAC OF WORLD CRIME. Cited above
  as item 19, p. 86.

Brief case history in a chapter on bombings.

438. PARRISH, JOHN (M)

Texas truck driver who went on a shooting rampage after
an argument with his employers, killing six persons and wounding three more before he was shot to death by police.

* "Body Count." Cited above as item 394.

Brief case history in an article summarizing recent
Texas multicides.

439. PEARSON, MOSES (M)

Drug abuser, high on cocaine, who spent an afternoon in
May 1976 driving through central Georgia, shooting three per-
sons to death and wounding 13 others. Cornered by police,
Pearson committed suicide.

* Nash, Jay Robert. MURDER, AMERICA. Cited above as item
  23, p. 443.

Case history presented in time line format.

439A. PEATRY, DARRELL (S): See "DE MAU MAU MURDERS"

439B. PEEL, JOHN KENNETH (M)

Alaska's worst simultaneous mass-slayer to date. In

early September 1982, Peel boarded a yacht near the remote
village of Craig, shooting to death all eight passengers and
crewmen, setting the boat on fire in an effort to disguise
his crime. Victims included the owner of the yacht, his wife,
their two small children, and four teenage crew members. Peel,
a former employee of the yacht's owner, was traced and arrested
in Washington state, two years after the murders. No rational
motive was determined. In the absence of an Alaskan death
penalty, Pell was sentenced to life.

423. McCall, Cheryl. "A Bloody, Baffling Mass Murder Shakes
        the Peaceful Spirit of a Small Town in Washington."
        PEOPLE WEEKLY 20 (September 12, 1983): 74-80.

        Describes reaction to the murders in the victims' home
      town.

424. Moody, Fred. "After a Two-Year Manhunt Police Arrest a
        Suspect in Alaska's Brutal Fishing Boat Murders."
        PEOPLE WEEKLY 22 (October 8, 1984): 127-128.

        Reports Peel's arrest and indictment.

                        440. PEETE, LOUISE (S)

        Convicted of murdering her fiancee, in 1920, Peete spent
eighteen years in a Colorado prison. Upon her release, she
moved in with an elderly California couple, spending six years
in their employ before she decided to take over their home.
After shooting the lady of the house to death and burying her
body in the garden, Peete signed papers committing the victim's
senile husband to a mental institution. Masquerading as her
female victim and raiding the couple's bank accounts, Peete
was betrayed by handwriting discrepancies. Convicted of murder
a second time, Peete was executed in April 1947.

    * Brian, Denis. MURDERERS DIE. Cited above as item 3,
        pp. 80-84, 259.

        Case history in an anthology of killers who were put
      to death.

    * Nash, Jay Robert. LOOK FOR THE WOMAN. Cited above as
        item 22, pp. 322-323.

        Case history presented in an encyclopedic format.

441. PETIOT, MARCEL (S)

French physician during World War II, who lured Jews and others to his home in Paris, offering to arrange their escape from German-occupied France. Instead of smuggling fugitives out of the country, however, Petiot murdered and dissected them, looting their bodies and bank accounts for personal gain. Corpses of his victims were disposed of at his home, or else dismembered and scattered around Paris, creating a minor reign of terror. Arrested by French police in March 1944, Petiot was not tried until after the war. He was ultimately charged with 27 murders, although police records indicate some 86 cadavers recovered with identical mutilations, the faces and fingertips expertly flayed to prevent identification. (Students of the case insist that Petiot's victims almost certainly numbered more than 100, with one estimate placing the body-count at 241.) At his trial, Petiot adopted the unusual tactic of confessing to more homicides than were charged against him —63 in all—and claiming that his victims had been Germans or collaborators with the enemy. In fact, the prosecution demonstrated that Petiot had never been a member of the French resistance, and had doubtless slain resistance fighters with his other victims. Guillotined in 1946.

* Boar, Roger, and Nigel Blundell. THE WORLD'S MOST IN-
    FAMOUS MURDERS. Cited above as item 2, pp. 142-147.

    Case history presented in sensational tabloid style.

* Brian, Denis. MURDERERS DIE. Cited above as item 3,
    pp. 89-97.

    Case history presented as an example of French capital
    punishment.

* CRIMES AND PUNISHMENT: A PICTORIAL ENCYCLOPEDIA OF ABER-
    RANT BEHAVIOR, Volume 5. Cited above as item 4, pp.
    123-130.

    Case history presented in an encyclopedic format.

* FACTS ON FILE. Volume 4, 1944. Cited above as item 7,
    p. 353.

    Reports Petiot's arrest in Paris.

* Gaute, J.H.H., and Robin Odell. THE MURDERERS' WHO'S
    WHO. Cited above as item 8, p. 185.

Case history presented in an encyclopedic format.

* Green, Jonathon. THE GREATEST CRIMINALS OF ALL TIME.
  Cited above as item 11, p. 282.

Brief case history in an encyclopedic format.

425. Grombach, John V. THE GREAT LIQUIDATOR. New York:
     Doubleday, 1980.

Definitive study of the Petiot case, based on French
and German police records.

* Nash, Jay Robert. ALMANAC OF WORLD CRIME. Cited above
  as item 19, p. 324.

Case history in a general discussion of mass murder.

* ————. CRIME CHRONOLOGY, 1900-1983. Cited above as
  item 21, p. 128.

Brief case history presented in time line format.

* Scott, Sir Harold. THE CONCISE ENCYCLOPEDIA OF CRIME
  AND CRIMINALS. Cited above as item 27, p. 257.

Case history presented in an encyclopedic format.

* Wilson, Colin. A CRIMINAL HISTORY OF MANKIND. Cited
  above as item 34, p. 617.

Case history in a general discussion of mass murder.

* ————, and Patricia Putnam. THE ENCYCLOPEDIA OF MURDER.
  Cited above as item 35, pp. 440-444.

Case history presented in an encyclopedic format.

442. PETRILLO, PAUL and HERMAN (S): See BOLBER, MORRIS

443. PHILLIPE, JOSEPH (S)

French "ripper" who anticipated London's Jack by a
quarter-century. Phillipe's usual method of operation involved
choking his victims—normally prostitutes—into unconscious-
ness, after which he slit their throats. Most of his victims
were robbed, although robbery itself was clearly not Phillipe's
driving motivation. The killer claimed his first victim in

1861, another in 1862, and five (including a young girl) in
1864. His last successful murder was committed in 1866, after
which three other intended victims managed to escape. One of
them remembered Phillippe's tattoo——"Born Under an Unluck Star"
——and the identifying mark led to his arrest. In custody,
Phillipe swiftly confessed and was executed.

* Logan, Guy B.H. MASTERS OF CRIME. Cited above as item
   17, pp. 66-78.

   Case history in an anthology of 19th-century murders.

* Nash, Jay Robert. ALMANAC OF WORLD CRIME. Cited above
   as item 19, pp. 272-273.

   Brief case history in a chapter on mass murder.

* Wilson, Colin. A CASEBOOK OF MURDER. Cited above as
   item 33, p. 250.

   Case hisoty discussed in sociological context.

444. PIASCENY, HANK (M)

Resident of Manchester, N.H., who stabbed his estranged
wife and her male friend to death at Christmastime, 1963.
Committed to a mental institution "for life or unless earlier
discharged," he was released after two years of therapy.

426. "U.S. Journal: Manchester, N.H." NEW YORKER 54 (July 24,
   1978): 71.

   Retrospective on the case, examining legal standards
   of judging sanity.

445. PIERCE, ALEXANDER (S)

Escaped convict in 19th-century Australia, who murdered
and cannibalized his five companions in the break-out. Food
supplies taken by the escapees were still intact when Pierce
was recaptured, and he told arresting officers that he pre-
ferred the taste of human flesh. Hanged.

* Wilson, Colin. A CASEBOOK OF MURDER. Cited above as
   item 33, pp. 91-92.

   Case study in a sociological history of murder.

446. Deleted.

447. PIERRE, DALE (M)

Native of Trinidad and member of the U.S. Air Force, responsible, with accomplice William Andrews, for the brutal torture and shooting of five victims during the robbery of an Ogden, Utah, record shop, in April 1974. All five victims were forced to drink acid, and were subsequently shot in the head, execution-style; one also had a ball-point pen hammered into his ear. Incredibly, two victims survived their ordeal to testify against the killers. Pierre is also a prime suspect in the 1973 stabbing death of an Air Force sergeant, although he was never charged in that case. Both Pierre and Andrews were sentenced to die for their crimes. Awaiting execution.

427. Kinder, Gary. VICTIM: THE OTHER SIDE OF MURDER. New York: Delacorte Press, 1982.

   Examines the Utah case in detail, with emphasis on the means through which survivors cope with the trauma of a brutal crime.

   * Wilson, Colin. A CRIMINAL HISTORY OF MANKIND. Cited above as item 34, pp. 638-639.

   Case history in a discussion of "motiveless" crimes.

   * ———, and Donald Seaman. THE ENCYCLOPEDIA OF MODERN MURDER. Cited above as item 36, pp. 190-191.

   Case history presented in an encyclopedic format.

448. PIPER, THOMAS W. (S)

Church sexton and sexual psychopath who bludgeoned and raped four women between December 1873 and May 1875. Three of his victims were killed, while the fourth suffered permanent brain damage. Following his conviction in one case, Piper confessed the other three, and was hanged in May 1876.

428. BELFRY MURDER IN BOSTON. Philadelphia: Old Franklin Publishing House, 1875.

   Contemporaneous report of Piper's crimes and trial.

   * Nash, Jay Robert. MURDER, AMERICA. Cited above as item 23, pp. 14, 92-94, 357.

   Case history in an anthology of "classic" murders.

* Sifakis, Carl. THE ENCYCLOPEDIA OF AMERICAN CRIME. Cited above as item 29, p. 570.

Case history presented in an encyclopedic format.

* Wilson, Colin, and Patricia Putnam. THE ENCYCLOPEDIA OF MURDER. Cited above as item 35, pp. 444-445.

Case history presented in an encyclopedic format.

429. Yerrington, James M.W. THE OFFICIAL REPORT OF THE TRIAL OF THOMAS W. PIPER. Boston: Wright & Potter, 1887.

Contemporaneous report of Piper's trial and execution.

449. PISKOWRSKI, RONALD F. (M)

With accomplice Gary Schraeger, Piskowrski shot and killed six persons during the October 1974 robbery of a bakery, in Connecticut. Both gunmen were subsequently sentenced to life.

* FACTS ON FILE. Volume 34, 1974. Cited above as item 7, pp. 932, 1103.

Reports the massacre and subsequent arrests.

450. PLEIL, RUDOLPH (S)

German habitual criminal, burglar, and rape-slayer who boasted of killing 50 women in the period from 1945 to 1957. A sexual sadist, Pleil used hammers, hatchets, knives, and stones to mutilate the bodies of his victims, relishing the terror which he inspired in female captives. Proud of his achievements in the field of crime, Pleil described himself as "the best death-maker." In a jailhouse interview, he told reporters, "Every man has his passion. Some prefer whist. I prefer killing people." Committed suicide in his cell, in February 1958.

* Wilson, Colin. A CRIMINAL HISTORY OF MANKIND. Cited above as item 34, p. 621.

Case history in a discussion of modern mass murder.

* ————, and Patricia Putnam. THE ENCYCLOPEDIA OF MURDER. Cited above as item 35, p. 445.

Case history presented in an encyclopedic format.

451. POMEROY, JESSE HARDING (S)

Boston street waif, whose hare lip and single functioning eye made him an outcast among his peers. Sentenced to a reformatory at age 13, for the brutal beating of a playmate, Pomeroy began abducting and killing younger children after his release. Although finally convicted of only two murders, plus a failed attempt, Pomeroy plainly claimed other victims, as well; two sources credit him with 27 murders, while others refer vaguely to "dozens" of slain children. Condemned to die, his sentence was subsequently commuted to life imprisonment, and he spent the next 52 years behind bars, dying in prison in 1932. (During his early incarceration, Pomeroy attempted to escape by setting fire to his cell block, and three other inmates died in the blaze.)

* Boar, Roger, and Nigel Blundell. THE WORLD'S MOST IN-
  FAMOUS MURDERS. Cited above as item 2, pp. 148-149.

  Case history presented in sensational tabloid style.

* CRIMES AND PUNISHMENT: A PICTORIAL ENCYCLOPEDIA OF ABER-
  RANT BEHAVIOR, Volume 13. Cited above as item 4, pp.
  38-40.

  Case history in a general discussion of mass murder.

* Green, Jonathon. THE GREATEST CRIMINALS OF ALL TIME.
  Cited above as item 11, p. 155.

  Brief case history in an encyclopedic format.

* Master, R.E.L., and Eduard Lea. PERVERSE CRIMES IN
  HISTORY. Cited above as item 18, p. 83.

  Case history in a general discussion of sadism.

* Nash, Jay Robert. ALMANAC OF WORLD CRIME. Cited above
  as item 19, pp. 277-278.

  Case history in a discussion of mass murder.

* ———. BLOODLETTERS AND BADMEN. Cited above as item
  20, p. 448.

  Case history presented in an encyclopedic format.
  Curiously omitted from the later Warner Books edition.

* ————. MURDER, AMERICA. Cited above as item 23, p. 357.

Sketchy case history presented in time line format.

430. Pomeroy, Jesse H. AUTOBIOGRAPHY OF JESSE H. POMEROY.
Boston: J.A. Cummings, 1875.

The killers tells his own story, for a contemporary
audience.

* Wilson, Colin. A CASEBOOK OF MURDER. Cited above as
item 33, pp. 203-205.

Credits Pomeroy with 27 victims, overall.

* ————. A CRIMINAL HISTORY OF MANKIND. Cited above as
item 34, p. 507.

Brief history within a survey of human criminality.

452. POMMERAIS, EDMOND DE LA (S)

19th-century French physician and compulsive gambler,
who settled his debts through murder. Pommerais poisoned his
mistress and his mother-in-law for their insurance money, but
was found out, convicted, and executed in 1863.

* Nash, Jay Robert. ALMANAC OF WORLD CRIME. Cited above
as item 19, p. 317.

Case history in a chapter on homicidal doctors.

* Wilson, Colin, and Patricia Putnam. THE ENCYCLOPEDIA OF
MURDER. Cited above as item 35, pp. 178-179.

Case history presented in an encyclopedic format.

453. POMMERENKE, HEINRICH (S)

German sex-slayer who killed at least ten women in the
late 1950s. Allegedly inspired by film versions of the Old
Testament, Pommerenke became convinced that women are the root
of all worldly troubles, and that they should be "taught a
lesson." This he accomplished by raping an estimated 30 women,
ten of whom he also murdered. Upon his arrest, in 1960, he
was charged with ten homicides, 20 rapes, and 35 other felonies,
including burglary. Sentenced to six life terms, Pommerenke
will be technically eligible for parole after serving 140 years.

* Gaute, J.H.H., and Robin Odell. THE MURDERERS' WHO'S
  WHO. Cited above as item 8, p. 187.

  Brief case history in an encyclopedic format.

* Wilson, Colin, and Patricia Putnam. THE ENCYCLOPEDIA OF
  MURDER. Cited above as item 35, pp. 447-448.

  Case history presented in an encyclopedic format.

454. POPE, DUANE EARL (M)

Recent college graduate and football star who shot four
persons, three of them fatally, following a bank robbery at
Big Springs, Neb., in June 1965. Pope's victims were forced
to lie on the floor, after which each was shot in the head
and back with a silencer-equipped pistol. (The sole survivor
remains paralyzed from his wounds.) Upon conviction, Pope was
sentenced to die.

431. "All-American Boy." NEWSWEEK 66 (December 13, 1965): 33.

Reports Pope's conviction and sentencing.

432. "College Football Hero's Postgraduate Course in Horror."
     LIFE 58 (June 25, 1965): 30-30A.

Pictorial layout covering the Big Springs massacre.

433. Lindeman, Bard. "Riddle of the Nice Killer." SATURDAY
     EVENING POST 238 (October 23, 1965): 98+.

Examines Pope's life in an effort to explain his sudden
shift to violent crime.

434. "Stranger in Big Springs." NEWSWEEK 65 (June 21, 1965):
     29-30.

Contemporaneous report of the Nebraska murders.

455. PRITCHARD, EDWARD WILLIAM (S)

British physician and megalomaniac, who poisoned his
wife and mother-in-law without apparent motive, in 1865. Ob-
servers of the case were inclined to believe that the murders
were an "exercise," designed specifically to demonstrate that
Pritchard could escape detection. On the night before his
scheduled execution, Pritchard confessed both slayings. When

asked his motives, the doctor merely smiled.

* Nash, Jay Robert. ALMANAC OF WORLD CRIME. Cited above
    as item 19, p. 317.

    Brief case history in a chapter on homicidal doctors.

456. PROBST, ANTON (M)

German immigrant and Philadelphia's first (known) mass-
murderer. In 1866, Probst used an ax and hammer to slaughter
seven members of the Dearing family, his employers, along with
a friend of the family who happened to be visiting their home.
Robbery did not appear to be his motive, although Probst did
steal a total of thirteen dollars from two of his victims.
Arrested five days after the massacre, Probst was quickly tried
and hanged, in June 1866.

435. THE DEARING TRAGEDY. Philadelphia: C.W. Alexander, 1866.

    Sensational contemporaneous account of the case.

* Nash, Jay Robert. MURDER, AMERICA. Cited above as item
    23, pp. 14, 86-89, 349.

    Case history in an anthology of "classic" murders.

457. PRUDOM, BARRY PETER (S)

British "Cop Killer," who ran amok in the north of England
during 1982. During a routine traffic check, Prudom shot a
police constable through the head for no apparent reason,
leaving him for dead. (The victim survived long enough to
write down Prudom's license number.) The killer subsequently
murdered a married couple in Yorkshire and stole their car,
eluding police in the midst of an intensive manhunt. On July 3,
Prudom murdered another policeman, who observed the fugitive
leaving a rural post office. That night, he was cornered by
a strike force of armed officers, and engaged them in a wild
battle, during which rifles, shotguns, and stun grenades were
used to root him out of cover. The firefight ended when Prudom, wounded 22 times, committed suicide by shooting himself
in the head.

* Wilson, Colin, and Donald Seaman. THE ENCYCLOPEDIA OF
    MODERN MURDER. Cited above as item 36, pp. 192-196.

    Case history presented in an encyclopedic format.

458. PRUYON, KENYON (M)

Sniper who, in 1976, killed two persons and wounded ten others while firing on a cafe, across the street from his apartment. Captured and convicted, Pruyon was sentenced to life.

    * Tobias, Ronald. THEY SHOOT TO KILL. Cited above as item 31, p. 74.

    Brief case history in a survey of criminal snipers.

459. PULLIAM, MARK (M)

Georgia resident who, in November 1942, sought to avoid familial responsibility by burning down his home, with his family inside. Pulliam's wife and five of their eight children died in the blaze. Convicted of arson and murder, the defendant was sentenced to life.

    * Nash, Jay Robert. ALMANAC OF WORLD CRIME. Cited above as item 19, p. 24.

    Brief case history in a section on arson.

460. PURVIS, THOMAS E. (S)

Son of a California policeman, who murdered two consecutive women in fits of raging jealousy. Sentenced to death, his punishment was later commuted to a term of life, much to the convict's dismay. "Men on death row bought their own one-way ticket to hell," he told a reporter. "For me, booze and women didn't mix. I loved the women I killed in a jealous rage. Even when I paced my cell, unable to sleep because I dreamed of the choking death of the gas chamber, I believed in the death penalty."

    * Brian, Denis. MURDERERS DIE. Cited above as item 3, p. 13.

    Case history in an anthology of killers facing execution.

461. PUTT, GEORGE HOWARD (S)

Abused as a child, Putt grew to become a habitual criminal, responsible for the brutal murders of five Memphis, Tenn., residents during a two-month period of 1969. (He was

also suspected, but never charged, in the April 1969 murder
of a man in Jackson, Miss.) State psychiatrists reported that
Putt nurtured "a morbid preoccupation with blood and gore."
Convicted on five counts of murder, in October 1970, Putt was
sentenced to die.

436. Meyer, Gerald. THE MEMPHIS MURDERS. New York: The Sea-
      bury Press, 1974.

      Traces Putt's brutal crimes back to his traumatic early
      years.

   462. RADCLIFF, DIXIE (S): See BOGGS, DONALD MELVIN

             463. RAIS, GILLES DE (S)

      Marshal of France and an intimate of Saint Joan, so
traumatized by her martyrdom that he abandoned Christianity
and devoted himself to a life of debauchery, sexual perversion,
and the pursuit of "forbidden knowledge" through occult rituals.
A pedophile and sadist, Gilles de Rais was reportedly responsible for the torture, sexual abuse, and murder of several
hundred children. Blood and portions of the murdered children's
bodies were allegedly employed in Satanic rituals, at which
Gilles was assisted by several accomplices. At his trial, in
October 1440, he "confessed everything," following the usual
period of torture and threats of excommunication. It has
become fashionable to regard Gilles de Rais as an innocent
victim of the Inquisition, but several sources record the
discovery of small, dismembered bodies, fifty to eighty in
number, on the grounds of his various estates. (Some sources
"credit" Gilles with 800 murders.) Strangled and burned, by
order of the court, in 1440.

437. Benedetti, Jean. GILLES DE RAIS. New York: Stein and
      Day, 1972.

      Informative biography of an enigmatic figure, report-
      ing the discovery of 40 corpses each, in two locations,
      on property owned and controlled by Gilles. Benedetti
      concludes that his final body-count probably exceeded
      100 victims.

  *   CRIMES AND PUNISHMENT: A PICTORIAL ENCYCLOPEDIA OF ABER-
      RANT BEHAVIOR, Volume 1. Cited above as item 4, p. 85.

      Case history presented in an encyclopedic format.

* Masters, R.E.L., and Eduard Lea. PERVERSE CRIMES IN
  HISTORY. Cited above as item 18, pp. 25-31, 159-160.

  Case history in a discussion of sadism.

* Nash, Jay Robert. ALMANAC OF WORLD CRIME. Cited above
  as item 19, pp. 266-267.

  Case history in a general discussion of mass murder.

* Reinhardt, James Melvin. THE PSYCHOLOGY OF STRANGE
  KILLERS. Cited above as item 70, pp. 10-12.

  Brief case summary employed to gain historical perspective on modern serial killers.

* Wilson, Colin. A CASEBOOK OF MURDER. Cited above as
  item 33, pp. 35-37.

  Examines the case from a sociological perspective.

* ————, and Patricia Putnam. THE ENCYCLOPEDIA OF MURDER.
  Cited above as item 35, pp. 452-453.

  Case history presented in an encyclopedic format.

464. RAMIREZ, RICHARD (S)

California's "Night Stalker," accused, in 1985, of 14
murders and numerous other felonies committed during an eight-
month reign of terror. (Authorities suspect Ramirez of at
least six other homicides, spanning a year, along with various
other crimes including child molestation.) A drug abuser and
self-styled Satanist, Ramirez left occult "signs" at the homes
of several victims, sometimes drawn in blood on the walls.
In at least one case, a victim's eyes were removed (and have
yet to be found). According to reports from friends and
relatives, Ramirez was obsessed with the lyrics of a song,
"Night Prowler," recorded by the mock-Satanic "heavy metal"
group, AC/DC. The song allegedly inspired Ramirez to invade
suburban homes in both Los Angeles and San Francisco, raping,
murdering, and mutilating the inhabitants before inscribing
pentagrams and other cryptic symbols on the walls. Captured
by an angry neighborhood crowd near the scene of an attempted
burglary, in July 1985, Ramirez was beaten and held for police,
who report that his fingerprints match those of the elusive
Night Stalker, found at several crime scenes.

Books

* FACTS ON FILE. Volume 45, 1985. Cited above as item 7, p. 651.

   Reports the Night Stalker manhunt in progress.

Articles

438. Givens, R. "The Night Stalker of L.A." NEWSWEEK 106 (August 26, 1985): 23.

   Reports Ramirez's arrest.

439. Plummer, William. "Night Stalker." PEOPLE WEEKLY 24 (September 16, 1985): 42-45.

   Family background on Ramirez, in the wake of his arrest.

440. Stengel, R. "Stalking the Serial Killer." TIME 126 (September 9, 1985): 43.

   Reports Ramirez's arrest in Los Angeles.

465. RANSOM, FLORENCE (M)

British murderess who shotgunned her estranged lover's wife, daughter, and housemaid in July 1940, leaving a monogrammed glove at the scene of the crime. Judged to be insane upon arrest, she was committed to a mental institution for life.

* Nash, Jay Robert. CRIME CHRONOLOGY, 1900-1983. Cited above as item 21, p. 116.

   Brief case history presented in time line format.

466. RARDON, GARY DUANE (S)

Chicago slayer of three, in a series of petty robberies during 1974. Upon arrest and conviction, Rardon drew a prison sentence of 40 to 100 years.

* Nash, Jay Robert. MURDER, AMERICA. Cited above as item 23, p. 442.

   Sketchy case history presented in time line format.

467. RAVEN, DANIEL (M)

London advertising executive, who beat his father- and mother-in-law to death with a television aerial, in October 1949. Hanged in July 1950.

    *   Nash, Jay Robert. CRIME CHRONOLOGY, 1900–1983. Cited above as item 21, p. 137.

        Brief case history presented in time line format.

468. RAYMOND, JAMES (M): See GIBSON, HUGH

469. REDDEN, LEONARD O. (M)

Indiana public shcool principal who shotgunned two of his teachers in their classrooms, then committed suicide. The murders occurred on the day before Redden's scheduled visit to a psychiatrist, with whom he planned to discuss his "persecution complex."

    *   FACTS ON FILE. Volume 20, 1960. Cited above as item 7, p. 52.

        Reports Redden's crimes and suicide.

470. REES, MELVIN DAVID (S)

Jazz musician and sadistic rape-slayer of the late 1950s, dubbed "the Sex Beast," after the ferocity of his attacks. In June 1957, Rees accosted a soldier and his girlfriend, in a lonely lover's lane near Annapolis, Md. The soldier escaped after Rees shot his female companion to death; upon returning with police, he found the killer had remained to rape her corpse. In January 1959, Rees used flashing "police lights" to force a family of four off the highway, near Apple Grove, Va. Two months later, bodies of the four victims were found, carelessly hidden in a rural area miles from the site of their abduction; two of the three female victims had been raped, before or after death. An anonymous tip, from one of Rees's friends, led to his arrest in 1960, whereupon he was identified by the survivor of the first attack. Evidence recovered after his arrest included notes which Rees had made, describing the murder of the family in 1959. "Caught on a lonely road," he wrote. "Drove to a select area and killed husband and baby. Now the mother and daughter were all mine. Now I was her master." Police subsequently linked Rees to the rape-slayings of four other teenaged girls, all in Maryland. He was tried, convicted, and executed in Virginia, during 1961.

* Browning, Norma Lee. THE PSYCHIC WORLD OF PETER HURKOS.
  Cited above as item 186, pp. 92-99.

  Following the Jackson family murders, Hurkos led police
  to an innocent sanitation worker, who falsely confessed
  to the crime. Embarrassed by the arrest of Rees, ten
  days later, the psychic's apologists belatedly insisted
  that Hurkos identified both the innocent man and the
  actual killer. A less than impressive performance, in
  any case.

* FACTS ON FILE. Volume 19, 1959. Cited above as item 7,
  pp. 88, 123.

  Reports the discovery of Rees's Virginia victims.

* FACTS ON FILE. Volume 20, 1960. Cited above as item 7,
  p. 240.

  Reports the arrest of Rees.

* FACTS ON FILE. Volume 21, 1961. Cited above as item 7,
  pp. 260, 404.

  Reports Rees's conviction and sentencing.

* Gaute, J.H.H., and Robin Odell. THE MURDERERS' WHO'S
  WHO. Cited above as item 8, p. 194.

  Case history presented in an encyclopedic format.

* Nash, Jay Robert. ALMANAC OF WORLD CRIME. Cited above
  as item 19, p. 289.

  Case history in a general discussion of mass murder.

* ———. BLOODLETTERS AND BADMEN. Cited above as item
  20, pp. 465-468.

  Case history presented in an encyclopedic format.

* ———. CRIME CHRONOLOGY, 1900-1983. Cited above as
  item 21, p. 155.

  Brief case history presented in time line format.

* ————. MURDER, AMERICA. Cited above as item 23, pp. 427-428.

    Sketchy case history presented in time line format.

* Reinhardt, James Melvin. THE PSYCHOLOGY OF STRANGE KILLERS. Cited above as item 70, pp. 165-177.

    Case history in an anthology of serial killers.

* Sifakis, Carl. THE ENCYCLOPEDIA OF AMERICAN CRIME. Cited above as item 29, p. 607.

    Case history presented in an encyclopedic format.

* Steiger, Brad. THE MASS MURDERER. Cited above as item 30.

    Sensational case history in a paperback discussion of multiple murder.

* Wilson, Colin. A CRIMINAL HISTORY OF MANKIND. Cited above as item 34, pp. 618-619.

* ————. ORDER OF ASSASSINS. Cited above as item 76, pp. 118-119.

    Psychological case study of Rees.

* ————, and Donald Seaman. THE ENCYCLOPEDIA OF MODERN MURDER. Cited above as item 36, pp. 198-200.

    Case history presented in an encyclopedic format.

471. REMETA, DANIEL (M): See WALTER, MARK

472. RENCZI, VERA (S)

20th-century murderess in Bucharest, who poisoned her two husbands, her son, and 32 lovers, preserving their bodies in zinc-lined coffins, stored in her basement. She enjoyed sitting among the caskets each evening, in an armchair, and most of her crimes appear to have been motivated by insane jealousy, provoked by the mere suggestion that "her" man might be interested in another woman. (Renczi's son was the lone exception; he was murdered after threatening to expose her previous crimes.) Police recovered the 35 corpses from her cellar, and Renczi was sentenced to life imprisonment.

* Wilson, Colin, and Patricia Putnam. THE ENCYCLOPEDIA OF
 MURDER. Cited above as item 35, pp. 458-459.

Case history presented in an encyclopedic format.

473. REID, PATRICK (M)

Yorkshire slayer who, with accomplice Michael McCabe,
murdered an elderly couple and their manservant in 1847, afterward looting the house. Both participants in the crime were
convicted of multiple murder and hanged, although the evidence
seemed to portray McCabe as a "mere bystander" during the
murders.

* Logan, Guy B.H. MASTERS OF CRIME. Cited above as item
 17. pp. 227-242.

Case history in an anthology of 19th-century murders.

474. RICHARDS, STEPHENLEE (S)

19th-century "Nebraska fiend," linked with at least nine
brutal murders around Lincoln, in 1879. Finally convicted and
condemned for slaughtering a family of five, near Minden,
Richards was hanged in April 1879.

* Nash, Jay Robert. MURDER, AMERICA. Cited above as item
 23, p. 362.

Sketchy case history presented in time line format.

475. RICHARDSON, JAMES (M)

Black migrant worker in Florida, convicted during May
1968 of poisoning his seven children for insurance money.
Sentenced to die.

441. Lane, Mark. ARCADIA. New York: Holt, Rinehart and
 Winston, 1970.

The author, a self-styled "radical" lawyer and ousted
member of the New York state legislature, calls the
deaths of Richardson's children a tragic accident, caused
by careless handling of pesticides by farmers for whom
Richardson worked. Lane attacks the (white) jury system, (white) agri-businessmen, (white) police, and cites
"compelling evidence" of Richardson's innocence. This,
from an author who, a decade later, blamed the Jonestown

suicides on agents of the CIA. Best taken with substantial quantities of salt.

476. RICHLAND, GA., CHILD MURDERS (S)

Nocturnal abductions and subsequent brutal murders of
three young girls at Richland, Ga., during 1981 and 1982. In
each case, the kindapper(s) invaded the victim's home, strategically removing light bulbs and thereby leaving family members
in the dark during the actual, frequently noisy abductions.
At this writing, local sources report no suspects in custody.

* Nash, Jay Robert. CRIME CHRONOLOGY, 1900-1983. Cited
   above as item 21, p. 202.

   Brief case history presented in time line format.

477. RILEY, CHARLES DAVID (M)

Murderer, with lover-accomplice Marlene Olive, of Olive's
parents in June 1975. Marlene's adoptive father was shot, and
her mother beaten to death with a claw hammer, at the family
home in Terra Linda, Calif., after which their bodies were
burned in a barbecue pit. Subsequent testimony revealed that
Marlene, who regarded herself as a "voodoo witch," had used
drugs and sex to dominate Riley over the past six months,
turning him into her "slave." Convicted on two counts of
murder, Riley was sentenced to die; his "master" and guilty
accomplice was dealt with as a juvenile.

* Godwin, John. MURDER USA. Cited above as item 10, pp.
   119-124.

   Case history in a discussion of multiple homicides.

442. Levine, Richard M. BAD BLOOD. New York: Random House,
      1982.

      Emphasizes the sexually-permissive, drug-and-occult-
      oriented youth subculture of Northern California. In-
      sightful and instructive.

478. RIJKE, SJEF (S)

Sadistic poisoner of Utrecht, Holland, who murdered two
finacees and attempted to kill two other women, including his
new bride, in 1971. Rijke was arrested after police learned
that he had purchased rat poison prior to each murder or

attempted murder. Under interrogation, he confessed deriving
pleasure from the sight of women suffering (although he denied
any murderous intent). Found sane and guilty during January
1972, Rijke was sentenced to life.

* Wilson, Colin, and Donald Seaman. THE ENCYCLOPEDIA OF
  MODERN MURDER. Cited above as item 36, pp. 200-201.

  Case history presented in an encyclopedic format.

479. RIVERA, MIGUEL (S)

Manhattan's "Charley Chop-off," believed responsible for
the murders of four young boys (and assaults on two others)
between March 1972 and August 1973. Three of the murdered
victims were found on rooftops, stabbed and slashed numerous
times, with their penises severed (and sometimes missing from
the scene). A fourth victim was killed in similar fashion,
but without sexual mutilation, and police theorize that the
killer was interrupted before he could complete his ritual.
(A fifth victim, stabbed and emasculated, managed to survive
his grievous wounds.) Rivera, a frequent inmate of local
mental institutions, was arrested in May 1974, following the
attempted abduction of another boy, who physically resembled
"Charley Chop-off's" prior victims. Returned to the asylum
in lieu of prosecution, Rivera was never officially charged
with any of the slayings, but homicide investigators maintain
their conviction of his guilt in the series of crimes.

443. Gelb, Barbara. ON THE TRACK OF MURDER. New York:
     William Morrow, 1975, pp. 141-199.

     Covers the "Chop-off" case in a general examination
     of NYPD's Manhattan Homicide Task Force.

* Nash, Jay Robert. OPEN FILES. Cited above as item 24,
  pp. 53-54.

  Typically garbled report of another "unsolved" case.
  Nash places all the "Chop-off" crimes in 1972 (when, in
  fact, the murders continued through August 1973), and
  reports, nine years after Rivera's arrest, that police
  "never managed to identify" the killer.

480. RIVIERE, PIERRE-MARGRIN (M)

French mass-slayer who murdered his mother, brother, and
sister with an ax in June 1835. Arrested in early July, Riviere

confessed his crimes, asserting that he acted under orders from
God, eliminating family members who conspired to persecute his
father. Condemned to die, his sentence was commuted by the
king to life imprisonment. Riviere died in prison, during
October 1840.

Books

444. Foucault, Michel. "I, PIERRE RIVIERE, HAVING SLAUGHTERED
      MY MOTHER, MY SISTER, AND MY BROTHER..." New York:
      Pantheon Books, 1975.

      Includes Riviere's lengthy "memoir," written in jail,
      together with reports of his interrogators, medico-legal
      opinions, and so forth. Foucault ably chronicles the
      early confusion of law and psychiatry, which continues
      unabated to the present day.

Articles

445. De Feo, R. "I, Pierre Riviere, Having Slaughtered My
      Mother, My Sister, and My Brother..." NATIONAL REVIEW
      27 (August 29, 2975): 950.

      Reviews item 444 above.

481. ROBERTSONE, CLARENCE (S): See NORTHCOTT, GORDON STEWART

482. ROBINSON FAMILY MURDERS (M)

Family of six, found shot to death in their summer home
near Good Hart, Mich., in July 1968. Victims included the
parents and four children, aged seven to nineteen. At this
writing, no solution to the mystery has been announced.

   * FACTS ON FILE. Volume 28, 1968. Cited above as item 7,
      p. 476.

      Reports the massacre and search for clues.

483. ROBINSON, LARRY KEITH (M)

Unemployed Texan who murdered and mutilated five persons
in two adjacent homes, near Ft. Worth, in August 1982. Robinson had been living with one of the victims while job hunting.
There was no apparent motive for the crimes. Sentenced to die.

* "Body Count." Cited above as item 394.

   Reports Robinson's case in a survey of recent Texas
multicides.

484. ROBINSON, SARAH JANE (S)

19th-century Boston murderess who poisoned at least six
persons. Known victims included her husband, her sister, a
brother-in-law, a nephew, and two of her own children. Sentenced to life in 1883, Robinson died in prison during 1905.

* Jones, Ann. WOMEN WHO KILL. Cited above as item 13,
   pp. 121-128.

   Case history in a feminist discussion of Victorian
murderesses.

* Nash, Jay Robert. LOOK FOR THE WOMAN. Cited above as
   item 22, pp. 334-335.

   Case history presented in an encyclopedic format.

* ————. MURDER, AMERICA. Cited above as item 23, p. 365.

   Sketchy case history presented in time line format.

* Pearson, Edmund L. "Rules for Murderesses." Cited
   above as item 25, p. 15.

   Brief case history in a satirical examination of female
killers.

485. ROBLES, RICHARD (M)

New York drug addict who stabbed, mutilated, and decapitated two female roommates in August 1963. A black suspect,
George Whitmore, falsely confessed to the murders in 1964,
but Robles, a Caucasian, was identified and arrested in 1965.
Although he denied the crime, circumstantial evidence was
sufficient to convict him, and he was sentenced to life.

Books

* Brussel, James A. CASEBOOK OF A CRIME PSYCHIATRIST.
   Cited above as item 63, pp. 106-135.

   Chronicles the effort to construct a psychological

"profile" of the killer, who was still at large when
Brussel went to press.

* CRIMES AND PUNISHMENT: A PICTORIAL ENCYCLOPEDIA OF ABER-
  RANT BEHAVIOR, Volume 4. Cited above as item 4, pp.
  119-126.

  Case history presented in an encyclopedic format.

446. Lefkowitz, Bernard, and Kenneth G. Gross. THE VICTIMS.
  New York: G.P. Putnam's Sons, 1969.

  Detailed examination of the case, including treatment
  of Whitmore's false confession.

* Nash, Jay Robert. CRIME CHRONOLOGY, 1900-1983. Cited
  above as item 21, p. 167.

  Brief case history presented in time line format.

* ————. MURDER, AMERICA. Cited above as item 23, p. 433.

  Sketchy case history presented in time line format.

447. Shapiro, Fred C. WHITMORE. New York: Bobbs-Merrill,
  1969.

  Examines police methods which produced Whitmore's
  erroneous confession to the double murder. (Whitmore
  was subsequently convicted of a non-fatal attack on
  another woman, and sent to prison for that crime.)

* Wilson, Colin, and Donald Seaman. THE ENCYCLOPEDIA OF
  MODERN MURDER. Cited above as item 36, pp. 201-202.

  Case history presented in an encyclopedic format.

                              Articles

448. "Girls in 3-C." NEWSWEEK 63 (May 4, 1964): 24.

  Reports the arrest and confession of Whitmore.

                    486. ROSSE, RICHARD (M)

  Personal chef of Britain's Bishop of Rochester, who
spiced his dishes with poison, murdering 17 persons at a
single feast. No motive was ascertained. Boiled alive.

* Green, Jonathon. THE GREATEST CRIMINALS OF ALL TIME. Cited above as item 11, p. 155.

Brief case history in an encyclopedic format.

487. ROTTMAN, ARTHUR (M)

German sailor, ashore in New Zealand, who axed three members of a local family to death in December 1914. Hanged in March 1915.

* Gaute, J.H.H., and Robin Odell. THE MURDERERS' WHO'S WHO. Cited above as item 8, p. 198.

Case history presented in an encyclopedic format.

* Nash, Jay Robert. CRIME CHRONOLOGY, 1900-1983. Cited above as item 21, p. 36.

Brief case history presented in time line format.

488. ROULET, JACQUES (S)

French "werewolf," who confessed, in August 1598, to murdering and devouring "numerous" local children, naming his brother and cousin as accomplices. Two murders, at least, were verified upon recovery of remains. Unlike other such cases, where torture was employed and swift execution decreed upon confession, Roulet was merely confined to a church hospital for life.

* Masters, R.E.L., and Eduard Lea. PERVERS CRIMES IN HISTORY. Cited above as item 18, pp. 61-62.

Brief case study in a chapter on lycanthropy.

489. RUDLOFF, FRITZ (S)

Male nurse in the East German town of Walterhausen, bitterly resentful of licensed physicians who received more respect and attention for their efforts. The chief surgeon at Rudloff's hospital became a particular target for hatred when he forced Rudloff to break off his affair with a female nurse on the staff. Thereafter, during 1954, Rudloff murdered four of the surgeon's patients, with arsenic, in an effort to destroy the doctor's professional reputation. Sentenced to death on the guillotine.

449. "Nurse's Resentment." TIME 64 (November 1, 1954): 35.

      Reports Rudloff's crimes and sentencing.

                490. RULLOFFSON, EDWARD HOWARD (S)

      Ex-convict and self-styled "herb healer" in upstate New
York, who murdered at least four "patients"—including his own
wife and daughter—in the mid-19th century. Bodies of his
victims were subsequently sold to medical schools, as specimens for dissection. Twice acquitted on murder charges stem-
ming from his "medical practice," Rulloffson was finally convicted of killing a man in the course of a burglary. Hanged
in May 1871.

450. Freeman, E.H. THE VEIL OF SECRECY REMOVED, THE ONLY
      TRUE AND AUTHENTIC HISTORY OF EDWARD H. RULOFF.
      Binghamton, N.Y.: Carl and Freeman, 1871.

      Examines the killer's case, using his most frequent
      alias.

451. LIFE, TRIAL AND EXECUTION OF EDWARD H. RULOFF. Phila-
      delphia: Barclay and Co., 1871.

      Another contemporary account of Rulloffson's crimes,
      again managing to ignore his actual name.

   * Nash, Jay Robert. MURDER, AMERICA. Cited above as item
      23, pp. 14, 45-55, 334.

      Case history in an anthology of "classic" murders.

                  491. RUPPERT, JAMES (M)

      Forty-year-old gun enthusiast who shot his parents and
eight siblings to death at the family home in Hamilton, Ohio,
on Easter Sunday, 1975. In custody, Ruppert pled not guilty
by reason of insanity; the prosecution countered with a claim
that Ruppert wiped out his family in hopes of hastening his
inheritance. Upon conviction, the killer received eleven
consecutive life sentences.

                           Books

   * Levin, Jack, and James Alan Fox. MASS MURDER: AMERICA'S
      GROWING MENACE. Cited above as item 15.

Brief case history in a discussion of mass murder.

* Nash, Jay Robert. CRIME CHRONOLOGY, 1900–1983. Cited
   above as item 21, p. 187.

Brief case history presented in time line format.

* ————. MURDER, AMERICA. Cited above as item 23, p. 442.

Sketchy case history presented in time line format.

Articles

452. Calio, Jim, and John Lowell. "Silent Slaughter." NEWS-
   WEEK 85 (April 14, 1975): 46.

Reports Ruppert's crimes and arrest.

492. RUSH, JAMES BLOMFIELD (M)

British murderer who shot and killed his landlord and
the landlord's son, wounding his wife and maid, during a
November 1848 dispute about his mortgage. Hanged in April 1849.

* Gaute, J.H.H., and Robin Odell. THE MURDERERS' WHO'S
   WHO. Cited above as item 8, p. 200.

Case history presented in an encyclopedic format.

493. RUXTON, BUCK (M)

Physician and resident of Moffat, Scotland——born in India
——who stangled his wife in September 1935, proceeding to kill
their maid when she witnessed the murder. Ruxton surgically
dissected his victims and dumped their remains in a local
river, but the various parts were retrieved and identified.
Convicted and hanged in May 1936.

* Gaute, J.H.H., and Robin Odell. THE MURDERERS' WHO'S
   WHO. Cited above as item 8, pp. 201–202.

Case history presented in an encyclopedic format.

* Nash, Jay Robert. ALMANAC OF WORLD CRIME. Cited above
   as item 19, p. 324.

Case history in a discussion of homicidal doctors.

*   ————.   CRIME CHRONOLOGY, 1900–1983.   Cited above as
     item 21, p. 103.

     Brief case history presented in time line format.

                    494. RUZICKA, JAMES (S)

        Sexual psychopath and slayer of at least two women in the
Pacific Northwest. The product of a traumatic childhood, combined with the affects of habitual drug abuse, Ruzicka first
practiced bestiality as a child, moved on from there to molesting young girls, and was finally convicted of raping two women
at knifepoint. His ten-year sentence was suspended by the
court, on condition that he participate in a program for sexual
offenders at the Western State Hospital, near Tacoma, Wash.
After nine months in the program, Ruzicka achieved the position
of trusty, and immediately fled while on a 48-hour pass. Within
the next four weeks, he raped and murdered two women in Seattle,
moving on to Oregon, where he was finally arrested for the
brutal rape of a 13-year-old girl. In custody, he told police,
"I asked her if she wanted to ball, and she didn't say 'no,'
so I figured she wouldn't mind." Sentenced to ten years in
Oregon, and receiving female hormone injections to control
his libido, Ruzicka subsequently confessed to the Washington
murders and was sentenced to two consecutive life terms, to
be served on completion of his Oregon sentence.

*   Godwin, John. MURDER USA. Cited above as item 10, pp.
     220–222.

     Case history in a discussion of "motiveless" crimes.

*   SERIAL MURDERS——HEARINGS BEFORE THE SENATE SUBCOMMITTEE
     ON JUVENILE JUSTICE. Cited above as item 28, p. 22.

     Brief case history within the transcript of author
     Ann Rule's senate testimony on serial murder.

                    495. SACH, AMELIA (S)

        Operator of a London "nursing home" for unwed mothers,
where, with accomplice Annie Walters, she disposed of unwanted
infants, for a price. The total number of her victims is unknown, but it was certainly considerable, as the operation
spanned a period of years. Suspicion was aroused when Walters,
rather than disposing promptly of their latest victim, took
the infant home "for company." Recovery of several infant
corpses cinched the case, and the two baby farmers were hanged

together in 1903, protesting their innocence all the way to
the gallows.

* Nash, Jay Robert. LOOK FOR THE WOMAN. Cited above as
    item 22, pp. 335-336.

    Case history presented in an encyclopedic format.

496. SANDER, ROBERT PAUL (M)

Mentally unbalanced drifter who drove from Ohio to California in 1975, checking into a motel in Smith River, then
shot and killed six strangers from his balcony. Sentenced to
life.

* Tobias, Ronald. THEY SHOOT TO KILL. Cited above as item
    31, pp. 30-31.

    Case history in a survey of criminal snipers.

497. SAN FRANCISCO "GAY" MURDERS (S)

Serial murders of male homosexuals, perpetrated by at
least two separate killers. These crimes, occurring at the
same time as the "Black Doodler" homicides, were placed by
local detectives in two groups. The first five slayings were
"ripper"-style mutilation murders of Tenderloin "drag queens,"
apparently committed by a killer whose pathological hatred of
transvestites drove him to murder. The second string of six
murders, generally considered unrelated to the first, were
aimed at "closet slaves," who patronized sadomasochistic
"leather bars" on Folsom Street, south of Market. At this
writing, police remain stymied by lack of cooperation from
the fringe gay community, and all the aforementioned crimes
are unsolved.

* Godwin, John. MURDER USA. Cited above as item 10, pp.
    176-177.

    Case histories in a chapter on homicides influenced by
    homosexual life-styles.

498. SCHAEFFER, GERRIT C. (S)

Resident of Rotterdam, Holland, arrested with his wife,
in November 1958, on charges of murdering four newborn infants
—their own—over a span of seven years. Sentenced to life
imprisonment.

* FACTS ON FILE. Volume 18, 1958. Cited above as item 7, p. 420.

    Reports Schaeffer's arrest and the investigation.

499. SCHMID, CHARLES HOWARD, Jr. (S)

The "Pied Piper of Tucson," a pampered only child and pathological liar, whose extravagant behavior and "macho" image made him a hero for many local teens in the early 1960s. Bored with mere sex, Schmid murdered two teenaged girls, in 1964 and 1965, committing the first crime before witnesses and boasting openly of the second. His crimes were common knowledge among local youngsters at the time of Schmid's arrest, in 1965, and he received two terms of life imprisonment. In 1972, Schmid escaped from prison, in the company of another inmate, but both were soon recaptured.

Books

* Gaute, J.H.H., and Robin Odell. THE MURDERERS' WHO'S WHO. Cited above as item 8, pp. 204-206.

    Case history presented in an encyclopedic format.

453. Moser, Don, and Jerry Cohen. THE PIED PIPER OF TUCSON. New York: New American Library, 1967.

    Examines the case in detail, with emphasis on Tucson's teenage sub-culture and parental responsiblity for the behavior of adolescents.

* Nash, Jay Robert. ALMANAC OF WORLD CRIME. Cited above as item 19, pp. 13, 362.

    Case history in a general discussion of mass murder.

* ————. BLOODLETTERS AND BADMEN. Cited above as item 20, pp. 485-488.

    Case history presented in an encyclopedic format.

* ————. CRIME CHRONOLOGY, 1900-1983. Cited above as item 21, p. 169.

    Brief case history presented in time line format.

* ———. MURDER, AMERICA. Cited above as item 23, p. 433.

   Sketchy case history presented in time line format.

* Sifakis, Carl. THE ENCYCLOPEDIA OF AMERICAN CRIME. Cited above as item 29, pp. 641-642.

   Case history presented in an encyclopedic format.

* Wilson, Colin. A CASEBOOK OF MURDER. Cited above as item 33, pp. 231-233.

   Presents a sociological case history of Schmid's crimes.

* ———, and Donald Seaman. THE ENCYCLOPEDIA OF MODERN MURDER. Cited above as item 36, pp. 206-208.

   Case history presented in an encyclopedic format.

Articles

454. "Killing for Kicks." NEWSWEEK 67 (March 14, 1966): 35+.

   Reports the case against Schmid in Tucson.

455. "Secrets in the Sand." TIME 86 (November 26, 1965): 27.

   Describes Schmid's arrest and confessions.

456. "Trial by Headline?" NEWSWEEK 66 (December 13, 1965): 70.

   Reports Schmid's arrest and indictment.

500. SCIERI, ANTOINETTE (S)

Self-styled nurse and poisoner-for-pleasure, who murdered at least six persons in Paris. At her trial, the judge who sentenced her to life declared, "You have been called a monster, but that expression is not strong enough. You are debauched. You are possessed of all vices." Died in prison.

* Nash, Jay Robert. CRIME CHRONOLOGY, 1900-1983. Cited above as item 21, p. 68.

   Brief case history presented in time line format.

501. SEARS, CHARLES (S)

New York City's "Skid Row Slasher," charged in July 1981 with killing two men and wounding thirteen others in the past two months. Like California killers Vaughn Greenwood and Bobby Joe Maxwell, Sears chose homeless transients as his victims, stabbing them as they slept in alleys and on sidewalks. Sentenced to life.

* FACTS ON FILE. Volume 41, 1981. Cited above as item 7, p. 524.

  Reports the arrest and indictment of Sears.

502. SEEFELD, ADOLF (S)

Nomadic German watchmaker and confessed homosexual slayer of at least twelve boys, between April 1933 and February 1935. First charged with the murder of a young boy in 1908, Seefeld was released on grounds of insufficient evidence. Twenty-three of his 65 years were spent in prison, serving time for sexual assaults against boys, and on one occasion Seefeld was committed to a mental institution, near Potsdam, where he remained for two years without speaking a word. Ironically, in spite of Seefeld's record, none of his young murder victims seem to have been sexually molested. Each was poisoned, with a concoction of wild plants and fungi, their bodies found in attitudes of repose. Brought to trial in 1936, Seefeld was executed by Nazi authorities three months later.

* Nash, Jay Robert. ALMANAC OF WORLD CRIME. Cited above as item 19, p. 288.

  Brief case history in a general discussion of mass murder. Nash erroneously states that Seefeld's murder victims were molested before they were killed.

* Wilson, Colin. A CRIMINAL HISTORY OF MANKIND. Cited above as item 34, p. 609.

  Brief case history in a discussion of sex crimes.

* ———, and Patricia Putnam. THE ENCYCLOPEDIA OF MURDER. Cited above as item 35, pp. 484-485.

  Case history presented in an encyclopedic format.

503. SEELEY, JAMES R. (M)

Resident of Flint, Mich., who stabbed his wife to death and drowned two of their four children in the family home, during March 1959. Sentenced to die.

* FACTS ON FILE. Volume 19, 1959. Cited above as item 7, p. 88.

    Reports Seeley's crimes and arrest.

504. SHANKARIYA, KAMPATIMAR (S)

Native of Jaipur, India, convicted of using a hammer to murder at least 70 victims between 1977 and 1979. Sentenced to death and hanged at Jaipur in May 1979. Shankariya's last words were a gallows lament: "I have murdered in vain. Nobody should become like me."

* Tobias, Ronald. THEY SHOOT TO KILL. Cited above as item 31, p. 178.

    Brief case history in a discussion of serial murder.

505. SHEARING, DAVID WILLIAM (M)

Canadian slayer of two vacationing families—six victims in all—who were massacred in the British Columbian interior, during September 1982. A 14-month investigation by the Royal Canadian Mounted Police led to Shearing's arrest and indictment in December 1983. Robbery is presumed as the motive in the murders, although Shearing offered no plea or explanation.

457. O'Hara, Jane. "Arrest in Camper Murders." MACLEANS 96 (December 5, 1983): 34.

    Report's Shearing's arrest, with a recap of the R.C.M.P.'s extensive manhunt.

458. Zwarun, Suzanne. "The Grisly Conclusion to a Summer Mystery." MACLEANS 95 (September 27, 1982): 15.

    Reports the British Columbia massacre, with coverage of the early search for evidence.

506. SHERMAN, LYDIA (S)

19th-century America's "Queen of Poisoners," whose 12

confirmed victims include three husbands, six of her own
children, and three step-children. Financial motives were
apparent in most of the homicides, and Sherman was arrested
after her third husband's death, in 1871. Sentenced to life,
she died in a Connecticut prison, in May 1873.

> * Boar, Roger, and Nigel Blundell. THE WORLD'S MOST IN-
>   FAMOUS MURDERS. Cited above as item 2, pp. 160-161.
>
>   Brief case history in sensation tabloid style.
>
> * Green, Jonathon. THE GREATEST CRIMINALS OF ALL TIME.
>   Cited above as item 11, p. 155.
>
>   Brief case history in an encyclopedic format.
>
> * Jones, Ann. WOMEN WHO KILL. Cited above as item 13,
>   pp. 116-121.
>
>   Case history in a feminist survey of female killers.
>
> * Nash, Jay Robert. LOOK FOR THE WOMAN. Cited above as
>   item 22, p. 342.
>
>   Case history presented in an encyclopedic format.
>
> * ———. MURDER, AMERICA. Cited above as item 23, pp.
>   14, 73-86.
>
>   Case history in an anthology of "classic" murders.
>
> * Pearson, Edmund L. "Rules for Murderesses." Cited
>   above as item 25, pp. 14-15.
>
>   Presents a tongue-in-cheek review of Sherman's case.

459. THE POISON FIEND! LIFE, CRIMES AND CONVICTION OF LYDIA
      SHERMAN, THE MODERN LUCRETIA BORGIA. Philadelphia:
      Barclay and Co., 1872.

      Sensational contemporary account of Sherman's case.

507. SHERRILL, PATRICK HENRY (M)

Disgruntled postal employee in Edmond, Okla., who responded to criticism from his supervisors by going on a shooting rampage inside the local post office, in August 1986.
Fourteen persons were killed and six others wounded before

Sherrill turned the weapon on himself, committing suicide.

460. Johnson, Terry E. "10 Minutes of Madness." NEWSWEEK
        108 (September 1, 1986): 18-19.

        Contemporaneous report of the Oklahoma massacre.

461. Lamar, Jacob V., Jr. "'Crazy Pat's' Revenge." TIME 128
        (September 1, 1986): 19.

        Reports the massacre and Sherrill's suicide.

508. SHOAF, MAMIE SHEY (M)

Despondent housewife in Lebanon, Ky., who drove her three
children to a local cemetery in May 1929, and there killed all
three by cutting their throats. Following the triple murder,
Shoaf took her own life, in identical fashion.

*   Nash, Jay Robert. CRIME CHRONOLOGY, 1900-1983. Cited
    above as item 21, p. 77.

    Brief case history presented in time line format.

*   ————. MURDER, AMERICA. Cited above as tiem 23, p. 401.

    Sketchy case history presented in time line format.

509. "SIDNEY SNIPER, THE" (S)

Unidentified hit-and-run sniper who killed five persons
and wounded seven others in a high-crime area of Richmond, Va.,
in the early 1960s. The random shootings served to clear the
streets and reduce local crime for a brief period, leading
police to suspect the sniper may have been a self-styled urban
vigilante. At this writing, the case remains unsolved.

*   Tobias, Ronald. THEY SHOOT TO KILL. Cited above as
    item 31, p. 136.

    Brief case history in a survey of criminal snipers.

510. SIMANTS, ERWIN CHARLES (M)

Invaded the home of his best friend, at Sutherland, Neb.,
in October 1975, shooting six family members to death with a
rifle, raping a child and an elderly woman. Simants was arrested next morning, as he tried to re-enter the house. Sentenced to death in January 1976, he won a new trial three

years later, and was deemed not guilty by reason of insanity.
Committed to a mental institution for life.

* FACTS ON FILE. Volume 35, 1975. Cited above as item 7,
  p. 932.

  Reports the Supreme Court's decision to bar television
  cameras from Simants' trial.

* FACTS ON FILE. Volume 36, 1976. Cited above as item 7,
  p. 492.

  Reports Simants' death sentence.

* FACTS ON FILE. Volume 39, 1979. Cited above as item 7,
  p. 890.

  Reports the results of Simants' second trial.

* Godwin, John. MURDER USA. Cited above as item 10, pp.
  308-309.

  Case history in a survey of atrocious crimes.

* Nash, Jay Robert. MURDER, AMERICA. Cited above as item
  23, p. 443.

  Sketchy case history presented in time line format,
  marred by sloppy scholarship. Writing five years after
  the Sutherland massacre, Nash can only manage to report
  that Simants killed "at least four victims," two short
  of the actual total.

511. SIMON, J.C. (S): See "ZEBRA MURDERS"

512. SIMPSON, CHARLES (M)

Mentally-disturbed Vietnam veteran in Harrisonville,
Mo., who shot and killed three persons, wounded three others,
and then shot himself to death in May 1972. Three of Simpson's
six victims were peace officers, and his outburst was reportedly inspired by recent harassment of his long-haired fellow
veterans.

Books

462. Eszterhas, Joe. CHARLIE SIMPSON'S APOCALYPSE. New
     York: Random House, 1973.

Highlights the clash of generations in small-town
America which paved the way for bloodshed. Instructive.

Articles

463. "Our Town." NEWSWEEK 79 (June 5, 1972): 42.

Reports the massacre, with an examination of conflict
between Harrisonville's conservative elders and young
war veterans gone "hippy."

513. SKINNER, KENNETH (M)

Teenaged newsboy in San Francisco, Calif., who torched
an aprtment complex in July 1951, killing eight persons. Sentenced to ten years in prison.

* Nash, Jay Robert. ALMANAC OF WORLD CRIME. Cited above
  as item 19, p. 25.

Brief case history in a chapter on arson.

514. SMITH, ALLEN R. (M)

Teenaged slayer of the married couple who secured his
release from a Michigan reformatory in December 1953. Smith
was arrested by police in Miami, Fla., and returned to Michigan for trial. Sentenced to die.

* FACTS ON FILE. Volume 13, 1953. Cited above as item 7,
  p. 416.

Reports Smith's crime and arrest.

515. SMITH, CHARLES (S)

Merchant seaman who shot and killed two Miami, Fla., men
without apparent motive, during October 1958. Arrested after
boasting of his crimes in saloons, Smith was sentenced to life.

* Browning, Norma Lee. THE PSYCHIC WORLD OF PETER HURKOS.
  Cited above as item 186, pp. 89-90.

Little work for "psychic" Hurkos in this case, given
the killer's prpensity for loose talk in public places.

516. SMITH, FRED (M)

Escaped convict and slayer, with accomplices David Thomas Blackstone and Frank Oliver, of four Ypsilanti, Mich., teenagers in August 1931. Smith and company accosted the two couples, parked in a rural lover's lane, and robbed the teens of two dollars, thereafter raping one of the girls and killing all four victims, setting the car afire with their bodies inside. Two innocent suspects, brothers, were first arrested for the crime and narrowly escaped death at the hands of a lynch mob before the actual killers were identified. Smith and his comrades entered pleas of guilty in the case, and were sentenced to life.

*   Wilson, Colin. ORDER OF ASSASSINS. Cited above as item 76, pp. 103-104.

    Psychological case history of the Ypsilanti murders.

517. SMITH, GEORGE JOSEPH (S)

British habitual criminal and professional "Bluebeard," slayer of wives for profit. Serving his first reformatory sentence at age nine, Smith was a hardened criminal by the time he reached adolescence. Between 1912 and 1914, Smith murdered three successive wives for their money, drowning each in a zinc bathtub specifically purchased as a tool of murder. Tried and convicted in June 1915, he was hanged two months later.

*   Boar, Roger, and Nigel Blundell. THE WORLD'S MOST INFAMOUS MURDERS. Cited above as item 2, pp. 175-183.

    Case history presented in sensational tabloid style.

*   CRIMES AND PUNISHMENT: A PICTORIAL ENCYCLOPEDIA OF ABERRANT BEHAVIOR, Volume 4. Cited above as item 4, pp. 71-78.

    Case history presented in an encyclopedic format.

*   Tullet, Tom. STRICTLY MURDER. Cited above as item 32.

    Case history in an anthology of Scotland Yard cases.

*   Wilson, Colin, and Patricia Putnam. THE ENCYCLOPEDIA OF MURDER. Cited above as item 35, pp. 496-499.

Case history presented in an encyclopedic format.

518. SMITH, MARK ALAN (S)

Rape-slayer of several young women across northern Illinois, beginning in 1966. Upon his arrest, Smith confessed to seven sexually-motivated murders, and was sentenced to 500 years in prison.

* Nash, Jay Robert. MURDER, AMERICA. Cited above as item 23, p. 435.

Sketchy case history presented in time line format.

519. SMITH, PERRY E. (M): See HICKOCK, RICHARD E.

520. SMITH, ROBERT BENJAMIN (M)

Entering a Mesa, Ariz., beauty parlor in November 1956, Smith forced five women, a three-year-old child and an infant to lie on the floor. He then proceeded to shoot and stab each victim, stopping only when he believed all seven to be dead. (In fact, the infant, shielded by her mother's body, would survive with a bullet in the arm.) Arrested at the scene, Smith informed police that, "I wanted to get known, just wanted to get myself a name." Sentenced to life without parole.

Books

* CRIMES AND PUNISHMENT: A PICTORIAL ENCYCLOPEDIA OF ABERRANT BEHAVIOR, Volume 1. Cited above as item 4, pp. 87-88.

Case history presented in an encyclopedic format.

* Nash, Jay Robert. ALMANAC OF WORLD CRIME. Cited above as item 19, p. 289.

Case history in a general discussion of mass murder.

* ————. CRIME CHRONOLOGY, 1900-1983. Cited above as item 21, p. 173.

Brief case history presented in time line format.

* ————. MURDER, AMERICA. Cited above as tiem 23, pp. 435-436.

Sketchy case history presented in time line format.

Articles

463A. "The Quiet One." NEWSWEEK 68 (November 29, 1966): 28.

Reports Smith's crimes and arrest.

464. "Slaughter in the College of Beauty." TIME 88 (November 18, 1966): 33.

Contemporaneous account of the Arizona massacre.

521. SMITH, RUSSELL LEE (M)

On probation from his first murder conviction, Smith went berserk in Dayton, Ohio, during 1975, launching a one-man reign of terror. He killed three persons and wounded eleven others in a single day of random shooting, then abducted two girls, raping both and killing one, before committing suicide.

*   Nash, Jay Robert. CRIME CHRONOLOGY, 1900-1983. Cited above as item 21, p. 188.

Brief case history presented in time line format.

*   ————. MURDER, AMERICA. Cited above as item 23, p. 443.

Sketchy case history presented in time line format.

522. SOBHRAJ, CHARLES (S)

Vietnamese swindler, thief, and drug runner, responsible for at least eight murders in five Asian countries. Victims were typically European or American tourists, who encountered Sobhraj and his several accomplices while traveling in the Far East. Sentenced to nine years at hard labor in India, upon his conviction there, Sobhraj continues his appeals, while several other nations wait to extradite him on capital charges.

465. Neville, Richard, and Julie Clark. THE LIFE AND CRIMES OF CHARLES SOBHRAJ. London: Jonathan Cape, 1979.

Includes portions of Sobhraj's confession in a general survey of his criminal career.

466. Thompson, Thomas. SERPENTINE. New York: Doubleday, 1979.

    The definitive study of Sobhraj. Instructive.

* Wilson, Colin, and Donald Seaman. THE ENCYCLOPEDIA OF
   MODERN MURDER. Cited above as item 36, pp. 211-215.

    Case history presented in an encyclopedic format.

523. SOMMER, FRED Jr. (S)

    Homicidal teenaged hitchhiker in Camerson Mills, N.Y.,
who shot and killed two motorists in December 1957, stealing
their vehicles for later use in armed robberies. Sentenced
to life.

* FACTS ON FILE. Volume 17, 1957. Cited above as item 7,
   p. 428.

    Reports Sommer's crimes and arrest.

524. SOMMERHALDER, RICHARD (M)

    Habitual criminal and operator of a "head shop" in Santa
Cruz, Calif., who abducted, raped, and beat to death two girls
in 1976. Sommerhalder was idolized by many local youths, whom
he supplied with drugs. Sentenced to a double term of life
in prison, where his brother was already serving time for
triple murder. As one prison official remarked, "They were
two great brothers. Sort of like Cain and Cain."

* Godwin, John. MURDER USA. Cited above as item 10, p. 317.

    Case history in a discussion of random, senseless crimes.

525. "SOUTH SIDE SLAYER, THE" (S)

    Unidentified torture-slayer of an estimated 18 prosti-
tutes in Los Angeles since 1983. Described by surviving witnesses as a tall black man, the sadistic killer stabs or
strangles his victims, and several bodies have shown evidence
of torture with some sharp object, like an ice pick, prior to
death. Victims are typically dumped from the killer's car,
on public streets, or otherwise discarded where they will be
quickly found. (One body was discovered in the stairwell of
an elementary school.) At this writing, police have no
viable suspects in the case.

467. Uehling, M.D. "The L.A. Slayer." NEWSWEEK 107 (June 9,
      1986): 28.

        Summarizes the case, examining the manhunt in progress.

526. SPECK, RICHARD FRANKLIN (S)

     Transient and habitual criminal, slayer of eight student
nurses in a Chicago hotel, on July 13, 1966. The victims were
variously stabbed or strangled, although only one was raped.
Speck was subsequently identified by a ninth intended victim,
who escaped in the confusion of the massacre, and upon conviction he was sentenced to die, with the sentence subsequently
commuted to a term of more than 600 years in prison. Later
investigation tentatively linked Speck with as many as eight
other rape-slayings, committed over five months prior to the
Chicago slaughter. Speck was never charged in any of the
other cases, and they remain technically unsolved.

                              Books

468. Altman, Jack, and Marvin Ziporyn. BORN TO RAISE HELL:
      THE UNTOLD STORY OF RICHARD SPECK. New York: Grove
      Press, 1967.

        Studies the case with emphasis on psychiatric evalua-
        tion of the killer. (Ziporyn was one of the doctors
        who examined Speck prior to trial.) Instructive.

  *   CRIMES AND PUNISHMENT: A PICTORIAL ENCYCLOPEDIA OF ABER-
      RANT BEHAVIOR, Volume 13. Cited above as item 4, p. 85.

        Case history presented in an encyclopedic format.

  *   FACTS ON FILE. Volume 26, 1966. Cited above as item 7,
      pp. 325-326.

        Reports the Chicago massacre and Speck's indictment.

  *   FACTS ON FILE. Volume 27, 1967. Cited above as item 7,
      pp. 144, 583.

        Reports Speck's conviction and sentencing.

  *   FACTS ON FILE. Volume 28, 1968. Cited above as item 7,
      p. 604.

        Reports Speck's stay of execution.

* FACTS ON FILE. Volume 32, 1972. Cited above as item 7, p. 794.

Reports the court order for Speck's new sentence.

* FACTS ON FILE. Volume 38, 1978. Cited above as item 7, p. 172.

Speck confesses to seven of the Chicago murders, blaming the eighth on an unnamed accomplice, whom he allegedly murdered and buried after the massacre. No evidence has been discovered to support this strange story.

* Gaute, J.H.H., and Robin Odell. THE MURDERERS' WHO'S WHO. Cited above as item 8, pp. 217–218.

Case history presented in an encyclopedic format.

* Green, Jonathon. THE GREATEST CRIMINALS OF ALL TIME. Cited above as item 11, p. 156.

Brief case history in an encyclopedic format.

* Levin, Jack, and James Alan Fox. MASS MURDER: AMERICA'S GROWING MENACE. Cited above as item 15.

Case history in a general discussion of multicide.

* Nash, Jay Robert. ALMANAC OF WORLD CRIME. Cited above as item 19, p. 289.

Case history in a general discussion of mass murder.

* ———. BLOODLETTERS AND BADMEN. Cited above as item 20, pp. 511–516.

Case history presented in an encyclopedic format.

* ———. CRIME CHRONOLOGY, 1900–1983. Cited above as item 21, pp. 118, 172.

Case history pursued through time line entries.

* Sifakis, Carl. THE ENCYCLOPEDIA OF AMERICAN CRIME. Cited above as item 29, p. 677.

Case history presented in an encyclopedic format.

* Wilson, Colin. A CASEBOOK OF MURDER. Cited above as
    item 33, pp. 243-247.

    Links Speck with eight slayings priot to the Chicago
    massacre.

* ————. A CRIMINAL HISTORY OF MANKIND. Cited above as
    item 34, p. 622.

    Case history in a general discussion of mass murder.

* ————, and Donald Seaman. THE ENCYCLOPEDIA OF MODERN
    MURDER. Cited above as item 36, pp. 217-220.

    Case history presented in an encyclopedic format.

                              Articles

469. "All Deliberate, Little Speed." TIME 89 (March 24,
     1967): 60.

     Describes pre-trial maneuvers in Speck's case.

470. Altman, Jack, and Marvin Ziporyn. "The Mind of a
     Murderer." SATURDAY EVENING POST 240 (July 1, 1967):
     27-31+; (July 15, 1967): 40+.

     Two-part series, excerpts from item 468 above.

471. "Confrontation." NEWSWEEK 68 (August 1, 1966): 26.

     Reports Speck's early court appearances.

472. Hamill, P. "Suddenly, Without Warning or Reason."
     GOOD HOUSEKEEPING 164 (April 1967): 98-99+.

     Retrospective on the Speck case.

473. "Headlines and Checkbooks." NEWSWEEK 68 (August 1, 1966):
     76.

     Criticizes journalists who purchased rights to Speck's
     story.

474. "House of Death." NEWSWEEK 69 (April 17, 1967): 43-44.

     Covers Speck's murder trial.

475. "Judgment on Speck." NEWSWEEK 69 (April 24, 1967): 29.

Reports Speck's conviction.

476. "Justice vs. Journalism." NEWSWEEK 69 (March 6, 1967): 37.

Criticizes the involvement of writers in Speck's defense.

477. "Man Who Liked Liquor, Women, and Knives." LIFE 61 (July 29, 1966): 24.

Reports Speck's arrest and criminal background.

478. "Mass Murder that Horrified the Nation." US NEWS & WORLD REPORT 61 (July 29, 1966): 8.

Contemporaneous report of the Chicago massacre.

479. Oberbeck, S.K. "Born to Raise Hell." NEWSWEEK 70 (September 25, 1967): 108+.

Reviews item 468 above.

480. "One By One." TIME 88 (July 22, 1966): 21.

Reports the massacre of nurses in Chicago.

481. "Press and Richard Speck." TIME 89 (March 3, 1967): 49.

Examines the role of the media in Speck's case.

482. "Speck: Handled with Care." LIFE 61 (July 29, 1966): 4.

Reports Speck's arrest in Chicago.

483. "They Are All Dead!" NEWSWEEK 68 (July 25, 1966): 20.

Contemporaneous report of the Chicago slaughter.

484. "Twenty-four Years to Page One." TIME 88 (July 29, 1966): 15-17.

Describes Speck's arrest and background.

485. Wainright, L. "Who the Gentle Victims Were." LIFE 61 (July 29, 1966): 18-27.

Profiles Speck's Chicago victims.

527. SPENCER, BRENDA (M)

San Diego high school student who opened fire with a rifle on the school near her home, killing two persons and wounding several others in January 1979. Interrogated by police, her stated motive for the shootings was bizarre. "It was Monday," she explained. "I don't like Mondays." Convicted of murder at her trial, in October 1979, Spencer was sentenced to a term of 25 years to life.

Books

* FACTS ON FILE. Volume 39, 1979. Cited above as item 7, p. 819.

   Summarizes the case, through Spencer's sentencing.

* Tobias, Ronald. THEY SHOOT TO KILL. Cited above as item 31, pp. 36-37.

   Case history in a survey of criminal snipers.

Articles

486. "It Was Monday." TIME 113 (February 12, 1979): 25.

   Contemporaneous report of the San Diego shootings.

528. SPISAK, FRANK G. (S)

Self-styled Nazi who murdered three male students at Cleveland State University during 1982 and early 1983. Ethnic bigotry was the apparent motive for Spisak's crimes. Upon conviction, in August 1983, he was sentenced to die.

Books

* Nash, Jay Robert. CRIME CHRONOLOGY, 1900-1983. Cited above as item 21, p. 205.

   Brief case history presented in time line format.

Articles

487. "Nazi Killer is Sentenced to Death." NEWSWEEK 102 (August 22, 1983): 22.

   Reports Spisak's conviction and sentencing.

529. SPREITZER, EDWARD (S): See KOKORALEIS, ANDREW and THOMAS

530. SPRINGFIELD, MASS., MURDERS (M)

Unsolved stabbing murders of babysitter Lynn Ann Smith, age 14, and her four-year-old charge, Steven Goldberg, found dead in the Goldberg family home on September 25, 1954.

* FACTS ON FILE. Volume 14, 1954. Cited above as item 7, p. 328.

    Reports the murders and manhunt in progress.

531. STANIAK, LUCIAN (S)

Poland's "Red Spider," a "ripper"-style slayer who disemboweled 20 women between 1964 and 1967. An artist and translator of literature for a Polish publishing house, Staniak displayed his fascination with violent death in certain morbid paintings, prior to the beginning of his crime spree. Before his first murder, he wrote to the state newspaper: "There is no happiness without tears, no life without death. Beware! I am going to make you cry." Ultimately charged in only six of the 20 "identical" cases, Staniak was sentenced to life.

* Green, Jonathon. THE GREATEST CRIMINALS OF ALL TIME. Cited above as item 11, p. 156.

    Brief case history in an encyclopedic format.

* Leyton, Elliott. COMPULSIVE KILLERS. Cited above as item 16, pp. 290-291.

    Brief case history, culled from item 33 above.

* Wilson, Colin. A CASEBOOK OF MURDER. Cited above as item 33, pp. 250-255.

    Sociological case history of Staniak's crimes.

532. STANO, GERALD EUGENE (S)

Confessed slayer of 39 women, mostly in the state of Florida, within a ten-year period from 1973 to 1982. Victims were variously strangled, beaten, shot, or stabbed to death, with frequent evidence of sexual abuse. A classic misogynist, Stano told police, "I can't stand a bitchy chick." Sentenced to die.

Books

* Levin, Jack, and James Alan Fox. MASS MURDER: AMERICA'S
  GROWING MENACE. Cited above as item 15.

Case history in a general discussion of multicide.

* SERIAL MURDERS—HEARINGS BEFORE THE SUBCOMMITTE ON
  JUVENILE JUSTICE. Cited above as item 28, pp. 10-11.

Brief case history within witness testimony.

Articles

* Gest, Ted. "On the Trail of America's Serial Killers."
  Cited above as item 46.

Brief case history in a survey of recent multicides.

533. STARKWEATHER, CHARLES (S)

Teenaged garbage collector in Lincoln, Neb., who, with
accomplice Caril Ann Fugate, murdered eleven persons in
December 1957 and February 1958. Starkweather's first victim
was a gas station attendant, murdered during an ill-conceived
robbery. The next explosion occurred at Caril Fugate's home,
where Starkweather murdered her mother, sister, stepfather,
apparently in the girl's presence (and, according to the
prosecution, with her full cooperation). In the next five
days, Starkweather and Fugate murdered seven other victims,
encountered at various points along an aimless joy-ride in
the vicinity of Lincoln. Wounded in a wild police chase,
Starkweather was captured and held for trial, which resulted
in a death sentence. His erstwhile girlfriend turned on
Starkweather in custody, claiming she had been his hostage
throughout the killing spree. Starkweather refuted her story,
insisting that Fugate had numerous opportunities to run, and
that the hostage alibi was "cooked up between us" prior to
their capture in early February. (He also blamed Caril, specifically, for the sexual mutilations suffered by one female
victim, although the question was never resolved.) Starkweather was electrocuted in June 1959; Fugate was sentenced
to life, serving 18 years before her eventual parole, in 1976.

Books

488. Allen, William. STARKWEATHER: THE STORY OF A MASS
     MURDERER. Boston: Houghton Mifflin, 1976.

Thoughtful, instructive biography of the ultimate teenage rebel, by one of Starkweather's contemporaries.
Allen ably recreates the 1950s atmosphere, in which a
"hoodlum rep" was not only desirable, but sometimes man-
datory. The author's personal perspective recreates an
era when rebellious youth had "nothing to do" in a
Midwestern town, and thoughts turned easily toward casual,
destructive behavior.

489. Beaver, Ninette, B.K. Ripley, and Patrick Trese. CARIL.
     Philadelphia: J.B. Lippincott, 1974.

     Presents a "sympathetic" portrait of Fugate, lobbying
     for her parole on the twin theories that (a) she was
     probably innocent, and (b) if she killed anyone, it was
     a long time ago.

* CRIMES AND PUNISHMENT: A PICTORIAL ENCYCLOPEDIA OF ABER-
  RANT BEHAVIOR, Volume 6. Cited above as item 4, pp.
  112-113.

  Case history presented in an encyclopedic format.

* FACTS ON FILE. Volume 18, 1958. Cited above as item 7,
  pp. 32, 176.

  Reports the murders and Starkweather's conviction.

* FACTS ON FILE. Volume 36, 1976. Cited above as item 7,
  p. 442.

  Reports Caril Fugate's parole.

* Gaute, J.H.H., and Robin Odell. THE MURDERERS' WHO'S
  WHO. Cited above as item 8, p. 218.

  Case history presented in an encyclopedic format.

* Godwin, John. MURDER USA. Cited above as item 10, p.
  308.

  Brief case history in a discussion of mass murder.

* Levin, Jack, and James Alan Fox. MASS MURDER: AMERICA'S
  GROWING MENACE. Cited above as item 15.

  Case history in a survey of modern multicide.

* Leyton, Elliott. COMPULSIVE KILLERS. Cited above as
    item 16, pp. 222-257.

    Cannibalizes items 487, 488, and 489 to produce a
    profile of Starkweather containing "no new data."

* Nash, Jay Robert. ALMANAC OF WORLD CRIME. Cited above
    as item 19, p. 289.

    Case history in a general discussion of mass murder.

* ————. BLOODLETTERS AND BADMEN. Cited above as item
    20, pp. 523-527.

    Case history presented in an encyclopedic format.

* ————. CRIME CHRONOLOGY, 1900-1983. Cited above as
    item 21, pp. 112, 155-156.

    Brief case history presented in time line format.

* ————. MURDER, AMERICA. Cited above as item 23, p. 428.

    Sketchy case history presented in time line format.

490. Reinhardt, James Melvin. THE MURDEROUS TRAIL OF CHARLES
     STARKWEATHER. Springfield, Ill.: Thomas, 1960.

     A criminologist examines Starkweather's rampage.

* ————. THE PSYCHOLOGY OF STRANGE KILLERS. Cited above
    as item 70, pp. 88-125.

    Includes Starkweather in an anthology of multicides.

* Sifakis, Carl. THE ENCYCLOPEDIA OF AMERICAN CRIME.
    Cited above as item 29, pp. 682-683.

    Case history presented in an encyclopedic format.

* Wilson, Colin. A CRIMINAL HISTORY OF MANKIND. Cited
    above as item 34, p. 618.

    Case history in a discussion of "motiveless" crime.

Articles

491. "Behind a Week of Terror. One Boy's Story." US NEWS & WORLD REPORT 44 (February 7, 1958): 15.

    Examines Starweather's crimes and background.

492. Coffey, M. "Badlands Revisited." ATLANTIC MONTHLY 234 (December 1974): 2+.

    Reviews Starkweather's case, in light of a recent film loosely based on his crimes. Art's imitation of life is weighed and found wanting.

493. "Eleven Lay Dead." NEWSWEEK 51 (February 10, 1958): 42+.

    Reports Starkweather's crimes and arrest.

494. "Even with the World." TIME 71 (February 10, 1958): 21-22.

    Recounts Starkweather's crimes and arrest.

495. "Teen-ager Becomes Brutal Killer. Why?" LIFE 44 (February 10, 1958): 20-24.

    Photo spread of Starkweather's family and crimes.

 * "These Brutal Young." Cited above as item 59.

    Examines Starkweather's case in light of other recent crimes by juvenile delinquents, seeking answers and solutions.

535. STEMBRIDGE, MARION (M)

West Virginia banker and grocery store proprietor who shot and killed two local attorneys before committing suicide, in May 1953. Stembridge blamed the lawyers for his recent conviction on tax evasion and manslaughter charges, along with his subsequent indictment on charges of bribery and perjury.

 * FACTS ON FILE. Volume 13, 1953. Cited above as item 7, p. 176.

    Reports the West Virginia shootings and their aftermath.

536. STONE, LOIS (M)

Religious fanatic of Kinsman, Ohio, who drowned her three young sons in May 1820. Sentenced to life.

* Nash, Jay Robert. MURDER, AMERICA. Cited above as item
  23, p. 323.

Brief case history presented in time line format.

537. STRAFFEN, JOHN THOMAS (S)

British slayer of at least three victims in the post-war
era. Committed to a mental institution at age 17, in 1947,
after an assault on a child, Straffen was released as "cured"
in February 1951. Shortly thereafter, he strangled two small
girls in an effort to "annoy the police." Returned to the
asylum, Straffen escaped six months later. He was recaptured
the same day, but not before he killed another girl. Sentenced
to die, this time, Straffen eventually had his sentence commuted
to life imprisonment.

* Gaute, J.H.H., and Robin Odell. THE MURDERERS' WHO'S
  WHO. Cited above as item 8, p. 221.

Case history presented in an encyclopedic format.

538. STUBBE, PETER (S)

16th-century German "werewolf," serial killer, and
cannibal, linked to the mutilation murders of one man, two
women, and 13 children over a period of several years. Many
of Stubbe's victims were sexually abused, before or after
death, and their bodies were so mutilated—with portions removed and apparently devoured—that wild animals were initially blamed for the deaths. After Stubbe began snatching
victims in front of witnesses (and as the sexual element of
the attacks became manifest), a new explanation was found in
the popular werewolf superstitions of the period. Upon his
arrest, Stubbe confessed everything—including the murder
of his own young son, whose brains he devoured—and was executed as a lycanthrope, in 1590.

* Aylesworth, Thomas G. WEREWOLVES AND OTHER MONSTERS.
  Cited above as item 266, pp. 44-53.

Case history in a survey of werewolf lore.

* Garden, Nancy. WEREWOLVES. Cited above as item 267,
  pp. 24-27.

Case history in a general study of lycanthropy.

* Hurwood, Bernhardt J. VAMPIRES, WEREWOLVES, AND GHOULS.
Cited above as item 12, pp. 147-152.

Case history in an anthology of "human monsters."

* Masters, R.E.L., and Eduard Lea. PERVERSE CRIMES IN
HISTORY. Cited above as item 18, pp. 62-76.

Case history in a discussion of lycanthropy.

* McHargue, Georgess. MEET THE WEREWOLF. Cited above as
item 268, p. 54.

Case history in a general survey of werewolf legends.

539. STULLER, NICKLAUS (S)

16th-century German murderer whose victims included a
cavalry soldier and three pregnant women. In each of the
latter cases, Stuller slashed open the victims' bodies, ripping out their unborn fetuses. Upon his arrest and conviction,
in 1577, Stuller was publicly broken on the wheel, his flesh
torn with red-hot tongs before he finally expired.

* Wilson, Colin. A CASEBOOK OF MURDER. Cited above as
item 33, pp. 109-110.

Case history in a sociological survey of homicide.

540. STULLGENS, ROBERT WILHELM (M)

Compulsive German sex-killer who massacred a family of
four in Dusseldorf, during June 1980. One of the victims,
missing from the family apartment, was discovered in Stull-
gen's flat. A review of the killer's record revealed that he
had been released from prison just a few months earlier, after
serving time for raping a young mother (and attempting to rape
her child) in a public park. Arrested at his mother's home,
Stullgens swiftly confessed and was sentenced to life.

* Wilson, Colin, and Donald Seaman. THE ENCYCLOPEDIA OF
MODERN MURDER. Cited above as item 36, p. 220.

Case history presented in an encyclopedic format.

541. SUTCLIFFE, PETER (S)

Northern England's "Yorkshire Ripper," responsible for

at least 13 murders and seven nonfatal assaults upon women,
between October 1975 and January 1981. Sutcliffe's early victims were known prostitutes, each of whom he bludgeoned with
a hammer, afterward slashing and mutilating their prostrate
bodies. As his killing frenzy escalated over time, Sutcliffe
no longer restricted himself to ladies of the evening, broaden-
ing his attack to include co-eds, businesswomen, even a female
doctor. Arrested by chance, in the company of another prostitute, Sutcliffe had already been questioned several times by
police, without attracting serious attention. (In the midst
of the manhunt, police were misled by letters and an audio
cassette tape from a hoaxer—never identified—who posed as
the Ripper. Investigators wasted countless hours trying to
identify the hoaxer's voice and handwriting.) At his trial,
in May 1981, Sutcliffe asserted an insanity defense, claiming
that his victims were selected and slain under orders from
God, but one of his jailers had overheard a conversation between Sutcliffe and his wife, in which the killer stated his
intention to escape punishment by spending a short period "in
a loony bin." His duplicity revealed, Sutcliffe was sentenced
to a term of life imprisonment.

Books

496. Beattie, John. THE YORKSHIRE RIPPER STORY. London:
      Quartet/Daily Star, 1981.

      The first full-length examination of Sutcliffe's
      case, prepared in sensational tabloid style.

  *   Boar, Roger, and Nigel Blundell. THE WORLD'S MOST IN-
      FAMOUS MURDERS. Cited above as item 2, pp. 162-174.

      Case history presented in sensational tabloid style.

497. Burn, Gordon. SOMEBODY'S HUSBAND, SOMEBODY'S SON. New
      York: Viking, 1984.

      A British journalist, who covered Sutcliffe's trial,
      examines the killer's background in detail. Sutcliffe's
      early fascination with death, deformity, and disease—
      particularly of the venereal variety—present an insight-
      ful portrait of a personality warped in childhood and
      adolescence, nursing a pathological hatred of females
      in general and "loose women" in particular. It appears
      that Sutcliffe's obsession with VD, including repeated
      assertions of his own infection by a prostitute, served
      as motivation in his later violent crimes.

498. Cross, Roger. THE YORKSHIRE RIPPER. London: Granada.
     1981.

     Another early examination of the case. Well worth
     reading, though it falls short of being "the last word."

499. Jouve, Nicole Ward. "THE STREET CLEANER": THE YORKSHIRE
     RIPPER CASE ON TRIAL. London: Marion Boyers, 1986.

     Feminist examination of the "brutalized culture of
     machismo" which allegedly produced Sutcliffe and others
     of his kind. Described by the publisher, perhaps un-
     fairly, as "a salutory corrective to previous studies
     of Sutcliffe, from which the voices of women were notable
     by their absence."

*   Nash, Jay Robert. CRIME CHRONOLOGY, 1900-1981. Cited
     above as item 21, p. 205.

     Sketchy case history presented in time line format.

*   Wilson, Colin. A CRIMINAL HISTORY OF MANKIND. Cited
     above as item 34, pp. 642-643.

     Case history in a discussion of modern sex crimes.

*   ————, and Donald Seaman. THE ENCYCLOPEDIA OF MODERN
     MURDER. Cited above as item 36, pp. 220-226.

     Case history presented in an encyclopedic format.

500. Yallop, David A. DELIVER US FROM EVIL. New York:
     Coward, McCann & Geoghegan, 1982.

     Highlights police failures in the hunt for Sutcliffe,
     contending that one of the "official" Ripper victims
     was actually murdered by the author of the "hoax" letters
     and audio tape. Yallop also tentatively links Sutcliffe
     with five other murders and seven attempted murders—
     including one attack in France and two in Sweden—which
     were never charged against him. (One of the five mur-
     ders was "solved" through the confession of another
     suspect, but as Yallop notes, the killer's methods were
     identical to Sutcliffe's, and the crime occurred only
     three miles—and three months—from the scene of an
     "official" Ripper slaying.)

Articles

501. Brecher, J., and T. Clifton. "Break in the Ripper Case." NEWSWEEK 97 (January 19, 1981): 50+.

 Reports Sutcliffe's arrest.

502. "Crime: Yorkshire Murderer." PEOPLE WEEKLY 12 (October 15, 1979): 117-118.

 Recounts police efforts in the continuing manhunt.

503. "Hang Him!" TIME 117 (January 19, 1981): 39.

 Describes public reactions to Sutcliffe's arrest.

504. Hauptfuhrer, F. "Olivia Reivers Has Reason to Wonder: Was She the Yorkshire Ripper's Last Date?" PEOPLE WEEKLY 15 (January 26, 1981): 70-71.

 Profile of the prostitute who was arrested with Sutcliffe.

505. Kennedy, C. "Jack the Ripper's Latest Disciple." MACLEANS 92 (July 9, 1979): 18.

 Reports the Yorkshire manhunt in progress.

506. ————. "Lynch-mob Journalism." MACLEANS 94 (January 19, 1981): 29.

 Critiques media handling of Sutcliffe's case.

507. Martin, G. "Ripper." ESQUIRE 95 (January 1981): 58-68.

 Recaps the manhunt and Sutcliffe's arrest.

508. "Ripper's Return." TIME 113 (April 23, 1979): 43.

 Reports the manhunt in progress.

509. "Striking Again." TIME 114 (September 17, 1979): 49.

 The murders and manhunt continue.

510. "13th Victim." TIME 116 (December 1, 1980): 47.

 More on the manhunt, a month before Sutcliffe's arrest.

542. SWANGO, MICHAEL (S)

Physician, compulsive poisoner, and closet occultist, convicted in Quincy, Ill., of attempting to murder hospital paramedic workers. According to testimony and scientific evidence, Swango spiked doughnuts and various other "free snacks" with ant poison before offering them to hospital co-workers. Sentenced to five years in prison, Swango is now suspected of murdering at least seven patients at Ohio University Medical Center, during his prior tenure there. Those victims were variously poisoned or asphyxiated—one with a gauze pad rammed down his throat—and Swango had been seen in the immediate vicinity before each unexpected death. Occult posters, literature, and writings recovered from Swango's home may provide the motive for his "motiveless" crimes.

511. ABC News. "20/20: A Trail of Poison." New York: American Broadcasting Companies, 1986.

> Transcripts of a "20/20" documentary on the Swango case, broadcast on February 13, 1986. Correspondent John Stossel interviews Swango, along with witnesses, acquaintances, and surviving victims.

543. SWIATEK (S)

19th-century Austrian beggar, convicted in 1850 of murdering and devouring several children near a small forest village. Swiatek confessed to the murders of six children, reporting that the victims had been eaten by himself and his family, but his own children recalled the number as being considerably higher. (Their recollection is supported by odd bits of clothing discovered in Swiatek's home.) In custody, the beggar explained that his taste for human flesh had developed years earlier, after a tavern burned down near his previous home. Poking around in the ashes, Swiatek had discovered a charred human body and sampled the meat, after which he could not get enough. The total number of his victims, spanning years, may well have been prodigious, but the investigation bogged down when Swiatek hanged himself, on his first night in jail.

* Garden, Nancy. WEREWOLVES. Cited above as item 267, pp. 76-78.

> Case history in a historical survey of lycanthropy.

544. TABORSKY, JOSEPH (M): See CULOMBE, ARTHUR

545. TAYLOR, DONALD and REUBEN (S): See "DE MAU MAU MURDERS"

546. TAYLOR, GARY ADDISON (S)

At age 13, in Florida, Taylor made a practice of loiter-
ing near bus stops, late at night, assaulting women with a
hammer as they disembarked. Upon release from custody, in
1957, he moved to Michigan and there became known as the "Royal
Oak Sniper," shooting at women in the Detroit suburbs during
a two-month reign of terror. Diagnosed as a paranoid schizophrenic, Taylor was shuttled from one mental institution to
another, assaulting and raping several Detroit women while
out on furloughs. Taylor was eventually released, with orders
to continue medication and return for weekly sessions, neither
of which he did. Fourteen months elapsed before authorities
noted him as "missing"; during that time, Taylor murdered
several Michigan women, burying them in his yard, and then
moved on to Seattle, Wash., where he was finally arrested for
questioning in the murder of a young bride. Released again,
when Kings County police found no outstanding warrants on him
from Michigan, Taylor moved to Oregon, then to Texas, murdering at least two more women and raping six others before his
eventual capture and conviction. Sentenced to life, Taylor
constitutes a classic example of a serial slayer who "slipped
through the cracks in the system."

Books

 * SERIAL MURDERS—HEARINGS BEFORE THE SUBCOMMITTED ON
    JUVENILE JUSTICE. Cited above as item 28, pp. 17-18,
    23.

    Brief case history presented in witness testimony.

 * Tobias, Ronald. THEY SHOOT TO KILL. Cited above as
    item 31, p. 136.

    Refers to Taylor's career as a sniper in Michigan.

Articles

512. "Freedom to Kill." TIME 105 (June 9, 1975): 19.

    Recaps Taylor's criminal career.

547. TERPENING, OLIVER Jr. (M)

Teenager charges with the "thrill killing" of four playmates, all of whom were shot at Imlay City, Mich., in May 1947.
Held in custody as a juvenile.

* FACTS ON FILE. Volume 7, 1947. Cited above as item 7,
    p. 172,

   Contemporaneous report of Terpening's arrest.

548. TESSNOW, LUDWIG (S)

German sex slayer of children, whose career spanned the
turn of the century. A traveling carpenter, Tessnow typically abducted children from the villages in which he stopped,
molesting boys and girls alike before dismembering their
bodies and scattering the remains in nearby woods. Definitely
linked with the murders of two girls in September 1898 and
two boys in July 1901, it is suspected that his final body-
count may have reached thirty or more victims. Executed upon
conviction for murder.

* Gaute, J.H.H., and Robin Odell. THE MURDERERS' WHO'S
   WHO. Cited above as item 8, p. 223.

   Case history presented in an encyclopedic format.

* Nash, Jay Robert. ALMANAC OF WORLD CRIME. Cited above
   as item 19, p. 279.

   Misspells Tessnow's name (as "Tessov") while presenting a brief case history in a chapter on mass murder.

* Wilson, Colin. A CASEBOOK OF MURDER. Cited above as
   item 33, p. 149.

   Places Tessnow's crimes in sociological perspective.

* ————. A CRIMINAL HISTORY OF MANKIND. Cited above as
   item 34, pp. 509-510.

   Brief case history in a discussion of mass murder.

549. "TEXAS RIPPER, THE" (S)

Unidentified mutilation-slayer of several black prostitutes during 1887, a year before Jack the Ripper appeared in

London. The coincidence of timing, together with the fact
that neither killer was ever captured, leas some students of
"Ripper-ology" to speculate on a possible connection. (At
least one London witness believed Jack to be "a Yank," based
upon his dress and accent.)

> * Masters, R.E.L., and Eduard Lea. PERVERSE CRIMES IN
>   HISTORY. Cited above as item 18, p. 93.
>
>   Regrettably brief case history, in a chapter on sadis-
>   tick "ripper" slayings.

550. "3X GUNMAN, THE" (S)

Unidentified lover's lane killer of Queens, N.Y., who
claimed two victims in separate attacks during June 1930. In
each case, the male occupant of a parked car was questioned
briefly, then shot to death with a pistol by his masked assailant. In the first attack, the dead man's female companion
was also raped; in the second case, the woman talked the killer
out of sexual assault by displaying a religious medal. Cryptic
notes, left at the scene of each killing, indicated that the
gunmen knew his murdered victims in advance. Subsequent letters
to police and the press, signed "3X," asserted that the killer
was employed by a mysterious international group, "the Red
Diamond of Russia," to recover certain "documents" which had
been stolen by the murdered men and various unnamed accomplices.
The letters—some mailed to relatives of the victims, as far
away as Pennsylvania—indicated that the attacks would continue
until the documents were surrendered. In fact, there were no
more killings after the initial incidents, and a subsequent
note to police said the gunman was "returning home," his business finished in America. At this writing, the case—which
prefigured the citywide panic later inspired by "Son of Sam"—
remains unsolved.

Books

> * Nash, Jay Robert. OPEN FILES. Cited above as item 24,
>   p. 250.
>
>   A ludicrous account, describing the 3X killer as a
>   "maniac bomber [who] plagued New York City ... by plant-
>   ing various homemade bombs throughout Manhattan" between
>   1930 and 1933. Literally nothing is correct in this
>   report, including Nash's statement that the "bomber"
>   killed no one. Efforts to trace the source of Nash's
>   bizarre information have proved fruitless; certainly,

contemporary press accounts and magazine articles bear
no resemblance to his final version of events.

Articles

513. Brundidge, H.T. "Three-X, The Man Behind the Gun."
     AMERICAN MERCURY 78 (April 1954): 59-63.

     Despite the title, no solutions to an enigmatic case.

514. Mauder, Jack G. "3 X Murders." AMERICAN MERCURY 50
     (June 1940): 222-228.

     Concise account of the case, including excerpts from
     the killer's letters and suggestions of a possible link
     to the (likewise unsolved) "lipstick murders" of 1937.

551. THOMAS, CHRISTOPHER (M)

     Slayer of ten persons in a 1984 Brooklyn massacre fueled
by drugs and jealousy. Believing, erroneously, that his estranged wife was having sex with a neighbor, Thomas invaded
the neighbor's apartment and shot ten persons—including eight
children and a pregnant woman—to death execution-style. Sentenced to life.

*   FACTS ON FILE. Volume 44, 1984. Cited above as item 7,
    p. 491.

    Reports the circumstances of the Brooklyn massacre.

552. THOMPSON, ROBERT J. (S)

     Slayer of female tourists in Mexico, during August and
September 1958. Thompson robbed, raped, and murdered at least
five women, allowing more to escape through his own clumsiness.
Eyewitness descriptions led to his arrest, and he was sentenced
to life.

*   CRIMES AND PUNISHMENT: A PICTORIAL ENCYCLOPEDIA OF ABER-
    RANT BEHAVIOR, Volume 4. Cited above as item 4, pp.
    60-61.

    Case history in a chapter on "lonely-hearts" killers.

553. THORPE, WILLIAM ALFRED (M)

Resident of Virginia who committed suicide after murdering

his mother, son, and sister, in June 1959. No apparent motive
for the family slayings was discovered.

>   *   FACTS ON FILE. Volume 19, 1959. Cited above as item 7,
>   p. 379.

>   Contemporaneous report of the Virginia shootings.

554. TISON FAMILY, THE (M)

Habitual criminal Gary Tison was serving life in Arizona,
for the murder of a prison guard, when members of his family
helped him escape in July 1978. With fellow inmate Randy
Greenawalt, Tison joined his three sons—Donald, Raymond, and
Ricky—on a dead-end flight into the Arizona desert. Stalled
with a flat tire the next day, the gunmen slaughtered a family
of four who stopped to offer help. The gang shot through one
roadblock, near Tison's home town of Casa Grande, but police
were primed and waiting at another checkpoint, down the road.
Donald Tison was killed in a furious exchange of gunfire,
lasting thirty minutes, and his brothers—along with Greenawalt—surrendered to authorities. Gary Tison fled, on foot,
into the desert, there eluding searchers for a month. In late
August, his rotting corpse was found by residents, less than
two miles from the scene of the shootout which ended his
rampage. Survivors of the gang were charged with six counts
of murder. (The van they were driving, when captured, belonged
to missing honeymooners from Texas, who have never been found.)
Gary Tison, in the words of Yuma County's coroner, had been
"released to a higher authority."

515. "Death in the Desert." TIME 112 (September 4, 1978): 19.

>   Recaps the manhunt, a week after discovery of Gary
>   Tison's remains.

555. TOFANIA (S)

18th-century Italian poisoner-for-hire, whose services
were reportedly in much demand by angry spouses, restless
heirs, and others with an urge to speed their various acquaintances along to their reward. No precise body-count is available for Tofania, but authorities suspected her of murdering
600 persons, give or take. Garroted in 1719.

>   *   Green, Jonathon. THE GREATEST CRIMINALS OF ALL TIME.
>   Cited above as item 11, p. 156.

Case history presented in an encyclopedic format.

556. TOOLE, OTTIS ELWOOD (S)

Homosexual sadist, arsonist, and confessed cannibal, convicted and sentenced to die for two slayings in Florida, indicted in several other cases now unlikely to be tried. By his own admission, Toole killed his first victim—another homosexual—at age 14, deliberately backing over the man with the victim's own car. A lifelong pyromaniac, Toole also torched an estimated 20 houses in his Jacksonville, Fla., neighborhood; later asked for an explanation, he replied, "I just hated to see them standing there." Almost certainly responsible for several murders in the early 1970s, as far away as Colorado, Toole met Henry Lee Lucas at a Jacksonville soup kitchen, circa 1976. The two became traveling companions and sometime lovers, reportedly killing at random on the road. Ironically arrested on an arson charge, in Florida, mere days before Lucas was seized in an unrelated Texas case, Toole was implicated by Lucas in subsequent confessions. The later decision by Lucas —or someone else—to change his story has not shaken Toole's admission of guilt in close to 100 cases. Transcripts of telephone conversations between Lucas and Toole, taped by Texas Rangers, make it obvious that the two men possess shared knowledge of numerous murders, including some where victims were partially devoured. This, despite the fact that there had been no unobserved communication between them in the weeks while Lucas "planned his hoax."

Books

* FACTS ON FILE. Volume 43, 1983. Cited above as item 7, p. 896.

     Relates Toole's confession to—and subsequent denial of participation in—the decapitation of six-year-old Adam Walsh. Florida detectives said they were "convinced" by Toole's confession, but abruptly changed their tune when he recanted a month later. The case remains open.

* Levin, Jack, and James Alan Fox. MASS MURDER: AMERICA'S GROWING MENACE. Cited above as item 15.

     Brief reference to the Walsh case, in a discussion of modern serial murder.

* Nash, Jay Robert. CRIME CHRONOLOGY, 1900-1983. Cited above as item 21, p. 206.

Typically garbled account, erroneously stating that
Toole killed his mother. In fact, she died of natural
causes, in June 1981.

Articles

516. Carlson, Peter. "Is an Innocent Man Behind Bars?"
      PEOPLE WEEKLY 22 (November 5, 1984): 89-90+.

Presents persuasive evidence of Toole's participation
in a 10-year-old murder for which serviceman Park Estep
is now serving life. Likewise interesting for the fact
that it places Toole in Colorado during a period of other
unsolved deaths and disappearances, some previously attributed to Ted Bundy.

* Darrach, Brad, and Joel Norris. "An American Tragedy."
   Cited above as item 40.

Case histories of Toole and Lucas, in a survey of
modern serial murder.

* Stanley, A. "Catching a New Breed of Killer." Cited
   above as item 56.

Highlights Toole and Lucas as examples of modern serial
killers, examining theproblems which transient slayers
pose for law enforcement agencies around the country.

557. TOPPAN, JANE (S)

New England nurse who poisoned patients and acquaintances
for pleasure, claiming dozens of victims between 1880 and her
arrest in 1901. In custody, Toppan recited the names of 31
victims from memory, but authorities suspected that her tally
might be closer to 70. (In fact, years later, Tappan revised
her estimate, claiming more than 100 victims; many of them,
killed in hospitals where she became a private nurse, were
described as "practice murders.") Sentenced to life.

* Nash, Jay Robert. CRIME CHRONOLOGY, 1900-1983. Cited
   above as item 21, p. 7.

Brief case history presented in time line format.

* ————. LOOK FOR THE WOMAN. Cited above as item 22,
   pp. 362-368.

Case history presented in an encyclopedic format.

* Pearson, Edmund L. "Rules for Murderesses." Cited above as item 25, pp. 15-16.

   Includes Toppan's case in a facetious review of classic female slayers.

* Sifakis, Carl. THE ENCYCLOPEDIA OF AMERICAN CRIME. Cited above as item 28, p. 716.

   Case history presented in an encyclopedic format.

558. TORONTO HOSPITAL MURDERS (S)

Bizarre, long-running case of infant deaths in the cardiac unit of Toronto's Hospital for Sick Children. Between June 1980 and March 1981, the cardiac ward experienced a dramatic 600% leap in infant mortality, with the number of actual deaths estimated, in various police and media reports, at between 21 and 43 babies. Upon examination, many of the infants showed high levels of digoxin, a form of the drug digitalis (which may also naturally increase in a body after death.) Late in March 1981, nurse Susan Nelles was charged with first-degree murder in four of the infant deaths, but charges were dismissed for lack of evidence in May 1982. (At that hearing, the presiding judge described Nelles as "an excellent nurse," with "an excellent reputation." He also declared that five, not four, infants had apparently been slain be persons unknown.) While Nelles remained on leave, with pay, for the next 27 months, investigators tried in vain to solve the riddle of the infant deaths. Lab reports, issued in February 1983, showed elevated digoxin levels in 28 deaths from the relevant period, and similar results were reported in the death of another infant, a month later. Ontario's attorney general immediately formed a special commission of inquiry, which described 18 of the infant deaths as "suspcious," while another ten were deemed "consistent with" digoxin poisoning, although no positive conclusion could be drawn from the existing evidence. In February 1984, another cardiac nurse accused nursing supervisor Phyllis Traynor of injecting an unknown drug into the intravenous line of one victim, who had been assigned to Nelles for care. A second nurse belatedly announced that she suspected Traynor in the murders prior to Nelles's arrest in 1981, but she possessed no evidence which would support indictments. New hearings, held in April 1984, provide the latest "last word" on the case: eight deaths are now conclusively described as murder, with another 13 termed "highly suspicious." At this writing, no further charges have been filed, and the case remains unsolved.

517. Block, Robert. "The Nurses and the 28 Infant Deaths."
      MACLEANS 97 (February 6, 1984): 44.

          Investigations continue, to no avail.

518. ————. "Who Killed the Babies?" MACLEANS 96 (Decem-
      ber 12, 1983): 50.

          Places the body-count at 36 infants, relating commis-
      sion findings that half of the deaths are "suspicious."

519. Hluchy, Patricia. "Nelles Takes the Stand." MACLEANS
      97 (April 16, 1984): 56.

          Suspects testify at yet another commission of inquiry.

520. ————. "Traynor Tells Her Story." MACLEANS 97 (April
      23, 1984): 44.

          The reported death toll stands at 36, as suspect
      Traynor maintains her innocence in public testimony.

521. Johnson, Arthur. "The Baby Murders." MACLEANS 97
      (April 9, 1984): 36-42.

          Best single overview of the convoluted mystery, with
      police estimates of the body-count quoted at 43 victims.

522. McKay, Shona. "The Letter to a Nurse." MACLEANS 97
      (May 7, 1984): 57.

          Fruitless investigations into the baby deaths continue.

523. ————. "A Limited Investigation." MACLEANS 97 (April
      30, 1984): 54.

          And the probe goes on.

524. ————. "New Questions About the Baby Deaths." MACLEANS
      98 (February 11, 1985): 44-45.

          The body-count sinks back to 36, as medical critics
      attack the methods used by investigators to determine
      "suspicious" digoxin deaths.

525. Ohlendorf, Pat. "The Mystery at Sick Kids." MACLEANS
      96 (July 25, 1983): 40-41.

Recaps the case to date, including an examination of the shifting body-counts.

526. Quinn, H. "The Unsolved Murders." MACLEANS 98 (January 14, 1985): 33.

Continuing coverage in the magazine's informative series.

527. Riley, Susan. "Baby Deaths Without Answers." MACLEANS 96 (March 7, 1983): 20.

Lab studies describe seven infants as definite murder victims, with another 21 "possibles."

528. Walmsley, A. "New Revelations in the Baby Murders." MACLEANS 97 (July 23, 1984): 13.

New lab reports juggle the body-count again. The muddled mystery continues.

529. Webb, Joann. "Another Death from Digoxin." MACLEANS 96 (May 9, 1983): 18.

A new victim is reported in Toronto, but never finally linked to the previous murders.

530. ————. "The Bough Breaks, the Cradle Falls." MACLEANS 94 (April 6, 1981): 23-24.

Reports the suspicious deaths and Nelles's arrest.

559. TROPPMAN, JEAN-BAPTISTE (M)

French killer-for-profit who befriended prospector Jean Kinck in September 1869. Convinced that Kinck had discovered a gold mine near Paris, Troppman murdered Kinck, his wife and six children, hoping to claim the bonanza for himself. In fact, there was no gold, and the remains of his victims were swiftly discovered. In custody, Troppman made a full confession prior to his November trial, and was guillotined in January 1870.

* Douthwaite, L.C. MASS MURDER. Cited above as item 6.

Case history in a general discussion of multicide.

* Gaute, J.H.H., and Robin Odell. THE MURDERERS' WHO'S WHO. Cited above as item 8, pp. 229-230.

Case history presented in an encyclopedic format.

* Green, Jonathon. THE GREATEST CRIMINALS OF ALL TIME.
  Cited above as item 11, p. 158.

Brief case history in an encyclopedic format.

* Logan, Guy B.H. MASTERS OF CRIME. Cited above as item
  17, pp. 35-52.

Case history in an anthology of 19th-century murders.

* Nash, Jay Robert. ALMANAC OF WORLD CRIME. Cited above
  as item 19, pp. 273-274.

Case history in a general discussion of mass murder.

560. TURNER, LEON (M): See WHITT, MALCOLM and WENDELL

561. "TYLENOL KILLER, THE" (M)

Deliberate contamination of patent medicine, for reasons
unknown, which resulted in at least seven Chicago fatalities
during September and October 1982. (An eighth possible victim,
never verified as Tylenol-related, died in Philadelphia.)
James W. Lewis and his wife, Lynn, were convicted of attempted
extortion in a sideline of the case, but they were cleared of
any involvement with the actual poisoning. The corporation
responsible for marketing Tylenol was found to be blameless
in the deaths, and in subsequent cases four years later. The
unsolved crimes inspired a host of "copy-cats," who played out
their sadistic fantasies by tampering with eye drops, cough
medicine, candy bars, and numerous other products. At this
writing, none of those responsible for any of the murders or
attempted murders through the years have been identified.

* FACTS ON FILE. Volume 42, 1982. Cited above as item 7,
  pp. 742-743, 776-777, 822, 823, 844, 971, 979.

Traces development of the case to its non-conclusion.

* Nash, Jay Robert. CRIME CHRONOLOGY, 1900-1983. Cited
  above as item 21, p. 202.

Brief case history presented in time line format.

562. ULMER, JERRY BEN (M): See MANGUM, RICHARD

563. UNRUH, HOWARD BARTON (M)

Veteran of World War II, who kept a daily journal of his military experience, listing the date, location, and appearance of each German soldier he killed. Infatuated with firearms, Unruh went berserk in home-town Camden, N.J., during September 1949, killing 13 persons in a twelve-minute shooting spree. Captured alive, Unruh defiantly insisted he was sane. "I'm no psycho," he declared. "I have a good mind." The court thought otherwise, consigning him to New Jersey's state hospital for life. In captivity, Unruh was asked if he regretted any of his killings. "I'd have killed a thousand," he replied, "if I'd had bullets enough."

Books

* Demaris, Ovid. AMERICA THE VIOLENT. Cited above as item 5, pp. 340-341.

Case history in a chapter on firearms and psychopaths.

* FACTS ON FILE. Volume 9, 1949. Cited above as item 7, pp. 296, 336.

Report's Unruh's crime and sentencing.

* Gaute, J.H.H., and Robin Odell. THE MURDERERS' WHO'S WHO. Cited above as item 8, pp. 233-234.

Case history presented in an encyclopedic format.

* Nash, Jay Robert. BLOODLETTERS AND BADMEN. Cited above as item 20, pp. 577-581.

Case history presented in an encyclopedic format.

* ————. CRIME CHRONOLOGY, 1900-1983. Cited above as item 21, p. 137.

Brief case history presented in time line format.

* ————. MURDER, AMERICA. Cited above as item 23, p. 420.

Sketchy case history presented in time line format.

* Sifakis, Carl. THE ENCYCLOPEDIA OF AMERICAN CRIME. Cited above as item 29, pp. 732-733.

Case history presented in an encyclopedic format.

* Tobias, Ronald. THEY SHOOT TO KILL. Cited above as item 31, pp. 143-169.

Detailed case study in a survey of criminal snipers.

Articles

531. "Camden 4-2490-W." NEWSWEEK 34 (September 19, 1949): 60.

Examines Unruh's state of mind. (The title is his telephone number, a reference to his conversations with police before he agreed to surrender.)

532. "Killer on a Rampage in East Camden, N.J." NEWSWEEK 34 (September 19, 1949): 21-22.

A companion article to item 531 above, reporting Unruh's crimes and arrest.

533. "Quiet One." TIME 54 (September 19, 1949): 28-29.

Contemporaneous report of Unruh's shooting spree.

534. "Twelve Minutes of Murder." LIFE 27 (September 19, 1949): 61-62+.

Pictorial layout from the Camden shooting gallery.

535. Yoder, R.M. "Strange Case of Howard Unruh." SATURDAY EVENING POST 223 (September 16, 1950): 24-25+.

A retrospective on Unruh's case, published on the first anniversary of the Camden massacre.

564. Deleted.

565. URSINUS, SOPHIE (S)

Daughter of an Austrian diplomat, married briefly to a German statesman in the early 19th century. Over a period of two years, she poisoned her elderly husband, her lover, and a maiden aunt, finally facing arrest in the latter case. Sentenced to a rather luxurious term of life imprisonment, at Glatz, Frau Ursinus died in April 1836 and was buried with great pomp. Clergymen lauded her generosity to the poor, and a children's choir sang as her casket was lowered into the earth.

* Nash, Jay Robert. LOOK FOR THE WOMAN. Cited above as
   item 22, pp. 370-371.

   Case history presented in an encyclopedic format.

566. VACHER, JOSEPH (S)

French "Ripper of the Southeast," active in the country
regions around Belley from 1894 to 1897. Born in 1869, Vacher
tortured animals as a child and also molested younger playmates.
Drafted into military service during 1890, Vacher cut his own
throat with a razor when he was passed over for promotion to
the rank of corporal. (Strangely, this act was viewed as a
sign of military zeal, and the promotion soon came through.)
Thereafter, his behavior grew steadily more erratic, unsettling
his fellow soldiers as he eyed their throats and muttered to
himself about "flowing blood." In 1891, possessed by jealous
rage, Vacher shot a female acquaintance and then turned the
pistol on himself, sustaining a face wound. He survived, and
was committed to a lunatic asylum, where he stayed until he
was discharged as "cured," in April 1894. Thereafter, he proceeded to attack and mutilate young victims of both sexes,
gnawing and disemboweling their bodies, raping the bloody
corpses in a necrophiliac frenzy. Vacher claimed at least 14
victims before his arrest, in 1897, whereupon he offered a
plea of insanity. Blaming his condition on the bite of a rabid
dog, years earlier, the slayer failed to impress a jury of his
peers. He was executed in December 1897.

* Masters, R.E.L., and Eduard Lea. PERVERSE CRIMES IN
   HISTORY. Cited above as item 18, pp. 88-91, 165-166.

   Case history in a survey of sadistic homicides.

* Nash, Jay Robert. ALMANAC OF WORLD CRIME. Cited above
   as item 19, pp. 529-530.

   Case history in a general discussion of mass murder.

* Wilson, Colin. A CRIMINAL HISTORY OF MANKIND. Cited
   above as item 34, pp. 508-509.

   Case history in a discussion of 19th-century murder.

* ————, and Patricia Putnam. THE ENCYCLOPEDIA OF MURDER.
   Cited above as item 35, pp. 529-530.

   Case history presented in an encyclopedic format.

567. Deleted.

568. VAN PENDLEY, JERRY (S): See MERRILL, HENRY BURTON

569. VAN VALKENBURGH, ELIZABETH (S)

Resident of Fulton, N.Y., who poisoned two successive husbands with arsenic in the mid-19th century. Charged with murder, Van Valkenburgh asserted she had only tried to cure her husbands of the drinking problem which they shared in common, allowing that, "I always had a very ungovernable temper." Hanged in January 1846.

*   Nash, Jay Robert. LOOK FOR THE WOMAN. Cited above as
     item 22, p. 372.

     Case history presented in an encyclopedic format.

570. VELTEN, MARIA (S)

German poisoner who confessed to murdering five persons —including her father, an elderly aunt, two husbands, and a lover—between 1963 and 1980. No final motive for the crimes was ascertained. Sentenced to life.

*   Nash, Jay Robert. CRIME CHRONOLOGY, 1900-1983. Cited
     above as item 21, p. 205.

     Case history presented in time line format.

571. VERZENI, VINCENT (S)

Italian rapist and "vampire" slayer, born of a family riddled with mental defectives, in 1849. As a boy, Verzeni slaughtered chickens for pleasure. Between 1867 and 1871, he assaulted several young women in the vicinity of Rome, raping them and biting their necks. At least two of his victims were killed and disemboweled, with physical evidence indicating that Verzeni had bitten their throats for the purpose of drinking their blood. Two murders were enough to earn him a life sentence in 1873, but authorities insisted he was guilty of at least ten other brutal homicides.

*   CRIMES AND PUNISHMENT: A PICTORIAL ENCYCLOPEDIA OF ABER-
     RANT BEHAVIOR, Volume 7. Cited above as item 4, p. 31.

     Case history presented in an encyclopedic format.

*   Masters, R.E.L., and Eduard Lea. PERVERSE CRIMES IN
     HISTORY. Cited above as item 18, pp. 96-99.

Case history in a section dealing with vampirism.

* Nash, Jay Robert. ALMANAC OF WORLD CRIME. Cited above as item 19, pp. 274-276.

Case history in a general discussion of mass murder.

572. VOIRBO, PIERRE (S)

French killer-for-profit of the 19th century, suspected of at least ten murders before his final arrest in the mutilation-slaying of an elderly Parisian man, in 1869. Unable to pay a debt, owed to his final victim, Voirbo killed and dissected his creditor, dumping most of the remains in a nearby well. (The skull was hollowed out, refilled with molten lead, and pitched into the Seine.) Upon discovery of the hidden corpse, Voirbo confessed his latest crime and subsequently killed himself, cutting his own throat with a razor smuggled into jail in a loaf of bread.

* Nash, Jay Robert. ALMANAC OF WORLD CRIME. Cited above as item 19, p. 273.

Case history in a general discussion of mass murder.

* Wilson, Colin. A CASEBOOK OF MURDER. Cited above as item 33, pp. 154-167.

Places Voirbo's case in sociological perspective.

573. WABLE, JOHN WESLEY (S)

Twenty-four-year-old resident of Greensburg, Pa., convicted in March 1954 of murdering a truck driver. Wable was subsequently found guilty of killing a second trucker and wounding a third, in a series of attacks known locally as the "Turnpike Murders," which terrorized Greensburg in July 1953. Sentenced to die.

* FACTS ON FILE. Volume 14, 1954. Cited above as item 7, pp. 88, 436.

Reports Wable's conviction and sentencing.

574. WAGNER, FRANZ (M)

German shoolteacher and product of an unstable family, a victim of severe depression, suicidal thoughts, and paranoid

fantasies. Married in 1903, he became the father of five children in swift succession, writing in his secret diary: "All
these children are coming against my wishes!" Transferred from
Muehlhausen to a new school in Radelstetten, Wagner became
obsessed with the notion that residents of the former town were
communicating vicious lies about him to citizens of the latter.
Purchasing several guns in 1908, he began to practice inces-
santly, but his mania did not explode until September 4, 1913.
On that evening, he murdered his wife and five children with
a knife, then traveled "home" to Muehlhausen, where he set
fire to several homes and barns, shooting down humans and
animals alike as they ran into the street. Wagner killed
nine persons outright, seriously wounding twelve others before
he was overpowered and beaten unconscious. Held to be insane,
he was committed to an asylum for life, and died there, in
1938.

Books

*   Leyton, Elliott. COMPULSIVE KILLERS. Cited above as
        item 16, pp. 277-282.

        Quotes at length from item 536 below, adding no new
        material.

*   Nash, Jay Robert. ALMANAC OF WORLD CRIME. Cited above
        as item 19, p. 288.

        Case history in a general discussion of mass murder.

*   ————. CRIME CHRONOLOGY, 1900-1983. Cited above as
        item 21, p. 34.

        Brief case history presented in time line format.

Articles

536. Bruch, Hilde. "Mass Murder: The Wagner Case." AMERICAN
        JOURNAL OF PSYCHIATRY 124 (1967): 693-398.

        Examines Wagner from a psychiatric perspective.

575. WAINEWRIGHT, THOMAS GRIFFITHS (S)

19th-century British killer-for-profit, who crossed the
line to murder for pleasure. Wainewright first poisoned his
grandfather, to hasten an inheritance, then repeated the process with his mother- and sister-in-law. His last known murder

was the sexually-motivated poisoning of a man, whose daughter
Wainewright hoped to seduce once familial obstructions were
removed. Eventually convicted on a charge of forgery, the
serial killer was transported to Australia.

* Wilson, Colin. A CASEBOOK OF MURDER. Cited above as
  item 33, p. 122.

  Places Wainewright's case in sociological and historical perspective.

576. WAITE, ARTHUR WARREN (S)

New York City dentist, who poisoned his father- and
mother-in-law in January and March of 1916, respectively. His
murders were committed for financial motives. Executed in May
1917.

* Nash, Jay Robert. CRIME CHRONOLOGY, 1900-1983. Cited
  above as item 21, p. 40.

  Case history presented in time line format.

577. WALLERT, FRANZ THEODORE (M)

Resident of Gaylord, Minn., who went berserk in August
1900, stabbing to death his wife and four step-children.
Hanged in March 1901.

* Nash, Jay Robert. CRIME CHRONOLOGY, 1900-1983. Cited
  above as item 21, p. 1.

  Brief case history presented in time line format.

* ————. MURDER, AMERICA. Cited above as item 23, p. 380.

  Sketchy case history presented in time line format.

578. WALTERS, ANNIE (S): See SACH, AMELIA

579. WANDERER, CARL OTTO (M)

Decorated hero of World War I and a closet homosexual
with violent tendencies. In 1920, repulsed by the news that
his wife was pregnant, Wanderer hired a Chicago bum for five
dollars, instructing the man to accost Wanderer and his wife
on the street, impersonating a robber. The "joke" turned
deadly when Wanderer drew a pistol, killed the tramp, and then

turned the weapon on his wife, claiming she was shot by the "robber" he had killed, in self-defense. Investigation by local journalists revealed the truth, and Wanderer was hanged in March 1921. He sang "Dear Pal O'Mine" on the gallows, before the trap was sprung.

* Green, Jonathon. THE GREATEST CRIMINALS OF ALL TIME. Cited above as item 11, pp. 264-265.

  Case history presented in an encyclopedic format.

* Nash, Jay Robert. ALMANAC OF WORLD CRIME. Cited above as item 19, pp. 141-142.

  Case history in a discussion of criminal "dual personalities."

* ————. BLOODLETTERS AND BADMEN. Cited above as item 20, pp. 403-409.

  Case history presented in an encyclopedic format.

580. WALTER, MARK (M)

Teenaged leader of a gang whose robbery and shooting spree left three persons dead and two others wounded at Colby, Kansas, in February 1985. Walter was killed by police at a road block; accomplices Lisa Dunn, James C. Hunter, and Daniel Remeta were captured alive and subsequently sentenced to life.

* FACTS ON FILE. Volume 45, 1985. Cited above as item 7, p. 163.

  Contemporaneous report of the Kansas shootout.

581. WARDER, ALFRED (S)

19th-century British phsyician who lost three successive wives under suspicious circumstances. The coincidence of a third death led police to investigate, discovering that the latest Mrs. Warder had been poisoned, over a period of time, with aconite. Forewarned of his impending arrest, Warder committed suicide at home, by drinking prussic acid, before police arrived.

* Nash, Jay Robert. ALMANAC OF WORLD CRIME. Cited above as item 19, p. 318.

Case history in a discussion of homicidal doctors.

582. WARREN, BENJAMIN (M)

Hired by landlord Albert Epstein, to burn a New York apartment building for insurance money, Warren subcontracted the arson job to three neighborhood youths. Once the fire was lit, Warren locked the three boys in a closet, where they burned to death. The killer-arsonist received a term of 20 years in prison; his employer, Epstein, was sentenced to ten years.

* Nash, Jay Robert. ALMANAC OF WORLD CRIME. Cited above as item 19, p. 26.

Case history in a section dealing with arson.

583. WATSON, CHARLES (M): See MANSON, CHARLES MILLES

584. WATSON, JAMES B. (S): See OLDEN, JOSEPH

585. WATTS, CORAL EUGENE (S)

Texas bus mechanic and woman-hater who viewed females as an "evil," in need of destruction. As the "Sunday Morning Slasher," Watts reportedly murdered four women in Ann Arbor, Mich., plus others in Kalamazoo, Detroit, and Windsor, Canada. Moving to Houston in 1982, he picked up his career in murder, killing at least eleven women in Harris County, with other victims suspected in Austin and Galveston. Authorities suspect Watts of stabbing, strangling, or drowning forty girls and women, selected at random and murdered on weekends, when Watts was off work. Some object of clothing or personal property was taken from each victim by Watts, and later burned in ritualistic fashion, to erase the "evil spirits" of the women he had killed. In August 1982, Watts struck a controversial bargain with Texas authorities, leading them to the bodies of eleven victims in return for dismissal of murder charges filed against him. Sentenced to 60 years for burglary, he will be eligible for parole in the year 2002.

Books

* SERIAL MURDERS—HEARINGS BEFORE THE SUBCOMMITTEE ON JUVENILE JUSTICE. Cited above as item 28, pp. 18, 22.

Brief case history in a transcript of witness testimony.

Articles

* "Body Count." Cited above as item 394.

    Describes Watts's plea bargain in a survey of recent
    Texas multicides.

537. Peer, E. "A Mass Killer Cops a Plea." NEWSWEEK 100
     (August 2, 1982): 29-30.

     Reports the Texas plea bargain, with a review of the
     case against Watts.

586. WEBER, JEANNE (S)

    Sadistic French slayer of children, suspected in at least
ten deaths between 1905 and 1907. After two of her own children died under suspicious circumstances, Weber began offering
her services to relatives and neighbors, as a babysitter.
One neighbor family lost three children to Weber in a three-
week period of March 1905, apparently without suspecting foul
play. (This, despite the fact that two of the children died
with bruises on their throats, produced by strangulation.
Doctors ascribed the sudden deaths to "convulsions" and "diptheria.") In April 1907, Weber murdered the young son of her
lover, then found work as a nurse's aide in a sanitorium.
Surprised in the act of throttling a bed-ridden child, she
was dismissed from her job, but no charges were filed. Weber
subsequently approached police, in Paris, with confessions
to the murder of her nieces, but the admission of guilt was
dismissed as a symptom of insanity, and she was briefly confined to an asylum. Upon her release, she murdered yet
another neighbor's child, and was returned to the asylum,
where she committed suicide.

* CRIMES AND PUNISHMENT: A PICTORIAL ENCYCLOPEDIA OF ABER-
  RANT BEHAVIOR, Volume 5. Cited above as item 4, pp.
  82-86.

    Case history presented in an encyclopedic format.

* Nash, Jay Robert. CRIME CHRONOLOGY, 1900-1983. Cited
  above as item 21, pp. 13-15, 18, 21.

    Follows Weber's career with time line entries.

* ————. LOOK FOR THE WOMAN. Cited above as item 22,
  pp. 377-381.

Case history presented in an encyclopedic format.

587. WEGER, CHESTER (M)

Chicago slayer of three middle-aged women, all of whom were beaten to death during a bungled robbery attempt in March 1960. Weger accosted the three in a suburban park, clubbing them when they resisted his demands for money, dumping their bodies in the mouth of a cave. Sentenced to life.

* FACTS ON FILE. Volume 20, 1960. Cited above as item 7, p. 100.

  Reports the murders, with Weger still at large.

* Nash, Jay Robert. CRIME CHRONOLOGY, 19-0-1983. Cited above as item 21, p. 161.

  Brief case history presented in time line format.

* ————. MURDER, AMERICA. Cited above as item 23, p. 430.

  Sketchy case history presented in time line format.

588. WEIDMANN, EUGEN (S)

French slayer-for-profit, guillotined in May 1939, after confessing to the murders of six persons, killed for pocket money or small kidnap ransoms.

* Nash, Jay Robert. CRIME CHRONOLOGY, 1900-1983. Cited above as item 21, pp. 109-110.

  Case history presented in time line format.

589. WEINBERG, HAROLD (M)

Slayer of a homeless New York novelist and the author's wife, in 1954. Weinberg's victims had been living with him, briefly, when he tired of their company and chose a permanent solution to the problem. Sentenced to life.

* FACTS ON FILE. Volume 14, 1954. Cited above as item 7, p. 48.

  Reports the murders and Weinberg's arrest.

* Nash, Jay Robert. MURDER, AMERICA. Cited above as
   item 23, p. 424.

   Erroneous case history presented in time line format,
   describing the murders as the result of a bizarre love
   triangle.

590. WERNER, KARL F. (S)

   Mutilation-slayer of three female victims near San Jose,
Calif., between 1969 and 1971. In early August 1969, two
teenaged girls were attacked and killed while picnicking on a
rural hillside, their bodies bearing a combined total of 300
stab wounds. The case remained unsolved for over two years,
with the murders variously attributed to Satanists, the
"Zodiac" killer, and unspecified members of the Manson Family.
In April 1971, another young woman was killed at the same
location, stabbed 49 times by her assailant. Suspicion eventually fell on Werner, a high school classmate of the first
two victims, and in September 1971 he confessed to all three
crimes, receiving a life sentence.

538. Graysmith, Robert. ZODIAC. New York: St. Martin's
     Press, 1986, pp. 119-120, 180-181.

     Describes the Werner case in a general discussion of
     the unsolved "Zodiac" murders.

591. WEST, JOHN COULTER (M): See DAVIS, MURL

592. WHITE, DANIEL JAMES (M)

   Disgruntled city supervisor in San Francisco, who shot
the city's mayor and a fellow supervisor to death in November
1978. The case became a rallying point for the local gay community, as the supervisor slain by White was homosexual (a
fact which, apparently, played no part in the crime). At his
trial, White claimed temporary insanity, blaming his mental
condition on excessive consumption of "junk food." White's
relatively lenient sentence, for manslaughter—and his early
parole, in 1984—enraged homosexual activists, making White
the target for death threats and villification. White died
in 1986, shortly after discharging his parole.

Books

* FACTS ON FILE. Volume 38, 1978. Cited above as item 7,
   p. 920.

Reports the murders and White's arrest.

* FACTS ON FILE. Volume 39, 1979. Cited above as item 7, pp. 385, 547.

    Reports White's conviction and sentencing.

* FACTS ON FILE. Volume 44, 1984. Cited above as item 7, p. 22.

    Reports White's parole.

* Nash, Jay Robert. CRIME CHRONOLOGY, 1900-1983. Cited above as item 21, p. 194.

    Brief case history presented in time line format.

538A. Weiss, Mike. DOUBLE PLAY: THE SAN FRANCISCO CITY HALL KILLINGS. Reading, Mass.: Addison-Wesley, 1984.

    Detailed examination of White's case, with background on the killer and his victims.

Articles

539. "Another Day of Death." TIME 112 (December 11, 1978): 24-26.

    Reports the murders and White's arrest.

540. "Bitter Legacy." TIME 122 (September 28, 1983): 19.

    California gays react violently to news of White's impending parole.

541. "Crime: Murder of George Moscone and Harvey Milk." PEOPLE WEEKLY 10 (December 11, 1978): 161.

    Reports the murders and White's arrest.

542. Krassner, P. "The Milk-Moscone Case Revisited." THE NATION 238 (January 14, 1984): 9+.

    Reviews gay outrage over White's parole.

543. Mathews, T., and G.C. Lubenow. "Day of the Assassin." NEWSWEEK 92 (December 11, 1978): 26-28.

    Reports the murders and White's arrest.

544.   Raine, G. "Gay Outrage Over a Parole." NEWSWEEK 103
          (January 16, 1984): 20.

          Describes homosexual reactions to White's parole.

545.   "Warning: Stay Away from the Bay." NEWSWEEK 105 (Janu-
          ary 21, 1985): 38.

          Reports gay threats against White at the end of his
          statutory parole period.

593. WHITEWAY, ALFRED CHARLES (S)

London's "Riverside Rapist," necrophile, and slayer of
at least two teenaged girls, whose bodies were dumped in the
Thames. Convicted and executed in 1953.

  *   CRIMES AND PUNISHMENT: A PICTORIAL ENCYCLOPEDIA OF ABER-
         RANT BEHAVIOR, Volume 7. Cited above as item 4, p. 92.

      Case history presented in an encyclopedic format.

594. WHITMAN, CHARLES (M)

Former Eagle Scout, Marine Corps veteran and student at
the Texas University, in Austin, who went berserk in 1966.
Consulting a psychiatrist in March, Whitman spoke of a compelling urge to climb the university's clock tower and shoot
passers-by with a deer rifle, but the doctor dismissed the
notion as a passing fantasy. On July 31, Whitman stabbed his
mother and wife to death, collecting his numerous guns and
preparing to launch a full-scale massacre. Next day, he
carried his weapons to the top of the tower and opened fire
on pedestrians below, killing 16 persons and wounding 30 before
he was gunned down by police. An autopsy revealed that Whitman suffered from an undetected brain tumor, but the growth
was finally deemed unrelated to his homicidal outburst. (Whitman held the record for American simultaneous mass murder
until 1984, when James O. Huberty topped his body-count in
San Diego.)

Books

  *   CRIMES AND PUNISHMENT: A PICTORIAL ENCYCLOPEDIA OF ABER-
         RANT BEHAVIOR, Volume 7. Cited above as item 4, p. 105.

      Case history presented in an encyclopedic format.

* Demaris, Ovid. AMERICA THE VIOLENT. Cited above as
  item 5, pp. 346-347.

  Case history in a discussion of guns and psychopaths.

* FACTS ON FILE. Volume 26, 1966. Cited above as item 7,
  p. 326.

  Reports the Texas massacre and Whitman's death.

* Gaute, J.H.H., and Robin Odell. THE MURDERERS' WHO'S
  WHO. Cited above as item 8, p. 248.

  Case history presented in an encyclopedic format.

* Godwin, John. MURDER USA. Cited above as item 10, pp.
  267-268.

  Case history in a discussion of mass murder.

* Levin, Jack, and James Alan Fox. MASS MURDER: AMERICA'S
  GROWING MENACE. Cited above as item 15.

  Brief case history in a discussion of mass murder.

* Nash, Jay Robert. BLOODLETTERS AND BADMEN. Cited above
  as item 20, p. 607.

  Case history presented in an encyclopedic format.

* ————. CRIME CHRONOLOGY, 1900-1983. Cited above as
  item 21, pp. 172-173.

  Brief case history presented in time line format.

* ————. MURDER, AMERICA. Cited above as item 23, p. 434.

  Sketchy case history presented in time line format.

* Sifakis, Carl. THE ENCYCLOPEDIA OF AMERICAN CRIME.
  Cited above as item 29, pp. 761-762.

  Case history presented in an encyclopedic format.

* Steiger, Brad. THE MASS MURDERER. Cited above as item
  30.

  Case history in a quickie paperpack survey of multicide.

*   Tobias, Ronald.   THEY SHOOT TO KILL.   Cited above as
     item 31, pp. 43-59.

     Case history in a survey of criminal snipers.

*   Wilson, Colin, and Donald Seaman.   THE ENCYCLOPEDIA OF
     MODERN MURDER.   Cited above as item 36, pp. 246-247.

     Case history presented in an encyclopedic format.

Articles

546.   "All-American Boy."   NEWSWEEK 68 (August 15, 1966): 24-26+.

       Reports the Austin massacre and Whitman's death.

547.   Coles, R.   "American Amok."   NEW REPUBLIC 155 (August
       27, 1966): 12-15.

       Laments Whitman's crimes as a symptom of endemic vio-
       lence in a "gun-ridden" country.

548.   Crews, H.   "Climbing the Tower."   ESQUIRE 88 (August
       1977): 38-39.

       A 12-year retrospective view of Whitman's rampage.

  *   McBroom, P.   "Can Killers Be Predicted?"   Cited above
       as item 89.

       Examines the missed signals in Whitman's case, with
       an eye toward heading off future carnage.

549.   ———.   "Tumor Found Innocent."   SCIENCE NEWS 90 (Aug-
       ust 13, 1966): 98.

       Reports clinical findings from Whitman's autopsy.

550.   "Madman in the Tower."   TIME 88 (August 12, 1966): 14-19.

       Contemporaneous report of the Austin massacre.

551.   "Mass Murder on a Campus."   US NEWS & WORLD REPORT 61
       (August 15, 1966): 6.

       Reports the Austin shootings and Whitman's death.

552. Nevin, D. "Under the Clock, a Sniper with 31 Minutes to
      Live." LIFE 61 (August 12, 1966): 24-31.

      Examines Whitman's crimes and background.

553. "Real Story of Austin's Mass Killer." US NEWS & WORLD
      REPORT 61 (August 22, 1966): 9.

      Relates Whitman's troubled background to his crimes.

594A. WHITT, MALCOLM and WENDELL (M)

      Escapees, with fellow inmate Leon Turner, from the Attala
County, Miss., jail, in January 1950. Previously charged
with burglary, robbery, and the attempted rape of a black
sharecropper's daughter, the three white prisoners broke out of
jail to seek revenge on their accuser. Before their recapture
by authorities, they murdered three of the farmer's children
—ages four, seven, and thirteen—wounding the sharecropper
and his oldest daughter, whom they had earlier trief to rape.
Sentenced to prison for murder.

  *   FACTS ON FILE. Volume 10, 1950. Cited above as item 7,
      p. 16.

      Follows the Mississippi case to its conclusion.

595. WILDER, CHRISTOPHER BERNARD (S)

      Florida race car driver and building contractor, linked
with the murders of eight young women and brutal attacks on
four others, committed between late February and mid-April
1984. Convicted of sexual assault in Florida, in 1977, Wilder
was scheduled for trial on similar charges in Australia when
he launched a wild, cross-country killing spree in the United
States. After slaying three Florida women and abducting a
fourth (who escaped from his clutches in Georgia), Wilder
drove to California and back again to New York, kidnapping,
raping, and murdering women at each stop along the way. Three
of his twelve victims managed to survive their wounds, while
a fourth was unaccountably released, provided with an airline
ticket to her home in Southern California. On April 13,
Wilder—then on the FBI's "Ten Most Wanted" list—was sighted
by police officers in Colebrook, N.H. The fugitive drew a
pistol, wounding one officer in the scuffle before a second
bullet from his own gun pierced his heart, killing him instantly. In the wake of Wilder's death, his name was tentatively
linked with the unsolved slayings of several other young women

in Florida, prior to his cross-country odyssey, but no positive connections were ever established.

Books

* FACTS ON FILE. Volume 44, 1984. Cited above as item 7,
  p. 283.

  Reports the manhunt for Wilder, ending with his death.

554. Gibney, Bruce. THE BEAUTY QUEEN KILLER. New York:
  Pinnacle Books, 1984.

  Sensational paperback study of Wilder's case, valuable
  for its verbatim inclusion of psychiatric reports on the
  killer. Careless inaccuracies include misidentification
  of Wilder's victims in photograph captions.

* Levin, Jack, and James Alan Fox. MASS MURDER: AMERICA'S
  GROWING MENACE. Cited above as item 15.

  Case history in a general discussion of serial murder.

* Leyton, Elliott. COMPULSIVE KILLERS. Citeda above as
  item 16, pp. 19-21.

  Brief case history based on media reports.

Articles

555. "The FBI: A Manhunt Ends in Violent Death." NEWSWEEK
  103 (April 23, 1984): 35.

  Describes Wilder's last days on the run.

556. "Journey of Terror." PEOPLE WEEKLY 21 (April 30, 1984):
  38-43.

  "Celebrity profile" on Wilder, with background and
  general coverage of his crimes.

557. Lamar, J.V., Jr. "Trail of Death." TIME 123 (April 16,
  1984): 26.

  Contemporaneous report of Wilder's final days.

558. Strasser, S. "A Long Trail of Death." NEWSWEEK 103
  (April 16, 1984): 38.

Reports the manhunt, with Wilder still at large.

596. WILLIAMS, ANN (M)

Deranged housewife in Algo, Texas, who strangled and dismembered her two sons, ages eight and nine, in February 1955.
In custody, Williams described her motive as humanitarian: the
boys, she said, "were suffering" over their father's arrest for
auto theft, and she had simply tried to end their misery.
Sentenced to life.

* FACTS ON FILE. Volume 15, 1955. Cited above as item 7,
  p. 72.

Reports Williams's crimes and arrest.

597. WILLIAMS, DALTON (M): See MANGUM, RICHARD

598. WILLIAMS, H. SANFORD (M)

Methodist minister, in St. Petersburg, Fla., who shot
his wife, two sons, and himself in December 1957. No motive
for the slaughter was determined.

* FACTS ON FILE. Volume 17, 1957. Cited above as item 7,
  p. 428.

Reports the St. Petersburg massacre and aftermath.

599. WILLIAMS, JOHN (M)

Irish sailor, believed responsible for Britain's notorious "Ratcliffe Highway murders," in 1811. On December 7, four
persons were robbed and slain in their home, in the East End
of London, apparently haveing been beaten to death. Two
weeks later, three more residents of the same neighborhood
were bludgeoned, slashed, and robbed. Accused of the crimes,
Williams hanged himself in jail, prior to trial, thereby con-
firming public opinions of his guilt.

* CRIMES AND PUNISHMENT: A PICTORIAL ENCYCLOPEDIA OF ABER-
  RANT BEHAVIOR, Volume 7. Cited above as item 4, p. 53.

Case history presented in an encyclopedic format.

559. Critchley, T.A., and P.D. James. THE MAUL AND THE PEAR
     TREE. London: 1971.

Argues that Williams was framed for the murders while his guilty shipmate—one Abass—escaped detection in the case.

* Logan, Guy B.H. MASTERS OF CRIME. Cited above as item 17, pp. 144-160.

Case history in an anthology of 19th-century murders.

* Wilson, Colin. A CASEBOOK OF MURDER. Cited above as item 33, pp. 112-114.

Places the Ratcliffe Highway crimes in sociological perspective.

* ————. ORDER OF ASSASSINS. Cited above as item 76, pp. 22-23.

Psychological profile of Williams.

* ————, and Patricia Putnam. THE ENCYCLOPEDIA OF MURDER. Cited above as item 35, pp. 554-555.

Case history presented in an encyclopedic format.

600. WILLIAMS, WAYNE BERTRAM (S)

Young, black music promoter, convicted on dubious evidence in two of Atlanta, Georgia's, so-called "child murders." (In fact, Williams was convicted of killing two adult men, ages 21 and 27; the cases of 21 other victims were then arbitratily closed and credited to Williams after his conviction, without benefit of trial.) Officially, the Atlanta murders took place between July 1979 and May 1981, claiming the lives of two young girls and 28 male victims, ages nine to 27 years. Most of the victims were dumped in or near local rivers, although one was left bound to a tree, another was run down by a car on the street, and so forth. Many were strangled or asphyxiated, but the cause of death could never be determined in a number of cases (thereby ruling out prosecution as a homicide). Williams fell under suspicion after police officers, staking out a local bridge, "heard a splash" in the river below, subsequently observing Williams as he drove across the bridge. Days later, when a corpse was found downstream—its point of entry to the river unknown—Williams became a prime suspect in the case. Charged in only two of 30 "similar" cases, he was convicted largely on the basis of fiber evidence and questionable testimony from convicted felons. In the wake

of his conviction, it was revealed that (a) the "unique" carpet
samples from his family home were, in fact, extremely common;
(b) the car in which he allegedly hauled his victims was not
in Williams's possession at the time of the murders; and (c)
five eyewitnesses had identified another suspect—subsequently convicted of child molesting—in one of the murders credited
to Williams. Likewise, despite official claims that the
Atlanta murders ceased with the arrest of Williams, there is
persuasive evidence that more than 20 local murders fit the
prosecution's "pattern" in the 18 months after Williams was
jailed. FBI documents, declassified in 1986, revealed that
a militant faction of the Ku Klux Klan had been suspected in
some of the murders which were later "closed" with the
conviction of Wayne Williams.

Books

560. Baldwin, James. THE EVIDENCE OF THINGS NOT SEEN. New
      York: Holt, Rinehart and Winston, 1985.

      Four years in the making, this insubstantial volume
      was not worth the wait. Celebrity author Baldwin uses
      the Williams case as a springboard for a sparse examin-
      ation of "the State of the Union in the 1980s." After
      noting that the state's case against Williams contained
      "enough holes to drive a truck through," Baldwin shies
      away from any real discussion of the evidence, conclud-
      ing that Williams was not proved guilty ... but he may
      not be innocent, either. Forgettable.

  *   Boar, Roger, and Nigel Blundell. THE WORLD'S MOST IN-
      FAMOUS MURDERS. Cited above as item 2, pp. 184-189.

      Case history presented in sensational tabloid style.

561. Dettlinger, Chet, and Jeff Prugh. THE LIST. Atlanta:
      Philmay Enterprises, 1983.

      Dettlinger worked with Atlanta police on the case,
      was dropped when he pointed out instances of official
      negligence, and was briefly harassed as a "suspect"
      when he refused to be silent. Latent bitterness shines
      through his narrative, but it is still compelling in
      its presentation of evidence that (a) more than 60 vic-
      tims were arbitrarily excluded from the "official"
      police listing; (b) the Atlanta murders continued, un-
      abated, after the arrest of Wayne Williams, and (c)
      vital evidence pointing to other suspects in the case

was deliberately suppressed by the authorities. Thought-provoking, in its view of how the justice system can go absolutely, hideously wrong.

* FACTS ON FILE. Volume 40, 1980. Cited above as item 7, pp. 927-928.

  Reports the Atlanta manhunt in progress.

* FACTS ON FILE. Volume 41, 1981. Cited above as item 7, pp. 46, 168, 367-368, 447, 567.

  The manhunt continues, through Williams's arrest.

* FACTS ON FILE. Volume 42, 1982. Cited above as item 7, p. 148.

  Reports Williams's conviction.

* FACTS ON FILE. Volume 43, 1983. Cited above as item 7, p. 965.

  Williams loses his first appeal.

* FACTS ON FILE. Volume 45, 1985. Cited above as item 7, p. 160.

  Reports the airing of a made-for-television movie based on the Atlanta case, highlighting discrepancies in the prosecution's case.

562. Jenkins, James S. MURDER IN ATLANTA! Atlanta: Cherokee Publishing Co., 1981, pp. 170-182.

  Brief case history in an anthology of local murders, accepting Williams's guilt as established fact.

* Levin, Jack, and James Alan Fox. MASS MURDER: AMERICA'S GROWING MENACE. Cited above as item 15.

  Case history in a discussion of modern serial murder.

* Sifakis, Carl. THE ENCYCLOPEDIA OF AMERICAN CRIME. Cited above as item 29, p. 37.

  Case history presented in an encyclopedic format.

* Wilson, Colin, and Donald Seaman. THE ENCYCLOPEDIA OF
  MODERN MURDER. Cited above as item 36, pp. 247-250.

  Case history presented in an encyclopedic format.

Articles

563. Adler, J., and V.E. Smith. "Atlanta Stirs a Nation."
     NEWSWEEK 97 (March 23, 1981): 18-19.

     Reports the continuing manhunt in progress."

564. ————. "Terror in Atlanta." NEWSWEEK 97 (March 2,
     1981): 34-37.

     Continuing coverage of the investigation.

565. "After 28 Murders, Atlanta Police Point an Accusing
     Finger at Wayne Williams." PEOPLE WEEKLY 16 (July 6,
     1981): 79.

     Reports the identification of a prime suspect.

566. "Another Body." TIME 117 (March 16, 1981): 38.

     Reports the discovery of another victim in Atlanta.

567. "Atlanta: A Break That Never Came." NEWSWEEK 97 (June
     15, 1981): 35.

     Reports the arrest of Wayne Williams.

568. "Atlanta Case: Murder Times Two." NEWSWEEK 98 (July 27,
     1981): 28.

     Reports Williams's indictment.

569. "Atlanta Clues: Will They Be Enough?" U.S.NEWS & WORLD
     REPORT 91 (July 6, 1981): 8.

     Speculates on the likelihood of indictment against
     Williams.

570. "Atlanta: More Victims, No Clues." NEWSWEEK 97 (Janu-
     ary 19, 1981): 29.

     Examines the stagnant search for suspects.

571. "Atlanta Murders." TIME 116 (December 1, 1980): 28.

      Describes the series of crimes to date.

572. "Atlanta Responds Angrily as a TV Show Opens the Old
      Wound." PEOPLE WEEKLY 23 (February 11, 1985): 62.

      Describes local reactions to a TV "docudrama" presum-
      ing Williams's innocence.

573. "At Last, At Least a Suspect." TIME 117 (June 15, 1981):
      16.

      Reports the interrogation of Williams by police.

574. Bonnett, M. "Tracking Atlanta's Phantom Killer of Chil-
      dren." PEOPLE WEEKLY 15 (March 23, 1981): 28-29.

      Examines FBI efforts to prepare a psychological profile
      of the killer.

575. "Break in the Investigation?" TIME 117 (April 27, 1981):
      30.

      FBI spokesmen create controversy with announcements
      that some Atlanta victims were probably killed by their
      own parents.

576. Browning, F. "Life on the Margin." PROGRESSIVE 45
      (September 1981): 34-37.

      Examines the dangers of life for underprivileged black
      children, in light of the Atlanta murders.

577. "Case of the Green Carpet." TIME 118 (July 6, 1981): 12.

      Reports Williams's arrest on the basis of fiber evi-
      dence.

578. "Caught in the Headlines." TIME 117 (July 29, 1981): 23.

      Describes the continuing investigation of Williams,
      prior to his formal arrest.

579. "Children." NEW YORKER 57 (March 30, 1981): 30-31.

      Describes a Harlem "vigil" for Atlanta victims.

580. "City of Fear." TIME 117 (March 2, 1981): 31.

    Describes the atmosphere of terror in Atlanta.

581. Clark, M., and V.E. Smith. "Epidemic of Murder."
    NEWSWEEK 96 (December 22, 1980): 62.

    Atlanta's Center for Disease Control takes a crack at
    the case, with negligible results.

582. Delloff, L.M. "Profiting from Tragedy." CHRISTIAN CEN-
    TURY 98 (July 1-8, 1981): 692-693.

    Describes shady fund-raising efforts billed as "relief
    funds" for the families of Atlanta victims.

583. Ecclesine, T. "Summer in Atlanta." ENCORE 96 (July
    1981): 16-21.

    Examines the Safe Summer '81 program.

584. Englade, K. "A Murder Mystery Still Unsolved." MACLEANS
    96 (March 28, 1983): 8.

    A Canadian journalist outshines American reporters by
    examining discrepancies in the prosecution's case.

585. Euchner, C. "Questions the Press Didn't Ask About the
    Atlanta Murders." WASHINGTON MAGAZINE 13 (October
    1981): 45-46.

    Belatedly examines discrepancies in the prosecution's
    case.

586. Farber, M.A. "Leading the Hunt in Atlanta's Murders."
    NEW YORK TIMES MAGAZINE (May 3, 1981): 62-67+.

    Profiles Atlanta Police Commissioner L.P. Brown.

  * Gest, Ted, and Douglas C. Lyons. "Behind a Nationwide
    Wave of Unsolved Murders." Cited above as item 47.

    Examines the Atlanta case with other then-unsolved
    serial murders in progress.

587. Gray, L.S. "Death in Atlanta." BLACK ENTERPRISE 11
    (May 1981): 15.

Describes the continuing search for a suspect.

588. Greene, B. "Targets." ESQUIRE 96 (July 1981): 23-24.

Interviews Atlanta children for their views on the
continuing murders.

589. "Grief and Exploitation." NEW REPUBLIC 184 (March 28,
1981): 5-6.

Describes various "relief funds" allegedly designed
to benefit the families of Atlanta victims.

590. Hinson, S. "Fiber Analyst Lunn Henson Helps Unravel the
Atlanta Murders." PEOPLE WEEKLY 16 (July 27, 1981):
33-34.

Profiles one of the forensic scientists involved in
building the case against Williams.

591. Horton, L. "City Beat: Atlanta." ENCORE 10 (December
1981): 10-11.

Examines the atmosphere in Atlanta after Williams's
arrest.

592. Jennings, T.W. "Our Children Are Dying." CHRISTIAN
CENTURY 98 (May 6, 1981): 502-504.

Covers the continuing manhunt in Atlanta.

593. Keerdoja, E. "Atlanta Killer: A Life of Isolation."
NEWSWEEK 100 (September 20, 1982): 18+.

Examines Williams in solitary confinement.

594. Khalid, S. "Atlanta Syndrome." WORLD PRESS REVIEW 28
(June 1981): 39-40.

Examines the continuing search for a solution in
Atlanta.

595. Klein, J. "Mystery of Atlanta's Murdered Children."
ROLLING STONE (March 5, 1981): 26-29+.

Covers the manhunt in progress.

596. Leavy, W. "Mystery of the Disappearing Blacks." EBONY 36 (December 1980): 136-138+.

   Examines the accelerated death and disappearance rate of black children in Atlanta, with brief views of other racial murders around the country.

597. Leo, J., and J.N. Boyce. "Growing Up Afraid in Atlanta." TIME 117 (March 2, 1981): 77.

   Describes the atmosphere of tension among Atlanta's black children.

598. Levin, B. "Atlanta's Long Nightmare." MACLEANS 98 (March 11, 1985): 6+.

   Reviews the Atlanta case in light of a recent television "docudrama."

599. Locklear, J. "Atlanta Churches React to Murders of Black Children." CHRISTIANITY TODAY 25 (April 10, 1981): 62-63.

   Examines the reaction of Atlanta's religious community to serial murder.

600. Lowther, W. "Murder the Little Children." MACLEANS 93 (November 3, 1980): 43-44.

   Coverage of the Atlanta manhunt in progress.

601. ————. "Ordeal That May Not Be Over." MACLEANS 94 (July 6, 1981): 32-34.

   Reports the arrest of Wayne Williams.

602. McGrath, E., and J.N. Boyce. "Exploiting Atlanta's Grief." TIME 117 (April 6, 1981): 18.

   Examines celebrity efforts to raise money "for the victims in Atlanta."

603. ————. "Siege in Atlanta." TIME 117 (March 9, 1981): 19.

   Describes the continuing murders and manhunt.

604. ————. "Is He a Suspect or Isn't He?" NEWSWEEK 97
      (June 29, 1981): 38.

      Examines the confusion preceding Williams's indictment.

605. ————, and V.E. Smith. "Atlanta: Profile of a Suspect."
      NEWSWEEK 98 (July 6, 1981): 22+.

      Covers the background and arrest of Wayne Williams.

606. Mitford, J. "How Will We Ever Teach Them to Trust Adults
      Again?" McCALLS 10 (June 1981): 32+.

      Considers the psychological repercussions of serial
      murder on Atlanta's black children.

607. Morganthau, T., and V.E. Smith. "Atlanta Goes on a Man-
      hunt." NEWSWEEK 96 (December 1, 1980): 40+.

      Covers the ongoing search for a killer.

608. "National Plot to Kill Blacks?" U.S. NEWS & WORLD REPORT
      89 (November 3, 1980): 7.

      Examines the Atlanta crimes in conjunction with then-
      unsolved slayings of blacks in Buffalo, N.Y., and else-
      where.

609. O'Hare, J.A. "Of Many Things." AMERICA 144 (March 28,
      1981): inside cover.

      Examines the Atlanta case prior to Williams's arrest.

610. Poole, I.J., and M. White. "Plot to Kill?" BLACK EN-
      TERPRISE 11 (January 1981): 13.

      Casts a fearful eye on murders in Atlanta, Buffalo,
      and elsewhere.

611. "River of Death." TIME 117 (April 13, 1981): 54.

      Murders continue, with no solution in sight.

612. Smith, V.E. "Atlanta's Nightmare Revisited." NEWSWEEK
      105 (February 18, 1985): 31.

      Re-examines the case in light of a recent TV movie
      based on the Williams case.

613. ———. "Inside the Atlanta Probe." NEWSWEEK 97 (April 20, 1981): 42.

   Reviews the continuing manhunt in Atlanta.

614. Sun, M. "Epidemiologists Try to Help Stop More Atlanta Murders." SCIENCE 211 (January 23, 1981): 366.

   Describes the ultimately futile efforts of Atlanta's Center for Disease Control.

615. "27th Victim." TIME 117 (May 25, 1981): 29.

   Reports the discovery of another murdered black.

616. Witherspoon, R. "Suffer the Children." ESSENCE 12 (July 1981): 64-65+.

   Another black periodicl covers the ongoing manhunt.

601. WILSON, CATHERIN (S)

   London nurse and poisoner-for-profit, active from 1853 to 1862. Wilson ingratiated herself with elderly patients, persuading them to name her in their wills before she administered various poisons, thereby hastening her inheritance. Acquitted of attempted murder in early 1862, the circumstances of her case led authorities to exhume seven other victims, all of whom were found to have died by poison. Convicted on seven counts of murder (and probably guilty of others), Wilson was hanged in October 1862.

   * Nash, Jay Robert. LOOK FOR THE WOMAN. Cited above as item 22, pp. 389-390.

   Case history presented in an encyclopedic format.

602. WILSON, ELIZABETH (M)

   Impoverished resident of East Bradford, Pa., who murdered her infant twins in 1785, when she could no longer afford to feed them. Wilson was sentenced to hang, but her brother obtained a reprieve from the governor, galloping back with the papers, on horseback. Slowed by rain and muddy roads, he arrived 23 minutes after his sister was executed, on January 3, 1786.

* Nash, Jay Robert. LOOK FOR THE WOMAN. Cited above as
  item 22, p. 390.

Case history presented in an encyclopedic format.

603. WILSON, JOHN GLEESON (M)

19th-century slayer of four victims, in Liverpool, England.
Gleeson murdered his landlady, her maid, and her two small children in the boarding house where he resided, bludgeoning the
women with a poker and slitting the throats of the children.
Arrested after pawning property belonging to the victims, he
was swiftly convicted and sentenced to hang. A crowd of 30,000
persons witnessed his execution in 1849.

* Logan, Guy B.H. MASTERS OF CRIME. Cited above as item
  17, pp. 110-126.

Case history in an anthology of 19th-century murders.

604. WILSON, KENNETH (M)

Teenaged sniper who opened fire on black picnickers in
Charlotte, S.C., during 1977. Two persons were killed and
two others wounded before Wilson turned the gun on himself,
committing suicide at the scene. He left behind a note, explaining that the shootings were inspired by his love for a
local girl.

* Tobias, Ronald. THEY SHOOT TO KILL. Cited above as
  item 31, p. 74.

Case history in a survey of criminal snipers.

605. Deleted.

606. WILSON, ROBERT (S): See "DE MAU MAU MURDERS"

607. WINDERS, WILLIAM (M)

Resident of Seneca, Ill., who shot and killed his wife,
three children, and himself in March 1960. No certain motive
for the slayings was determined.

* FACTS ON FILE. Volume 20, 1960. Cited above as item 7,
  p. 100.

Describes the Seneca massacre and Winders's death.

608. WINSTANLEY, HAROLD (M)

Deranged British servant who killed two butlers and wounded two others in a wild shooting spree at the Earl of Derby's home, near Liverpool, in October 1952. Sentenced to life.

* FACTS ON FILE. Volume 12, 1952. Cited above as item 7, p. 356.

    Reports the shootings and Winstanley's arrest.

609. WISE, MARTHA HAZEL (M)

Homicidal widow in Medina, Ohio, who poisoned eight of her relatives, three of them fatally, in January and February 1925. Each of the victims had ridiculed Marthas's love affair with a younger man, touching off violent hatred which surfaced in murder. In custody, Wise also confessed to numerous local burglaries and arson fires, explaining that "the devil" had compelled her to commit the crimes. Sentenced to life, she died behind bars.

* Nash, Jay Robert. CRIME CHRONOLOGY, 1900-1983. Cited above as item 21, p. 66.

    Brief case history presented in time line format.

* ————. LOOK FOR THE WOMAN. Cited above as item 22, pp. 390-391.

    Case history presented in an encyclopedic format.

* ————. MURDER, AMERICA. Cited above as item 23, pp. 397-398.

    Sketchy case history presented in time line format.

610. WOOD, FREDERICK G. (S)

Paroled in June 1960, on a 1942 conviction for beating a man to death, Wood was arrested for two more bludgeon murders a month later, in New York City. In all, he confessed to a total of five homicides, committed since 1926, when he was 14 years old. Sentenced to die, Wood inspired New York's governor to ban future parole for all killers and major sex criminals, pending intensive review of their cases.

* Brian, Denis. MURDERERS DIE. Cited above as item 3, p. 260.

    Another case of careless parole, cited as an argument in favor of capital punishment.

* FACTS ON FILE. Volume 20, 1960. Cited above as item 7, p. 252.

    Reports Wood's latest arrest and confessions.

611. WOOD, ISAAC (M)

Seeking to cinch his inheritance by wiping out the members of his immediate family, Wood poisoned his brother, sister-in-law, and their three children at Dansville, N.Y., in early 1858. A short time later, he dispatched his own wife and child, in New Jersey, by similar means. Convicted of multiple murder before he could collect the cash, Wood was hanged in July 1858.

* Nash, Jay Robert. MURDER, AMERICA. Cited above as item 23, p. 342.

    Brief case history presented in time line format.

* Sifakis, Carl. THE ENCYCLOPEDIA OF AMERICAN CRIME. Cited above as item 29, pp. 771-772.

    Case history presented in an encyclopedic format.

612. WOODFIELD, RANDALL BRENT (S)

Native of Newport, Ore., member of Campus Crusade for Christ, and a draft choice of the Green Bay Packers, believed responsible for a brutal series of robberies, rapes, and murders in the Pacific Northwest, between December 1980 and March 1981. Dubbed the "I-5 Bandit," after his highway of preference, Woodfield began his criminal career while in Wisconsin, with the Packers, racking up a series of arrests for indecent exposure. In 1975, he was convicted of mugging an undercover policewoman; several suspected cases of robbery and sexual assault were never prosecuted. Convicted of one murder, charged in two others, and suspected of at least two more, Woodfield was sentenced, in June 1981, to a term of life plus 90 years in Oregon's state prison. The states of California and Washington are prepared to try other cases against him, in the unlikely event that he should ever be paroled.

* SERIAL MURDERS—HEARINGS BEFORE THE SUBCOMMITTEE ON
  JUVENILE JUSTICE. Cited above as item 28, p. 21.

  Brief case history in transcripts of witness testimony.

617. Stack, Andy (pseud.). THE I-5 KILLER. New York: New
  American Library, 1984.

  Last in a series of "Andy Stack's True Crime Annals,"
  actually written by author Ann Rule. Worth reading.

613. YOUNG, GRAHAM (S)

Compulsive British poisoner, obsessed with observing the
effects of poison on the human body. Young began poisoning
members of his family in 1961, killing his stepmother and making several other persons gravely ill before his actions were
discovered. Confined to an asylum for the criminally insane,
he was released in February 1971. Throughout the remainder
of that year, he poisoned several coworkers at a photo devel-
oping firm, killing two. Upon his arrest, police discovered
a diary with details of his "experiments." Young initially
described the diary as an outline for a novel he planned to
write, but he eventually confessed and was sentenced to life.

* Boar, Roger, and Nigel Blundell. THE WORLD'S MOST IN-
  FAMOUS MURDERS. Cited above as item 2, pp. 190-192.

  Case history presented in sensational tabloid style.

* CRIMES AND PUNISHMENT: A PICTORIAL ENCYCLOPEDIA OF ABER-
  RANT BEHAVIOR, Volume 3. Cited above as item 4, pp.
  31-34.

  Case history presented in an encyclopedic format.

* Gaute, J.H.H., and Robin Odell. THE MURDERERS' WHO'S
  WHO. Cited above as item 8, pp. 251-252.

  Case history presented in an encyclopedic format.

* Green, Jonathon. THE GREATEST CRIMINALS OF ALL TIME.
  Cited above as item 11, pp. 255-256.

  Brief case history in an encyclopedic format.

* Wilson, Colin, and Donald Seaman. THE ENCYCLOPEDIA OF
  MODERN MURDER. Cited above as item 36, pp. 255-256.

Case history presented in an encyclopedic format.

614. YOUNGMAN, WILLIAM GODFREY (M)

19th-century British slayer-for-profit who stabbed his mother, fiancee, and two young brothers to death in July 1860, at Walworth, England. In his report to police, Youngman claimed that his mother had gone berserk, murdering the other victims, after which he was forced to kill her in self defense. A bungled attempt to cash in on his fiancée's life insurance brought Youngman to trial, where he was convicted and sentenced to die.

* Logan, Guy B.H. MASTERS OF CRIME. Cited above as item 17, pp. 190-198.

Case history in an anthology of 19th-century murders.

615. YUKL, CHARLES (S)

Convicted, in 1966, of strangling a young woman and mutilating her corpse, Yukl was paroled after only five years in prison. Two years later, he strangled another woman, and was returned to prison for life.

* Brian, Denis. MURDERERS DIE. Cited above as item 3, p. 260.

Yet another case history used as an argument in favor of capital punishment.

616. "ZEBRA MURDERS, THE" (S)

Random, brutal assaults upon white residents of San Francisco, which terrorized the city during a 179-day period of late 1973 and early 1974 (so-called because all victims were white, and all attackers were black). At least fifteen persons were killed, and another eight wounded, in the series of attacks perpetrated by members of a Black Muslim splinter group, the "Death Angels." Murders of white strangers were required for "Angels" to obtain their "wings," a badge of achievement within the secret organization. Eight men were eventually taken into custody for the murders and assaults, but available evidence permitted the trial of only four: Jesse Cooks, Larry Green, Manuel Moore, and J.C. Simon. All four were convicted, in a trial lasting one year and six days, receiving sentences of life imprisonment. In the wake of the conviction, California authorities announced that unnamed

"Death Angels" might be responsible for as many as 60 other homicides, throughout the state, as well as untold others, nationwide. At this writing, no other members of the cult have been publicly identified, and the group's status is unclear.

Books

* FACTS ON FILE. Volume 34, 1974. Cited above as item 7, pp. 318, 399.

Reports the continuing manhunt for suspects.

* FACTS ON FILE. Volume 35, 1975. Cited above as item 7, p. 367.

Reports the beginning of the "Zebra" trial.

618. Howard, Clark. ZEBRA. New York: Richard Marek, 1979.

Fascinating "inside" account of the Death Angels, prepared from extensive interviews with fringe participants in the "Zebra" crimes.

Articles

619. "Fear in the Streets of San Francisco." TIME 103 (April 29, 1974): 18.

Reports the continuing terror by the Bay.

620. Mann, E.B. "Gun in the Zebra Murders." FIELD AND STREAM 83 (August 1978): 20+.

An outdoorsman's magazine examines ballistic aspects of the case.

621. "Nothing Personal." NEWSWEEK 83 (February 11, 1974): 26.

Reports the random murders and manhunt in progress.

622. Shields, J. "Why Nick?" NEWSWEEK 91 (May 8, 1978): 23.

Retrospective on the random selection of victim Nick Shields, written by a surviving relative. Ironically, Shields is not included in the "comprehensive" tabulation of victims presented in item 618 above.

623.   "Zebra Dragnet."   NEWSWEEK 83 (May 6, 1974): 50.

        Reports the continuing manhunt in progress.

624.   "Zebra Killers."   NEWSWEEK 83 (April 29, 1974): 27.

        The search for suspects continues.

617. ZIMMER, ANDREW J. (M)

        Inmate of a Tennessee jail who, in June 1977, set a fire
which claimed the lives of 42 fellow inmates. Zimmer pled
guilty to arson and manslaughter in December 1978, with additional time added to his previous sentence.

   *   FACTS ON FILE. Volume 38, 1978. Cited above as item 7,
        p. 992.

        Reports Zimmer's guilty plea, with a review of his case.

618. "ZODIAC, THE" (S)

        Unidentified serial slayer of at least six victims in
California, between October 1966 and October 1969 (two other
victims survived stab or gunshot wounds). In a series of
taunting letters to the media and homicide investigators,
written between July 1969 and April 1978, the killer claimed
an ever-escalating body-count, which finally reached 37 victims.
None of these subsequent murders were ever verified, but students of the case have granted Zodiac a "possible" death toll
of 43 victims, outside the official tally. The "Trailside
Murders," committed by Richard Carpenter, were initially believed to be the work of Zodiac, but Carpenter's arrest eliminated any possible connection, after he was ruled out as a
suspect in the known Zodiac slayings. Still at large.

                              Books

   *   CRIMES AND PUNISHMENT: A PICTORIAL ENCYCLOPEDIA OF ABER-
        RANT BEHAVIOR, Volume 2. Cited above as item 4, p. 113.

        Brief case history in an encyclopedic format.

   *   Graysmith, Robert. ZODIAC. Cited above as item 538.

        Intriguing, detailed survey of the evidence, naming
        43 "unofficial" Zodiac victims, with details of their
        cases which lead him to believe all were attacked by the

same man. The full text of various Zodiac messages is also presented for the first time anywhere. Essential to a serious study of the case, whether or not you agree with the author's conclusions.

* Nash, Jay Robert. CRIME CHRONOLOGY, 1900-1983. Cited above as item 21, p. 178.

Brief case history presented in time line format.

* ————. OPEN FILES. Cited above as item 24, pp. 276-279.

Case history presented in an encyclopedic format.

* Purvis, James. GREAT UNSOLVED MYSTERIES. Cited above as item 36, pp. 33-39.

Case history in an anthology of unsolved crimes.

* Sifakis, Carl. THE ENCYCLOPEDIA OF AMERICAN CRIME. Cited above as item 29, p. 784.

Case history presented in an encyclopedic format.

* Wilson, Colin. ORDER OF ASSASSINS. Cited above as item 76, pp. 85-89.

Attempts to sketch a psychological profile of the killer, in absentia.

* ————, and Donald Seaman. THE ENCYCLOPEDIA OF MODERN MURDER. Cited above as item 36, pp. 258-260.

Case history presented in an encyclopedic format.

Articles

625. Oakes, George (pseud). "Portrait of the Artist as a Mass Murderer." CALIFORNIA MAGAZINE (November 1981): 111-114+.

Another effort to identify the Zodiac, with the suspect's name strategically deleted. Author "Oakes"—a pseudonym, employed for "self-protection"—connects Zodiac's coded messages to an alleged fascination with binomial mathematics and the writings of Lewis Carroll. Interesting in theory, although the editors admit cryptographers found Oakes's conclusions unconvincing, and

agents of the FBI "weren't very impressed, either." The
adoption of a pen name for security purposes is curious,
since "Oakes" asserts that Zodiac has called him on the
telephone, at home.

619. ZON, HANS VAN (S)

Bisexual necrophile of Utrecht, Holland, who murdered at
least six persons between 1964 and 1967. Identified after a
seventh intended victim survived the assault, Van Zon was
arrested and swiftly confessed to his crimes. He was sentenced
to life, while an accomplice in some of his lesser felonies,
one Oude Nol, received a term of seven years in prison.

* Green, Jonathon. THE GREATEST CRIMINALS OF ALL TIME.
  Cited above as item 11, p. 159.

  Case history presented in an encyclopedic format.

* Wilson, Colin. ORDER OF ASSASSINS. Cited above as item
  76, pp. 94-98.

  Presents a psychological profile of Van Zon.

* ————, and Donald Seaman. THE ENCYCLOPEDIA OF MODERN
  MURDER. Cited above as item 36, pp. 260-261.

  Case history presented in an encyclopedic format.

620. ZWANZIGER, ANNA MARIA (S)

19th-century German poisoner who traveled throughout the
country, working as a housekeeper and cook. Believed responsible for the murders of several employers and their families,
apparently motivated by jealousy or pure sadism in the majority
of cases. Convicted of a single homicide, Zwanziger was beheaded in July 1811.

* Feuerbach, Anselm Ritter Von. NARRATIVES OF REMARKABLE
  CRIMINAL TRIALS. Cited above as item 152, pp. 128-162.

  Case history in an anthology of German murder cases.

* Green, Jonathon. THE GREATEST CRIMINALS OF ALL TIME.
  Cited above as item 11, p. 159.

  Brief case history in an encyclopedic format.

* Nash, Jay Robert. ALMANAC OF WORLD CRIME. Cited above as item 19, pp. 270-271.

    Case history in a general discussion of mass murder.

* Wilson, Colin. A CASEBOOK OF MURDER. Cited above as item 33, p. 125.

    Places the case in sociological perspective.

SUBJECT INDEX